SHEFFIELD HALLAM UNIVERSITY
LEARNING CENTRE
COLLEGIATE CRESCENT
SHEFFIELD S10 2BP

D0547957

101 936 800 4

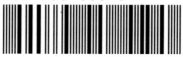

THE WORLD'S BANKER

Sheffield Hallam University
Learning and Information Services
Withdrawn From Stock

ALSO BY SEBASTIAN MALLABY

After Apartheid: The Future of South Africa

THE
WORLD'S
BANKER

A STORY OF FAILED STATES,
FINANCIAL CRISES, AND THE
WEALTH AND POVERTY
OF NATIONS

SEBASTIAN MALLABY

YALE UNIVERSITY PRESS
New Haven and London

First published in the USA by The Penguin Press, 2004

This edition published by Yale University Press, London, 2005

Copyright © Sebastian Mallaby, 2004

All rights reserved. This book may not be reproduced, in whole or in part, in
any form (beyond that copying permitted by Sections 107 and 108 of the U.S.
Copyright Law and except by reviewers for the public press), without written
permission from the publishers.

For information about this and other Yale University Press publications, please
contact:
U.S. Office: sales@yale.edu www.yalebooks.com
Europe Office: sales@yaleup.co.uk www.yalebooks.co.uk

Designed by Marysarah Quinn

Printed in Great Britain by St Edmundsbury Press Ltd, Bury St Edmunds

ISBN: 0-300-11676-4

Library of Congress Cataloging-in-Publication Data

Mallaby, Sebastian
The world's banker : a story of failed states, financial crises, and the wealth and
poverty of nations / Sebastian Mallaby.
p. cm.
Includes bibliographical references and index.
1. Wolfensohn, Jim.   2. World Bank—Presidents.   3. Economic
development—Finance.   4. Developing countries—Economic policy.
5. Financial crises.   I. Title.

HG3881.5.W57M35 2004
332.1'532'092—dc22

2004040100

SHEFFIELD HALLAM UNIVERSITY
WL
332.1532
MA
COLLEGIATE LEARNING CENTRE

TO ZANNY

CONTENTS

PREFACE: The Prisoner of Lilliput 1

CHAPTER ONE: A Tale of Two Ambitions 11

CHAPTER TWO: "World Bank Murderer" 41

CHAPTER THREE: The Renaissance President 65

CHAPTER FOUR: A Twister in Africa 84

CHAPTER FIVE: Mission Sarajevo 116

CHAPTER SIX: Narcissus and the Octopus 145

CHAPTER SEVEN: The Cancer of Corruption 174

CHAPTER EIGHT: Uganda's Myth and Miracle 207

CHAPTER NINE: A Framework for Development 232

CHAPTER TEN: From Seattle to Tibet 261

CHAPTER ELEVEN: Waking Up to Terror 286

CHAPTER TWELVE: A Plague upon Development 313

CHAPTER THIRTEEN: Back to the Future   336

CHAPTER FOURTEEN: A Lion at Carnegie   374

ACKNOWLEDGMENTS   395

NOTES   399

INDEX   447

THE WORLD'S BANKER

THE PRISONER OF LILLIPUT

I DIDN'T WRITE THIS BOOK to pick an argument. I wrote it for the romantic match between the two main characters. On one side there is Jim Wolfensohn—screamer, schemer, seducer; Olympian, musician, multimillionaire; by no means a saint but by any standards a fantastic force of nature. On the other side there is "development," an umbrella term for humanity's most intractable headaches—ignorance, illiteracy, malnutrition, AIDS—the toughest challenges of globalization. As president of the World Bank since 1995, Jim Wolfensohn has grappled with these challenges, an outsized character pitted against outsized problems. I wanted to write a book that followed Wolfensohn through the villages and capitals where he fought his battles, and to see what larger truths those battles illuminated.

The persistence of extreme poverty has fair claim to being the greatest outrage of our times, and the World Bank is the main instrument that rich nations have to fight it. We live in an age when millions of people die because they were born in the wrong place: one section of humanity enjoys $2 lattes and disposable cameras; the other section lives on $2 a day and appears itself to be disposable. It costs $2.50 to buy a bed net to keep out malarial mosquitoes, but the United States, which spends more than $9 billion on movie tickets annually and lands rockets on Mars, somehow can't get bed nets to the African children who die from malaria at a rate of roughly two per minute.[1] What struggle is more noble than the battle against this waste of human lives? Jim Wolfensohn feels this with a consuming passion: "It's all I think about," he said, early in his tenure; "I wake up in the morning thinking about it and I go to bed thinking about it." And yet, what struggle is more difficult either? More than any other institution, the World Bank has strived to understand the challenge of development: to create a delivery mechanism that can turn a sliver of the rich world's wealth into progress against poverty.

The World Bank was conceived six decades ago, along with the International Monetary Fund, when Franklin Delano Roosevelt and his allies were engaged in mortal combat with Germany and Japan. The founders' purpose was twofold: to relieve human suffering, certainly, but at the same time to control the economic chaos that threatened the rich world's security. The hyperinflation and mass unemployment of the interwar period had fueled the rise of fascism and communism in Europe: desperation had led to desperate *isms*. The International Monetary Fund was meant to head off a repetition by fighting currency crises; the World Bank had a broader mandate to develop broken-down economies. As the world changed, the Bank's functions evolved, but its role in international-security strategy has persisted. With the onset of the cold war, the Bank's mission was to prevent Latin Americans and Africans and Asians from joining the Soviet column. In the new age of terror, the Bank's efforts in the poor world offer the best chance of preventing the proliferation of failed states that serve as havens for terror. Meanwhile poverty is the vector for other threats to our security—global diseases, drug trafficking, and environmental degradation—which can thrive unchecked in desperate countries. In Kosovo, in East Timor, in Afghanistan, and to a lesser extent in Iraq, the World Bank has also emerged as a key player in the nation-building efforts that have become a feature of the past decade.

The World Bank is a strange kind of a bank, extremely good and frustratingly bad, not unlike its president. It lends money to poor countries—some $20 billion a year—but its real importance lies in its influence over the developing world's policies. In the words of one critical account, the Bank has "more to say about state policy than many states,"[2] and while that goes a little far, the general point is valid. The Bank's ten thousand professionals form the brightest concentration of development thinkers anywhere, and they combine brain power with practical experience; they spend years in the toughest corners of the earth, fighting to get children into schools or water into villages. In many poor countries, World Bank economists drive government strategy on everything from AIDS to civil-service reform to macroeconomic policy. Other big aid donors—the United States, Japan, and the leading European powers—can be influential, too. But the Bank is almost always in the lead, partly because a multilateral institution is best placed to coordinate rival flag-waving programs, but mostly because the Bank's analytical machine has more intellectual juice in it.

Jim Wolfensohn came to the Bank with his own kind of juice, and the mix has been explosive. He grew up in Australia, represented his country at the 1956 Olympics, then went to Harvard Business School. He became a master deal maker in the City of London and on Wall Street, leading the rescue of the Chrysler car company in 1979 and amassing a fortune of well over $100 million. He chaired New York's Carnegie Hall and Washington's Kennedy Center for the Performing Arts while running his own firm, and he performed concerts himself alongside the world's best musicians. He had a swashbuckling energy that took the World Bank by storm, lifting it out of a dark time when it was surrounded by critics of both left and right who called for its abolition. But the Bank is a proud institution, and its formidable technocrats did not always take kindly to Wolfensohn's high-voltage style. And so there followed a titanic clash: in one corner, a plutocratic financier who

always got his way; in the other, a phalanx of superqualified experts with
years of development experience. It was unstoppable force versus
immovable object, and both sides finished up in unexpected places.

There could scarcely be a better time to tell this story, for however
excellent the Bank's professionals, and however vital their mission, the
World Bank shares the fragility common to most multilateral institutions. We veer between contempt for international bodies—the United
Nations, the International Monetary Fund, and likewise the World
Bank—and unrealistic pronouncements on what they ought to do:
forge peace, banish financial instability, lift every person out of poverty.
It has become commonplace to say that our global institutions are not
up to the challenge of our unprecedented global interdependence. But
the reason for this mismatch lies partly in our schizophrenia. Sometimes we pour scorn on the Bank and other international bodies, and
starve them of resources. Sometimes we talk as though they must have
superhuman strength, and we lumber them with impossible objectives.

When President George W. Bush took office, it was the contempt
that seemed most threatening. In 2001 and 2002, the Bush Treasury
assailed the Bank with a mixture of aggression and plain ignorance, as
this book will describe later. In early 2003, the Bank was left out of the
planning for Iraqi reconstruction by the Pentagon, even though it had
valuable experience from other nation-building exercises. The Pentagon's attitude did not prevent the Treasury from attacking the Bank for
doing too little in Iraq; days after Jim Wolfensohn visited Baghdad in
the summer of 2003, and days before a World Bank expert was killed by
Iraqi insurgents, *The Wall Street Journal* published an editorial broad-
side about the Bank's lack of involvement in the country. Throughout
this period, the very idea of the international system was called into
question; some parts of the administration believed we lived in a *unipolar*
world—that the United States *was* the international system. The
unipolar fantasy is a trap, for it is only in military matters that American
power is overwhelming. In the economic realm, the United States is the

leading power, but it is not the only power; it depends on foreigners to open up trade, to prime the pump of global growth, and to provide the savings that pay for the federal government's spending habits. In other fields—the ones that occupy this book—the limits to American dominion are even more pronounced. You cannot fight AIDS or migration or environmental challenges unilaterally.

By 2004, the setbacks in Iraq had made the limits to American power obvious, and the contempt for international institutions had faded. In the meantime, however, multilateralists sometimes made the opposite mistake, insisting that the World Bank should tackle poverty as though by magic. The roots of this magical unrealism are understandable: When you know that Africans die for want of $2.50 bed nets, you want to yell and scream that the problem must be fixed; surely all you need is will and money? But those ingredients are sadly not enough. To get bed nets to children, you need a distribution network run by competent people; you need systems for handling the finances involved; you need peace where the children are living; and it helps if parents and health workers have not been carried off by AIDS or war or famine. The World Bank can make advances against poverty, as this book will describe; anybody tempted to dismiss development as hopeless should remember that between 1990 and 2015, the world is likely to halve the proportion of people who live below the $1-a-day line. But it doesn't help to set ambitious humanitarian targets if meeting them is going to be impossible. The world has committed itself, for example, to reaching a set of targets known as the Millennium Development Goals, which include universal primary school enrollment and a two-thirds cut in child mortality. When those goals are not met, the World Bank and other development agencies will be branded as failures. The critics of the multilateral system will be back, their contempt more poisonous than ever.

The Bank is large, lavish, and has lasted sixty years; it may seem outlandish to suggest that it is vulnerable. Yet it is not just our schizophrenia that threatens its future; the Bank is under constant attack from feisty nongovernmental organizations (NGOs) that ought to be its natural allies. At first sight this is paradoxical: the Bank's combination of powerful minds and noble motives is glorious, or at least ought to be; this book will introduce you to the dedicated pros who flew into war-torn Bosnia on military transports, who battled poverty amid Indonesia's revolution, who thought up new ways of combating human suffering in Africa. And yet, if the World Bank is unpopular, it is not difficult to see why. In large parts of the world it has promised heaven and left people in hell: 3 billion people, or half of all humanity, continue to live on less than $2 daily. Its intellectual dominance has made it arrogant, fueling the resentment of NGOs that feel locked out of the big decisions on development. Encased in their palatial headquarters in Washington, observed at their annual meetings hobnobbing with global finance's A-list, World Bankers have been too easily portrayed as pin-striped pointy heads, cut off from the real problems of the world's poorest people.

The clash between the Bank and NGOs ought to concern all of us, because the Bank may not survive it. Over the past decade—the first Internet decade—it has been fashionable to predict upheaval in the business world: noisy, nimble, entrepreneurial upstarts, with flat structures and low overheads, would destroy the lumbering hierarchies of the old era. But the triumph of the nimble is actually more a public-sector thing, and I believe it is a worry. In many of the world's rich capitals, and especially in Washington, public policy is decided by a bewildering array of lobbies and interest groups and advertising sneak attacks, and generally by people who campaign single-mindedly for narrow goals: benefits for veterans, subsidies for farmers, tax loopholes for businesses. A similar army of advocates pounds upon the World Bank's doors, demanding that Bank projects bend to particular concerns: no damage to indigenous peoples, no harm to rain forests, nothing that might hurt human rights, or Tibet, or democratic values. These constant NGO offensives tie up the World Bank, frequently disabling its efforts to fight poverty; despite their diminutive stature, the Lilliputians are winning. Unless we wake up to this danger, we will lose the potential for good that big organizations offer: to rise above the single-issue advocacy that small groups tend to pursue, and to square off against the world's grandest problems in all their hideous complexity.

So if the first threat to the multilateral system lies in our alternating bouts of millenarianism and contempt, a second one hides in the cacophony of our advanced democracies. I encountered this problem in May 2003, on a visit to East Africa. The World Bank was promoting a dam near the source of the river Nile, at a beautiful spot called Bujagali. Western NGOs were in revolt: the International Rivers Network, based in Berkeley, California, proclaimed that the Ugandan environmental movement was outraged at the likely damage to the Bujagali waterfalls, and that the poor people near the site would be uprooted from their land and livelihood. The activists' resistance had tied up the Bank for several years, delaying a project that would get electricity to clinics and schoolrooms that lacked lights and to industries whose productivity was wrecked by a lack of reliable energy. It is true that the Bank has a bad history with dams, backing schemes that have harmed both people and the environment, so journalists based in America or Europe often believe the NGOs' charges without being able to check them. But now I was in Uganda, a few hours' drive from the proposed dam, so I called up the Berkeley activists and asked for some advice. Who ran this Ugandan environmental movement that was so outraged? Where were these villagers who would be cruelly dislocated?

Lori Pottinger, the International Rivers activist who led the Bujagali campaign, was not exactly forthcoming. Her local counterparts were preoccupied, she said; and snooping around the villages at the Bujagali site would get me into trouble with the Ugandan authorities. I tracked down the environmental group that she worked with anyway, and telephoned the office; I was invited to come over straight away, and the group's young director sat me down in his office and plied me with leaflets and reports, which gratefully acknowledged the sponsorship of a group called the Swedish Society for Nature Conservation. After half an hour of conversation, I asked the question that really concerned me: What kind of organization was this?

"This is a membership organization," I was told.

"How many members?" I asked. My host kindly got up and rummaged about in his desk, returning with a blue notebook.

"Here is the list," he said triumphantly. I looked. Uganda's National Association of Professional Environmentalists had all of twenty-five members—not exactly a broad platform from which to oppose electricity for millions.

My next move was to visit Bujagali. I hooked up with a Ugandan sociologist who knew the region well, and who promised to translate for me. At a little cluster of buildings on the edge of the dam site, she stopped and checked in with the local government representative; far from threatening to call the cops, he grinned and climbed into the car with us. For the next three hours, we interviewed villager after villager, and found the same story; the dam people had come and promised generous financial terms, and the villagers were happy to accept them and relocate. My sociologist companion said maybe we had sample bias; we were interviewing men, who might be only too willing to spend cash compensation on booze, leaving their families with nothing. So we interviewed some women, too, and they offered the same pro-project line. The only people who objected to the dam were the ones living just outside its perimeter. They were angry because the project was *not* going to affect them. They had been offered no generous payout, and they were jealous of their neighbors.

This story is a tragedy for Uganda, since millions of Ugandans are being deprived of electricity—deprived by Californians whose idea of an electricity "crisis" is a handful of summer blackouts. But it is also a tragedy for the antipoverty fight worldwide, since projects in dozens of countries are being held up for fear of activist resistance. This would not happen if American and European politicians could tell good NGOs apart from unreasonable ones, and could close their ears to unjustified complaints. But this apparently is hard: time after time, malicious Internet-enabled groups make scary claims about the iniquities of Bank projects, and the government officials who sit on the Bank's board believe them. In the face of this pressure, the Bank is often forced to go to absurd lengths to prove that its projects will do no harm—even commissioning, in the case of one project I will describe, an environmental and anthropological study that ran to nineteen volumes. Small wonder that the Bank is attacked for being maddeningly slow. It is indeed slow, but the reasons lie mainly outside it.

With great fireworks shows of energy, Jim Wolfensohn has fought to rejuvenate the Bank; the battle has been messy. He has shaken the institution by the hair, booting almost every senior manager out of the door, and recasting the Bank's structure and mission. He would stroll down the Bank's corridors in the early days and accost a random official—"I'm surprised you're still here!" he'd say, leaving the unfortunate target to wonder whether it was time to start clearing out his office. And yet, under Wolfensohn, the Bank has made headway. In the Balkans, it has demonstrated that it can be a marvelous tool of Western strategy; in Uganda, despite the frustrations of the Bujagali dam, it has helped to lift one in five people out of poverty; all over the world, the Wolfensohn Bank has opened up the development agenda to new players and subjects. But for all Wolfensohn's ferocious personality, there are limits to what he can achieve. He cannot succeed—nobody can succeed—unless the rest of us wake up to the Lilliputian menace and contain our tendency to oscillate between contempt for multilateral outfits and excessive expectations. I have recounted Wolfensohn's struggles mostly for the joy of the story, but also to show why, if the World Bank is worth criticizing, that's because it's so well worth defending.

Jim Wolfensohn is the most ambitious man I know, and the Bank is the most ambitious institution. A dreamer who wants to do everything in the world stands atop an organization that wants to change every-thing within it. We live in an era of technologists who shrink the globe and biologists who clone species and a superpower that seeks to remake the Middle East in its own image. Surely Wolfensohn's story is a sort of saga of our times? It is a tale of ambition multiplied by ambition, and of ambition's limits.

CHAPTER ONE

A TALE OF TWO AMBITIONS

ON FRIDAY, SEPTEMBER 14, 2001, President George W. Bush led a televised prayer service in Washington's National Cathedral. He invoked the heroes of three days before: inside the World Trade Center, a man who could have saved himself had stayed and died beside his quadriplegic friend; a priest died giving the last rites to a firefighter; two office workers, finding a disabled stranger, carried her down sixty-eight floors to safety. We feel, said the president, what Franklin Roosevelt called the "warm courage of national unity." And he spelled out the next steps. "Our responsibility to history is already clear: to answer these attacks and rid the world of evil."

Meanwhile another memorial service was under way in another part of Washington. In what passes for the capital's business district, two blocks west of the White House, two thousand people gathered in the glass-fronted atrium of the World Bank's headquarters. In an institution with employees from more than a hundred countries, including a large number of Muslims, the attacks of September 11 had induced a trauma of a special kind. Along with the fear felt by everyone in Washington—that more and nastier attacks might follow soon—there was the fear that life in the United States would become less secure for people with Pakistani or Saudi or Afghan passports. And there was the fear—which only grew as the president's rhetoric evolved—that friends and family abroad could somehow find themselves on the wrong side of a new global divide—the side that President Bush now classified as "evil."

The World Bankers gathered in the atrium, where the walls rise, cathedral-like, thirteen stories above the marble floor to a roof composed of glass; and where, in place of the baptismal basin and Christian inscription, there is an internal lake fed by an internal waterfall, and a sign proclaiming, OUR DREAM IS A WORLD FREE OF POVERTY. The staff packed into this atrium, displacing the kiosk displays on work stress and business communication that often furnish its vast space, and watched their president face them from a stage: a silver-haired, barrel-chested, twinkly eyed man—a sort of Santa Claus without the beard and costume. "I am not a preacher and I surely don't represent all the religions here," the president began, "but in this room we have a microcosm of the world. We have one hundred forty nations. We have Christians and Muslims and Jews and Buddhists and Sikhs. . . . We as a family can be a light for each other and for our community and for the world, because we are charged with the most significant challenge of all: to relieve poverty, and to improve the lives of our fellow men, and give our children a chance for peace and hope. . . . Ours is a noble task," he added.

To relieve poverty and so create a space for peace: Over the next few weeks James Wolfensohn, who is more of a preacher than he allows, built upon this theme, offering a response to 9/11 that contrasted markedly with President Bush's promise to "rid the world of evil." In Wolfensohn's view,[1] an understanding of the terrorist attacks began with the big picture: In a world of 6 billion people, half lived on less than $2 per day, and a fifth subsisted with not even a dollar. In the next twenty-five years, moreover, the world's population would swell by a further 2 billion, and all but 50 million of these would live in poverty-afflicted countries. Even if no simple link existed between poverty and terrorism, these population numbers surely meant something. In a world with so much poverty, you couldn't just identify a few pockets of terrorism and vow to root them out. Security lay in bringing the excluded in, not in dividing the world into two camps and rooting out the evil one.

In the past, Wolfensohn would say, you might have overlooked this link between security and poverty. For the fortunate fifth of the world's people, who lived in the countries with four-fifths of the world's income, it had been possible to imagine that a wall separated "them" from "us," that sheer distance—psychic, geographical, or otherwise—could insulate us from the billion people who lacked drinkable water, or the women who perished in childbirth at the rate of one a minute. But after September 11, it was time to realize that global poverty had global reach, whether because it created the failed states that nurtured terrorists, or because it incubated disease, environmental damage, and migration pressures. "There is no wall," Wolfensohn declared. "We are linked by trade, investment, finance, by travel and communications, by disease, by crime, by migration, by environmental degradation, by drugs, by financial crises and by terror."[2]

If the rich world was going to get serious about fighting global poverty, there was no doubt that the World Bank would lead the effort. It was a presence in almost every poor country in the world, supplying around $20 billion in loans a year, for projects ranging from irrigation systems to anticorruption efforts, from AIDS control to a victorious campaign against river blindness in Africa. The Bank's money, moreover, was just part of its significance; more than any other institution in the world, it understood the complex web of influences that keep people poor, and it set the intellectual agenda for other development agencies. Its ten thousand–strong staff combined raw brain power with practical experience of four continents. It advised developing countries on which problems they should tackle and how they should proceed, spreading the lessons from these efforts around the world, so that Madagascar might learn from Thailand or Tunisia. Every time the rich world's leaders confronted global problems—whether it was AIDS or female illiteracy or environmental pressures—they turned instinctively to the World Bank. Now, in the wake of 9/11, they were bound to do so once again, and with a new sense of urgency.

Reacting to the new challenge of terror, President Bush had invoked Franklin Roosevelt. In setting forth his own reaction, Wolfensohn was invoking Roosevelt as well, even though he never mentioned him.

THE WORLD BANK was conceived six decades before the terrorist attacks, in the teeth of another violent threat to American security. In December 1941, scarcely a week after the Japanese assault on Pearl Harbor, Roosevelt's long-time friend and treasury secretary, Henry Morgenthau, commissioned a blueprint for the postwar economic order. Morgenthau was incapable of designing such a thing himself—he was a gentleman-farmer, not a financier—so he turned to Harry Dexter White, a driven, brilliant Harvard PhD whose service was later rewarded with persecution at the hands of Senator Joseph McCarthy. White's brief was nothing less than to prevent another war, and to do so by forestalling the kind of economic storm that had brought about the current one. As Morgenthau put it a little while later, "all of us have seen the great economic tragedy of our time. We saw the worldwide depression of the 1930s. We saw currency disorders develop and spread from land to land. . . . We saw unemployment and wretchedness. . . . We saw bewilderment and bitterness become the breeders of fascism, and, finally, of war."[3]

White's first priority was to prevent more such "currency disorders." The postwar economic system would be anchored by the gold standard, which would shield commerce from the twin evils of exchange-rate shocks and inflation. If this system came under pressure—if a balance of payments deficit exhausted a nation's gold reserves—a new international lender of last resort would bail the country out rather than leaving it to devalue. This new bail-out lender ultimately took shape as the International Monetary Fund, which today stands across the street from the World Bank in Washington, and which still fights financial crises from Argentina to Turkey. But White's creativity did not stop there. He also conceived the idea of a new public bank that would promote the rebuilding of Europe, so ending the "unemployment and wretchedness" that Morgenthau lamented. At first, the new institution's proposed name—the "Bank for Reconstruction of the United and Associated Nations"—made no reference to the plight of developing countries. But a member of White's team suggested that this bank could play a role beyond the reconstruction of Europe. In a memo circulated in November 1943, the words "and Development" were inserted after "Reconstruction" in the title.[4]

Without World War II, and the extraordinary leverage that it afforded the United States, White's plans might have faltered. His main ally abroad was John Maynard Keynes, the preeminent economist of the time, who was then advising Britain's Treasury. Keynes agreed with the outline of the American ideas, but he disagreed on the detail. He took a dim view of White's proposal to convene an international conference to discuss plans for a new world bank; observing that forty-four governments would come, he warned of "the most monstrous monkey-house."[5] But White insisted on the gathering, and Keynes swallowed his distaste: he knew that Britain depended upon American support, both economic and military. In July 1944, when the Allied forces had still not broken out of their Normandy beachhead, several hundred delegates convened in the sprawling Mount Washington Hotel in Bretton Woods, New Hampshire.

Even then, the creation of an international bank was by no means certain. The conference invitation proclaimed currency stabilization as the primary goal; creating a bank for reconstruction was a secondary objective.[6] Keynes headed the commission charged with discussing the potential bank's design; he liked the idea of a fresh source of reconstruction funds for Europe, and saw no positive harm in lending whatever might be left to Latin America or India. After a few days of deliberation on whether the new creation might best be termed a "corporation" rather than a "bank," a drafting committee drew up the Bank's Articles of Agreement, opening the way for the long process of amendment. On the last day of the conference, the Soviet delegation demanded five changes—an affront that in retrospect seems doubly irksome, since the Soviets subsequently refused participation in the Bretton Woods institutions. But the Soviets were contained. The drafting was finished. And the conference ended with an agreement on a new International Bank for Reconstruction and Development to work alongside the International Monetary Fund.

The link between security and poverty had been stressed throughout the conference. As White said to his colleagues, "There is nothing that will serve to drive these countries into some kind of ism—communism or something else—faster than having inadequate capital."[7] But White, like Keynes, was thinking of economic misery in Europe rather than in the developing world; at most, both men regarded development as a useful rationale for the Bank once reconstruction was over. In this, they reflected the spirit of their times. Poverty was even worse then than it is now: in India, life expectancy for the poor was twenty-five years, and 90 percent of the population aged ten or older was illiterate.[8] But this was seen as a fact of life rather than an urgent challenge. In 1948, Paul Samuelson published the first edition of his classic economics textbook. It contained less than three sentences on development.[9]

And yet, even in the 1940s, it was easy to see how time would soon expand the economists' horizons. The link between security and poverty logically applied to developing countries as well as the developed ones; and the statesmen of the time could see this. "The economic health of every country is a proper matter of concern to all its neighbors, near and distant," said the message read out to delegates at the start of the Bretton Woods conference; "there is no wall," it might just as well have stated. That message—a premonition of Wolfensohn's response to twenty-first-century terror—came from none other than Franklin Roosevelt.

JAMES DAVID WOLFENSOHN knew all about walls: he had spent his life crashing straight through them. He was born on December 1, 1933, and grew up in a modest suburban apartment in Sydney, Australia. His parents had emigrated from England during the Depression, and later helped to resettle the flood of fellow Jewish émigrés who arrived in Australia during and after World War II.[10] His mother, Dora, was a musician, and sang every week on the radio; his father adored music, too, and the young Wolfensohn took piano lessons. The parents lavished attention on their two children, and especially their son, who was ten years younger than his sister and so almost an only child. Wolfensohn remembers himself as "pudgy, a very fat little boy. I was indulged by my parents, spoilt probably, and I ate far too much chocolate."[11]

This indulgence was mixed with something else—something that instilled in the young Wolfensohn a vast and raw ambition. There was a scent of disappointment in the home, of financial stress and thwarted aspiration. The young boy's father—Hyman Wolfensohn, known universally as "Bill"—was proud and intellectual and profoundly frustrated. Early in life, he had studied medicine in London, but his plan to become a doctor had been interrupted by World War I. Later he had begun a law degree, but was distracted from his studies by James Rothschild, a scion of Europe's great banking family, who hired him as his private secretary. Bill Wolfensohn thrived in the service of the Rothschilds, and accumulated enough savings to set off on his own; he moved his family to Australia in search of independent fame and fortune. But by the time his son was entering his teens, Bill Wolfensohn's quest had clearly failed.

He had lost the money he had made in London, and had discovered how much harder it was to prosper when severed from the Rothschild name; the small business consultancy he ran made barely enough for the family to survive on. Cut off from his native Europe, Bill Wolfensohn brooded on the far fringe of the world. He lived in a state of financial worry, having rubbed shoulders with plenty. He rued his lowly professional status, having once aspired to join both the medical and legal priesthoods. He could not live his life again. But he was determined that his son should not repeat his errors.

Half a century later, Jim Wolfensohn still remembers the extraordinary paternal expectations of his youth. He was shoved through his early school years, jumping ahead two grades; when a famous tennis coach suggested that he interrupt his schooling to train for international tournaments, his father wouldn't hear of it. Somewhere in his mid-teens, the pressure grew too much; having entered Sydney Boys High School as a star student, he matriculated four years later with the lowest grades you could get while still qualifying for college. In his first year at university, he failed all his subjects and felt miserable.[12] He was plump, teased by his older classmates, ignored by the girls. His only success was to land a string of leading roles in the Gilbert and Sullivan comic operas. He sang the female parts because his voice had not yet broken.

Isolated, unhappy, and unsuccessful: by an irony familiar to parents, Bill Wolfensohn was turning his son into a facsimile of his own frustrations. But after the low point of that first university year, Jim's fortunes bounced back. He found a mentor in the form of Julius Stone, a family friend and eminent law professor. Stone invited Jim out to his country house on weekends, and the young man helped to lay cement paths in the garden while the grand professor offered advice on organizing note cards and other tricks of academic life. When Wolfensohn returned for his second year of university, he had gathered enough confidence for his innate ability to show through. His studies started to go better, and he

won a place in the university air squadron, an achievement that con-
ferred alpha male status. It was a mark of his new popularity that, as he
was watching the university fencing team practice on the veranda by
the tennis courts one day, the captain called out to him. A member of
the squad had fallen sick; would Wolfensohn like to stand in the next
day at the national championships?[13]

The way Wolfensohn tells it, he did not know how to hold a sword,
and he could not even afford the train ride to the tournament. He went
home to his father, who liked the idea of his son winning a sporting
accolade without the distractions of training, and the family scraped
together the money for the train ticket. On the way to the tournament,
Wolfensohn and his teammates worked out a code; the drop of a handkerchief would be a signal for Wolfensohn to charge at his opponent
with his sword extended. It made little difference, since Wolfensohn
lost all his bouts. But he had discovered a sport that he adored. As he
completed his studies—including the graduate law program that his
father urged on him—his fencing went from strength to strength. Five
years after his debut, he represented Australia in the Melbourne Olympics of 1956. Two years later he became Australia's team captain.

If the suburban apartment in Sydney was not an obvious springboard for international fame, the Olympics made up for that. Fencing
taught Wolfensohn that he could compete on a grand stage. The year
after his Olympic appearance, the youth who had flunked his first year
of university applied for a Rhodes Scholarship to Oxford; when the
Rhodes Trust turned him down, he applied to Harvard Business School
and was accepted. He called Australia's minister for air, Frederick
Osborne, and used his exceedingly modest status as a member of the
university air squadron to talk his way into a free seat on a London-
bound air force jet; "Fred thought the request was so preposterous he
granted it," Wolfensohn said later.[14] In London he begged a steerage-
class passage on the *Queen Elizabeth* from a benevolent uncle and set
sail for New York, where another relative took him in and bought him a

cheap radio. He arrived at Harvard broke but excited. "I was too stupid to know I was poor," he later told one interviewer.[15]

Wolfensohn's difficulties in the United States were not only financial. He faced a cultural challenge, too: his first day at Harvard he met a woman who, learning of his Australian origin, complimented him on his newfound mastery of English. The goading pressure of his father was still there; during his years of study at Harvard, Bill Wolfensohn wrote to him every single day, even though he usually had nothing to report beyond banal everyday details.[16] To survive financially, Wolfensohn and an Irish buddy set up Teddy's Laundry Service, which serviced the future chief executives in the management program at Harvard. The young entrepreneurs went around on a crummy bicycle, which they had picked up for a few dollars; in a neighborhood notorious for bike theft, the laundry service's official steed never attracted thieves' attention. The laundry business yielded enough money for Wolfensohn to go out occasionally, and he sometimes bought admission to rehearsals of the Boston Symphony Orchestra for 25 cents. At one of those rehearsals, he got into conversation with Elaine Botwinick, a Wellesley student who shared his love of Judaism and music. They married in New York in November 1961, and Elaine's father held a reception for the couple at the Waldorf-Astoria hotel. Afterward the young Wolfensohns set off for a honeymoon in Malaga, a Spanish resort, where Jim had found a bargain-rate hotel. On arrival he discovered to his surprise that Malaga is freezing in the winter.[17]

ON THE LAST WORKING DAY of the Bretton Woods conference, July 21, 1944, a delegate rose to emphasize the curious quality of the World Bank: "It was accidentally born with the name Bank, and Bank it remains, mainly because no satisfactory name could be found in the dictionary for this unprecedented institution."[18] The Bank would take no deposits, unlike a normal bank; it would obtain its seed capital from founding governments,[19] then use this collateral to raise extra cash by issuing bonds on Wall Street. The Bank would lend the money at a slightly higher interest rate than it paid the bond holders; the resulting profits would cover the cost of staff and other overheads and perhaps yield a small surplus. In the ensuing years, this surplus served to expand the Bank's capital base, a process that was accelerated from time to time by capital injections from shareholding governments. The stronger the Bank's capital base grew, the more bonds the Bank could issue and the more the Bank could lend. Lending duly grew at an impressive clip throughout the Bank's first decades.

The Bank's governance structure was unusual, too. Its founding governments appointed representatives to sit on the Bank's board. But, unlike at the United Nations, the Bank's professional staff asserted considerable independence. The first president, Eugene Meyer, battled the board's intrusions, and six months later he resigned;[20] his successor took the job on condition of the board's subordination. From then on, the board had the power to vote on loan proposals, but the staff retained control over what to propose; even then, the board's design saved the Bank from the woes of other multilateral institutions. There was no one-country, one-vote system, like the one adopted for the UN General Assembly at the San Francisco conference in 1945. Instead, each country's weight on the board reflected its contribution to the Bank's capital, giving the United States and its allies a firm grip on all decisions.

Having brought the board under control, John McCloy, the Bank's second president, signed off on the first loan, to France for reconstruction. The request for $500 million arrived as a letter attached to an outline of the government's reconstruction plan. It explained that $106 million was needed for equipment, $180 million for coal and petroleum products, and $214 million for raw materials such as animal fats and copper. The Bank's fledgling staff was thoroughly flummoxed. "Nobody knew where to begin," one official recalled. "We were inexperienced. We didn't know what kinds of questions to ask, what kind of investigation to make."[21] In May 1947, the Bank agreed to half the $500 million requested, and went on to make more reconstruction loans—to the Netherlands, Denmark, and Luxembourg.[22] But the Bank's efforts were soon swamped by the much bigger Marshall Plan, launched a month after the French loan. Sooner than it had expected, the Bank's original reason for being was gone. It graduated from reconstruction and advanced into the uncharted waters of developing countries.

At first the Bank was deliberately cautious. It sought not to transform the conditions of its clients, but rather to finance a handful of sound projects. The Bank's financial masters on Wall Street favored infrastructure developments, preferably ones that could charge a tariff and so generate an income. The idea was that a dam could produce electricity, and electricity could be sold, and selling it would make the loan repayable; the same logic held for rail networks and irrigation systems. Wall Street's logic was questionable, since the Bank's loans were made to governments, not free-standing projects, and there was no guarantee that a government would apply a project's revenues to debt repayment. But Wall Street saw the world through a commercial-banking lens, and as long as the World Bank pretended to be a commercial bank, the markets remained friendly. The Bank duly secured its AAA credit status at the end of the 1950s.

There was another reason for the Bank to stick to infrastructure, beyond the preferences of Wall Street. The reigning orthodoxy of the time held that the accumulation of fixed capital—of factories, machinery, and roads—was the key to development. Poor countries, after all, had large numbers of underemployed people, so labor scarcity did not appear to hold them back; capital scarcity was the bottleneck. The impressive industrialization of the Soviet Union in the 1950s, achieved by a program of forced saving to pay for factories and machines, only encouraged the belief that economic growth was determined by investment. In 1960, the economist Walt Rostow propounded the accepted wisdom in his bestselling volume, *The Stages of Economic Growth,* which argued that developing countries would take off into self-sustaining progress provided they had enough capital; he proposed that their "financing gaps" be bridged by generous foreign assistance.[23] But neither the financing-gap theory nor the World Bank's narrow infrastructure focus was destined to last long—for reasons that Jim Wolfensohn was soon to experience.

AFTER LEAVING HARVARD in 1959, Wolfensohn worked for a short time in Switzerland, then moved to New York the following August to take up a post with Rheem International. It was not the most glamorous of moves: Rheem made steel drums for oil as well as air-conditioners. But Wolfensohn was given a grand title—director, growth and development—and allowed to go out and find customers. The young director headed off to India, a country then borrowing heavily from the World Bank. But the trip that proved most memorable was to Nigeria, a place whose combination of oil wealth and appalling heat seemed to scream out for air-conditioner investment.

Wolfensohn set off for Lagos in 1961, the year that the World Bank established an Africa department to assist newly independent countries. The continent's prospects seemed bright. Its economies were growing as fast as Asia's, and it seemed relatively stable. Many African countries had oil or other natural resources as well as ample land; Asia's high population density, by contrast, was regarded as a serious handicap. Adventurous business executives were beating a path to countries like Nigeria, and their enthusiasm seemed to promise rapid advance. If Rheem International built an air-conditioner factory in Nigeria, it would be helping to bridge the "financing gap" that kept Nigerians in poverty.

On arrival in Nigeria's capital in September 1961, Wolfensohn found that the health minister wanted to see him. This seemed a little odd; he was not proposing to sell medicines. The minister explained that he was "in charge" of Wolfensohn's project since it was "his turn"; he observed that, in order to build a factory, Wolfensohn would undoubtedly need land; he had the perfect land for him. The minister then declared that he was due to speak in Parliament, so the meeting adjourned. Wolfensohn promised to come back to discuss the price his host was asking.

Not knowing how to fill the time, Wolfensohn wandered over to the Parliament building, thinking he might watch his new associate in action. He walked into the proud new structure, put up to mark Nigeria's independence the previous year, and almost laughed out loud: there, in the relentless 110-degree heat, was the speaker of the Nigerian Parliament, decked out in a full-bottomed wig and gown copied straight from England. To a young Australian, this colonial mimicry was half ludicrous, half sad; it was certainly worth a photograph. Wolfensohn drew from his pocket a miniature Minox camera that he had borrowed from Elaine's father, and took a couple of pictures. A quarter of an hour later, the sergeant at arms appeared at Wolfensohn's elbow and said he should come with him.

Assuming he was off to see his newfound friend the health minister, Wolfensohn agreed gladly. The sergeant led him out of the building and held on to his arm; a crowd had assembled in the street, but Wolfensohn wasn't sure it warranted close police protection. The people in the crowd were saying something, and Wolfensohn strained to make it out; "Spy! Spy!" they seemed to cry, so Wolfensohn turned to his guide and asked who the spy was. "Sir, you are," came the reply. "You took pictures illegally and you have a spy camera."

Wolfensohn protested, but to no avail; the hand on his arm was in no mood for negotiation. He was led into the office of the leader of the opposition and imprisoned there—evidently, Nigeria's opposition got no respect even in those early days of independence. Ten minutes later the sergeant returned, this time with another policeman and a photographer. The young director, growth and development, was staring disaster in the eyes: There was going to be a spy scandal, and his photo would appear in all the local newspapers. Forced to choose between respecting Nigeria's law enforcers and respecting his own reputation and prospects, the director pushed past his captors and sprinted down the corridor, pursued by the law enforcers in question and by the man trying to take his photograph. Seeing a door marked PRAYER ROOM, he rushed inside, and into an enormous figure washing his feet in preparation for spiritual devotion. "My dear chap, what do you want?" the enormous figure demanded. Wolfensohn panted that he wanted asylum.

The enormous figure never had a name, at least not one that Wolfensohn remembers, but he was obviously the product of Oxford or Cambridge. "Oh, these people have to have their fun," he said, telling the breathless sergeant to calm down. But the sergeant's colleagues had already seized Wolfensohn's passport from his hotel, and he hotly stood his ground; the spy-cum-director was informed that he must offer his apologies at the bar of the House, and since the House had just adjourned, that meant three weeks of unwanted Nigerian vacation. In the end, Wolfensohn was allowed to write a letter of apology in return for his passport.[24]

The story of the spy made the front pages of the Nigerian newspapers the next day: "The camera was tucked inside the lapel of his coat and was no bigger than a box of matches," the *West African Pilot* reported.[25] The affair ensured that Wolfensohn never did develop his air-conditioner factory, and he quit Rheem a few weeks later on the eve of his wedding. But Nigeria had given him some feel for the challenges confronting the World Bank in newly minted nations. It was all very well saying that developing countries would take off into self-sustaining growth if only they had sufficient investment capital. But development experts would have to take the argument to the next step: How do you create the conditions that allow investors to do business?

. . .

THE YEAR OF Wolfensohn's Nigerian visit, a future Nobel laureate named Theodore Schultz offered a partial answer to this question. Development was not all about physical capital, he said; you needed literate, healthy workers to make a country function right; without them your new machines were useless. Schultz coined the term "human capital" to describe this other ingredient of development. In the decade that ensued, the World Bank started to branch out into education, training, and other sorts of human-capital projects.

This transformation was accelerated by a change in the Bank's structure. In 1960, the new International Development Association—a subsidized lender that would specialize in the very poorest countries—was grafted onto the Bank's existing operation. For more than a decade, the Bank had preached the virtues of market-based lending; if money cost something, then money would be soundly used, at least according to the theory. Now, with the addition of the International Development Association (or IDA, as it is painfully known), the Bank would offer its poorest borrowers money at a much cheaper rate: in many cases there was a ten-year repayment holiday followed by a further forty years in which the loan would be paid back, and even then at a token interest rate. Because inflation eroded the value of the loan, the Bank would recoup only a small fraction of what it lent; it would therefore depend on regular infusions of capital from donor governments. The Bank's resemblance to a normal bank was now more tenuous than ever.

The creation of IDA reflected shifts in the mind-set of the Bank's leading shareholders. It was the height of the cold war, and U.S. policy makers looked upon cheap World Bank credits as a useful tool for propping up sympathetic governments. The tide of independence was sweeping across Africa, and there was no telling whether these new countries would look to the communists or to the United States and its allies. Fidel Castro's Cuban revolution, in 1959, did not encourage complacency among Western strategists; and it was a mark of the contemporary mood that Walt Rostow's pro-development "financing-gap" book, published the following year, was subtitled *A Non-Communist Manifesto*. Meanwhile, the miraculous recoveries of postwar Germany and Japan had boosted faith in technocrats' ability to bring about progress; if IDA was endowed with enough money, and if it recruited enough intellectual whizzes, there seemed every reason to hope that the ex-colonies' progress would be rapid. When, in the year following IDA's creation, President John F. Kennedy called for a development decade in a speech to the United Nations, he combined technocratic hopes and cold war fears in almost equal measure.

IDA rapidly transformed the Bank. In the 1950s, it had been effectively barred from helping countries that could not afford commercial loans; now it could help everyone. The staff grew quickly: having started the 1960s with 283 professionals, it ended the decade with 917; the economics department grew fourfold, and the total administrative budget tripled.[26] The ambitious mandate that came with IDA encouraged a messianic self-image: the Bank had been told to save millions from poverty, and no cause could be more virtuous or more pressing. At the same time, the Bank's leaders became fund-raisers: the IDA kitty needed refilling every three years, and the Bank discovered straight away that governments would not cough up the money easily. George Woods, the Bank's president from 1963 to 1968, found himself in a position that his successors would repeat: delivering speeches on the urgency of third-world poverty, in the hope that rich governments could be shamed into financing IDA more generously.

Woods's last speech, in Stockholm in October 1967, marked the high point of his advocacy. He declared that "the plight of the developing peoples—of the two-thirds of humanity who are striving to cross the threshold of modernization—is *the* central drama of our times." He spoke of "the risk of stark crisis—in food, in work, in hope—for over half the human race."[27] It was a startling performance, but it was merely a taste of stronger things to come. In 1968, Woods was succeeded by Robert Strange McNamara, the U.S. defense secretary who had presided over America's early intervention in Vietnam. McNamara pushed Woods's rhetoric to the emotional edge, causing his audiences to cry, and sometimes crying with them.

AFTER HIS STINT with Rheem International, Wolfensohn returned to Australia with his new bride. He set up his own business advisory firm and ran it for a year, then dropped it to join Ord Minnett Thomson, Sydney's leading brokerage. But his career really took off when Ord Minnett invested in a start-up merchant bank called Darling & Co. Wolfensohn moved over to Darling's in 1964, and discovered he had a golden gift for pleasing the corporate chiefs who provide merchant bankers' business. He was a magnetic listener, which is another way of saying he possessed a powerful charm; he gave his clients the warm sense that he had understood, that his mind was headed down exactly the same path, and that he was brimming with ideas to help his friend along this mutual journey. Perhaps Wolfensohn's own insecurity, the product of his father's goading and his experience as a young Jewish outsider in the United States, created within Wolfensohn an instinctive grasp of people's needs; he understood the human craving to be heard because he felt it so acutely. Whatever the secret of Wolfensohn's personality and charm, the art of relationship banking came to him naturally.

Wolfensohn was also lucky. He joined Darling's just as Australia was opening up as a market for U.S. and European firms, whose bosses discovered the joys of business trips to Sydney during the Southern Hemisphere's summer. These businessman-tourists would stop by at Darling's, and the firm's elder statesmen would introduce them to young Jimmy Wolfensohn, an Australian who knew how an American executive thought and planned: who could calculate the return on capital in the American fashion, and who knew everything that the hot

B-school graduates knew back in New York or Chicago. Wolfensohn could walk them through the Australian business landscape, and he could show them other things as well; Australia was too remote to be visited in a rush, so there was time to go sailing, go out to a restaurant, maybe visit the Wolfensohns at their apartment. And so, though still in his early thirties, Wolfensohn built a network of exalted business relationships that stood him in good stead. David Rockefeller of Chase Bank became a friend. Maurice Strong, the chairman of a big Canadian holding company called Power Corporation, recruited Wolfensohn to run his Australian subsidiary, which Wolfensohn did in parallel to his work at Darling's.

Wolfensohn's chief failing was impatience. He was burning to advance, not tomorrow but today; he wanted the success that had eluded his father, and he wanted enough cash to ease his parents' financial worries.[28] His impatience got the better of him in 1967, when he helped Maurice Strong's Power Corporation launch a hostile bid for a mining concern called Mount Morgan. This was not a tactful move: John Broinowski, a formidable industrialist who sat on Darling's board, was determined that if Mount Morgan was ready to be gobbled up it would be he who did the swallowing.[29] In the ensuing battle, Broinowski sued Wolfensohn for conflict of interest, which prompted Wolfensohn to countersue, which resulted in a victory for Wolfensohn, which did not stop Broinowski from gaining control of Mount Morgan in the meantime. Whatever the legal merits of Wolfensohn's conduct, he had picked a costly fight: Broinowski pulled himself up to his full establishment height and declared that he would crush this young upstart. Wolfensohn's fast-track career faced the prospect of deceleration.

Deceleration was not what Wolfensohn believed in. Rather than remain at his post until the storm passed, Wolfensohn preferred to quit—both the firm and Australia. He had a personal motive; Elaine, who had by now given birth to their second child, did not want to settle in Sydney. But there was also the fact that Wolfensohn had possibilities elsewhere. On business trips from Sydney, Wolfensohn had attended the court of Gordon Richardson, the wildly successful chairman of Schroders, then one of the leading financial houses in the City of London; and he had befriended Siegmund Warburg, founder of the eponymous bank, who took a shine to the young man because of his sophisticated feel for music. After the battle with Broinowski, Gordon Richardson took Wolfensohn off for a weekend at his country home, and one evening the job negotiations grew so furious that Peggy Richardson burst in on the two men; she ordered them off to bed, handing each a hot-water bottle. The next morning Wolfensohn and Richardson came to terms, and Wolfensohn told Warburg that he would not accept his rival offer.

Wolfensohn's period with Schroders, from 1968 to 1977, followed the same pattern as his time in Australia. He wooed his clients masterfully: he listened, empathized, and understood their needs; he offered "intelligence, imagination, lateral thinking, good contacts, focused energy and a very good memory," according to one Schroders contemporary. His stamina allowed him to take in more parties, exhibitions, and concerts than ordinary mortals could manage; his looks, cultural appetites, and exotic Aussie charm made him a popular figure on the London circuit. The more he got about, the more his network grew, and the more he would pop up in the right place at the right time with an I-can-solve-your-problem attitude. He brought in some prize clients—there were the Americans and Europeans whom he had known in Australia, as well as the Australians who were starting to venture in the opposite direction, but there were others, too. One day Wolfensohn got a call from the father provincial of the Jesuits in England, who had somehow come by an estate in Tahiti and didn't know what to do with it. "Father, I have some partners who are Jesuits, couldn't I get them to work for you?" Wolfensohn inquired, while also recommending that the land be used to develop a hotel. He was assured that being Jewish was no obstacle at all; half of Christendom had recommended him.[30]

In September 1970, less than three years after joining Schroders, Wolfensohn was appointed head of its American branch, which was judged a bit too sleepy. Wolfensohn moved his family to New York— by this time with three children—and brought the needed fizz, not least thanks to the musical passions that had endeared him to Sieg-mund Warburg. During his period in London, Wolfensohn had backed a small company that represented concert artists, and many became his friends: men like Vladimir Ashkenazi, the great Russian pianist-conductor, and Daniel Barenboim, his Argentine-Israeli rival. The Wolfensohns kept a grand piano at their London home, and Ashkenazi and Barenboim would drop by to practice on their visits to Britain; one summer the Wolfensohns shared a holiday in Greece with the Ashke-nazi family. And so in 1970, when Wolfensohn was preparing to open the new Schroders building in New York, he conceived the idea of an inaugural concert. He called up Ashkenazi and asked him how he would like to be the first Soviet musician to open a commercial bank on Wall Street.[31]

Wolfensohn quickly turned the New York position into something of an empire. He dreamed up extraordinary projects; there was a scheme to develop a large chunk of Tehran and name it in honor of the shah, and another to design a development plan for western Nigeria.[32] After oil prices jumped in 1973, Wolfensohn persuaded Venezuela's government that he could advise them on their newfound wealth, and he began to visit Caracas monthly. "His ideas were totally grandiose," recalls a colleague of the time; "he was a tremendous creator of transac-tions, but not much of a manager."[33] Yet the energy that Wolfensohn showed in his banking ambitions were only part of the total.

If you visit the Wolfensohn Family Foundation, forty-nine stories above Park Avenue in Manhattan, you may be shown into the spec-tacular corner office where the news clips from the Wolfensohn career have been painstakingly assembled. There are two bulging blue folders relating to Wolfensohn's banking adventures, beginning with a pair of disintegrating Nigerian newspapers that date from his ill-fated trip in 1961 to Lagos. But there are two equally large folders relating to his musical and charitable exploits, along with two more folders of photographs that relate largely to his life in music. Wolfensohn's musical and charitable interests amounted to a kind of secondary career, parallel to his hectic life in finance. It was a way to network—to bring contacts and sparkle to the American arm of Schroders—but even more it was a way to pursue personal interests.

If his financial career had taken off a decade earlier in Australia, Wolfensohn's musical career began to flower in New York in the early 1970s. He maintained the musical friendships he had formed earlier in London, and accumulated many more after 1972, when he joined the board of Carnegie Hall, the grandfather of New York's musical venues. The bond that came to matter most was with Daniel Barenboim, who had married a magical cellist called Jacqueline du Pre after a lightning two-week courtship. When Wolfensohn met her, du Pre was a global sensation: she was intense and impetuous, and she played with a rare flame; her performances went from glory to glory until one day when, rehearsing for the New York Philharmonic Orchestra, she found that she could not feel the bow in her fingers. The conductor, Leonard Bernstein, thought she was throwing a spoiled-genius fit, but the odd signs persisted; the feeling in her fingers never came back, and she would sometimes lose her balance. Eventually the inevitable diagnosis came: it was multiple sclerosis. She was only twenty-eight, and her career was finished.

On the day that hope gave out, du Pre and Barenboim had dinner with the Wolfensohns. Jacqueline was in despair, at a loss for what to do now that her concert days were over. Wolfensohn suggested she could teach, but Jacqueline retorted that no one would want to study under her; to cheer her up, Wolfensohn said he would. The next day she called him in his office at Schroders and said she had found him a cello; she was ready to start teaching right away if he would grant her one condition. The condition was that he must promise to play a concert on his fiftieth birthday. Wolfensohn was barely forty at the time, so he said yes without thinking.[34]

The way Wolfensohn tells it, Barenboim called years later with a message from his wife, whose illness had by then worsened. Jacqui was asking, "Where is the concert?" and since she was now deeply sick it wouldn't do to disappoint her. Wolfensohn had completely forgotten his promise, but didn't like to let her down; he would hold a concert at his home, he offered. "That's not a concert," Barenboim replied, before declaring that the venue should be nothing less than Carnegie Hall, of which Wolfensohn had conveniently become chairman. Barenboim started making calls, and lined up a musical who's who to play with Wolfensohn at the concert; Leonard Rose and Isaac Stern performed, and Vladimir Ashkenazi canceled another concert in order to join them.[35] And so it was that Wolfensohn, who had taken up the cello when on the verge of middle age, played with the stars in Carnegie Hall, New York City's most glittering venue.

After four years of running Schroders in New York, Wolfensohn returned to London in triumph as his bank's number two and heir apparent. The firm's chairman, Michael Verey, was expected to retire soon, and the word within Schroders was that Wolfensohn would succeed him.[36] But, just as in Australia, Wolfensohn pushed a little hard; he had so many ideas, and was so anxious to implement them now, that the traditionalists at Schroders took passionately against him. For the old guard at the firm, he was all fizz and flash; his style would damage the firm's name, and it was possibly un-British. Wolfensohn's U.S. operation, for all its razzmatazz, had never generated much in the way of profits, or so the old-boy network said; it didn't help that he was Jewish. Out of this cauldron of jealousy, traditionalism, and xenophobia, an anti-Wolfensohn movement took shape; the fittingly titled Earl of Airlie, whose wife was a lady-in-waiting to the queen, emerged as Wolfensohn's chief rival. When Verey stepped down from the top job at Schroders, the noble earl became the chairman.

ONE PERSON who wasn't stepping down was Robert McNamara. At the time of Wolfensohn's disappointment, in 1977, McNamara had spent almost a decade at the World Bank and showed no sign of slowing. In his first major speech after leaving the Department of Defense, at the Bank's annual meetings in the fall of 1968, he had announced an astonishing sea change: The institution would press beyond its focus on poor countries to focus on the poor people within them. Promoting economic growth would no longer be enough: The Bank had moved from physical capital to human capital, and now to a direct focus on poverty. As McNamara put it, a country's GDP numbers might look good, "and yet . . . you know and I know that these cheerful statistics are cosmetics which conceal a far less cheerful picture. . . . The growth is concentrated in the industrial areas, while the peasant remains stuck in his immemorial poverty, living on the bare margin of subsistence."[37]

McNamara's rhetoric put the Bank on the front end of a wave: the notion that economic growth could not be relied upon to "trickle down" gained broad acceptance at the end of the 1960s. There were no good data to support this view—in fact, growth does reduce poverty.[38] But there was an emotional need for new approaches after years in which growth targeting had failed to put an end to human misery; and there was an accurate sense that the postwar emphasis on dams and factories had involved a basic error. The way to enrich a peasant may not be to move him to a steel mill, it was now realized; it may be to give him better seeds, advice on agricultural techniques, or land tenure. In 1970, Peru's left-wing government launched a radical land redistribution program, to broad applause from development thinkers; on the other side of the world, India's Indira Gandhi built an election campaign on a promise to fight poverty directly. Meanwhile in the United States and Europe, redistributive ideas dominated the countercultural movement that had risen up in opposition to the Vietnam War, and similar notions percolated through the salons and the conference circuit. In 1970, David Morse, the head of the International Labor Organization, announced, a bit too gleefully, "the dethronement of GNP"; and a distinguished development economist named Hollis Chenery urged countries to target "optimum growth," a rate that might be different from maximum growth but that would include direct interventions against poverty.

In May 1970, shortly after making that remark, Chenery was hired to join the Bank as McNamara's chief economist.[39] The challenge for the two men was to choose the direct actions against poverty that would prove most effective. The Bank started to fund conferences, retrospectives, seminars; it tackled subjects as diverse as fishing, tourism, and land-holding patterns; the ambition was imperialistic. It didn't matter that the United Nations already had a Food and Agriculture Organization; McNamara created an overlapping group within his institution.[40] It didn't matter that the UN's International Labor Organization had researched employment patterns; McNamara created a division within the Bank to ponder the same issue. He created a Rural Development Department in 1973, an Urban Development Department in 1975, and a Population, Health and Nutrition Department in 1979: Nothing was excluded.[41] Through all this expansion, McNamara expanded the Bank's rhetoric as well; the planning for his annual meeting speech became increasingly elaborate. At the Nairobi gathering in 1973, McNamara delivered his best-remembered lines. He spoke to the world about "absolute poverty," a "condition of life so degraded by disease, illiteracy, malnutrition and squalor as to deny its victims basic human necessities. . . . The extremes of privilege and deprivation are simply no longer acceptable," he concluded. "We should strive to eradicate poverty by the end of this century."

McNamara's ambitions were especially aimed at small-holding farmers, who accounted for a large share of the world's poor. His staff wrestled with ways of reaching this group, eventually coming up with a creature known as the "integrated rural development project." The idea was that rural poverty had many roots, from farmers' poor health to the poor quality of their seeds, from the long distances they walked to fetch water to the lack of transport to urban markets and the number of children in their families: McNamara's integrated projects set out to tackle all these problems simultaneously. Though theoretically persuasive, this fix-everything approach proved overambitious, especially in countries without competent administrators; and the Bank's technocrats made too little effort to design projects in ways that would enlist poor farmers' willing cooperation. By the end of the 1970s, McNamara's rural development projects had ended in failure, and the Bank's project managers were grumbling behind his back. After more than three decades of continuous expansion—in staff numbers, loan volumes, and ambition—the World Bank had begun to seem overextended. The institution's war on poverty, like America's war on communism in Vietnam, was proving all too much for it.

Without pressure from outside, McNamara might have soldiered on, preaching the cause of development at the Bank's annual meetings each autumn, and driving his staff to come up with new ways of advancing it. But outside pressure did arrive—in the form of two successive oil shocks. McNamara's speech in Nairobi in 1973 had been followed almost immediately by the Yom Kippur War and the Arab oil embargo; oil prices shot up, and the Bank's oil-importing clients suddenly found their trade balance deteriorating. For a while, the pain could be postponed. The Arabs parked their windfall in Western banks, so credit became cheap; countries simply borrowed to finance imports. But sooner or later countries would have to cut imports and boost exports in order to pay their petrodollars back. In a speech in Manila in May 1979, soon after the Iranian revolution had set in motion a second oil-price rise, McNamara offered a response to this problem. The Bank, he said, should do some "structural adjustment lending" to cushion the shock of paying for expensive energy. In order to generate trade surpluses, countries were going to have to devalue their currencies. In order to wean themselves off petrodollar loans, they were going to have to cut public spending. Both adjustments were sure to be painful, and the Bank would stand ready to support reformers.[42]

It was, in retrospect, a momentous suggestion. McNamara had presided over the heyday of the Bank's project approach, believing that agricultural training and irrigation systems could directly improve the lives of poor people. Now he was proposing to shift from projects to loans that would support macroeconomic adjustment—adjustment, moreover, that would impose hardship on poor people. Although it still had two more years to run, the McNamara era was effectively over; a new phase in the Bank's history was beginning. A period of expansive agendas—of initiatives on everything from population control to slum upgrading to agricultural research—was giving way to a new and narrow focus on exchange-rate policies, budget balances, and other macroeconomic challenges. For the next decade and more, the "structural adjustment" that McNamara had innocently proposed became a furious battlefield.

THE YEAR OF THAT MANILA SPEECH, Jim Wolfensohn was wrestling with debt adjustments, too, though from a different vantage point. The cheap credit of the 1970s had seduced corporations as well as governments, and the hangover was just as nasty. By the end of the decade the Chrysler car company, one of the great icons of American manufacturing prowess, found itself suffocating under the weight of its excessive debts. In the summer of 1979, Lee Iacocca, Chrysler's folk hero-boss, went cap in hand to Washington seeking a federal bailout.

Wolfensohn was by now at Salomon Brothers. After failing to get the top job at Schroders, he could have stayed on as number two; but just as in Australia one decade before, he preferred to quit both firm and country. In 1977, Wolfensohn negotiated a generous severance package with Schroders, and left London for New York, a city that properly values graduates of Harvard Business School. He signed with Salomon, a rough-hewn trading firm whose owner saw in him some needed international polish: "He spoke French!" a former colleague recalls in astonishment. An Australian journalist who visited Wolfensohn at the Salomon headquarters at the time was struck by the contrast between Wolfensohn and his new firm. On one floor of the New York Plaza building, the traders sweated over the video terminals, screaming into their telephones and spilling plastic cups of coffee: this was the heart of Salomon's business. On another floor a relatively new team of relationship bankers tried to woo clients: a butler was on hand to take your coat, and the coffee came in fancy porcelain. As the new head of the firm's corporate finance department, Wolfensohn was the chief denizen of the silver-candlesticks section of Salomon Brothers.

Chrysler's collapse allowed Wolfensohn a chance to show more than sophisticated manners. Two months after asking help from Washington, Chrysler hired Wolfensohn to hold its creditors at bay, and ultimately to persuade them to accept a debt restructuring. It was a challenge almost without precedent. Normally debt workouts are done with the help of the bankruptcy laws: a judge orders banks to wave good-bye to some of their money. But Chrysler refused to take that route, on the theory that nobody buys cars from a bankrupt car company. That left Wolfensohn with the task of persuading the banks to cancel, voluntarily, $1 billion worth of loans, and to do so in a way that would share out the pain fairly. He worked as he had never worked, shuttling between four-hundred-plus lenders in Europe and the United States and Japan; at one point he collapsed with internal bleeding and spent a week in hospital, his papers always with him. As the deal approached completion, a few small creditors still refused to go along; the treasury secretary, William Miller, was forced to get on the phone to the president of the Twin City Bank of Little Rock, Arkansas, and a couple of other holdouts were brought to heel by labor union demonstrations. In June 1980, the odyssey bore fruit. Wolfensohn herded the lenders into a restructuring deal, and the treasury secretary praised "the most complex financing operation in U.S. history."[43] In a front-page article on the signing ceremony, *The New York Times* introduced the unknown, square-jawed banker who had made it all happen. "No one here has had personal lives for the last 10 months," the square-jawed figure commented.[44]

Wolfensohn's sudden prominence came at a propitious time. McNamara was nearing his sixty-fifth birthday and was preparing his succession. He had come to know of Wolfensohn through a variety of channels. Maurice Strong, Wolfensohn's business patron from his Australia days, was a confidante of McNamara's on environmental issues, and Strong had introduced Wolfensohn to Barbara Ward, an eminent development thinker who was also close to McNamara. Wolfensohn had accompanied Strong and Ward on walks in the mountains near Geneva, combining high-minded discussion of the environment with direct appreciation of its charms; he had also joined the board of the Population Council, which promoted family planning in the poor world, and was a director of the Rockefeller Foundation. He was, in other words, a keen amateur participant in development discussions, as well as a frequent visitor to Washington during the Chrysler crisis. For these reasons, or perhaps for others that the participants no longer recall, McNamara put Wolfensohn at the top of a list of non-Americans to be considered for the World Bank presidency.[45] The list was largely moot, since an American would almost certainly be chosen. But McNamara invited Wolfensohn over, showed him the office and where to park the car, and managed to give Wolfensohn the impression that he had a real chance of succeeding him.

Wolfensohn was beside himself with excitement. As an investment banker he had often attended the World Bank's annual meetings; they were an opportunity to hatch deals and entertain clients, since the presence of finance ministers from all around the world attracted a rich caste of corporations and investors. During the 1970s, Wolfensohn had been among the many who responded to McNamara's speeches with tears, and the idea of standing in the great man's shoes thrilled and tormented him. To boost his chances for the job, Wolfensohn gave up his Australian nationality: with the help of a contact at the Jimmy Carter White House, he scheduled a citizenship interview at two weeks' notice, and spent a weekend in New York studying a manual that listed the presidents and the names of the state capitals. When he appeared for his interview, he was ushered past the waiting hordes to a special room at the back, where a polite woman asked him to sign a sheet of paper. There, said the woman, you have passed the literacy test; now tell me the name of the first president. When Wolfensohn answered, she congratulated him upon becoming an American. The brand-new citizen protested that he had spent hours preparing for questions about those state capitals. The official was adamant that the interview was over.[46]

Not long afterward, however, something else was over, too. Elaine Wolfensohn got up one morning and retrieved the newspaper from outside the door of the family's New York apartment; she scanned the headlines and returned to find her husband.

"It seems you're not going to be World Bank president after all," Elaine told him. It was October 31, 1980, and Carter had announced the appointment of a rival candidate.

CHAPTER TWO

"WORLD BANK MURDERER"

JAMES DAVID WOLFENSOHN has many faults, as we shall presently discover. But one of his great merits must be proclaimed up front: He actually wanted to be the World Bank's president. He didn't want this coyly or bashfully or in a covert, grown-up kind of way. He desired it with a 10-million-volt passion, with the same supercharged, bulldozing lust that had made him an Olympic sportsman, a Wall Street titan, and an accomplished cellist. "You've got to have a passion for development, and I've got a passion which grows," Wolfensohn once said. "It's like a new love. It's all I think about. I wake up in the morning thinking about it and I go to bed thinking about it."[1]

You might imagine, not unreasonably really, that every hard-pushing highflyer who makes it to the presidency of the World Bank must have craved the job—must have plotted and campaigned and schemed, outdoing some rivals by the sheer caliber of their résumés and sinking others by sheer cunning. But the world is more bizarre than that. Even though there is probably no cause more compelling than the struggle to lift billions out of crushing poverty, and even though McNamara's ambition made the Bank the central player in this fight, the Bank has frequently been led by people who earlier spent long, illustrious careers cordially ignoring it. When opportunity came knocking—when they were offered the chance to lead the institution at the center of one of the biggest issues of our times—these men nobly obliged, and this was awfully good of them. But never, ever did they come to the office with the rush of Romeo to Juliet's balcony.

Alden "Tom" Clausen, the man whom President Jimmy Carter picked instead of Wolfensohn in 1980, was the very model of the no-rush president. Clausen had spent his entire career at BankAmerica, and had been chief executive since 1970; BankAmerica had done well, but then its base in booming California made this less than totally remarkable. Clausen had some experience of lending to poor countries, but he knew little of development; he could judge the credit quality of Ecuador, but he had never had cause to consider the caloric intake of the average Ecuadorian farmworker. What's more, he had no apparent desire to leave the world of private banking in which he had spent more than three decades; when he was first sounded out for the World Bank, he responded that he had no public-sector experience and no urge to acquire any. But Carter was determined to find somebody who, while acceptable to fellow Democrats, would pass muster with Republicans as well; the polls strongly suggested that the White House would soon be occupied by Ronald Reagan. In August 1980, McNamara traveled to California to persuade Clausen to think again, and two months later Carter announced the selection of this traditional banker to run an out-fit that was a bank only in name.[2] From the time Clausen took up the post in July 1981, the world's premier spokesman on development was a newcomer to the subject.

Five years later Clausen's successor was chosen in an even more peculiar manner. The Reagan administration, which cared little for the Bank or its mission, refused Clausen a second presidential term but had no idea whom it liked better. Paul Volcker, the chairman of the Federal Reserve, refused to take the job. So did some other likely figures. The Reagan folk started to worry that if they didn't come up with a candidate fast, then the Europeans might name one, shattering the tradition that the top job at the Bank gets filled by American appointment. Suddenly the Reaganites did care: though they were indifferent to the Bank, they were passionate about the prerogatives and power of the U.S. presidency. So James Baker, the treasury secretary of the time, called up a retired congressman from New York and demanded permission to put his name forward.

The ex-congressman was Barber Conable. He was being offered a chance to influence the agenda of the world, but he was not at all excited. He did not want to return to Washington, where he had served in Congress for twenty years; he was reluctant to leave behind his hobbies. Among the great topics that occupied his mind were animal-hide tents and arrowheads; he was an amateur historian of the Native Americans indigenous to the Finger Lakes of New York State and a devoted collector of their relics.[3] Like Clausen before him, Conable knew nothing of poverty or development, and he was disinclined to learn. He stoutly refused to be considered for the World Bank job until Baker assured him that proposing his name was just a tactical ploy, designed merely to show that the Treasury was not bereft of candidates. Two weeks later Baker returned to Conable with unhappy news. "Barber," he said, "I'm sorry to tell you that you're the only guy we can agree on."[4]

Conable continued to protest. He declared that he was totally unqualified, a description that was only honest. He hoped vaguely that his voting record in Congress might bar him from the job; the World Bank was so marginal in his mind that he could not remember whether he had voted pro or con on issues that affected it. But it turned out that his voting record was no bar. When Baker urged that Conable's refusal would allow the Europeans to usurp a traditional American prerogative, the old congressman allowed his sense of duty to prevail.[5] In March 1986, the appointment of Barber B. Conable was announced to a mystified world. An *Economist* journalist made some calls to gauge the reaction. "Barbara who?" people responded.[6]

The weakness at the top of the World Bank—two consecutive presidents who knew little of development—compounded the challenges from outside it. Just as the development optimism of the early 1960s had set the institution on an expansionary course, so, too, the ideological polarization of the Reagan-Thatcher 1980s subjected the Bank to a curious right-left pincer movement. Right-wingers assailed the Bank as a presumably bloated public-sector institution; at the U.S. Treasury, Undersecretary Beryl Sprinkel commissioned a report to determine whether the World Bank had "socialistic" tendencies.[7] Meanwhile left-wingers assailed the Bank with even more passion, accusing it of forcing free-market orthodoxy down the throats of poor countries. Not many other organizations were attacked simultaneously by the Right and the Left. But the Bank was on the one hand a public-sector institution, and on the other hand a promoter of free-market reform. It therefore qualified as a target for both ends of the political spectrum.

In this ideological climate the "structural adjustment" lending that McNamara had proposed as a pragmatic response to the oil shock became bitterly contentious. The Bank rightly urged developing countries to devalue their currencies, a policy that they should have embraced much sooner after the 1973 shock; expensive oil was affordable only if countries boosted their exports, and that meant making their goods competitive by having a low exchange rate. The Bank simultaneously urged developing countries to cut government spending, a harsh policy but also an unavoidable one: governments had lived far beyond their means during the 1970s. Little by little, these two core prescriptions were broadened: the Bank started to urge Latin Americans and Africans to cut trade barriers, to free prices, and generally to undo the state-directed development model that many had followed for the past two decades. Poor countries had not much choice but to comply, or at least to promise to do so. The Bank, acting in concert with the International Monetary Fund, refused to lend to countries that rejected its advice; and if the Bretton Woods sisters refused to lend, American and European donors withheld support also.

The pressure on poor countries to reform was justified. At the start of the 1980s, when the first structural-adjustment loans were made, many developing countries had no control of their budgets and were printing money to pay for government spending. In 1982, the year that it defaulted to its foreign creditors, Mexico's public spending accounted for an extraordinary 45 percent of GDP, up from around 20 percent in 1970; in Brazil and Argentina, meanwhile, the habit of printing money had driven inflation into triple digits. The "financing-gap" theory of development, which encouraged the idea that economic progress depended upon Soviet-style accumulation of fixed capital, had driven countries to build state-owned industries; and while limited state direction of a developing economy does not have to be a bad thing, as East Asia's experience shows, Latin Americans and Africans went on to make a crucial error. The East Asian formula was to back industries that exported successfully; by using foreign markets as a test of firms' mettle, they avoided backing losers. But Latin Americans and Africans backed industries to supply their own markets; since these markets were often protected by trade barriers, their flagship firms escaped a competitive test of their efficiency. Pretty soon, Latin Americans and Africans found themselves pouring subsidies into white-elephant factories. In the 1960s, Ghana's government built a shoe factory, a sugar factory, and a glass factory that never went into production; it erected a pharmaceutical factory where experimental animals were housed better than most Ghanaians. In the 1970s, Peru nationalized much of the country's industry and put incompetent military officers in charge of it. The World Bank and its allies were only pointing out an obvious truth when they said these policies should be ended.

The trouble was that the Bank wrapped its sound advice in evangelistic market rhetoric. Echoing the free-market faith of its leading shareholder in Washington (and to a lesser extent of conservative governments in London and Bonn), the Bank declared that structural adjustment would take no longer than five years; after that, liberalized prices would attract private investment; growth would pick up, and poverty would recede accordingly. This, like many development promises, proved wildly optimistic. Having grown 39 percent richer in the 1970s, the average Latin American grew 10 percent poorer in the subsequent decade; the average African experienced a 9 percent advance in the 1970s followed by an 11 percent fall during the 1980s. Measures of human welfare like literacy and infant mortality continued to improve, but it was easy to lose sight of that amid tough cuts in government spending.[8] Budget austerity, urged by the IMF and the World Bank, triggered riots in Zambia, Morocco, Bolivia, and the Dominican Republic; in Sudan they precipitated the fall of a government. The Bank was accused of prescribing toxic medicine for the poor; and to large chunks of public opinion, these attacks sounded convincing.

The Bank compounded the mistake of overselling structural adjustment with two further errors. Under the leadership of Tom Clausen, it all but abandoned McNamara's antipoverty rhetoric, viewing it as an unwarranted distraction from the challenge of correcting statist economic policies; this shift in the public message of the Bank made it all too easy to paint it as heartless. At the same time, the Bank played into the hands of its critics by lending copiously to America's cold war allies like Zaire, claiming that the loans were to support structural adjustment. These clients knew perfectly well that their access to the Bank's money depended on geopolitics, not economic policy, so they saw no need to implement the reforms that the Bank's technocrats negotiated with them. Mutually assured hypocrisy ensued. The borrowers pretended to promise economic reform, and the Bank pretended to believe them.

The result was a huge blow to the Bank's credibility. The popular view of structural adjustment was summed up a few years later by the

authors Susan George and Fabrizio Sabelli: "Virtually everyone affilli-
ated with a non-governmental organization," they wrote, "says that
adjustment is an unmitigated social and ecological disaster."[9] Clausen's
deliberate downgrading of McNamara's antipoverty rhetoric had given
the Bank an inhuman, technocratic face, and even though Barber
Conable reemphasized poverty in the second half of the decade, he was
too late to dislodge the widespread skepticism about the Bank's real
motives. The image of the World Bank economist flying first class from
Washington to some third-world capital and handing out cash to a corrupt strongman became engraved in the public mind: structural adjustment came to be seen as a nefarious pact between bureaucrat and
autocrat. The truth was that most Bank staffers had joined the institution because they wanted to fight poverty; they could have taken their
economics PhDs to Goldman Sachs or McKinsey if their priorities had
been different. But if you listened to the critics, you could easily come
away with the idea that Bank officials woke up each morning bent on
entrenching poverty in every corner of the planet.[10]

The rise of this hostility reflected the growing presence of a new
kind of player on the international stage: nongovernmental organizations. These entrepreneurial outfits, which came into their own a
decade later thanks to the Internet, were already barging their way into
public policy debates, often winning arguments in the press and among
parliamentarians. They were frequently tiny, but they were always
fierce; they would swarm at big organizations such as the World Bank,
like the mini-warriors of Lilliput who bound Gulliver and showered
him with arrows. In September 1987, NGOs organized a press conference to demand a greater focus on poverty from the Bank; the statement released at the conference carried the signatures of no fewer than
153 members of the U.S. House of Representatives plus an impressive 40
senators.[11] Kris Zedler, who was hired by the Bank to help manage
NGO relations in 1984, recalls how unfamiliar this challenge appeared.

The security guards at the Bank's front desk would call her in consternation when an NGO staged a protest outside. "Ms. Zedler, your No-
Gos are making a noise," they would complain. "Please come and talk
to them."[12]

The toughest NGOs hailed from the environmental movement,
which moved from the political fringe to the mainstream during the
1980s. The Bank deserved criticism on this front—it employed only five
environmentalists in 1985, an absurdly small number for an institution
that financed huge infrastructure projects with equally huge environmental consequences. The NGOs homed in on a few loans that had
gone environmentally astray, sending investigators to collect photo-
graphic evidence of forest destruction, persuading Congress to hold
hearings, and generally treating the Bank to its first taste of expert hostility. The cause célèbre for these campaigners was a project called
Polonoroeste, conceived under McNamara as an effort to develop the
poorest reaches of the Brazilian Amazon. Beginning in 1981, the Bank
lent nearly half a billion dollars for this highway-building and coloniza-
tion program; within a few years, fifty thousand square miles of rain
forest had been destroyed, an area roughly the size of Wisconsin, and
many of the region's indigenous peoples had died as a result of disease
or violence.[13] The Bank countered that such projects might have turned
out even worse if the government had gone ahead on its own: the
Bank's project design for Polonoroeste had called for the establishment
of multiple Indian reserves, two biological reserves, and a national park.
But the Bank's defense could not change the fact that it had financed an
environmental catastrophe; coming on top of structural adjustment, the
damage to its reputation was horrible. In 1987, the Bank admitted that it
had "stumbled" on Polonoroeste and, acknowledging the merit of the
NGO critique, created an environmental department.[14]

Given stronger leadership, the World Bank might have weathered
the ideological polarization of the 1980s, and would perhaps have
responded to the rise of Lilliputian NGOs with more dexterity. But, after

being run by just three presidents between 1950 and 1981, the Bank spent the 1980s in the care of two short-term bosses who saddled it with long-term problems. "The average congressman doesn't understand the World Bank," Barber Conable observed, "and I was the average congressman."[15]

AS YOU LEAF THROUGH the photos in the Wolfensohn foundation files, something happens around 1980. Somewhere near the turn of that decade—when the Bank was embarking on structural adjustment and the Chrysler saga was at its all-consuming peak—Wolfensohn reached a turning point as well: it is physically visible. The handsome Olympian, with chiseled face and thick black hair, fades gradually from view; the face widens; the neck recedes; the hair is longer, streaked with gray, and quite often unruly.

In January 1981, three months after President Carter had passed him over for the World Bank job, Wolfensohn went to the hospital for a minor operation that involved a blood transfusion in his arm. Work, as usual, pursued him. As he surrendered one arm to the needle, his free hand held a telephone with an open line to several Chrysler managers. The conversation over, he put the phone down and stared up at the hospital ceiling. "I realized then," he said later, "that it was time for a reappraisal."[16]

The reappraisal began with a decision to leave Salomon Brothers, and by the autumn of 1981, he and Salomon had parted company. For the third time in his banking career, Wolfensohn had walked away from a senior position at an established firm; and for the third time there was talk of friction with his senior colleagues. Wolfensohn insisted that there was nothing to this talk, but Salomon's boss, John Gutfreund, later huffed to one interviewer that "Salomon clients came to think of themselves as Jim Wolfensohn clients."[17] Whatever the truth of the matter, Wolfensohn turned the parting with Salomon Brothers into a triumph. By sheer luck, his decision to leave coincided with Salomon's decision to dissolve the partnership, generating enormous payouts for the top executives who jointly owned the firm. Wolfensohn's reward was reported variously at $8 million, $10 million, $12 million, and $14 million. His own memory (which he claims, somewhat implausibly on this particular issue, may not be precise) is that he walked off with $10 million—a return of 10,000 percent on the $100,000 he put down to buy the partnership four years earlier.[18]

Wolfensohn used his new millions to fulfill a long-held ambition: to create his own firm, and to run it in a way that would unite his disparate musical, charitable, and financial interests. "I always had this image of a brownstone, with ten clients and a piano upstairs where I could practice, and a cello, and one or two people working on my non-business things," Wolfensohn said later.[19] In interviews given at the time, Wolfensohn made another point as well: He was sick of acting as other people's adviser, and wanted instead to take stakes in natural-resource and real-estate deals, using his own money.[20] The one thing he did not want to do was to continue to make his living the way he had done so far. "I've had 20 years of being a traveling salesman," he said. "That's enough . . . I don't want to make a new business call ever again."[21]

The firm that Wolfensohn created lay somewhere between his past and his imagined future. He did not acquire a brownstone; the upstairs-downstairs layout was no good for an office, and he deemed the rents excessive.[22] Instead, he set up shop in a suite above Park Avenue; JAMES D. WOLFENSOHN INCORPORATED, announced the large metal letters on the door; the peephole was concealed in the first O of Wolfensohn. When a writer visited the firm in its early years, he was impressed by a mildly erotic painting in the reception area, but the next time he stopped by, the painting had vanished. "I thought I'd better move it in case it alarmed visitors," Wolfensohn explained. "Especially the English."[23]

Despite his ambitions to get away from offering advice, Wolfensohn was simply too good at networking to withdraw from it. He could scarcely meet a chief executive without locking in, empathizing, and mentioning another chief executive who might make a fine partner; it might be someone he knew from his countless charitable interests, or it might be someone he played tennis with.[24] Pretty soon, the idea of natural-resource or property investment took a backseat; the real business of Wolfensohn's new firm was serving a select roster of clients who each paid an annual retainer of $250,000. In return, the ten initial subscribers—four American, four Australian, and two German—got the right to call on Wolfensohn and his few colleagues for advice. It was a mark of the trust that Wolfensohn inspired—and the lack of trust engendered by the bigger Wall Street firms—that a growing roster of clients considered this a bargain.

Wolfensohn's firm soon became a mirror of his personality. Ray Golden, one of Wolfensohn's early recruits, recalls that "you would never know whom you would run into in the lobby. You might meet Jimmy Carter, or the Queen of the Netherlands, or an opera star, or a famous basketball player, or a dance group from Harlem, or a South American president."[25] Some of these visitors were there to discuss business; others were part of Wolfensohn's musical and charitable network; the boundaries were blurry. The firm devoted a large slice of its profits to charities of various kinds, and these ventures were discussed at the management meeting "in an unselfconscious way, alongside the mergers and acquisitions," Wolfensohn boasted.[26] To be sure, this had its business advantages. The boards of charities are useful places to meet big shots, and knowing big shots generates big business. Making money and giving it away blended into each other.

In 1988, Wolfensohn pulled off a coup that took his young firm to a new level. He hired Paul Volcker, the departing chairman of the Federal Reserve, beating out the many rivals who had sought to snag him. It was a typical triumph: by a combination of charm and deal-clinching instincts, Wolfensohn had lured an almost legendary financial official into his tiny operation. Volcker remembers meeting Wolfensohn at a friend's house in upstate New York; Jim was holding forth about his new firm, and somehow it all sounded exciting. When he left the Fed a bit later, Volcker resumed discussions with Wolfensohn, whom he still barely knew; again, the infectious enthusiasm drew him in, and the offers from the grander firms seemed strangely less alluring. In the end, Wolfensohn clinched the deal by promising Volcker that he could combine banking with teaching at Princeton. More than any of his rivals, Wolfensohn had courted his target and understood what it would take to get him.[27]

Volcker's arrival married one vast Rolodex to another, and soon the reception room at Wolfensohn Inc. buzzed with more traffic than ever. On one occasion, the chairman of Ford Motor Co. and the chairman of Chrysler showed up in the office within minutes of each other, one to see Volcker, the other to see Wolfensohn; it took quick action on the part of the receptionist to prevent the two rivals from running into each other. But although Volcker carried the title of chairman, there was no question about who was the driving force; the man with his name in metal letters on the door had a feel for relationships that nobody could match, and Volcker himself recognized it. When he had first decided to work with Wolfensohn, Volcker's wife had assured him that he would have Wolfensohn around his little finger before long. But although this prediction was based on a sound reading of Volcker's long career, it proved utterly wrong. People who knew Volcker—but not people he regarded as friends—would stop by to see him in the office, and they'd have a businesslike discussion. But then Jim Wolfensohn would put his head around the door, and pretty soon Volcker would feel like a junior staffer at the far edge of a meeting. After some introductory banter, some mutual mentioning of A-list names, Wolfensohn would be inviting the Fed chairman's visitor to stay at his place out in Wyoming, or perhaps to come to a concert at Carnegie Hall, or maybe to join him on an Alaskan fishing trip. Volcker's acquaintances of ten years became Wolfensohn's firm friends in fifteen minutes.

You couldn't blame the visitors. Wolfensohn was after all chairman of Carnegie Hall, and had even performed there: Who better to go to a concert with? Who better, for that matter, to invite you on a fishing trip? Each summer, a group organized by Wolfensohn would fly from New York to Anchorage, and from there travel by seaplane into the Alaskan wilderness. There would be musical friends as well as financiers, and fathers often brought their sons; the conversation around the campfire at night was as good as the fishing in the morning. Anthony Loehnis, who ran the Bank of England's international operations at the time, remembers listening to Mstislav Rostropovich, the celebrated cellist and conductor, reduce the entire group to hilarious giggles with a succession of lewd jokes delivered in his thick Russian accent. Another year Kerry Packer, an Australian tycoon who loved fishing and betting, insisted that he could cast his fly farther than his host. The bet was accepted, and a contest was arranged; after three casts each, Wolfensohn was declared the winner. Packer cheerfully paid his betting debt, which meant picking up the cost of the week's fishing for the entire Wolfensohn party.

Adventures like these turned clients into loyal friends—and generated plenty of snide swipes from rivals. Wolfensohn was dismissed as a sycophant with a Rolodex, a charmer with no substance; it was said that vain corporate captains who went in for trophy wives were smitten with this trophy banker. "He's one-third psychiatrist, one-third concierge, and one-third business adviser," said an anonymous source in *Business-Week* in 1992; "if your jet breaks down, he will lend you his."[28] But the carping missed the serious reasons for Wolfensohn's success. The big Wall Street houses were hobbled by conflicts of interest; they got paid for organizing a merger or an acquisition, so they always advised in favor of merging or acquiring. Wolfensohn, by contrast, was paid primarily by retainer—though as time went by he did transactions, too—and his firm made it a point of honor to advise against deals that seemed unpromising. One time Ray Golden was asked by a client to organize the sale of a subsidiary—an invitation worth at least $3 million in fees—but Golden replied that the sale did not make sense; the client took his advice and waited for a better offer. Other Wolfensohn partners tell similar stories; Jeff Goldstein, who later joined Wolfensohn at the World Bank, reckons that "nine times out of ten we told clients not to do a deal," and the firm's code of loyalty often drove it to turn away new customers if they competed with existing ones directly.[29] The larger the fees that Wolfensohn passed up, the greater the clients' loyalty became, so that forgone fees were more than earned back after a short interval.

By 1990, Wolfensohn had achieved success beyond imagination. James D. Wolfensohn Inc. had sprouted an offshoot called Fuji-Wolfensohn to do business with the Japanese, and was soon to sprout a European branch called J. Rothschild, Wolfensohn & Co.—a particularly sweet moment, given Bill Wolfensohn's long-ago service as a Rothschild secretary. Wolfensohn was the chairman of the Institute for Advanced Study at Princeton as well as of Carnegie Hall, where the James D. Wolfensohn wing was soon to be named after him. Wolfensohn was also an adviser to Harvard's John F. Kennedy School of Government; he was a trustee of the Howard Hughes Medical Institute and a recipient of the Gay Men's Health Crisis Award for Distinguished and Pioneering Philanthropy. He had raised millions to fight multiple sclerosis out of his friendship for Jacqueline du Pre, and he continued to practice the cello; he frequently bought two seats on the Concorde so that the ungainly instrument could travel with him. He was on so many boards and knew so many people that it was assumed he didn't sleep. And yet, when Wolfensohn was asked to chair the John F. Kennedy Center for the Performing Arts in Washington, D.C., he could not resist the temptation.

There was something a bit crazy about all this. The newspaper profiles of the time began to broach a new question: What drove Wolfensohn so fiercely? By one reckoning, he was putting forty hours a week into his firm plus another thirty or so into Carnegie Hall and his other extracurricular interests; he would come to his firm in the evening after working a full day elsewhere, and stay until two the next morning.[30] Friends wondered whether this made Wolfensohn happy; he had long ago passed the point at which more money would make a serious difference to his life, and he was too thinly stretched to permit much savoring of all his rich experiences. "I don't know what drives him. I suppose it's recognition," said Andrew Knight, himself a media executive of legendary drive. But there were other possibilities that Knight did not mention. Perhaps the angel of his father still hovered over Wolfensohn. Perhaps, as Wolfensohn himself put it later, he just found everything so interesting.[31] Or maybe, just maybe, there was an ulterior motive for accepting the Kennedy Center position. Ever since 1980, when he had his first brush with the World Bank, Wolfensohn had had his eye on public office.

The Kennedy Center provided Wolfensohn with a springboard into Washington, a chance to woo the world of politics as he had wooed the corporate chieftains of New York—and so perhaps to win "a unique position . . . from which you can influence whole segments of the world," as he had once described the World Bank presidency.[32] When Wolfensohn accepted the Kennedy Center position, in March 1990, Conable was just over a year away from completing his first term; it was already clear that there might not be a second one. The job for which Wolfensohn had given up his Australian nationality might come up again soon. The Kennedy Center chairmanship, a terrific position in its own right, may also have been a stepping-stone to the future.[33]

If that was Wolfensohn's hope, he was sorely disappointed. As Conable's term at the Bank drew to a close, there was brief speculation about a Wolfensohn candidacy, but it came to nothing. Faced with a clear need for a dynamic leader, someone who could articulate a fresh vision and purpose for the ailing World Bank, the administration of President George H. W. Bush deliberated long and hard—and appointed Lewis Preston.

LEWIS THOMPSON PRESTON was a blue-blooded Episcopalian, New York born and Harvard educated. He joined the Marine Corps during World War II at seventeen; he was selected for the U.S. Olympic hockey team; he spent four decades at JP Morgan. He was a consummate Wall Streeter of the old school, and his upright bearing seemed calibrated to convince the wariest of clients that their money would be cared for prudently. His intelligence, courtesy, and inner steel propelled him to the top; he was enthroned as chief executive and chairman of JP Morgan in 1980. By 1989, when Preston relinquished his chief-executive role, Morgan had emerged stronger than all its traditional rivals—the only big American lender to retain its AAA credit rating through the dark years of the Latin debt crisis. Morgan was the country's preeminent commercial bank, and Lew Preston was the country's preeminent commercial banker.

Yet it was by no means clear that Preston was cut out to be the poor world's chief spokesman. He was used to exercising power privately, in a backroom kind of way; he was no seeker of the limelight. He hated addressing large audiences and had difficulty reading from a text; his eyes were weak, and he suffered from dyslexia. He would sit in meetings with his half-glasses riding down his nose, speaking in the soft tones of a man who knows that others need to hear him. Sometimes he wouldn't speak at all, leaving visitors to glean his answers in his eyes. "He didn't object," a novice would say after a meeting with the great banker—only to be told by an experienced reader of the man that his objection had been firm and final.[34]

JP Morgan prided itself on being the most discreet of banks, so none of this hindered Preston's rise to eminence. But the World Bank, a public institution operating in the media glare, was a different proposition. A flair for the bully pulpit, an ability to spar publicly with irreverent critics, a feel for the emotional stakes in debates on global poverty: all these mattered more at the World Bank than a résumé that commanded awe on Wall Street. In the Bank's early years, it had made sense to appoint a financier to the top job—the World Bank could be effective only if it could raise money cheaply in the capital markets. But by the time of Preston's appointment in 1991, the Bank enjoyed the highest possible credit rating and had done so for years. Other qualities mattered more, and Preston did not have them.

How or why Preston got the World Bank job is something of a mystery. The leading theory is that the elder George Bush felt comfortable with blue-blooded World War II veterans like himself; and that Preston's sense of duty compelled him to accept the post when his president offered it to him. Whatever the case, it was clear that Preston was not running the World Bank because he had a compelling vision of its role; his anxiety about the Vision Thing mirrored that of the man who had appointed him. He lurked in his office on the twelfth floor of the Bank's headquarters building, his door guarded by Pat O'Hara, a devoted secretary who had spent years with him at JP Morgan. O'Hara wielded a pencil and a big leather-bound *Economist* diary; she would note down two or three appointments every day, and that was considered adequate.[35] Even two or three years into the job, Preston could ride the World Bank elevator twelve stories down to the ground floor without being recognized by anyone. It is hard to believe that so private a man could ever have inspired and fired so public an institution.

Unlike Tom Clausen in the early 1980s, Preston prudently proclaimed that poverty was the Bank's "overarching objective." But he utterly failed to deliver this message with punch or conviction. Early on in his tenure, he signaled his talent for publicity by trying to avoid journalists; he seldom gave an interview, and when he did he regretted it. A *New York Times* writer was admitted to his penthouse office, and described him "slouched in the corner of a carved-wood sofa," more interested in his priceless paintings of wild birds than in combating global poverty.[36] In an interview two weeks later with the *Financial Times*, Preston declared that "the bully pulpit doesn't interest me a bit,"[37]—an extraordinary statement from a man who occupied the world's best platform for urging action against poverty. A month after that, Preston submitted to an interview with Hobart Rowen, a *Washington Post* columnist. Rowen lobbed the sort of softball that public figures usually hit out of the park: Why, Rowen asked, had Preston taken on the World Bank challenge? Rather than invoking the moral affront of poverty or the thrill and terror of postcommunist transition in Europe, Preston could only say that after four decades on Wall Street he wanted to perform "a public service."[38]

Statements like that performed a service to no one, least of all the impoverished public in the Bank's client countries. The Bank was too vulnerable an institution to shrug off a leader with negative communication skills, particularly since Polonoroeste-type controversies kept crashing down upon the institution. The noisiest battle of Preston's term concerned the Narmada Valley development in India, a scheme to provide drinking water, irrigation, and electricity for 40 million people. The Narmada project had been seized upon by critics as the ultimate expression of the Bank's scary "techno-cult"—it would comprise four big dams and thousands of smaller ones; the construction of the first big dam alone would displace forty thousand households.[39] The project provoked noisy resistance: there were hunger strikes, threats of self-immolation, and battles between police and villagers resisting relocation. In the end the Bank commissioned an independent review of the project by Bradford Morse, a former boss of the United Nations Development Program, who claimed to discover "fundamental failures in the implementation" of the project, including inadequate compensation for relocated villagers, violations of human rights, and breaches of the Bank's own environmental guidelines. Nonetheless, it took another year for Preston to end the Bank's support for Narmada, by which time it was too late to repair the hit to the Bank's image.

Meanwhile other fires were breaking out. Preston had commissioned an independent review of the quality of the Bank's projects, and the verdict came in one day before the board vote on Narmada. The report's devastating tone wiped out any credit he might have hoped to get for having the guts to ask for it. "There is reason to be concerned!" it began, before going on to announce that the proportion of unsatisfactory projects had increased from 11 percent in the early 1980s to 37.5 percent for projects completed in 1991. There were two exculpatory reasons for this decline. Project performance is determined partly by the economic climate, and the 1980s had been grim. And "unsatisfactory" was a subjective measure, based largely on comparing project outcomes with what project managers had promised going in; as the promises grew more extravagant, reflecting the Bank's efforts to build social and environmental objectives into its projects, the ratings naturally deteriorated.[40] But for the rising chorus of NGO critics, the report amounted to insider confirmation of their darkest fears. The Bank was staffed by a dangerous breed of technocrats, whose overweening confidence in prescribing policies for the poor world was matched only by their manifest incompetence. For the first time, NGOs began to think the unthinkable: "The World Bank is not reformable," declared a representative of Friends of the Earth to a Senate committee in June 1993.[41] In other words, abolish it.

There were other episodes that encouraged this verdict. In 1989, the Bank's board had authorized $186 million for the construction of a new headquarters building, but in May 1993, the Bank confessed that the project would cost $250 million. Two months later the figure was revised up to $290 million, and soon it hit $314 million, nearly double the original budget.[42] The irony was not lost on the critics: the World Bank, which presumed to design infrastructure projects all over the poor world, could not even manage the construction of its own building. Meanwhile the Bank unveiled a report on resettlement in April 1994 that got it into more trouble. In 1986, the Bank had promised to avoid resettlement schemes where possible, and the following year it had withdrawn from an abusive resettlement effort in Indonesia. The new report, done by the Bank's chief internal critic of resettlement, reported substantial progress.[43] Yet, in a pattern that anticipated battles to come, the Bank's critics ignored the good news, noting that between 1986 and 1993 the Bank had approved almost two hundred projects involving resettlement, but not noting that the people who were moved had been treated better than in the past, nor that it is often impossible to build necessary infrastructure without relocating anyone.[44] Reasonable criticism of the Bank was morphing into unreasonable slander.

PRESTON'S SHYNESS, his aloof distaste for the bully pulpit and his public role, came to a head in the last week of September 1994, when the World Bank held its annual meetings. In ordinary years, this gathering is an extravagant affair, famous for the garish parties thrown by visiting investment bankers. The 1994 meetings were bound to be especially florid: they marked the Bank's fiftieth anniversary, and there would be much harkening back to that founding conference in Bretton Woods, New Hampshire. Besides, the 1994 meetings were to be held in the Spanish capital, Madrid, whose fine weather and old European charm seemed certain to attract an even larger crowd than usual.

Long before Preston arrived in Madrid that September, it was clear to the Bank's staff that the crowds would not be uniformly friendly. As the fiftieth anniversary approached, Oxfam, the unofficial leader of the nongovernmental aid groups, had charged that World Bank and International Monetary Fund policies were "jeopardizing prospects for sustainable recovery and poverty reduction."[45] Other NGOs made similar statements; the press was reporting on their views, and their street protests were growing. After the Reagan-Thatcher 1980s, the pendulum was swinging back: the mood of 1994 echoed the mood of 1970, when people felt ready to celebrate the supposed "dethronement of GNP"; and the old emphasis on economic growth was thrown aside amid calls for more direct attacks on poverty. This time, however, the Bank was more exposed. Back in 1970, the Bank had been on the front end of the wave, thanks to Robert McNamara's rhetoric. But a quarter of a century later, the Bank was firmly associated with structural adjustment, and there was no way it could escape criticism. Indeed, to mark the half century since Bretton Woods, the critics united under the slogan "Fifty Years Is Enough," and demanded that the World Bank's doors be shuttered.

In an attempt to calm the brewing storm, the Bank ramped up its public-relations efforts. In September it dispatched Geoff Lamb, an engagingly hip South African, to serve as its emissary in London. Britain was arguably the epicenter of the anti-Bank revolt, and Lamb arrived there in early September, spending two weeks before the Madrid meetings telling anyone who would listen that the Bank was not bent on killing babies. Around the same time, the Bank hired Mark Malloch Brown, who had proved his mettle running political campaigns in developing countries, to take over its communications shop in Washington. Malloch Brown remembers arriving to find an institution in a state of "frozen fear"; the reports from Madrid were ominous. A group calling itself the Alternative Forum was planning a rival set of meetings at Madrid's Autonomous University. Another outfit called A SEED (Action for Solidarity, Equality, Environment and Development) was threatening traffic blockades; still others promised to obstruct the passage of delegates entering the World Bank's conference center. The Rainforest Action Network attacked the Bank with advertisements on the op-ed page of *The New York Times;* "How to Borrow Billions of Dollars and End Up Homeless" read the headlines above a picture of a poor woman with a begging bowl. Malloch Brown cornered Preston and persuaded him to undergo speech coaching at a Washington consulting firm. Then he boarded the plane for Madrid, bracing for a battle.[46]

He could not have known quite what would follow. As Preston and his entourage drove into Madrid from the airport, they found that the median strip of the highway resembled a refugee encampment; lines of ragged tents had been pitched there on the grass, each sheltering a posse of equally bedraggled protesters. The following day, A SEED activists staged a "die-in" near the site where delegates collected their registration cards; others dressed in rough blankets blocked the entrance to the conference site, proclaiming that their outfits signaled solidarity with indigenous peoples uprooted by the World Bank's projects. In the Plaza Mayor in the heart of Madrid's old town, a man in a top hat handed out fake dollar bills. "We are trying to cause inflation and disrupt the money supply," the man explained to an inquiring journalist.

Preston's first test came on Saturday, October 1, when he appeared before a press conference. At first things went pretty well; an "unhappy birthday" cake, intended as a projectile, was seized before it could be hurled in his direction. As Preston began to speak, a heckler called out that "fifty years of the Bank is really too much," but security guards quickly bundled the man out; "I'm sixty-eight so I don't think that fifty years is too much," Preston observed wryly. But the third attempt at sabotage was successful. As the security guards were grappling with the heckler at the back, a woman ran forward from the audience, ducked behind Preston, and unfurled a banner that proclaimed, WORLD BANK MURDERER. A hundred cameras flashed. The rest of the conference hardly counted after that: Preston's image in the next day's press had been cruelly determined.

The Bank made a fair effort to fight back. The day of the ill-fated press conference, Malloch Brown's public-relations team rounded up journalists who had attended an activist briefing on a controversial dam project in Nepal; the reporters were taken off to see three senior Bank officials who bristled with disarming arguments. The next day Malloch Brown, an impressive giant of a man, marched into the press center and called an impromptu conference; he denounced Oxfam and other

NGO critics for getting many of their facts wrong. But then, on Tuesday, October 4, the effort to snatch back the media initiative suffered a deathblow. At the official opening ceremony of the annual meetings, held in a spectacular new glass-and-marble conference center named in honor of the Spanish king, Preston rose to make his keynote speech. As he labored through the text, battling dyslexia and weak eyes, fake dollar bills began to tumble on the audience; "World Bankenstein" ran the inscription on one of the notes; "This note is redeemable for ozone destruction" read another. The crowd's attention shifted first to the fluttering paper, then to its source: two athletic activists had scaled the steel girders high up in the roof, and were looking down on the armed police officers below with mocking impunity. There were some tense moments; Malloch Brown briefly wondered what might happen if the police opened fire, causing the climbers to crash down upon the U.S. delegation. Alone at the speaker's podium, Preston soldiered on; because of his weak eyes, he could not see enough to be sure exactly what was happening.[47] But when the speech was over, the truth quickly sank in. Lewis Preston and his Bank had utterly lost the audience.

Preston, in fact, had lost more than the audience. He had lost the bigger game as well; the world had been changing around the Bank, and the Bank had responded slowly and awkwardly. Preston's qualities—his reserve, his modesty, his gentlemanly style—were no match for the theatrical talents of his NGO critics; the old Marine was up against guerrilla activists who didn't know or care what "gentlemanly" meant, and they had overwhelmed him. It was as though the new forces unleashed by the end of the cold war made the veterans of Hitler's war cruelly passé. The values and virtues of a former time were being shoved aside; deference was dead; and debates could be settled with banners saying WORLD BANK MURDERER.

In a loose kind of a way, Preston's humiliation in that fall of 1994 echoed the fate of the patrician-president who appointed him. Two years earlier the reserved and courteous George H. W. Bush had suffered electoral defeat at the hands of a baby boomer—an adversary who sensed how arguments could be won and publics could be wooed in an era when telegenic charm counted more than anything. Now it was Preston's turn·to face defeat by media-savvy foes who shared the war-room style that Bill Clinton had introduced to presidential politics. As time passed, and as two emotional persuaders took their turns as president of the United States and president of the World Bank, a certain nostalgia would creep in: the reserved men who had fought in World War II would be hailed as the "Greatest Generation." But that is to anticipate our tale. At that moment in Madrid in 1994, there was not much sympathy for the gentlemanly values of a former age. The need for fresh energy at the World Bank seemed nothing less than obvious.

CHAPTER THREE

THE RENAISSANCE PRESIDENT

TWO MONTHS AFTER that disastrous summit in Madrid, another grand festival of world statesmen convened, this time for the Summit of the Americas in Miami. As with the World Bank's Madrid meetings, the main business—an earnest discussion of trade barriers, immigration, and the like—was eclipsed by a parasite display, strong on color and theatrics. But the source of this eclipse had nothing to do with the ragtag legions of the Fifty Years Is Enough campaign. What stole the stage from the Summit of the Americas that December was a concert, called the Concert of the Americas. It was the work of the John F. Kennedy Center for the Performing Arts. And the chief impresario of this takeover was a barrel-chested bear-hugger of a man. It was, of course, James Wolfensohn.

Wolfensohn's job as Kennedy Center chairman had been going famously. He had restored financial stability to the Kennedy Center and lured major stars to Washington to lead the National Symphony Orchestra and the Washington Opera. In September 1994, he had heard about the Summit of the Americas and sensed a chance for a big splash; he had called over to the Clinton White House and proposed that the formal talks on trade and such be rounded off with some musical diversion. Wolfensohn had then recruited Quincy Jones and David Salzman,

who had put on the Lincoln Memorial concert at Clinton's inaugura-
tion party the previous year, and the pair proceeded to arrange what *The
Washington Post* described as "the biggest multi-culti bash' since the
Olympics."[1] The show began with a procession of children drawn from
the thirty-four participating countries; then the thirty-four heads of
state appeared onstage, to be serenaded by Liza Minnelli. For the next
hour and a half, 180 entertainers filed on and off: salsa stars like Tito
Puente and Celia Cruz, gospel singers like BeBe and CeCe Winans,
the Ballet Gran Folklorico de Mexico—even Bob Marley's widow. The
evening ended with a reading by Maya Angelou, who had interrupted
a film project in order to be there, and then with a few words from
President Clinton, who was introduced by actor Michael Douglas.
Sandwiched between Angelou and Clinton, Wolfensohn himself appeared onstage. Before an audience of four thousand he announced the
creation of a new Kennedy Center Fellows program, to be funded by
James D. Wolfensohn Inc. and various corporate partners, including an
energy company called Enron.[2]

At the reception that evening, Wolfensohn was in his element. His
outsider's insecurity was forgotten; the Jewish kid from the suburbs of
Sydney was playing host to nearly three dozen heads of state, not to
mention fifteen dozen hot musicians. As he worked his way through
the crowds, greeting and squeezing and glowing, Wolfensohn ran into
Bobby Danino, an attorney who (in a manner not untypical of his
friends) was destined for great things—in this case to be prime minister
of Peru and then ambassador to Washington. There, at that reception in
Miami, Danino greeted Wolfensohn and said something that made
him stop. The *Financial Times* was reporting that Lewis Preston would
soon be leaving the World Bank, and that Wolfensohn was on the short
list to replace him.[3]

Years later, during an interview in his palatial Wyoming "cabin,"
Wolfensohn assured me that he was intrigued but not electrified by this
news; his life as a private banker and musical patron was going more

than well, and he wasn't sure if change was warranted. It is a claim that fits the pattern of the stories that Wolfensohn tells about himself: he is always the happy bystander, propelled ahead to glorious things by the urging of others—the university fencing captain who recruited him on the spur of the moment to fill in for a sick member of the team; the dying cellist who made him promise to perform a concert on his fiftieth birthday; and now the unknown power brokers who whispered to the *Financial Times* that, if there was to be a succession at the World Bank, Wolfensohn would be on the short list. But Bobby Danino has a different memory of that Miami encounter. It is one that fits better with the recollections of many of Wolfensohn's old friends, who recall a man whose appetite for fame exceeded his gargantuan appetite for fortune.[4]

The way Danino tells it, Wolfensohn listened to the news of Preston's possible departure and made his friend stay put; then he brought over his wife, Elaine, and made Danino repeat the news a second time so that she could hear it. Danino recalls being astonished by the openness with which Wolfensohn displayed his excitement, and thought it remarkable that someone of his stature would let down his guard so obviously. Wolfensohn explained to Danino his long relationship with the World Bank: how McNamara had once invited him over to his office, shown him where he parked the car, inspired him to give up his Australian citizenship. The World Bank job was not just any job. It was the one for which Wolfensohn had waited almost fifteen years. It was the one that offered an unrivalled chance to make a difference to the world: to lead humanity's campaign against unspeakable poverty.

The prospect of a second shot at the World Bank set Wolfensohn's huge engines roaring. As soon as the Concert of the Americas was done, he raced back to Washington and called all his friends: There was Donna Shalala, President Clinton's health secretary and a Kennedy Center board member; there was Vernon Jordan, a lawyer with Wolfensohnian networking skills who was a favorite Clinton golf partner. Shalala thought Wolfensohn would be perfect for the World Bank; he could operate on a high level internationally; he spoke excellent French; and his dizzying variety of interests included involvement in population policies and environmental causes.[5] Over the space of a few days, Sha-lala took soundings as to Preston's future, but she came back with the answer that he had no plans to leave the Bank. Indeed, Preston had responded to the *Financial Times* rumor of his imminent departure by raising the idea of a second five-year term.[6] Wolfensohn returned to New York and to his overflowing private interests.

A month later, on a Friday afternoon in late January 1995, Preston emerged from his penthouse on the Bank's twelfth floor and wandered down the corridor to the small office occupied by Gerry Rice, his speechwriter. Rice was one of the few people among the World Bank's ten-thousand-strong staff who genuinely knew the boss, and Preston would often stick his head round the door to talk to him. On this occa-sion, however, Preston had not come to ruminate about the Bank's vari-ous affairs. He told Rice that he'd been feeling odd, that he'd coughed up a bit of blood; he'd be seeing doctors over the weekend. Early the next week, Rice got a call from Pat O'Hara, Preston's loyal secretary. The medical priesthood had spoken: Preston had terminal cancer; he would be dead before the year was over.[7]

Around the same time,[8] Jan Piercy, who represented the U.S. gov-ernment on the World Bank's board, received a phone call in her office. It was Lew Preston, speaking in his usual chipper voice, wishing her a good morning. "Well, Jan," she remembers him saying, "I'm in the Mayo Clinic for three days of tests, but I don't know what we're going to do with the next two days because everything they checked so far is not checking out." Preston was speaking briskly, his tone almost wry; it was as though he were reporting that some household implement had worn out and was in need of replacement. As Preston's real message began to emerge through the camouflage of his courage, Piercy began to cry.

"Lew, what are you telling me?" she asked.

"Jan," he answered, "this is very bad. You need to tell the president that he should think of a successor."[9]

Piercy ended the conversation and sat numbly for a while. Michael Marek, her deputy, walked into her office and found her sobbing. The two talked—Marek had come in to say something about the death of another development titan, UNICEF's Jim Grant—and then Piercy started making calls to administration colleagues. She spoke to the treasury secretary, Robert Rubin, and his deputy, Frank Newman; she reached several White House contacts. In all these conversations, Piercy delivered a message that reflected her sense of the World Bank's history and her close contact with European members of its board. In the past, the United States had exercised its unwritten prerogative to select the president of the World Bank in an opaque and arbitrary way; the appointments of Clausen, Conable, and even Preston were just short of notorious. Piercy sensed that times had changed: if the administration did not proceed quickly and convincingly, the Europeans might revolt and put forward their own candidate. By the end of that first day of phone calls, the Clinton team had agreed to create a formal search committee, staffed by a treasury official who had previously been a headhunter. The group would brainstorm about the challenges for the Bank. It would think out of the box and consider all possible candidates.[10]

Piercy's instincts were at least half right. The chances of the Europeans unifying around a non-American candidate were probably remote; the Europeans seldom muster unity on anything. But there certainly was a case for hard thinking about who might run the Bank: the institution cried out for strong leadership, and despite everything it remained a crucial building block in the international order. It was still without question the premier development actor; it was only a small exaggeration to say, as one critical book did, that the Bank "influenced, directly and indirectly, more lives in those countries euphemistically called less developed than any other institution since the Second World War";

and that it had "more to say about state policy than many states" in the Southern Hemisphere.[11] The Bank's lending came to a bit more than $20 billion annually in the mid-1990s, which meant it was pumping out around $2.5 million per hour; its lending program was twice the combined size of its three regional cousins—the Asian Development Bank, the Inter-American Development Bank, and the African Development Bank. The Bank's annual flow of lending also seemed substantial compared to government aid programs, though this depended a bit on how you looked at the numbers. If you subtracted repayments to the Bank and considered only net transfers, these were roughly similar to the grants pumped out by USAID, the biggest of the government aid agencies.[12] But the Bank's gross transfers were arguably a better way of measuring its clout, since developing countries tend to care about the new money they receive today more than the repayments they may make tomorrow. The Bank's gross transfers came to double the size of America's bilateral aid, a dramatic turnaround from the late 1960s, when the U.S. aid budget had been appreciably bigger than the Bank's lending program.

The Bank's dominance, moreover, was not just about money. Whatever the institution's shortcomings—its weak communication skills under Preston, its sluggish response to the environmental movement—there was no question about its intellectual caliber. The environmental issue was a case in point. After a slow start, the Bank had by the mid-1990s assembled a strong environmental staff; it had helped virtually all its borrowers to prepare National Environmental Action Plans; it was producing, in the view of one frequently hostile observer, "an outpouring of high-quality research reports on environment-development interactions, making the Bank arguably the largest center for such research in the world."[13] Meanwhile, on questions of development economics, the Bank's research department enjoyed a clear intellectual supremacy over nongovernmental aid groups, United Nations agencies, and even top-flight universities; it hired some of the best academics in the world, supplied them with copious research funds, and left them to push back the horizons of development thinking. From the time that McNamara recruited the Harvard professor Hollis Chenery to act as chief economist, that position had been held by world-class figures: Stan Fischer and Anne Krueger, who went on to dominate the International Monetary Fund from the number-two slot that is reserved for an American; Larry Summers, who went on to run the U.S. Treasury and serve as president of Harvard; and later Joseph Stiglitz, enfant terrible and Nobel laureate. You could certainly find brilliant development economists outside the Bank, but they tended to be scattered about the famous campuses; nobody could match the Bank's concentration of talent, nor could any other research team claim access to the wealth of real-life development experience that the Bank's lending operations generated. As a result, the Bank's annual World Development Report often established the accepted wisdom among development thinkers. Commentators outside the Bank spent much of their time reacting to World Bank ideas and citing World Bank data.

The combination of financial and intellectual clout made the World Bank durably important. In a strange way, the vision of the Bretton Woods founders remained intact: the reconstruction of war-torn Western Europe was long since complete, but the United States and its allies still needed to shoot down economic trouble round the world, especially in places where instability threatened their own interests. In February 1995, when the Clinton administration began its search for Preston's successor, the strategic importance of the Bank was clear: Mexico's peso crisis threatened to destabilize America's two-thousand-mile-long southern border, and the Bank was preparing to pump $1 billion and a bevy of experts into Mexico to stabilize the country's banking system. In the previous half decade, the institution had helped to guide the economic transition of ex-communist Europe, and was still engaged in an attempt to stabilize the states of the ex–Soviet Union. Russia, teetering under the drunken leadership of Boris Yeltsin, was particularly on the administration's mind, and the Clintonites were pressing the Bank to step up its lending to the country. Meanwhile, the Clinton team, prodded especially by Vice President Al Gore, was waking up to a range of security issues that had been pushed off the radar screen during the cold war. Environmental degradation, refugee flows, AIDS, drugs, financial crises: all ended up affecting the proverbial Peoria voter, and all caused administration officials to turn to the World Bank for expertise and money.

For all its importance, however, the Bank was in a delicate state. It had suffered a string of short-lived and unsuccessful presidents. It was vilified by the Left, as the Madrid summit had demonstrated. And the threat from right-wing critics seemed newly menacing, thanks to the recent victory of Newt Gingrich's troops in the 1994 congressional elections.

Like the left-wingers, who could point to real instances of Bank lending that had damaged the environment or harmed indigenous peoples, the right-wingers had a serious case. The World Bank had been created for a world of capital controls and infant financial markets in borrowing countries, a world in which there was a clear role for an institution that borrowed money on Wall Street and passed it along to developing nations. But now that role had ended, or so the conservatives maintained: private capital flows were exploding, and there was no need for public-sector lenders. The Bank pumped out $22.5 billion in loans during 1995,[14] a large number when compared to other aid budgets. But in the same year net private capital flows to developing countries amounted to $206 billion.[15] Naturally, much of this money went to corporate ventures rather than the poverty-fighting schemes that the Bank financed. But the right-wing critics were correct that developing country governments were borrowing private capital, too—and could use it to construct schools and wells and clinics. If commercial lenders were now willing to finance development, perhaps fifty years of the World Bank was indeed enough.

The Clintonites were right to be unpersuaded by this argument. Private capital flows had indeed grown marvelously, but they were concentrated in "emerging markets" like Brazil or Thailand, to the exclusion of the poorest regions of the world, most notably Africa. Of the $206 billion in private flows that the conservatives cited, two-thirds went to developing countries with an average income per person of $760 or more, and a fifth went to poor but booming China.[16] The rest of the poor world combined received just $23 billion; sub-Saharan Africa minus South Africa got almost nothing.[17] Moreover, private flows were volatile, so there was still a need for the World Bank during bad times—a point that Mexico's crisis had freshly demonstrated. But the weaknesses in both right- and left-wing arguments did not necessarily insulate the Bank from political damage. Piercy and her colleagues needed a leader who could take on the critics of both wings.

As the Clinton search committee contemplated these issues, it drew up a list of criteria. Preston's successor should be someone with the energy to serve more than one five-year term, not a fading private-sector lion looking for a quiet finale. The new leader should know about development—an apparently obvious qualification, perhaps, but one lacking in all recent presidents; he or she should have international stature, to avoid another "Barbara who?" embarrassment. The new leader should also be bold enough to lead the Bank into the new challenges of the post–cold war era: the Clinton team wished that Preston had been quicker to open the Bank's coffers to Russia, and they were worried by his standoffish approach to the prospect of reconstructing Bosnia. At one point, the search committee considered Michael Porter, the Harvard management guru, whose ideas on organization might help the Bank to get a grip on its bureaucracy. But, as they worked diligently through the various options, the committee members developed an uneasy feeling. Their deliberations were being overtaken by outsiders who had no doubt as to the right choice—outsiders who, in almost all cases, thought the right choice was Jim Wolfensohn.

There are no clear rules about how jobs get dished out in Washington. You call someone who owes you one, or perhaps someone who would like to be owed one; and that someone calls another someone who owes somebody else one; and the calls ripple this way and that way until, if you are successful, they reach the Oval Office in the West Wing of the White House. This is what Wolfensohn was doing, except that he was not calling a few friends, or even quite a lot of friends; he was wielding a vast switchboard of entangled lines that looped and curled and stretched around the world, each ending up with a devoted and distinguished associate in finance, or music, or academia, or politics, or any of the dozen other areas that Wolfensohn's activities encompassed. Wolfensohn was bent over this switchboard, coaxing and tickling the dials like an engineer at NASA. A lever over here connected him to Donna Shalala, the health secretary, who prowled Washington parties, ready to pounce upon unsuspecting administration colleagues to explain why Wolfensohn would make an excellent World Bank president.[18] A switch over there connected him to Vernon Jordan, who was out on the golf greens, talking directly to Bill Clinton. A small dial in the center hooked him up to Paul Volcker, the former chairman of the Federal Reserve whom he had lured into James D. Wolfensohn Inc. Maurice Strong, the Canadian businessman who had been Wolfensohn's patron in Australia and later McNamara's confidante at the World Bank, persuaded Canada's prime minister to weigh in with the Americans in support of the Wolfensohn candidacy.

In short, Wolfensohn was playing the Washington game with an energy that amazed even the city's grizzled veterans. Jan Piercy reckons she got calls from nearly every member of the Clinton cabinet, telling her why Wolfensohn was perfect. He had cared about environmental causes since 1972, when he had been involved in the United Nations conference on the environment in Stockholm; he had been committed to family planning through his service on the board of the Population Council in the 1970s and 1980s; he knew anybody who was anybody in virtually any country; he had the energy of a dozen normal beings. All these cabinet members were for Wolfensohn, but so were others, too: foreign finance ministers, Wall Street power brokers, cultural pooh-bahs, all bursting to explain what a truly remarkable person their friend was.[19]

There was one member of the cabinet who did not seem so impressed, and, unfortunately for Wolfensohn, he was the most important one. Robert S. Rubin, the treasury secretary, was another Wall Street success story who had come to Washington, and who shared some of Wolfensohn's passion for development. In style and temperament, however, Rubin and Wolfensohn could not have been more different. Rubin made his fortune at Goldman Sachs, where he ran the department that took risks with his own and his partners' money; Wolfensohn had made his fortune by impressing clients, who paid him millions for advice that entailed no risk to his own fortune. Rubin was quiet and deliberative, and he prized clear thinking; Wolfensohn was outgoing and impulsive, and he prized human relationships. Rubin instinctively disliked this pushy networker, and he had ties to other aspirants for the World Bank post. There was Ken Brody, the president of the Export-Import Bank, who had known Rubin at Goldman, and Felix Rohatyn, another Wall Streeter. Above all there was Lawrence Summers, the wunderkind Harvard economist who headed the international side of Rubin's Treasury. Summers had served as chief economist at the World Bank and was now angling for the top job, or at least for the prestige of being offered it.

By the end of February 1995, the struggle to succeed Preston had created two camps in Washington, and two visions of the selection process. In one camp there was Rubin, who had blessed the creation of the formal search committee and instructed his deputy to lead it; this camp wanted to give the search process more time, and regarded Wolfensohn's campaign as insufferably arrogant. Rubin's stature was second to none in Clinton's cabinet; and, in ordinary circumstances, the idea that

he might fail to prevail on an economic issue would have seemed outlandish. But the circumstances were not quite ordinary this time. For in
the rival, anti-Rubin camp there were Wolfensohn's many fans, who
saw no need whatever for a long selection process when the perfect candidate was standing right in front of them.

The more time went by, the more people found themselves running
into old-time friends who fitted, by some mysterious logic, into the
twisting wires of Wolfensohn's vast network. Mark Malloch Brown,
Preston's public-relations guru, was quietly hoping that Larry Summers
might get the presidency; Summers had after all been chief economist
at the World Bank and understood the institution well, whereas the
idea of another Wall Streeter ascending to the top smacked of Preston
succeeding Preston. But then Malloch Brown went to a birthday party
in Sag Harbor, New York, and stayed with his friend Peter Jennings, the
TV anchor. Jennings was singing Wolfensohn's praises, and so indeed
were many at the gathering that weekend, and Malloch Brown began to
reconsider his pro-Summers assumptions. Jennings even suggested
arranging a lunch for the "three colonials"—Jennings the Canadian,
Wolfensohn the Australian, and Malloch Brown, who, though British,
had pretended to be South African when he'd worked in Argentina
after the Falklands War. Jennings was sure that if Malloch Brown only
met his friend, he would not be so opposed to him.

Early the next Monday, Malloch Brown picked up the phone in his
office and heard a completely fake-sounding Australian accent.

"Hello, this is Jim Wolfensohn; I understand you think I wouldn't
make a great president of the World Bank," the voice declared.

"Oh Peter, fuck you and drop that accent," Malloch Brown retorted.

"No," said the voice, "this really is Jim Wolfensohn." He was calling
from Paris, and he wanted to make sure that the Bank's public-relations
boss understood his development credentials.[20]

Around the same time, Jan Piercy, the Clinton administration's representative on the World Bank board, went to visit Robert McNamara.

Piercy had taken a visceral dislike to Wolfensohn when they'd first met. "Who does he think he is?" she remembers thinking; "the egocentric quality here was so offensive. . . . It was boorish almost."[21] It was evident to Piercy that Wolfensohn meant to short-circuit the official search committee by activating his switchboard of friends, and she deeply resented it. But when Piercy went to consult McNamara about the institution he'd once led, she got a lecture on Wolfensohn's virtues, and she left feeling more neutral.[22] Jack Quinn, Vice President Al Gore's chief of staff, was another who called McNamara for counsel in this period. The first time he tried to get in touch, he was told that the old man (McNamara was seventy-eight by then) was out hiking in the Colorado mountains. But when McNamara later returned the call, he talked for nearly an hour about Wolfensohn's great qualities.[23] Soon afterward Quinn drafted a memo for Al Gore, saying he should back Wolfensohn, and Gore passed the message on to Bill Clinton himself at one of their private weekly lunches. The multiple ripples of the Wolfensohn campaign were finally nearing their target.

Years later, in a conversation with a World Bank colleague, Wolfensohn compared the art of landing deals to the art of fishing. If there's a big fish on the line, you sometimes have to give it play; you let the line run out and bide your time, letting the hooked monster swim this way and that way until it begins to exhaust itself. The trick is to know when to switch tactics; you feel the fish on the line, sense the moment that its energies begin to sag, and—snap!—you pull, sinking the hook deeper into its mouth and reeling it back toward you without pause or mercy.[24] At the beginning of March 1995, Wolfensohn decided it was time to sink the hook. With astonishing chutzpah, he delivered an ultimatum to the White House: If it failed to make a decision by the end of the following week, he would be forced to withdraw his candidacy. Wolfensohn declared that his banking clients were getting antsy: figures like Juergen Schrempp, the boss of Daimler-Benz, were reading of Wolfensohn's candidacy in the press, and were demanding to know whether they should find themselves a new banker; the situation put intolerable pressure on a small company like Wolfensohn Inc. To ram home his ultimatum, Wolfensohn departed the country, saying he had business that mattered more in various capitals of Europe.

On Monday, March 6, the administration's search committee convened in the White House for its first and only meeting with the president. Jan Piercy had prepared a decision memo, which laid out the leading candidates, chief among them Wolfensohn and Larry Summers. Several people at the meeting were furious at Wolfensohn's ultimatum, though Gore, under the influence of his chief of staff, remained a fierce Wolfensohn proponent. Bob Rubin sounded a cautionary note, but he was less assertive: he regarded Summers as a genius, but was reluctant to have the Treasury lose him, particularly so soon after Summers had proved his usefulness by leading the response to Mexico's financial crisis. At the same time, Rubin had been induced to have dinner with Wolfensohn and had come away feeling that, however unattractive Wolfensohn's campaign methods, his boundless enthusiasm for the World Bank job counted in his favor.[25] Besides, Rubin sensed the worldwide web of the Wolfensohn campaign everywhere around him, and he could see that he was up against Al Gore. Resistance would cost him more effort and allies than the issue justified.[26]

The White House meeting broke up without a conclusion. Some felt the committee ought to carry on looking; others urged a quick decision, which was code for choosing Wolfensohn. The team decided that in order to clarify the options Wolfensohn ought to meet Gore; if he failed to impress him, those who wanted more time to search would get what they demanded. Wolfensohn was duly summoned back from Europe; he flew on the Concorde to New York and arrived in Washington on Wednesday morning. He was met there by Mark Malloch Brown, who had been picked up by the Kennedy Center driver; Malloch Brown remembers a disheveled figure emerging from the aircraft, with the book by Susan George and Fabrizio Sabelli, two of the Bank's

most vociferous left-wing critics, bursting out of his overcoat pocket.[27]
The two men talked in the car and then in Wolfensohn's suite at the
Watergate Hotel, and soon Malloch Brown's doubts were utterly dispelled. Wolfensohn was a charmer, a seducer, a force of nature. He was
no Lewis Preston.

Malloch Brown left the Watergate, and was soon followed by a delegation from the Clinton administration. Wolfensohn was expecting
senior visitors—he had flown halfway around the world for this meeting—and was not amused by what he saw when the door opened. There
was Jan Piercy, the World Bank board member whom he had brushed
off early in the selection process; and there was Bob Nash, the assistant
to the president for personnel, whom Wolfensohn took for the junior-
most lawyer in the White House. Nash proceeded to explain that, in
order to get clearance for the World Bank nomination, Wolfensohn
would need to go through various background checks, and that, just by
way of a first step, he would need to supply the dates of all entries to and
exits from the United States over the past decade. Wolfensohn objected
that this was preposterous: he spent his life entering and exiting the
country, and a requirement to list all trips over a ten-year period was
virtually prohibitive; it would effectively disqualify any frequent flyer
from the job, condemning the Bank to be led by some no-passport iso
lationist. Nash held his ground, and even pushed forward a few yards:
Wolfensohn would need reasons for all those foreign travels as well as
all the dates; Nash had checked into the law, and there was no getting
around this.

Wolfensohn protested that the World Bank presidency was not like
a cabinet appointment; it did not require confirmation in Congress,
and the usual background checks did not apply to it. But his entreaties
made no difference: He had come all the way back from his make-
believe business in Europe, and his reward was bureaucratic torture.
The bold one-week ultimatum was about to backfire; there was no way
Wolfensohn could assemble a record of his foreign trips in the next

seventy-two hours, and he had a feeling that his tormentors were aware of this constraint and not necessarily displeased by it. Wolfensohn, whose temper we shall presently explore, was ready to explode in plate-smashing anger—and if he had allowed that to happen, his chances of ever reeling in his fish would have exploded in the same moment. But just then the phone rang.

"Don't say anything," said the voice on the other end of the line. "I know who's there, and I think I know what's happening." It was Jack Quinn, the vice president's chief of staff. "Come round to the White House this afternoon. But say nothing to the people who are with you."[28]

His mood now pleasantly transformed, Wolfensohn cruised through the remainder of his meeting. By the time he was done, Nash was most impressed: Wolfensohn, it seemed to him, regarded the World Bank less as a job than as a mission.[29]

After Nash and Piercy left, Wolfensohn had a cup of coffee and went over to the White House. Al Gore received him and led him earnestly through a checklist of issues: the environment, the role of women in development, the Bank's managerial challenges, and so on. Wolfensohn had read the literature on the Bank; he knew the left-wing criticism and he knew the right-wing criticism, and he somehow conveyed a sense that he understood everybody's arguments and could embrace the reasonable bits of each of them. Gore listened and concentrated and moved on down through the checklist; Wolfensohn had the sense that the vice president was covering all the issues that he thought Clinton might raise with him. After running through his list, Gore thanked him and led him out into the corridor. Instead of showing him the way out he walked him into the Oval Office and left him with the president.

The way Wolfensohn recalls the subsequent meeting, Clinton asked nothing about the World Bank and little about development. The Gore checklist was forgotten, and the two men chatted about everything in general and not much in particular. They touched upon the state of the world, the challenge of global poverty, and the policy conundrums caused by global capital flows, a subject that had clearly exercised the president since Mexico's recent peso crisis. The conversation swam along, with one curious and agile mind playing off against the other, until, after more than an hour, Clinton indicated he had heard enough. But Wolfensohn insisted he had one last point to make. Even if Clinton wanted him for the World Bank, he might not be available; his banking clients were pressing to know what his plans were, and he needed to give them an answer. If Clinton chose to appoint him, he would have to find a way of cutting through the background checks that his staff apparently thought necessary. In fact, he would have to announce a decision no later than the coming weekend.[30]

Wolfensohn left the White House feeling buoyant. He called Malloch Brown, who had somehow morphed from stranger to right-hand man in the space of a single morning meeting, and reported that the White House conversations had gone well.[31] Then he left Washington for Frankfurt, where he was determined to attend a concert marking the fiftieth birthday of Deutsche Bank. Early on Thursday afternoon, Wolfensohn emerged from the concert with a group of friends, including George Mallinckrodt, a craggy, handsome patrician-financier, who presided over Schroders, Wolfensohn's old bank. Wolfensohn's party went off for lunch, and then Wolfensohn found he had a message from the White House. He hurried over to the offices of Metzler Bank, a private firm on whose board Wolfensohn sat, and returned the call; he was put through to an official who informed him that the president had chosen to support him. Wolfensohn asked how long the background checks would take.

"Don't worry," came the reply. "The president has given instructions for the checks to be completed this morning."

Wolfensohn put down the phone. His dream of leading the anti-poverty crusade articulated by Robert McNamara had finally come true. He was beaming.[32] He called Elaine and told her the good news. Then he opened some champagne with Mallinckrodt, and they toasted victory together.[33]

Back in Washington, Jan Piercy heard the news from Robert Rubin. She was surprised by the speed of the denouement.[34] Her selection committee, which had sifted and labored and pondered, had in the end been sidestepped by a candidate who barely concealed his contempt for it. Her misgivings soon found an echo in the first public comments after the news leaked out on Friday evening. President Clinton issued a statement praising Wolfensohn for his "long-standing, broad and active interest in the developing world and development issues." But the next morning the news wires were carrying the reaction of Juliette Majot, an activist from the International Rivers Network and a founding member of the Fifty Years Is Enough campaign. "It is Mr. Wolfensohn's international commercial banking connections and not his knowledge of the very real needs of poverty-stricken women, men and children of the developing world that brings him to the World Bank," Majot said. "Mr. Wolfensohn is becoming captain of a sinking ship," she declared ominously.[35]

Mark Malloch Brown, who spoke regularly to the big hitters at the major newspapers, fielded a series of calls on Friday evening and Saturday morning. It was clear to him he had a problem. His early skepticism about Wolfensohn was being played back to him: Wasn't Summers the candidate who knew development? Wasn't this Preston succeeding Preston? The *Financial Times*, which had editorialized in favor of Summers on March 1, was now preparing to give Wolfensohn a skeptical welcome. The first rule of public relations is not to let your enemies define you, and Malloch Brown decided that the press story could not be left unguided over the weekend. He lined up a list of Wolfensohn admirers who might impress the commentariat: his star witnesses were Robert McNamara and Maurice Strong, the prominent Canadian environmentalist who had lined up the support of his country's prime minister. Then he passed on their phone numbers to Jurek Martin, the Washington bureau chief of the *Financial Times*, and Peter Truell, a

New York Times business writer. On Monday morning Malloch Brown was rewarded with two large profiles of Wolfensohn. "Renaissance Man Gets the Nod" ran the title of the *Financial Times* analysis. "The Renaissance Banker" ran the title on the *New York Times* article. As Malloch Brown expected, the early definition stuck. Wolfensohn was described as a Renaissance man in countless articles and profiles thereafter.

The World Bank board meeting, held on the day these articles appeared, was a victory lap for Wolfensohn. Not only did the Europeans and other shareholders acquiesce to the American choice, they seemed positively thrilled by it. As the directors took their turn to speak for the record, each had a story about Wolfensohn; he was known to them because of some act of philanthropy, some banking tour de force, or some appreciated cultural gesture.[36] The wide ripples of the Wolfensohn campaign had affected every one of them.

CHAPTER FOUR

A TWISTER IN AFRICA

GABRIEL GARCIA MARQUEZ, the great Colombian writer, tells the story of Florentino Ariza, who lives a life of unrequited love for the beautiful Fermina Daza. Early on in his romantic career, Florentino thinks he has a chance to marry Fermina, but then she spurns him for a man of professional distinction and blue blood and not an ounce of passion. For the next fifty-one years, nine months, and four days, Florentino is condemned to live without his life's true love, although he doesn't waste his time. Deprived of the one thing that he craves, he accumulates 622 lovers. At the end of the story, Fermina's blue-blooded husband dies, and Florentino returns. He woos her urgently—propositioning her even at her husband's funeral—and at first she remains cold. But, by dint of sheer insistence, Florentino eventually wins his life's desire. He finally sees her, Garcia Marquez tells us, "naked to her waist, just as he had imagined her. Her shoulders were wrinkled, her breasts sagged, her ribs were covered by a flabby skin as pale and cold as a frog's."

For Florentino Ariza, substitute Jim Wolfensohn. Earlyish in his career, he thought he had a chance to lead the Bank, but then he was spurned in favor of gray men with fine credentials and no passion. For the next fourteen years, three months, and eleven days, he lived without the job he craved, though he probably accumulated 622 awards, board seats, and clients. Eventually his opening came, and he pressed too ardently at first, but then he finally prevailed through sheer implacable insistence. And yet there was a sad taste to his triumph. The World Bank that he had first courted—the Bank of Robert McNamara, of messianic speeches and ambition with no bounds—was like a woman in her youth; the Bank of 1995 was embattled and exhausted. Right from the outset, Paul Volcker told him that the institution was a mess, and that he'd have a hard time fixing it.[1] George Mallinckrodt, the chairman of Schroders, asked Wolfensohn why he wanted to be CEO for ten thousand people; "It's a nightmare!" Mallinckrodt warned him.[2]

Wolfensohn's early tenure at the Bank was colored by this fear of disappointment. In 1980, when he first wooed his bride, their dual ambitions were in step. McNamara's fire and expansionism gave the Bank a dynamic image; it would have been a balanced marriage. By 1995, however, Wolfensohn's star had risen even more, but the Bank's fortunes were drooping. Everything Wolfensohn read in the weeks after the triumph of his appointment told him that the Bank was in trouble: its professionals were arrogant; its structural-adjustment prescriptions were cruel; its relevance was threatened by the boom in private capital flows; its projects were deemed unsatisfactory by its own internal assessors. The suspicion that he had made a mistake in coming to the Bank—that it was too worn out and flabby to match his energy and pace—drove Wolfensohn through a series of emotional turns, but none of them was calm. He quarreled with his senior managers, whom he held responsible for the Bank's unpopularity. He quarreled especially with any who showed loyalty to the Bank's old ways, which he resented like a jealous husband. He could not stand the possibility that his sacrifice in coming to the Bank might not be appreciated fully. Didn't this institution understand that it needed a good shake? Couldn't people see he was the man to do it?

The answer was that many couldn't. From the point of view of the Bank's professionals, Wolfensohn was a showboating newcomer, long on glitzy contacts and short on gritty development experience, and the gap between how Wolfensohn expected to be greeted and the Bank's grudging welcome created repeated explosions. Soon after his appointment, Wolfensohn butted heads with the Bank's board, which reacted in disbelief at Wolfensohn's request that a private jet be put at his disposal: Many of the board members represented countries where the prime minister himself did not have standing access to an aircraft. In the fights over this issue, Wolfensohn would leap up in a furious rage, flinging his keys down on the table; "In that case I don't want this job," he'd shout, while making for the exit. But then he'd do an about-face and come back to collect the keys, and in the end the two sides reached a deal. Wolfensohn settled for a salary of $190,000 a year plus a $90,000 entertainment allowance. "It's an enormous financial sacrifice," he told a *Washington Post* journalist.[3]

As he had done in his previous lives, Wolfensohn responded to professional challenge by going into overdrive. He was determined that the Bank he imagined could somehow be revived: the Bank that served as the supreme commander in humanity's noblest mission, to lift billions out of poverty. His new job, he believed passionately, was unlike any that he'd held before—it was "a unique position . . . from which you can influence whole segments of the world," as he had told an interviewer fourteen years previously. Even if his senior managers struck Wolfensohn as surly, he was sure that further down the ranks he would find idealism and talent. Long before his formal accession on June 1, he ordered his top lieutenants to set up brunches at the Watergate Hotel with "bright young staff," a request that triggered electric convulsions up and down the Bank's bureaucracy. Who was bright? What was young? Who should decide anyway?[4] Wolfensohn then declared that he wanted to meet all seventeen vice presidents and their teams; he meant to go over and see them on their own turf, so he could walk the corridors and feel the institution. Nothing like this had ever happened in the reign of Lewis Preston, and maybe not in any previous reign either; the president was supposed to be aloof, ceremonial almost; you wheeled him out to meet visiting heads of state so that the veteran experts on the staff could proceed with the real work of the institution. But Wolfensohn would never settle for that role. By the time he assumed office, he had talked to more World Bankers than Preston probably had done in his entire presidency.

Meanwhile Wolfensohn set out to woo the Bank's NGO antagonists. The Bank that he imagined—the Bank of Robert McNamara—took a backseat to nobody in its indignation about global poverty, and Wolfensohn was not going to cede the moral high ground to the Fifty Years Is Enough battalions. Instead, he was going to meet them, charm them, and make them feel that they ought to be the Bank's allies—that they shared the same poverty-fighting goals, and that Wolfensohn could even help them on their mission. As soon as his appointment was public, he began to stage meetings with environmental groups and other critics, and he soon instituted a new approach to answering their correspondence. The Bank got thousands of letters every month complaining about what it was doing; most went in the trash or got dumped on a junior official who seldom answered properly. Wolfensohn declared that henceforth vice presidents would respond to the letters; when the vice presidents sent back bland replies, Wolfensohn hollered that he wanted to read all these responses himself and add a personal note at the bottom. "Thank you for writing and please keep in touch," he would say, and sure enough the flattered letter writer would soon write again, and before you knew it the Bank would be locked into a game of Ping-Pong, back and forth, back and forth, with some tiny NGO in the Philippines or Guyana.[5]

It didn't take long for the Bank's old guard to mock the new boss's frenetic energy. Wolfensohn had replaced Lewis Preston's three-meetings-a-day desk diary with an electronic schedule that kept him busy from seven till seven, but there was no way he could possibly keep up with all his passions and ambitions. On June 1, the day that Wolfensohn formally took over the institution he had by now inhabited for two months, an anonymously published staff magazine called *Bank Swirled* sneered that he'd arrived with

> his collection of rapiers and swords, two cellos, a large cage containing his trademark koala, his personal library of 150,000 volumes, a drafting board, several easels, five unfinished oils, two watercolor landscapes, a marble bust in progress, a working model of a cold fusion reactor, several 12 meter yacht designs, his Gulfstream jet, a Bloomberg terminal, a model of the set design he is finishing for the San Francisco Opera's production of Semele, costumes from his staging of Titus Andronicus at Stratford, Ontario, last year, his collection of 11,000 autographed celebrity photos, a Gutenberg press, a keg of Castlemaine beer and a refrigerated tap. In addition, adjacent office space was allocated to his court composer, his chamber orchestra, his biographer and the 1996 Australian men's Olympic fencing team.[6]

But to many in the Bank, Wolfensohn seemed wonderful. He was a whirlwind of fresh air, upending the old hierarchy with his newcomer's questions and his brunches with the younger staff; he was precisely what was needed to restore the Bank's idealism and sense of mission. On the day of his accession, he held a press conference. "Poverty alleviation is the single most important problem" for the world, he declared, adding that the Bank must be a force for "social justice." To staff members who bridled at the Bank's bloodless technocratic culture, the emphasis on poverty and social justice was like rain after a drought; Kris Zedler, the official who had been recruited to deal with those pesky groups that front-desk security officers called No-Gos, remembers "skipping down the halls" in her excitement.[7] The Bank's public-relations officials watched the press conference in amused shock. Earlier that year their boss, Mark Malloch Brown, had spent a good deal of energy trying to shift the Bank's image away from a direct focus on poverty and toward hardheaded growth promotion; he had taken note of the Gingrichite

revolution in Congress and decided that the Bank needed to differentiate itself from "loser" outfits like the United Nations.[8] After Wolfensohn's first press conference, Malloch Brown commented that the
newcomer was not "on message."

"He's the president," someone observed. "I think you'll find that *is*
the message."[9]

AS WELL AS MEETING the Bank's staff and external critics, Wolfensohn set out to meet its clients. He had come to the helm of a global
institution, with projects in nearly one hundred countries, and he was
determined to travel, to see the Bank's work on the ground and hear
about its performance directly from its borrowers. In early April, he told
Kim Jaycox, the imposing vice president for Africa, that he wanted to
visit his region as soon as he became president.[10] He didn't care that
such trips normally took months to prepare. He didn't care that some
would find it odd if he hit the road so soon after assuming office. And
he didn't want to be constrained by the normal conventions of such
missions, which were usually confined to government meetings plus a
token field trip to a model project. Wolfensohn wanted to meet students, church leaders, nongovernmental groups. He wanted to get out
into the fields and the slums: "To walk with the poor," was how he put
it. "I'll be walking the streets, smelling it myself," he declared in an
interview shortly before he set off. "I can't get that from listening to
commentary in Washington."[11]

For a president seeking to revive the messianic energy of Mc-
Namara's Bank, the choice of Africa was fitting. Soon after his arrival in
1968, McNamara had reversed the policy of playing second fiddle in
Africa to the former colonial powers, and determined that the Bank
should become a leading player on the continent. During the 1970s, the
Bank duly lent Africa three times as much as it had in the previous
decade,[12] and its presence there jumped from two to fifteen field offices.

McNamara's engagement was driven by Africa's evident misery, by a determination to identify the Bank with the poorest of the poor; in the mid-1990s, when Wolfensohn arrived, this imperative had grown even stronger. East and South Asia had made big strides, and in the early 1990s Latin America was undergoing a revival; but Africa had stagnated.[13] The region was being almost totally bypassed by the vaunted boom in private capital flows to developing countries. Farmers in parts of the continent pushed plows by hand, lacking even animals. Women walked hours to collect firewood, because deforestation had denuded the landscape of trees. AIDS spread across the continent.

Wolfensohn's urge to fight this suffering was reinforced by another motive for his early trip to Africa: a sense that the Bank's reputation depended on the continent. Ever since McNamara made the Bank a leading player in the region, the institution's fortunes had been tied to Africa's repeated setbacks. This was only fair: the Bank shared some responsibility for the continent's mistakes. In the McNamara period it was too willing to back leaders who were well meaning but misguided, such as Tanzania's scholarly socialist leader, Julius Nyerere, who translated Shakespeare's *Julius Caesar* into Swahili. Nyerere nationalized Tanzania's businesses and forcibly moved peasants to collectivized farms, yet he retained the Bank's support and McNamara's personal friendship throughout the 1970s. Eventually, at the turn of the decade, the Bank reversed course. It realized that its projects in Tanzania would never succeed unless the surrounding economic policies were sound, and that subsidizing Nyerere's confusion was a cruel sort of charity. From January 1980, when McNamara journeyed to Tanzania to tell his friend to forget socialism and decontrol prices, the Bank stuck to a new line. If Africans wanted the Bank's help, they would have to accept pro-market "structural adjustment" as a condition.[14]

The new insistence upon structural adjustment only increased the Bank's reputational stake in Africa. Adjustment was controversial from the outset, as we have seen: it was enthusiastically supported by the

Bank's Bretton Woods sister, the International Monetary Fund, but agencies like the United Nations Development Program and UNICEF were less inclined to blame Africa's problems on policies that needed adjustment, and more apt to point the finger at the oil shock, falling commodity prices, and other misfortunes not of Africa's own making. African leaders, not surprisingly, sided with the United Nations, and denounced the Bank's new orthodoxy as anti-African: They wanted aid, not policy lectures.[15] The Bank soon found itself prescribing the bitter medicine of economic austerity while others declared that its diagnosis was all wrong; and the sense that its credibility was on the line drove the Bank to redouble its efforts on the continent. In the course of the 1980s, the Bank churned out twice as many reports on Africa as it had in the previous decade; it devoted a third of its regional staff to Africa, even though Africa represented less than a sixth of its lending.[16] And in its eagerness to show that its prescriptions worked, the Bank assumed a growing role as a coordinator of donors.[17] If an African country accepted the Bank's economic conditions, the Bank would arrange regular meetings of its backers, coaching the country's officials on what to say in order to elicit extra aid money. The more the Bank waded in, the more it encouraged the idea that it was a sort of shadow government for the continent.

Of course, this only increased the Bank's reputational risk still further. The Bank was telling Africans what to say to donors; it was telling donors what to give to Africans; if its advice failed to bring progress, both sides would resent it. By the time of Wolfensohn's arrival in the mid-1990s, the resentment was boiling; with a few exceptions like Ghana, structural adjustment had failed to revive Africa's economies, and the main thing that donors had to show for their efforts was a large mountain of debt that Africans could never service. Never mind that the Bank's prescriptions—free prices, a sound budget—were broadly correct; and never mind that Africa's continuing misery was explained to a large extent by the failure to implement reform faithfully. The Bank had pushed its prescriptions arrogantly, and now its critics were exacting their revenge. And to the World Bank's brand-new president, the lesson was quite clear. If he was ever to rejuvenate his bride, he would have to bury the legacy of structural adjustment the moment he set foot in Africa.

WOLFENSOHN'S DETERMINATION to get out of Washington immediately had set the Africa department humming. Headquarters memos went out to the Bank's field offices in the region, inviting each to make a case for inclusion on the presidential itinerary. There would inevitably be stops in the countries favored by the big European donors—the French insisted on Côte d'Ivoire, the British insisted on Uganda—but Wolfensohn also wanted to break the mold a bit. Linda McGinnis, the Bank's young representative in the remote Sahelian country of Mali, made a pitch. Mali was one of the poorest countries in the world, but its democratically elected government was fresh and idealistic and committed to development; moreover, in the warmth of its people and the color of its textiles, Mali was the perfect introduction to Africa. Other country representatives made similar appeals, and by early April five countries had been chosen. "Be careful what you wish for," McGinnis told her husband one evening. Mali was going to be the first stop on the visit.[18]

On April 18, another headquarters memo went out about the briefing books for Wolfensohn's first odyssey. "Each brief should start with a poem or saying that captures some aspect of the drama in each nation," the memo instructed.[19] "Mighty farmer, salute! / Master of the hoe / Runner in the morning / Walker in the evening . . . " began the poem on the cover of the Mali briefing book; it continued for another dozen lines, but without noticeable improvement. A bit later Linda McGinnis wrote to her friend Victoria Kwakwa, the World Bank official who had written the briefing book's first draft: "Nice Job!!! Enjoyable, readable, NON-BANKESE prose," she exalted, before suggesting a few upgrades to the manuscript. Kwakwa might want to know that the storied Malian town of Timbuktu dates back to the eleventh century and was named after the nomad woman who first guarded it; in the Tuareg language, *Timbuktu* means "old mother with a large navel." The wealth of Timbuktu was built on gold and salt, the two being considered of almost equal value at the time, so that you could trade a pound of one for a pound of the other. "You may wish to add something along these lines in the second paragraph," McGinnis continued, before launching into a love letter to her adopted land: "All of your senses will feel sharpened, if not assaulted. Color is everywhere."[20] The memo went on for seven pages, and the next day another one arrived. "More on Wolf Brief," announced the title.[21]

As the date of the trip approached, the preparations threatened to break down into chaos. Headquarters bombarded Linda McGinnis with phone calls, often waking her at night; an electrical surge wrecked much of the equipment in her office, making communication difficult. On June 2, she sent a reassuring memo to Washington in a bid to calm everybody: The presidential villa, where Jim and Elaine Wolfensohn would stay, had a fabulous view of Bamako and the Niger River, and it came "with cooks, laundry services, telephones, TV, and your hearts' desire (almost)."[22] But the headquarters folk remained jumpy, and almost at the last moment they called McGinnis with an impossible request; they wanted to be sure that Wolfensohn could have constant phone access. McGinnis explained that this was Mali, 1995: the GDP per capita was $240, half the level of India and a third of the level of China; you'd be lucky to find a working telephone of any kind, and there were certainly no cell phones in the country. This provoked consternation back in Washington, until eventually McGinnis had an inspired idea. Mali boasted one satellite phone, housed in a silver briefcase and almost never used, which belonged to the country's president. McGinnis suspected that the device might not work; it was carried about proudly on presidential trips and was mainly ornamental.[23] But she used her warm relations with the government to borrow the phone, and headquarters relaxed a bit.

By the eve of the trip, a cautious optimism was creeping in. On June 15, Hasan Tuluy, a member of the headquarters team, sent a memo to Linda McGinnis: "GOOD LUCK TO YOU ALL! *Entre nous*, Mr. W. is lucky to be introduced to Africa by a great country team." Then Tuluy gave McGinnis a bit of advice about the boss she would be dealing with. "Whoever described Mr. W. as the 'tornado' was right on," the memo confided; in his first weeks at the Bank, Wolfensohn had made a strong impression. "He is very intense, but not in an intimidating manner . . . he will move and move the Bank along—better be on board, or get off now," the memo advised ominously. Tuluy concluded by invoking John F. Kennedy. "As I remember JFK once said something along the lines of: 'There are costs and risks to every course of action, but they are far less than the long-range risks and costs of comfortable inaction.' It probably applies to JDW as well," Tuluy contended.[24]

A DAY AFTER being compared to JFK, JDW arrived in Bamako. He lowered his head as he emerged from the aircraft and came carefully down the steps, his white hair bushy and a touch unruly, his burly Father Christmas frame cheerful, his khakis just a little short for him.[25] He proceeded down the red carpet laid out on the tarmac, greeting a line of waiting dignitaries: a crisp handshake for the men, a gallant air kiss for the hands of all the ladies; "Enchanté, enchanté," he said over and over. A short while later, he was whisked into the VIP section of Bamako's airport, a cramped, musty room with an air-conditioner that made no impact on the heat, but which asserted its relevance by blaring out the noise of a truck blasting hard along a highway. There, sitting on the seedy velvet couches, after not more than ten minutes in Africa, Wolfensohn gave his first interview, laying himself open to questions before he had even seen the country, and doing it in fluent French as well. "The future of Africa is the most important thing of all," he declared passionately.[26]

The country that Wolfensohn was visiting was one of the world's poorest. One in four children died before the age of five, three in four adults were illiterate, and the average life expectancy was just forty-seven years. But the bright hope for Mali was President Alpha Oumar Konaré, a big man in boldly colored suits with a physique to match his name; "Alpha! Alpha!" the crowds would cry when he went about the capital. In the bad old days of Mali's Leninist dictatorship, Konaré had founded an independent newspaper and cowritten two pamphlets that had inspired the democracy movement. In 1992 he had won power in a clean election, and since then he had happily tolerated rivals. Mali bustled with ten opposition parties, over forty private newspapers, and hundreds of active civil-society outfits.[27]

This was more than merely heartwarming. As it picked over the lessons of structural adjustment's failure, the Bank was developing a new interest in politics. Its sound economic prescriptions had failed to lift the continent because of political failures: aging autocrats, lacking electoral legitimacy, had been too weak to push through currency devaluations or cuts in government spending. The autocrats were often corrupt, and corruption was another reason for structural adjustment's failure: it scared away job-creating investment and deprived the poor of decent services. The defeat of structural adjustment was a defeat for the idea that you could ignore this political context and proceed by technocratic means alone, calling in the finance minister and imposing your program.

Because of this lesson, the Bank was on the threshold of a transformation. It was a sequel to the one it had undergone ten years before, when it gave up on the idea that its projects in Tanzania could work if the surrounding economic policies were rotten. Now, in the mid-1990s, the Bank was coming to see that economic policies could not stick either if the surrounding politics were rotten: its concept of development had broadened one step further. American and European aid donors were making the same shift, declaring that they would cut off aid to the corrupt African strongmen whom they had bankrolled. The end of the cold war made it easy to be pure: The old motive to prop up kleptocrats like Zaire's President Mobutu Sese Seko was fading, since the CIA no longer needed him to funnel arms to anticommunist rebels in Angola. The lessons of structural adjustment and the logic of geopolitics converged. Both pointed to a new emphasis on supporting African democracies. Encouraged by donor pressure, autocrats stepped aside in Zambia and Benin in 1991, in Congo-Brazzaville in 1992, in Burundi and Niger the year after.

Mali's Alpha Oumar Konaré was part of this new wave, and his tolerance for civil society and freewheeling debate offered a chance for a new relationship with Africa. In the new democratic Mali, the World Bank could break out of the narrow dialogue with finance-ministry people; it could sell its ideas to NGOs and parliamentarians and journalists; it could build a broad consensus for its economic program. If the Bank could speak to a whole nation, rather than just to a few technocrats, perhaps its policies might actually be implemented for a change, and perhaps its image might improve as well. Given the right leadership from its new president, the World Bank could be a partner, not a scold. It could be at once more popular and more effective.

The morning after Wolfensohn's arrival in Mali, Linda McGinnis led a cavalcade of cars over to the presidential guesthouse, where the Wolfensohns were staying. McGinnis had called in several favors to assemble such a fleet; cars were scarce in Mali. It was early in the morning, and the Wolfensohns were still having breakfast, so the cavalcade parked and waited, and then McGinnis saw something that made her heart stop. In keeping with Malian tradition, President Konaré had laid on a group of praise-singers to chant Wolfensohn's virtues, and the praise-singers had assembled outside the visitors' window, wailing out their message in a screeching, jarring, atonal din. Sam Carlson, McGinnis's husband, remembers thinking that this was "the last freaking thing that the Wolfensohns wanted. They're jet-lagged. They're stressed. They were out late last night at the reception. This is their first stop in Africa. And it's six-thirty in the morning."[28] Then out of the guesthouse bounded Jim Wolfensohn, his eyes bleary and his shirt collar open, a huge grin plastered all over him. Unembarrassed by the cavalcade of spectators, he accepted a scarf from one of the singers, wrapped it around his shoulders and began to sway, holding the singers' hands and improvising a line dance like a delighted father at a wedding. McGinnis had seen other visiting officials get the praise-singer treatment, and she'd seen them flinch, clap slightly, and dive into the nearest car. Wolfensohn alone was brave enough to risk looking ridiculous.[29]

The breakfast-time dance set a pattern for the visit. The Wolfensohns went off to see a school in Bamako; they squeezed along a mud street between lines of curious onlookers, children in plastic flip-flops and women with heads that balanced trays of mangoes.[30] They visited a clinic, and Wolfensohn gamely exchanged his shoes for sanitary slippers and donned an absurd-looking hair cap; then he struck up a long conversation with a nurse about one of his own children who had been born prematurely. He and Elaine toured a public-works project, and were greeted by a festival of Malian diversity: there were Bambara dancers with red pants and yellow cloths wrapped around the groin; there were Tuaregs in flowing blue robes; there were dancers from the Dogon tribe on six-foot stilts painted in wild stripes, disguised in fantastical face masks. The Wolfensohns loved all of it, and they were not shy about expressing their delight. This was not the aloof, arrogant, structural-adjustment-pushing World Bank that Africans so frequently encountered.

Toward the end of the morning there was a long meeting with President Alpha Oumar Konaré. His office was a proud symphony of orange and lime green, with deep shag carpets, and Wolfensohn and his entourage waited on big, low-slung chairs made out of sweaty foam until presently Konaré walked in wearing an electric blue polyester

Nehru jacket and a big smile, and held forth on his vision for the future of his country. The meeting went on and on, the garrulous visitor warming to his equally expansive host, and after a long time the two were winding up, patting each other on the back and squeezing each other on the arm, and then President Konaré said there was one final thing he had for Wolfensohn. From behind the visitors, an enormous goat appeared, a fantastic alpha of a beast with splendid, looping, curly horns. It stood there on the shag carpet like a late-arriving guest, macho and confident. For the first time during the visit, Wolfensohn appeared speechless. Konaré laughed his big alpha laugh. The goat, he explained, was a gift to his visitor.[31]

The next morning the Wolfensohns headed out of Bamako to a village called Koro-Koro. It was an hour's drive, and the heat was monstrous. When they arrived the whole village had lined up to greet the visitors under a banner specially made for the occasion. The Wolfensohns were invited to sit down in low-slung chairs made out of plastic straps that press and sweat against the flesh, and were honored with the rare luxury of Coca-Cola. Little girls with kauri shells in their hair stared curiously at the white strangers. The villagers brought out some enormous muskets and began to fire into the air. Then there was a dance, and afterward Wolfensohn was taken off to meet the chief of the village, a wizened white-bearded figure in a faded pink turban, straight out of central casting. Wolfensohn squatted down with the chief, who was holding court under a baobab tree, and they ate kola nuts together. The old man gave Wolfensohn a red tunic with black geometric patterns and a square red hat to match, and instead of just saying thank you Wolfensohn put them on right there, pulling the tunic over his button-down shirt, looking utterly delighted.[32]

The Mali trip was going more than well; Wolfensohn was bowled over. Back in Washington, he had confronted so many problems: the Bank was complicated, bureaucratic, controlled by arrogant barons. But here in Mali, he had found the soul of the World Bank he knew was there, hidden under the encrusted layers of head-office formality. He was being shown around by this young Linda McGinnis, a smart, attractive, poverty-fighting idealist, who spoke impeccable French and seemed to be the best friend of everybody in the government. He was meeting the ordinary people as well as the president, and he was getting on with all of them. He was living and breathing Africa, and he was showing that the Bank didn't have to be aloof and inaccessible; it could be passionately human. The acid fights over structural adjustment seemed a world away, and Wolfensohn was starting to form a theory of his presidency. The World Bank—his Bank—should throw out the headquarters arrogance and get out to the field, where air-conditioners roared like trucks and you danced before you finished breakfast and goats paraded on shag carpets. The World Bank—his Bank—should get out and embrace its clients, the poor people for whom it existed; it should get so close to them it was practically wearing the same clothes, much as Wolfensohn himself had forged familial bonds with corporate clients during his career in private banking. If you became part of the client's family, your critics could carp until the moon turned green, but you'd be the one who was in there at the center of the action, rescuing Chrysler or merging two vast companies. It was easy to see how the World Bank's sedentary barons, lurking in the gleaming headquarters in Washington, could be mocked and undermined by NGOs. But nobody would dare attack the Bank for callous structural-adjustment arrogance if its face was Linda McGinnis, a front-line poverty fighter who lived and worked right here with the client. Nobody would dare attack a Bank that visibly delivered clinics and public-works projects, and schools, where kids with plastic flip-flops learned a life that didn't end in death at forty-seven.[33]

The Wolfensohns had asked to see the maternity ward in the village, and as they were led toward the small mud structure they could see a rectangle of brown paper just above the entrance. Elaine was asked to tear away the paper, and underneath was another Malian surprise: A proud sign had been affixed to the wall, naming the clinic after her. The villagers were cheering, and Elaine was looking up at her name, and then she was realizing that she'd have to make a speech, which she did, a bit shyly. Inside the clinic was a single bed frame with no mattress: there was no electricity, no running water, no medical instruments beyond some gauze and a bucket. Perhaps the old man under the baobab tree was cannier than he appeared; there was no way the Wolfensohns would leave Mali with a clinic named after Elaine that contained nothing but a bed frame. Linda McGinnis had to spend the next month ordering hospital beds and supplies for the clinic, all paid for by a contribution from the Wolfensohns' personal foundation.

There was one other thing that McGinnis had to do: "Take care of my goat," Wolfensohn instructed. At first the boss wanted it shipped out to his ranch in Wyoming, where it would have endured some snowy winters in the shadow of the Grand Tetons, but McGinnis quickly discovered that shipping goats live from Mali is no easy matter. She was left with no alternative but to bring the goat home to Bamako, where her husband, Sam, tied it to a stake on the front lawn, and where the goat contemptuously pulled free and charged around the yard, eating all the pomegranate bushes and papaya trees and defecating copiously. In the end the goat was herded into the back of the family land cruiser and driven out to Koro-Koro, and Linda and Sam presented it to the village chief as a gift from Mr. Wolfensohn. The chief promptly organized a barbecue. For months and months afterward, messages would arrive periodically from Wolfensohn in Washington, inquiring how the goat was. Great, great, they always said; in fact it had sired several babies. It was several years before Linda McGinnis admitted to her boss that the goat had long ago been eaten.

The reviews of the Mali trip could not have been more positive. The country had been captivated "by the conquering charm of the World Bank boss," declared an article on the front page of a Malian newspaper. "By his easy manner and profound humanity, he had projected an image of a World Bank more eager to please than to recoup its loans," the paper commented.[34] The visit had been ceremonial, but the ceremony mattered. For Africa, it signaled that the World Bank's new leader would go out of his way to visit a promising new democracy, and that he would listen to its people; the years of harsh structural-adjustment conditionality were over. For nongovernmental organizations, including the many that had assailed the Bank in Madrid the previous year, it signaled that the Bank's new president had instincts much like theirs: that he wanted to sit under baobab trees, eating nuts with village leaders. For Wolfensohn, meanwhile, the Mali visit created an image of what the Bank could be: unstuffy, unhierarchical, and above all human.

On June 19 a memo went out from the World Bank's head office to Linda McGinnis, offering a postmortem on the trip. "Congratulations to you and everyone are indeed in order," it declared; the reports were coming in from Wolfensohn and his entourage in Abidjan, and "the glow of the Mali visit is still with them."[35]

THE TRUTH WAS that Abidjan, capital of Côte d'Ivoire and the next stop on Wolfensohn's grand tour, was something of a battlefield. On the plane from Mali, Wolfensohn had been reading the Côte d'Ivoire briefing book and felt it lacked detail; "he blew a fuse," in the words of another memo from headquarters in Washington.[36] Wolfensohn turned to Olivier Lafourcade, the Bank's director for Côte d'Ivoire and its neighbors, and demanded to know the female literacy rate in the country. Lafourcade hesitated, tried to bluff, then found to his horror that Wolfensohn already knew the answer. The full wrath of Wolfensohn descended upon him, and the visit to Côte d'Ivoire never quite recovered. As soon as the Wolfensohns touched down in the airport, they could feel the difference from Mali; they had left the exotic magic of the Sahel and entered ersatz Europe. An official limo deposited them outside the Hotel Ivoire, a flashy structure with huge glass doors and a semicircular driveway. Elaine was taken off to see a school that could hardly have been more different from the huts she had visited in Mali. It had an art room and a swimming pool.[37]

Compared to Mali, Côte d'Ivoire was a development success story; its GDP per head was nearly three times bigger. But its government, led by Henri Konan Bedié, was as unappealing as Mali's Alpha Oumar Konaré was seductive. Konan Bedié was a small Napoleon, stiff, corrupt, and inordinately vain; he was promising an election soon, but his cronies had drawn up an electoral code that banned his chief rival from running. To make matters worse, Côte d'Ivoire epitomized all that had gone wrong in the Bank's relationship with Africa. The Bank had lent to the country until it was swamped in debt, and now it was having to pour in cheap IDA credits so that the Ivorians could repay old loans from the World Bank's market-rate lending operation. This refinancing operation didn't make the Bank feel good. It was pumping in new money not out of belief in the government's program but out of fear that the alternative was default. Kim Jaycox, the Bank's Africa vice president, would have preferred the Wolfensohn itinerary to skip Côte d'Ivoire altogether, but the French government would not hear of that. So here was Wolfensohn, visiting wannabe France because the French wanted him to. It was not a promising scenario.

While Elaine was visiting the school, Wolfensohn was taken off to meet civil-society leaders. It was what he wanted; he was breaking out of the pattern of meeting only with officialdom, and he was continuing his campaign to defuse NGO criticisms. But the setup for the meeting was oppressively formal; a terrifyingly elegant lady from the government's protocol office presided over the scene with an officious walkie-talkie. Shigeo Katsu, the Bank's resident representative in Abidjan, tried to persuade Madame Protocol to change the arrangements, but his adversary bore down on him like some haughty Parisian catwalk queen; there was no question of last-minute adjustment. The meeting began with a stultifying speech from an Ivorian official, long on philosophical reflections about the nature of the World Bank, and then Wolfensohn had his turn to speak. But the lady from protocol had allowed press cameras into the middle of the meeting room, so that people seated around the rectangular layout could not see the speaker. The cameras flashed and whirred, mocking Wolfensohn's hopes to make eye contact with the NGOs. In an effort to satisfy the press crews, Wolfensohn made a joke about speaking French like an Australian; and, finding that the photographers were still exploding flashbulbs in his face, he made another about not wanting to be a movie star. Finally his patience snapped. "I think that's enough," he said brusquely, waving to the cameras to get out of the meeting.[38]

That evening the Wolfensohns went off to dinner at the president's private residence. There was no trace of Mali's charmingly retro 1970s decor; instead, the home of Henri Konan Bedié derived its inspiration from Versailles, or perhaps from Konan Bedié's idea of it. There were gold trimmings and plush carpets and ivory tusks and fine china; each dinner place was set with five or six glasses. Lafourcade, who had felt the lash of Wolfensohn's displeasure earlier in the plane, could feel another storm approaching; here was the World Bank president who had promised to "walk with the poor" trapped under a French chande-lier drinking French wine out of a French glass. Wolfensohn was trapped there, and his captor was making things still worse; he was explaining that his chef was, naturally, French, and that he belonged to an association of "chefs des chefs d'état," a pun he found inordinately amusing. In a last attempt to forge a relationship, Wolfensohn caste aside the prepared text of his dinner speech and instead spoke to Konan Bedié informally. But the little Napoleon refused to bend. Instead of replying to Wolfensohn in kind, he stood up and read a written speech, a stream of meaningless pomposities.[39]

Wolfensohn returned to the Hotel Ivoire in a testy mood. Elaine went up to bed, but he and a handful of Bank staff sat down in a cluster of chairs a few steps from the reception desk. After some preliminary chatter, Wolfensohn asked about the Bank's education-adjustment loan in Côte d'Ivoire. Where were the schools that it had financed?

There was a brief silence, and then one lieutenant ventured: "Jim, this is an adjustment operation, not an investment operation."

"Well, what's the difference?" Wolfensohn asked. "Where are the textbooks? Where are the schools? You're putting in $100 million!"

"No, this is an adjustment operation," came the response. The money was really supposed to plug a hole in the government's budget. It didn't directly finance concrete schools or textbooks.

This revelation blew the cork on Wolfensohn's frustrations. He gushed and bubbled about this terrible country; he didn't know what the hell the Bank was doing there, but he knew he didn't like it. Jaycox told him he didn't like it either, but Wolfensohn went on. He said this couldn't possibly continue, this business of pouring out free "adjustment" money that had nothing to do with education or any other legitimate purpose; the Bank should lend only to countries that would use its resources well, and get out of the rest of them. The whole situation in Côte d'Ivoire was ridiculous, preposterous, monstrous, he told Jaycox, as though Jaycox were pure stupid. Finally, seated there in the Hotel Ivoire, a few yards from the reception desk, Wolfensohn lost control. "You tell me we are taking this grant money from IDA and just throwing it away?" he thundered.

Jaycox did not take this meekly. He was an imposing character, well over six feet tall and strong as well, with the tough look of a man who'd spent years trying to get sewers and water into Africa's meanest shanties. For nearly a decade, he had presided over the Bank's Africa programs as the baron of barons; no country south of the Sahara could hope for a Bank loan without Jaycox's say-so. The baron wasn't going to be lectured by a newcomer, never mind his rank; what Wolfensohn was saying was insulting and naïve, and Jaycox was not afraid to say that. Côte d'Ivoire could not service its market-rate loans from the World Bank, so there was no choice but to pump in soft IDA cash in order to refinance the country; and by the way the French government, which was providing a fair chunk of the IDA funds, insisted on this policy. When Wolfensohn yelled at Jaycox, Jaycox just yelled back: "Wake up, Jim. Wake up. That's the way it works. You may not like it, but that's the way it works," he screamed. "We can't forgive the debt, so how do we get out of it?"

The argument raged on, the two men hollering at each other in full view of the reception desk. Olivier Lafourcade and several of the others present felt they were witnessing the end of the Jaycox era in Africa, but Jaycox carried on, apparently unbothered by the threat to his career prospects. He had been accused of throwing IDA money down the drain, but what was the alternative? In theory, the alternative was to forgive unrepayable old loans, and Jaycox was all for that. But the subject of debt relief was virtually taboo within the Bank; Ernie Stern, the number two during much of the period since McNamara's reign, had long forbidden talk of debt relief, and the International Monetary Fund was equally against it.[40] As a result, there was no alternative to "defensive lending" in countries like Côte d'Ivoire. To defend against default, you lent money to absurd Napoleons.

"I agree it's pretty damn stupid," Jaycox told Wolfensohn. "But that's the way it is around here. If I talked about debt relief I'd have my balls cut off by Ernie Stern, so I'm not going to take this."

Wolfensohn looked at Jaycox for a moment. The two men calmed down, conscious of the other guests in the hotel lobby. Then Wolfensohn replied that debt relief was the only way forward.

"Sure, we've done the analysis," Jaycox answered. "But the fund doesn't agree with any of this."

"Leave that to me," Wolfensohn told him.[41]

THE YELLING at the Hotel Ivoire exposed an issue that loomed large in Wolfensohn's first years in office. For roughly a decade, the Bank had been ducking the issue of debt relief. Wolfensohn's arrival changed that.

Africa's debt problems—like Latin America's even larger ones—had begun with the first oil shock. To pay for newly expensive oil, Africans had borrowed lavishly: in the course of the next decade, the region's debt grew sixfold. In the early 1980s, private lenders, which had always been leery of Africa, refused to stump up further cash; so Africa fell back on official creditors, notably the IMF, which waded into Africa with short-term loans, on the theory that the continent's troubles would be over in three years or so. After that, Africa was stuck. It could not service its debts, so the unpaid interest got added to the amount it owed; and it had to borrow even more to repay old lending.[42] An elaborate Kabuki play transpired, with Côte d'Ivoire being just one example of many. The World Bank made long-term loans to Africa so that the IMF's short-term loans could be paid back; the Bank's soft-loan arm made loans so that the market-based arm could be paid back; when all else failed, Britain, France, and other donors made grants to prevent Africans from defaulting.

There are those who argue that, sooner or later, the World Bank was bound to end this smoke-and-mirrors style of business. It had been clear since the late 1980s that Africa needed debt relief; most of the Kabuki moves merely deferred the day of reckoning. Recognizing the inevitable, the big donor governments began to forgive some debt-service payments starting in 1988; then in the 1990s, they began to cancel debt outright, and by 1994 these efforts had yielded debt forgiveness worth a bit over $15 billion for sub-Saharan Africa.[43] Still, that sum was only a fraction of the $235 billion that the region owed to foreigners, and the obvious next step was debt relief by multilateral lenders—led by the World Bank and the International Monetary Fund. The more other kinds of debt were written off, the more obvious this became, since multilateral debt accounted for a growing share of Africa's burden.[44] The Bank claimed that its own lending bore little responsibility for Africa's debt crisis, since its loans carried low interest rates. But African debt to the World Bank nonetheless accounted for around a sixth of the region's debt-service payments.[45]

Moreover, the World Bank had its own motive to embrace debt relief, as Côte d'Ivoire demonstrated. Festering bad debts threatened the Bank's own financial structure. The more it lent money to bad debtors, the more indebted they became—and the greater the calamity would be if one of these bad debtors defaulted. Besides, the more the Bank was forced to keep dud countries from defaulting by plying them with defensive loans, the less it could direct money to fresh openings in the battle against poverty. By the late 1980s and early 1990s, the Bank's so-called structural-adjustment programs were failing to promote adjustment because that was often not their real purpose; they were really about getting fresh loans to Africa so that Africans could repay old ones. Time and again, the Bank would give these defensive loans a structural-adjustment coating by projecting that they would kick-start growth; time and again, these projections proved wrong, discrediting structural adjustment still further. When internal critics questioned the realism of these growth projections, they were told to be quiet. "Realism" required getting the Bank's own loans serviced.[46]

And yet, however compelling the arguments for debt relief, they were heresy at the World Bank when Wolfensohn arrived there. The Bank stuck to its line that rich governments were welcome to forgive debts, and that such relief would be sufficient to relieve Africa's crisis. The Bank also argued that debt forgiveness would harm other developing regions: it would amount to a public admission of trouble in the Bank's portfolio, and this would undermine its AAA credit status, raising costs for Latin American or Asian borrowers. It was a strange argument, since every banker knows that dealing promptly with problems is the best way to protect your credit status, but it was nonetheless the Bank's position.[47] Only a few heretics, such as Ravi Kanbur, the Bank's chief economist in the Africa region, opposed this orthodoxy. As Kanbur put it in a private memo to Wolfensohn, "We have been seen to be dragged into this issue kicking and screaming—pointing to everybody else's debt problem and asking for solutions to those, but please God not multilateral debt stock reduction."[48]

For all the logic of debt relief, therefore, Wolfensohn broke the mold by recognizing it.[49] He came to the Bank with the practical instincts of a corporate financier: if debts were unpayable then they ought to be restructured. Sure, there would be people who said this was impossible, and they would bleat and moan; but Wolfensohn had encountered that with Chrysler's creditors, and in the end he had corralled them all into a successful debt restructuring. Shortly before becoming World Bank president, Wolfensohn had raised the debt issue with the Treasury in London. Her Majesty's officials had regretted that it would be "very, very difficult, in their view, to persuade the G7 to write off multilateral debt," and Wolfensohn had seen he faced an uphill battle.[50] But he had not given up, and what he saw in Côte d'Ivoire only redoubled his determination. A few hours before the shouting match with Kim Jaycox, at the civil-society meeting organized by Madame Protocol, Wolfensohn had been struck by an articulate mullah: "If you put money in the pocket of my white robe and you take an equal amount out of the other pocket of my white robe, what good does that do for me?" the mullah had demanded. "It made a profound impact on me," Wolfensohn said later; "the simplicity with which this guy stated it, and the obvious truth."[51]

If the first consequence of Wolfensohn's Africa trip was that he imagined a Bank like Linda McGinnis, the second was that he resolved to tackle debt relief.

BOTH THESE THEMES—the refashioning of the Bank's style in Africa and the challenge of bad debts—came to the fore in Uganda, the next stop on Wolfensohn's odyssey. As in Mali and Côte d'Ivoire,

Wolfensohn had demanded that NGOs be fitted into his schedule, and he was duly taken off to see Katwe, a slum of light-industrial workshops on the edge of Uganda's capital. Once again, Jaycox was impressed by his boss's energy and guts: Wolfensohn marched across an open sewer on a makeshift bridge consisting of rough planks, not pausing to notice that a single slip would earn him enough ailments to entertain a faculty of medics. The boss proceeded past a huge area of carpenters making nothing but coffins—long ones for grown men, miniatures for children— all stacked up in a macabre monument to Uganda's AIDS victims. As he walked along above the stinking sewer, his feet stuck in the mud of the pathway and he looked happier than he'd been in a long while; after the stiff formality of the Ivorians, he was in his element again, marching past the hopeless shacks, shaking hands and kissing babies, his big face sunburned and his shirt drenched in sweat; he was more like Douglas MacArthur landing at Inchon than like any recent World Bank president, Jaycox reflected.[52] Stopping at an NGO health clinic, Wolfensohn gave the nurse a full-bodied bear-hug that appeared the next day on the front page of the newspaper, doing wonders for the World Bank's image.[53] Not far from the clinic, Wolfensohn came upon a scene that somehow stuck with him in the months ahead. There, in the shadow of the AIDS coffins, was a woman baking green banana skins, turning them into charcoal. In his address to the World Bank's annual meetings in October, Wolfensohn invoked this symbol of the will to live. The banana-skin lady "had all the pride of the chairwoman of a multi-national company as she shared with me her pencil-written records."

The Bank's team in Uganda hoped that the Katwe trip was sufficient exposure to the NGOs, particularly since it had been instructed at the last moment to jam some tennis into Wolfensohn's schedule. But, at a reception that evening, Wolfensohn was briefly introduced to Tony Burdon, the Oxfam representative in Uganda.

"We're sorry you don't have time to meet with us," Burdon said innocently.

Wolfensohn looked first astonished, then furious. "I'll make sure that I do see you," he responded.[54]

The following day Wolfensohn told the finance minister that their scheduled meeting would have to begin late, and he spent two hours with Kampala's NGO leaders. The debt issue kept coming up. As Oxfam frequently noted, Uganda spent around $2.50 per citizen on health annually, against $30 on debt repayment. How could a poor country like Uganda, which was pursuing all the orthodox economic reforms that the World Bank had urged, make headway against poverty if it was saddled with old debts? And how could government debt forgiveness rescue Uganda from its hole, given that a large chunk of its debt was owed to multilateral lenders? Oxfam and its allies were just then working up an international, high-decibel appeal for multilateral debt relief, and Uganda was going to be the poster child of this campaign. Again, the lesson to the World Bank's brand-new president was unmistakable. To escape the encirclement of Madrid—to revive the Bank's old energy and fire—the debt question must be settled.

WOLFENSOHN AND HIS ENTOURAGE stopped briefly in Malawi and then flew on to South Africa. This last stop on the tour did nothing to brighten Wolfensohn's view of the Bank's prospects. The local representative had been accused of rape; and though he was later exonerated in full, Wolfensohn did not relish appearing constantly in public with him. More serious still, South Africa presented a kind of mirror-image threat to the one that Wolfensohn had confronted in Côte d'Ivoire. Rather than borrowing massively to finance dubious policies, South Africa's new government had yet to borrow anything at all, even though it was a model candidate for the World Bank's services. By the standards of most developing countries, South Africa had sound leaders, a functioning new democracy, and strong institutions. The chances that it would use development loans productively seemed much better than average.

Wolfensohn could not have known it at the time, but of all the challenges he encountered on his trip, the issues raised by South Africa
were to prove the most troubling. The legacy of structural adjustment
and the tangle of bad debt were problems that Wolfensohn tackled vigorously and early on. But South Africa's refusal to borrow raised a fresh
set of questions, ones that emerged as the central weakness of the Bank
during Wolfensohn's second term in office.

Initially, the South Africa problem seemed to stem from familiar
concerns: one section of the new government had spent the years of
apartheid in exile in Zambia, where structural-adjustment austerity had
triggered urban riots and the World Bank was anathema. But soon other
obstacles surfaced. The South Africans objected that the Bank was an
infuriating business partner: it was bureaucratic and slow-moving, and it
required its borrowers to make repeated trips to Washington. Even if
the World Bank's market-based loans were slightly cheaper than those
from private banks, the hassle of dealing with it was more than the
South Africans could stomach. This raised fundamental questions about
the Bank's future in healthier developing countries like South Africa,
those that were too rich to qualify for subsidized IDA loans, and that
did have access to private capital markets. If the World Bank simply
wasn't attractive to South Africa-type borrowers—to countries like
Brazil, China, and Mexico—its lending there would progressively dry
up, in which case the Bank's whole financial model was at stake, since
the small profits on market-based loans paid for a large part of the
World Bank's overheads and salaries.[55]

This problem of the Bank's appeal to strong developing countries
never excited public interest at the time of Wolfensohn's Africa visit.
But most of the world's poor continued to live in the big emerging markets with access to private capital, and the Bank's global mission would
be incomplete if it ignored so many natural clients. For one thing, the
emerging markets' access to private capital was to prove volatile later in
the decade, showing why the Bank's continued involvement could be

valuable. For another, the Bank could contribute to the struggle against poverty through the force of its ideas. Even in countries with first-rate technocrats, there was a role for a friendly outside institution that could distil global experience. In Brazil, for example, the Bank had helped the government to put in place a successful AIDS program in the early 1990s,[56] and around the same time it improved the design of Brazil's land reform.[57] Moreover, the Bank had used its engagement in Brazil to enrich its own stock of development experience—which it then passed along to Africans and others lower down the development ladder. Keeping the Bank in middle-income countries strengthened the Bank's role as a factory of ideas.[58] But to remain relevant in such countries, the Bank would have to deliver faster.

WOLFENSOHN AND HIS ENTOURAGE returned to Washington on June 25. He assembled his top managers and tried to sum up his impressions; he told the story of the mullah in the white robe in Côte d'Ivoire, but he sensed that his audience was cold to it.[59] He told of how he had visited villages and slums and felt development happen, and the managers looked back with a blank stare that had "so what?" written all over it. "How could you tell all those projects were working?" one member of the audience asked. "By the smile on a child's face," Wolfensohn answered. The Bank's assembled barons concluded that the new kid was laughably naïve. Jaycox called an ex-colleague in a despondent mood: Wolfensohn understood nothing about Africa and didn't want to learn from him.[60]

The boss understood more than the barons were admitting. His visit to Mali had taught him that the Bank could be popular when it put good people in the field; and he soon embarked on a radical decentralization. His stop in Côte d'Ivoire had sealed his determination to tackle debt, and over the next year he hammered on this issue, ultimately bringing the IMF and reluctant rich-country shareholders around to his position.

His time in Uganda had confirmed his suspicion that the Bank's NGO critics could sometimes be correct, and that the Bank's own staff could be too arrogant to admit it. Here were these dedicated NGOs, running projects in Katwe; if they could see the need for debt relief, why couldn't his own staff see it? By the end of his trip to Africa, Wolfensohn was plotting Jaycox's removal from the Africa vice presidency.

For the next three months, Wolfensohn carried on in the same vein, courting the Bank's outside clients and beating up the insiders. He kept up a ferocious travel schedule, visiting twenty-four countries in his first one hundred days as president; his staff developed a code to alert the country teams if he was in a screaming mood: "The Twister has landed." Returning from a trip to Latin America in July, Wolfensohn convened another meeting with his top managers and launched into an attack on the Bank's performance in the region, where structural adjustment had muddied the Bank's name just as much as in Africa. When Shahid Hussein, the former vice president for Latin America, rose to defend the Bank's record, he was writing his own retirement notice just as surely as Jaycox had done before him. Before long, Hussein handed in his resignation.[61]

Meanwhile the Twister charmed the NGOs, building his relationship with them at the expense of his relationship with his own institution. After looking into a Nepali dam that had been controversial at the Madrid annual meetings, Wolfensohn canceled the project in August, infuriating the Bank's engineers, who pointed out that only 12 percent of Nepal's 20 million people had the benefit of electricity. The following month, Wolfensohn attended the UN Conference on Women in Beijing, where he did his best to charm the Bank's feminist critics, who blamed structural adjustment for pushing women into poverty. In an attempt to win his audience over, Wolfensohn admitted that the Bank was not perfect. "Have we made mistakes? Yes!" he exclaimed. "Have we had some disasters? Yes!" he conceded.[62] That was about the worst thing he could have said in the eyes of his own staff. The feminists' criticisms were outrageously ill informed, and Wolfensohn was chiming: Yes! Yes! Yes! We'll punish all the culprits! "We thought we were getting a tough investment banker," the Bank's managers told one another afterward; "but in fact we've been saddled with the political correctness of the Kennedy Center."[63]

There were times when this carping was justified. Wolfensohn had taken over a troubled institution, but not an outright basket case; the Bank had failed miserably at public relations, but it was not as though its entire approach to developing countries was crazy. On the Nepali dam, for example, the Bank's engineers had had a point: the NGOs that had campaigned against the dam did not come from the area where it would be built, and their claims to represent the poor were spurious.[64] As Wolfensohn would later discover, siding with the external critics against his own staff did not always produce the right outcome. The Bank's problems often reflected the difficulty of its mission rather than its own mistakes, and blaming the Bank's incumbent managers was too simple. In time, Wolfensohn's inability to see the strength of others' contributions would emerge as a theme of his leadership; it would turn natural allies into enemies and colleagues into psychoanalysts: Why could the boss not share credit? Why could he not trust anyone? The strange demon inside Wolfensohn—the insecurity that had lurked within him since his youth—made him thin-skinned, quick to anger, and hungry for approval. Running an institution surrounded by uproarious critics and staffed by thousands of disputatious PhD's seemed a risky proposition.

And yet in those early months Wolfensohn was making progress. The Bank's relationship with NGOs, which had seemed almost terminally poisonous in Madrid, was improving at a rapid clip; at the annual meetings in Washington in October 1995, Oxfam marked the extent of the progress by staging a joint press conference with Wolfensohn. Even more remarkably, Wolfensohn was pushing forward with the drive for debt relief. He was taking on the IMF, several of his big shareholder governments, and some of his own brass, and he was making headway against all of them. The truth was that the opposition to multilateral debt relief reflected bureaucratic inertia rather than good sense, and when Jacques de Larosiere, the former boss of the IMF, protested to Wolfensohn that his initiative might undermine the world's financial stability, his plea sounded so shrill that it persuaded no one. At the World Bank's annual meetings in 1995, Britain and the United States threw their weight behind Wolfensohn's debt-relief idea; and Michel Camdessus, de Larosiere's successor as IMF chief, declared himself a convert. It was an open secret that the scheme would get the formal go-ahead at the Bank's next gathering in April, and that Uganda was likely to become one of the first countries to benefit.

After four months in the job, Wolfensohn could boast some remarkable achievements. In Madrid one year before, Oxfam had denounced the Bank for "jeopardizing prospects for sustainable recovery and poverty reduction." Now Oxfam was sharing a platform with the World Bank president. In Madrid one year before, the World Bank had refused to countenance the mere hint of debt relief. Now that same policy was the Bank's official position, thanks almost entirely to its tumultuous new president. He was just getting started.

CHAPTER FIVE

MISSION SARAJEVO

DESPITE HIS TRAVEL SCHEDULE in those first few months, Wolfensohn managed to find time to take a summer break in Jackson Hole, Wyoming. The headquarters barons, anxious for face time with the new boss, were reduced to hopping planes out west and checking into the Hitching Post motel a few miles from his spread. For Wolfensohn, those days in his "log cabin"—actually, a log cathedral built around astonishing spruce columns that soar thirty feet up to the roof—were not merely downtime. They were a chance to connect with the World Bank's main shareholder, President Bill Clinton, who had morphed from stranger to firm friend in the few months since Wolfensohn's appointment. The shareholder in chief was also vacationing in Jackson Hole, testing his wits against Wolfensohn's neighborhood golf course and dining with Wolfensohn's friend Harrison Ford. The World Bank president had introduced the American president to a president from Hollywood, since Ford was soon to appear in the movie *Air Force One* as President James Marshall. On August 19, Wolfensohn threw a party at his home to celebrate Clinton's forty-ninth birthday. The photos show the two men kitted out in denim shirts and bolo ties, surrounded by senators and film stars and other natural soul mates.

The day of the party, half a world away, a team of American negotiators set out for the besieged Bosnian city of Sarajevo. They took off by
helicopter from a Croatian town called Split, then landed in a soccer field
and switched to armored vehicles for the last part of the journey. Their
convoy set off toward Mount Igman, the only peak around Sarajevo not
controlled by the encircling Serbs. The road wound up the mountain's
flank, narrowing precariously, a steep drop beckoning on one side, the
surface treacherously bumpy. Somehow the second vehicle bounced
into the void, somersaulting through the trees as it descended. A few
hours later Richard Holbrooke, the traumatized leader of the American
negotiators, was on the phone to President Clinton in Wyoming, telling
him that three members of the team were dead. Clinton interrupted his
vacation to fly east to the memorial service for Holbrooke's fallen com-
rades.[1] The Bosnian crisis had turned personal, and it had done so just
when Clinton was spending personal time with Wolfensohn.

Wolfensohn's predecessors at the Bank had resisted getting sucked
into the Balkans, not least out of a sense that the Bank was spread too
thin already. "This institution never turns down an assignment," Lew
Preston once remarked; "it must learn to say no."[2] Preston's reluctance
was shared by Ernie Stern and other members of his senior team; when
Kemal Derviş, the Bank's director for the region, pressed the case for
helping Bosnia, they told him to forget it.[3] But if there was any doubt in
Wolfensohn's mind that he would reverse Preston's policy, the Mount
Igman accident ended it. Here he was, partying with President Clinton
in Wyoming the very day when Bosnia was Topic A; his relationship
radar was flashing red alert, and he was not going to miss this opening.
The World Bank's chief shareholder was pushing for a Bosnian peace
deal, and a peace deal would mean reconstruction, and reconstruction
would mean a chance for Wolfensohn to help. What was the World
Bank's official name? The International Bank for *Reconstruction* and
Development.

Without particularly realizing what he was doing, Wolfensohn was taking sides in a debate that was to loom large in his presidency. Preston's reluctance to get sucked into Bosnia had been entirely rational. The Bank is cumbersome and slow because it tries to do so many things; it is unpopular because it promises more than it delivers. Each time the Bank takes on a new challenge, both problems expand: its sprawling bureaucracy sprawls a little more; its resources stretch a little thinner. Unlike the International Monetary Fund, which has a fairly clearly defined mandate to battle financial instability, the areas into which the Bank can charge are practically unlimited. In the 1970s, Robert McNamara had set up departments to deal with everything from population control to agricultural research, and since then the world's rich governments had developed a habit of issuing communiqués on illiteracy or migration or AIDS, and telling the World Bank to do something about them. Preston was right to see advantages in saying no. Saying yes to everyone always can be a recipe for breakdown. Hadn't McNamara's ambitious expansion ended up in disappointment?

When he resolved to charge into the Balkans, Wolfensohn had barely thought about these arguments. He was committing his institution to a vast task, and ultimately to a vast series of tasks, since the Bank's involvement in Bosnian reconstruction set it up for later episodes: in Kosovo and East Timor and Afghanistan and, though in a rather different way, in Iraq after Saddam Hussein's eviction. And yet, though Wolfensohn launched the Bank into this territory without deliberating too hard, there is a powerful comeback to the Preston view, and over the next years Wolfensohn expounded on it frequently. Committing the Bank to multiple assignments may certainly cause stress, but the fact is that poverty has multiple causes, and you have to fight on many fronts: the organizational stress is worth it. Moreover, the Bank is simply more competent than the underfunded UN agencies, so if you've got a problem you want fixed, it makes sense to get the Bank involved: again, the institutional consequences for the Bank are a price worth paying. You can argue, as did Preston, that charging into postconflict reconstruction may be bad for the cohesion of the Bank. But, as we shall see, charging in was clearly good for Bosnia.

This debate—between an expansive and a conservative mission—runs throughout the history of the Bank, and we shall be returning to it. At the start of the 1950s, the Bank's president rebuffed a plea to boost lending to $1 billion a year, saying that $400 million would be adequate; a decade later the Bank easily surpassed the $1 billion milestone.[4] At the start of the 1960s, the Bank refused to make inequality within countries part of its mandate, only to rush into that terrain when Robert McNamara became president. Again and again, the argument that there's a problem out there that needs fixing has proved stronger than the urge to fix the Bank itself: The messianic impulse has nearly always trumped the managerial one. And there is good reason for this outcome. The Bank was created by its founders precisely to tackle the biggest problems in the world: the threat that poverty might lead to war, that desperation might lead to desperate *isms*. To retain the backing of its shareholders, the Bank needs to understand this impulse and respond. Saying no can leave the Bank vulnerable and all alone—as Preston himself discovered.

In the summer of 1995, Wolfensohn had no doubt of the need to please his shareholders. He was campaigning all out for contributions to the soft-loan IDA fund; he needed to look useful. Besides, his new Wyoming buddy faced a big test in the Balkans, and Wolfensohn was determined to get in there and help him. Sure enough, the World Bank soon found itself at the center of the Bosnian drama; and the story that ensued showed how, in the last analysis, Wolfensohn's half-considered expansionism was right. The Bosnian experience became a model of how invaluable the Bank can be as a tool of enlightened foreign policy, and won it valuable new friends inside the U.S. administration. At the same time, Bosnia helped defend the Bank against some of its NGO detractors in the Fifty Years Is Enough movement. Less than a year before the Mount Igman accident, the critics had been yammering that the Bank had outlived its original purpose of rebuilding Europe after war. Bosnia showed that reconstruction in Europe still justified the Bank's existence.

Yet Bosnia was more than just a demonstration of the Bank's contemporary usefulness. In a paradoxical way, given the Preston camp's worries about expanding the mission, Bosnia came to suggest a route out of the Bank's deepest long-term difficulty. As Wolfensohn had seen during his visit to South Africa, the Bank's cumbersome bureaucracy could deprive it of strong clients, countries like Brazil, India, and China, which are home to the majority of the world's poor, but which increasingly have the option of borrowing on private capital markets. The Bank's morale and professionalism—its clear superiority over UN agencies— depend on retaining those strong borrowers, because the small profits that the Bank collects on its market-based operations pay for a large part of the institution. If strong developing countries defect, and the Bank becomes mainly a provider of soft IDA credits, its financial independence will erode and it will depend increasingly on handouts from its shareholders. In a worst-case scenario, it could decline, gradually but inexorably, into the cash-strapped dependency of the United Nations.[5] Its best people will drift off, and its professionalism will fade—accelerating the defection of the South Africas of the world, and sucking the Bank into a vicious downward spiral.

The World Bank's performance in Bosnia showed that it *is* capable of escaping its habitual slowness and delivering for important clients fast. It showed that a downward spiral of decline is not at all inevitable.

THE BANK'S BOSNIA ADVENTURE would not have happened without Wolfensohn, at least not the same way, but he was not its main protagonist. After the accident at Mount Igman, and on several occasions thereafter, Wolfensohn resolved that the Bank should help in Bosnia, and that it should move fast; his outlook sent a signal to his staff, and without that signal progress would have been more difficult. But the front-line figures in this drama were to be found further down the Bank, starting with Kemal Dervis, the Bank's director for the part of Europe that contained ex-Yugoslavia. It was Dervis who had pressed the case for helping Bosnia in the Preston period, and who had been told firmly to forget it.

Luckily for Bosnia, Kemal Dervis ignored that directive. He was Turkish, which gave him a more-than-ordinary concern for the plight of the Balkans; and moreover he was a formidable figure, not yet a vice president but nonetheless a classic baron in the old mold—strong, clever, and determined above all to call the shots on the countries in his fiefdom. He was bald and burly and reassuringly solid; a few years later, when he returned to Turkey to take up an appointment as his country's finance minister, the stock market jumped as his plane landed in Ankara and he was greeted as a savior. But in 1994, it was Bosnia that needed saving most. Sooner or later the country would reach some sort of cease-fire, and the Bank would be expected to help out; Dervis was determined to prepare a reconstruction plan ahead of time. Denied a budget to do that, he appealed successfully to the Dutch director on the Bank's board, who spoke for the Balkans under the Bank's system of pooled representation.[6] Dutch money paid for the World Bank and the Bosnians to hold a series of meetings at the Bank's offices in Warsaw.

The first Warsaw encounter took place in January 1995, and it was a charged experience. The World Bank's people were used to meeting the comfortable elites of the poor world, but the Bosnians who showed up in Warsaw were different. They were the survivors of a war that had displaced 2 million people since 1991, killing 250,000. The territory of Bosnia, once a model of a multiethnic society with high rates of intermarriage, had become the bloodiest slaughterhouse in Europe since World War II. A relatively affluent society had been reduced to burning books and furniture and shoes for heat; there was little food to be found, and snipers struck at any moment. To get to the Bank's meetings in Warsaw, the Bosnian delegation had escaped out of Sarajevo via a tunnel that snaked under the airport; they had emerged on the far side through the basement of a farmhouse and then dived into a trench before sniper fire could harm them. They had climbed up the side of Mount Igman and made their way eventually to Warsaw, where they encountered a world that seemed utterly alien. The telephones worked, and so did the lights; nobody had used the chairs for firewood. Kasim Omićević, the grandfatherly central bank governor who led these missions, recalls the emotion of arriving in a town where food was plentiful. Like many citizens of Sarajevo, Omićević had lost a fifth of his body weight during the war. His clothes hung loose on his body, and his eyes gazed out of sunken sockets.[7]

The first Warsaw meeting began to assess the extent of Bosnia's wartime destruction. It was followed by a second one in June, so by the time of the Mount Igman accident in August 1995, the World Bank had already started to compile plans for reconstruction. Just as Dervis had predicted, the advance work paid off: now that the Clinton team was sending negotiators to risk their lives for Balkan peace, it was delighted to find that the Bank could contribute to its objective. The Clinton Treasury, which had felt no great enthusiasm for Wolfensohn's appointment to the Bank, was pleasantly surprised. The standard joke at Treasury was that when countries approached the World Bank for assistance, the Bank carried out a multiyear study; it took the Bank longer to get off its chair than it took FDR to dispense with Hitler. But now for once the Bank was out in front. David Lipton, the Treasury official who dealt most closely with the Balkans, remembers Kemal Dervis and his deputy, Christine Wallich, as "wonderful, energetic; they were the best game in town."[8] This was rare praise coming from Lipton, who was to demonstrate his contempt for the usually sluggish World Bank during the Asian crisis two years later.

It helped that the Clinton Treasury, unlike the subsequent Bush team, was led by people who understood multilateral institutions—how they could be maddening but also how they could be helpful. Lipton himself had worked at the International Monetary Fund, as had a number of other Clinton Treasury officials, and he reported to former World Bank chief economist Larry Summers. On August 30, 1995, when NATO air strikes on Serb positions signaled the start of the pressure that would push the parties to peace talks, Lipton knew immediately how he could get the Bank to help: he wanted the Bank's money, certainly, but he wanted more than that; the Bank offered expertise in infrastructure, microfinance, and all the nuts and bolts of reconstruction. Just as important, the Bank offered political legitimacy. Transatlantic relations were in appalling shape. A reconstruction effort led by the World Bank would be more likely by far than an American-led one to attract international sympathy and money.

The contrast with the subsequent Bush Treasury, which began talking to the Bank only *after* the invasion of Iraq, could not be more revealing. But, from the point of view of Wolfensohn's South Africa challenge—the challenge of speeding up the sluggish Bank—the way that the institution responded to Lipton was even more significant. Within a week of his call, Christine Wallich and her team of experts returned to Warsaw for a third meeting; and in October, when NATO air strikes forced the warring parties into a cease-fire, Dervis called up the UN chief in the Balkans and talked him into providing a plane to get a team of donors into Bosnia.[9] To many at the Bank, this seemed a bit crazy. Nobody knew whether this Bosnian cease-fire would hold, and Bosnia was neither a member of the World Bank nor even a real state; it was a broken fragment of the old Yugoslavia. And yet, to an extent that even Dervis might not have foretold, the next six months were to prove that unhesitating speed could pay off handsomely.

A few days after the start of Bosnia's October cease-fire, Dervis set off for Sarajevo accompanied by Christine Wallich and representatives of four other development agencies.[10] It was nighttime when the team landed; there was no electric light and not even any moon; and the cars headed into town through falling snow, their headlights off in order to avoid snipers. The convoy drove along streets that ran parallel to the mountains, so that buildings on either side afforded some protection from the unseen marksmen in the hills. Instead of stopping at junctions, the drivers accelerated straight through them. After an adrenaline-soaked quarter of an hour, the convoy stopped outside the grand outline of Sarajevo's presidency building.[11]

The presidency was a proud monument to the Austro-Hungarian empire, but if empires stand for order and wars stand for mayhem, the building bore a double signature. Its ornate entrance was protected with sandbags; there were blankets over the cavities that had been windows; there were bullet marks all over the exterior walls and even some *inside* the building. The foreign visitors filed into this historical carcass and were impressed by what they saw inside: their hosts had managed to create the semblance of a state dinner. Under a surviving chandelier, in a room framed by gilt mirrors left over from Austrian times, a long table had been covered with a long white cloth; waiters in white gloves ar-rived to serve the guests, and each place had been laid with crystal and silver. The elegance of the setting was all the more poignant because of the food that the gloved waiters served—processed cheese and other UN relief rations.

For the Bosnian hosts that evening, the arrival of a delegation from the World Bank was fraught with symbolism. For the past four years, the outside world had ignored the plight of the Balkans, as though the end of the cold war entitled them to shrug off foreign crises. The coun-try's Muslim majority—known, confusingly, as Bosniaks—had suffered attack first by the Orthodox Christian Serbs, then by the Catholic Croats; they had hunkered down in their encircled capital, stoking their resentment at the civilized world's indifference. Scarcely three months before Dervis and Wallich arrived for their state dinner of processed cheese, Serb aggression—and Serb contempt for the outside world's restraining pleas—had climaxed in a small town called Srebrenica, where the Bosnian Serb army slaughtered more than seven thousand Bosniaks, herding some into execution sites and hunting others as they fled from the carnage. The United Nations, whose peacekeepers were supposedly monitoring this "safe zone," was buried in black shame: The United Nations, said one Bosniak leader, "was just monitoring our disappearance."[12] But now the arrival of the World Bank in Sarajevo's bombed-out presidency building signaled that the outside world was waking up. At the end of the dinner Bosnia's prime minister rose and kissed Dervis on the lips.[13] The long years of neglect were finally ending.

The next day Dervis left the country, leaving Christine Wallich and her team to flesh out the reconstruction plan that the U.S. Treasury wanted. Wallich and her colleagues set up shop at the Hotel Bosna, where dirty gray plastic sheeting did duty as windows. There was not much electricity and no running water; in the course of her two-week mission, Wallich took just one shower, and that was only because a U.S. embassy official took pity on her. The Bank's meetings took place in underground shelters, in a small section of the city that was deemed safe. One of Wallich's colleagues was overheard on the lone phone in the lobby of the hotel, reassuring his wife that Paris was beautiful—he hadn't had the heart to confess his true location.[14]

In her seventeen years at the Bank, Wallich had not come up against anything quite like this. She was in many ways a typical World Bank whiz, with a PhD from Yale and an international outlook that came from her background: a Czech mother, a German father, and a British American education. She had worked previously on Russia and India and China, challenging assignments all, but not ones requiring that you drive though a city with your headlights off, accelerating through the intersections for fear of stray bullets.[15] The physical challenge that Wallich confronted was nothing compared with the political one: the hatreds that had fueled the war were very much in evidence. In that first dinner at the presidency building, the Bosniak officials were outraged when the Bank announced that it would reconstruct more than just the

Bosniak towns; it would reconstruct Croat and even Serb ones. The Bosniaks reacted in fury; they had fought a war against the Croats as well as against the Serbs, and now the World Bank wanted to reward aggressors. Shortly after that dinner, the World Bank convened a reconstruction conference in the Croat town of Medjugorje, and hostilities threatened to erupt again. Medjugorje was the site of an alleged visitation by the Virgin Mary in 1981, and the Muslim Bosniaks regarded the city as a bastion of Catholic chauvinism. At first they threatened to boycott the conference. It took several shouting sessions before they agreed to send a delegation.

These were the typical frustrations of postwar efforts, and the wonder is that, even after the experience of Bosnia and East Timor and Afghanistan, people still appear surprised when reconstruction proves difficult. In all postwar settings, you will hear the same refrain—that the Afghans or Iraqis should sort out their own problems, and that foreigners should leave them to it. But all these experiences show how, without the neutral presence of a foreign institution, progress is unthinkable. In Bosnia in 1995, there was no way the warring parties could discuss reconstruction; they could not even agree where the discussion should be located. It took the World Bank's mediation to focus the Bosnians on practical problems: Should there be a central bank? How to reconcile conflicting tax and customs systems?[16]

One morning two weeks into her mission, Christine Wallich had breakfast with Dan Serwer, the U.S. official who had arranged for her to use the embassy shower in Sarajevo. Wallich's trip was coming to a close, and she was looking forward to a period of comfort in Washington. But over breakfast that morning, Serwer asked Wallich if she could put off her thoughts of going home. His boss, Richard Holbrooke, had spoken to her boss, Jim Wolfensohn. She was needed as soon as possible at the Balkan peace conference in Dayton.[17]

This was the first reward for Kemal Dervis's unhesitating speed. When the stakes were at their highest—when nearly four years of

Balkan bloodshed might finally be coming to a close—the peacemakers summoned the World Bank into the heart of the action.

THE FIRST THING that greeted the negotiators at the Wright-Patterson Air Force Base in Dayton was a team of sniffer dogs, which probed and snorted and wheezed until the visitor was declared free of explosives. The French delegate at Dayton was outraged by this treatment; it was an insult not merely to him but to "all of France"; "I will not be sneefed!" he protested.[18] By the time Wallich arrived, this indignity had been suspended for the most senior negotiators, but Wallich got the full treatment. After the mission to Bosnia, it barely registered on her discomfort meter.

There were two reasons why Holbrooke had called Wolfensohn for help in Dayton. He wanted someone who could help write the economic parts of Bosnia's new constitution; and his Treasury counterpart, David Lipton, had told him that the World Bank staff was ahead of everybody else in thinking through the future shape of Bosnia's financial institutions. Second, Holbrooke needed a way to reassure the Bosniaks that the West would not abandon them all over again if they signed on to a peace deal. Having a World Bank official at Dayton—an official who'd already held multiple meetings with the Bosnians and dined in Sarajevo's sandbagged presidency building—was a good way for Holbrooke to show the West's commitment to reconstruction and prevent the Bosniaks from quitting.

Wallich plunged immediately into the job of constitution writing. Along with David Lipton, she grappled with the new country's tax system, aiming to strike a balance between the two forces at Dayton. On the one hand, she wanted a viable central government that would rule over a united state; on the other, she knew that ethnically based local government would wield most of the power for the foreseeable future. Based on her experience with Bosnians, Wallich drafted language giving as much power to the center as she thought salable; then she set out to negotiate. The Wright-Patterson air base was divided into four barracks, one for the foreign diplomats and one for each of the war's three parties, so Wallich trudged from one barrack to the next, seeking comments on her text and penciling in suggested changes. She could go through ten or twelve drafts in a single day, inching nearer to consensus with each one. Sometimes she would track the negotiators down in Packy's All-Sports Bar, the main source of recreation at the base, where the Croats gathered to cheer their hero, Toni Kukoc of the Chicago Bulls; where the Serbs waited to cheer Vlade Divac of the Los Angeles Lakers; and where the warring parties united fleetingly to watch *America's Favorite Home Videos.*

At the end of ten days, Wallich produced a formulation that all the parties could agree on.[19] But this would count for naught if the wider negotiations foundered. The Bosniaks, as Holbrooke had expected, were skittish; they feared that if they signed a peace the rich world would abandon them. In the final days of the peace conference, Wallich drafted a "comfort letter," addressed to Bosnia's three parties and signed by Wolfensohn, expressing the Bank's commitment to reconstruction. The promise of financial backing helped to reassure the Bosniaks and keep them at the table.[20]

It is just possible, indeed, that the Bank's presence at Dayton saved the entire exercise from failure. On November 20, after three weeks locked up at the air base, Holbrooke was prepared to disband the talks and declare defeat. A slew of orchestrated calls from world leaders had pushed the three parties closer together, but there was still no breakthrough. Holbrooke gave the negotiators a final deadline, and scheduled a press statement announcing the breakup of the talks for ten o'clock the next morning. This ultimatum extracted a final round of concessions from the Serbs, which persuaded the Croats to sign on; it remained for the Americans to sell the deal to the Bosniak president, Alija Izetbegovic. With an hour or so to go before the scheduled press statement, Holbrooke and Secretary of State Warren Christopher went to confront the Bosniak. He could accept the deal and so finish the war, or he could condemn the Dayton talks to failure.

The Americans outlined the final offer, and Izetbegovic sat silently. There was a pause, and Holbrooke described the deal again; the silence from the Bosniaks stretched on interminably. "It is not a just peace," Izetbegovic finally declared, and Holbrooke's heart was in his mouth. But the yearning for reconstruction, for a return to normalcy after four years, seemed to push Izetbegovic on. "My people need peace," he said slowly. Christopher and Holbrooke took that for a yes and made swiftly for the exit.[21]

Returning to Sarajevo from Dayton, Izetbegovic sought to explain his final compromise. Among the main benefits of Dayton, he explained, was "a substantial aid package for the reconstruction of Bosnia-Herzegovina."[22] His acceptance of the deal had been balanced on a knife edge, and without the promise of substantial World Bank aid, he might have rejected it.[23]

As soon as Dayton's outcome was announced, Kemal Dervis dispatched another mission to Bosnia. The team flew into Sarajevo on a UN transport; the back of the plane opened up as they touched down, and the passengers were ordered to *run, run, run!*—the snipers were still in business. Every night of the mission, bullets rained down on the city from the hills, and once a shell exploded just outside the Holiday Inn where the World Bankers were staying. On December 14, 1995, the World Bankers watched the formal signing of the Dayton deal on CNN. As they listened to the encomiums to peace, they could hear shells exploding outside their window.[24]

Fast action had won the Bank a chance to help broker a peace, but Dervis and his colleagues needed to keep sprinting. Starting on December 20, the Bank was due to chair the first pledging conference of donors, which would test David Lipton's faith that the Bank was the right agency to lead the postwar effort. In Washington, Christine Wallich worked on the last details of the Bank's reconstruction blueprint; in Sarajevo, the Holiday Inn team worked eighteen-hour days, riding in an armored car to meetings held in underground shelters and battling with the satellite phone to get information back to headquarters. The Bank's task was rendered especially difficult by the problem that Lipton had foreseen. The Europeans were in a foul mood, which in turn threatened to foul the approaching donor conference.

Holbrooke's tactics at Dayton had deepened the transatlantic rift still further. He cut the Europeans out of the key talks, instructing his staff to engage them endlessly on secondary issues so that the big stuff could be done without their tiresome meddling. At one point Pauline Neville-Jones, the British representative, exploded in fury at these American "bastards," threatening to call Prime Minister Major to protest Holbrooke's behavior. The Americans reasonably believed that Europe had earned its marginalization by dithering for years over the Balkans; but that didn't change the fact that the Europeans were furious with Holbrooke. "He flatters, he lies, he humiliates," declared a French diplomat, quoted in *Le Figaro*. "He is a sort of brutal and schizophrenic Mazarin."[25]

There was no way, in this climate, that the Americans would persuade Europe to pay the costs of reconstructing Bosnia. Much as in Iraq in 2003 and 2004, the international community would underwrite the peace only if the peace process was internationalized. But though it was clear that Bosnia could not be rebuilt by the United States alone, it was yet to be shown that the World Bank could do much better, for the crisis in transatlantic relations raised the question of whether the Bank could function in the post–cold war era. The Bank had been created at a moment of unquestioned American ascendancy in 1944, and for nearly half a century the cold war had obliged Western Europe to depend on American security. This Western cohesion had been reflected in the

World Bank's board: so long as the Soviet threat loomed, few Europeans were inclined to second-guess American guidance of the World Bank's policies. But now the Bank was in a tricky position: it was being asked to chair a donor conference for Bosnia after an "American" peace, and some Europeans on the World Bank's board hated this.

On the eve of the conference, several European Union members agreed on a common position: They would refuse to pledge anything at this meeting on the ground that it was premature, a product of American-imposed deadlines. The next day a Spanish delegate rose to explain the no-pledge position. The cause of Bosnia was dear to Europe, the delegate declared, but it was imprudent to rush in with cash before a thorough review of the country's destruction. A panicked Christine Wallich slipped out of the room to fetch the Dutch development minister, Jan Pronk, who was ensconced in another meeting. Wallich quickly explained the crisis that was brewing, and Pronk came to the rescue: the needs of Bosnia were not a mystery, he told his fellow donors; they were painstakingly laid out in the conference documents prepared by the World Bank, which had held multiple meetings with the Bosnians over the past year; there was no excuse for delaying reconstruction. Pronk's intervention and the Bank's preparatory work combined to rescue the moment. With one exception, every government at the conference pledged money. The lone holdout was France, perhaps still smarting from the sniffer-dog incident.

The Bank's fast move into Bosnia had now helped to secure two victories. The Bosniak president had been persuaded to accept a peace he termed "unjust." And the Europeans had backed an "American" project with immediate pledges of assistance.

SOON AFTER THE BRUSSELS CONFERENCE, the Bank started to station staff permanently in Sarajevo. Again it faced the pressure of deadlines; having extracted $500 million from the Brussels donors, the

Bank was morally obliged to show that reconstruction was doable. The Bank's task managers—engineers and economists and financial experts—piled into makeshift offices at the top of Sarajevo's central bank, often playing musical chairs since there were not seats enough for everybody. But the chaos outside their office was far worse. Donors were tripping over one another and competing for control: the European Union wanted to be coequal with the Bank, and a new Dayton-created outfit called the Office of the High Representative wanted to be superior to both of them. The chaos among donors was compounded by the chaos among the Bosnians. A convoluted constitution had just been dropped on the country by some Middle American conclave; multiple layers of government competed for aid funds, including some layers that had supposedly been abolished by Dayton.[26] Ordinary Bosnians mobbed the World Bank, too. People would hear of this rich newcomer and show up in its offices, asking for loans to fix up their apartments. "Aren't you a bank?" people would ask. "If you are a bank, why can't you lend to me?"

Despite all the chaos, something wonderful was happening. For a glorious moment, a whole chunk of the Bank felt like Linda McGinnis, the feisty country rep in Mali. People wanted to be in the field; they wanted to work hard; they wanted above all to deliver for the clients. Early on in the process of assembling his team, Kemal Dervis had worried that it might be difficult to find people willing to forsake the comfort of Washington. But word had gone around the Bank about the adventure that was revving up in the Balkans, and candidates were lining up to join the effort. Dervis diffidently asked one applicant, a young microcredit expert named Sarah Forster, whether she'd be prepared to live in Sarajevo full time. He got a sharp response: Forster was only interested in the job if she could move to the region. Within a few months, Forster was organizing a lending cooperative for widows of the Srebrenica massacre, who were setting up small businesses, investing in farm animals or sewing clothes, and beginning to look to the future.[27]

It helped Dervis's recruitment drive that the early Sarajevo missions had returned with inspiring stories. But the enthusiasm that seized the Bosnia team reflected something else as well—something obvious but generally forgotten. The vast bulk of the Bank's staff had joined the institution because they wanted to fight suffering. Years of setbacks in shambolic countries, years of hectoring by NGOs, and years inside the Bank's own velvety bureaucracy had combined to dull idealism. But somewhere deep within them the embers still glowed, and a dramatic challenge like Bosnia was enough to relight them. They positively wanted to work in an office where you seldom left until the ten o'clock curfew, but where you could quickly reduce suffering. Even the support team in Washington was buzzing with adrenaline. During the Washington snowstorm of January 1996, the whole city closed down, and virtually nobody was working. But for the World Bankers on the Bosnia team, staying home was inconceivable; they faced a frozen metro system, but their clients on the far side of the world faced an entire winter without heating. One official trudged two and a half hours to work from the Maryland suburbs, hoping to complete a deal to get gas into Sarajevo. "I don't think anybody felt particularly heroic about any of this," he said later in a quiet tone. "Nobody thought of not doing it."[28]

It was not just the hours that people worked, nor their willingness to board C-130 relief transports and fly into a war zone. It was their readiness to tear up the normal procedures that often made the Bank so cumbersome. The usual hierarchical decision process was replaced by a daily meeting in Washington at six P.M.: The day's issues were raised and resolved immediately. The usual paper-clogged disbursement process, which could delay projects for months and add thousands of dollars to their cost, was replaced by a streamlined alternative. The Bosnia team also took an ax to the Bank's usual procurement rules. Instead of insisting upon original copies of every document, faxed versions were sometimes allowed. Instead of insisting upon international competitive bidding—a virtuous process, but not a speedy one—the Bank allowed some tenders to be limited to national bidders only.

The result was just about unprecedented. In January and February—at a time when the Serb part of Sarajevo was literally in flames—the Bank finalized its Emergency Recovery Project, a $160 million scheme to finance emergency imports, loans to enterprises that could jump-start production, a rudimentary social safety net, and basic equipment for government ministries. In March and April, another slew of projects went to the Bank's board: there was one to rebuild the transportation network, another to fix the sewerage system, others for farm reconstruction, urban heating, mine clearance, and the rehabilitation of war victims. Loans that normally might have taken two years to prepare were rushed through in three months or so, and after project approval, the sense of urgency did not let up. If implementation was hampered by the slow processing of documents, the Bank's staff would march over to the minister's office and tell him what to sign; if his printer had run out of paper they would refill it for him. The Bank was operating at a pace that would have made the defection of middle-income clients like South Africa far less likely. The freedom to damn protocol and get things done was gloriously exhilarating.

Without anybody really planning it, the Bank's speed on Bosnia had yielded a third victory. It was transforming the morale of the staff, turning bureaucrats into adventurers.

THE BIGGEST BATTLE against the Bank's conventions played out elsewhere: not in the rubble of Sarajevo, but in the financial conclaves of the United States and Europe. Along with other new states in the Balkans, Bosnia had inherited its share of the ex-Yugoslavia's old debts, including $650 million in World Bank lending. This was a problem for Bosnia, but it was also a problem for the Bank: What if the Bosnians defaulted? Dervis knew that the Bosnians would accept responsibility for old loans only in exchange for a reconstruction plan involving large volumes of fresh money. But the Bank's traditionalists resisted. Bosnia was not entitled to fresh money because it was not formally a member of the World Bank, and membership would depend on shouldering the debts inherited from Yugoslavia. Putting Bosnia in that catch-22 greatly increased the risk of its default; and with the help of Wolfensohn and the Dutch representative on the World Bank's board, Dervis pulled and stretched at the Bank's rules, determined to save both Bosnia and the Bank's own balance sheet. Gradually a solution formed. The Bank would begin by helping Bosnia, then Bosnia would accept the old Yugoslav debts and become a Bank member—but its membership would be back-dated, rendering the early reconstruction assistance legal in retrospect. The only problem with this plan was that the Bosnians might reject it.

In the first week of February 1996, Kemal Dervis and Christine Wallich booked a restaurant in a Swiss resort called Bad Ragaz, an hour's drive away from the World Economic Forum in Davos. Their guests were four Bosnians—two Bosniaks and two Croats—and their dinner was to stretch from seven that evening to three o'clock the next morning. The Bosnian group was led by the new prime minister, Hasan Muratovic, a charmer with a lopsided smile that faintly recalled Robert de Niro. Dervis laid out the terms of the proposed deal, and Muratovic countered: Most of his countrymen thought any repayment immoral. "They were saying look, our country is destroyed, the roads you built are destroyed, the hospitals are destroyed, the factories are destroyed, and you're asking us to say that we will pay the debt attached to these assets," Dervis recalls. "They're gone, so you should forgive this debt," Muratovic was urging.

"You're getting a lot more money than you're paying back, so you have a net gain, plus you get technical assistance," Dervis protested. He suggested the Bosnians could expect $900 million in cheap IDA credits.

"Okay, sign a piece of paper that you will give us this $900 million."

"I can't do this," Dervis replied. "These are board decisions; it's not my decision." Every IDA transfer would need separate authorization from the World Bank's board. "I can't promise you. I can't sign a paper that the Bank will give you the money."

At this, Muratovic exploded. "Are you crazy or what?" he demanded. "You want me to sign the paper that I owe you $650 million and you're not willing to sign anything?"[29]

In the end, it all came down to trust: the Bosnians had to believe that Dervis and Wallich would deliver on their side of the deal, even though they could not put anything in writing. Given the World Bank's poor reputation with many of its clients—given the Bank's vilification in Madrid—it was remarkable that the Bosnians had faith in their dinner hosts that evening. But Dervis and Wallich had climbed aboard that C-130. They had dined in Sarajevo's sandbagged presidency building before Dayton was signed, and they had corralled the donors in Brussels into pledging $500 million for Bosnia. In sum, they had earned the right to be trusted. By the small hours of the morning, Muratovic had come around; and for the fourth time in six months, the risk of plunging into Bosnia early was amply rewarded. Rather than facing a default, the World Bank was now set to acquire an enthusiastic new member.

THE FAST MOVE into Bosnia was a victory for the World Bank, but it was also a victory for Jim Wolfensohn. The old Bank under Lewis Preston and Ernie Stern had had a reputation for caution; the new Bank—Wolfensohn's Bank—was a place where risk takers could take wing, and where the payoffs could be spectacular. Yet somehow Wolfensohn could not savor this success, not when he could claim only one part of the credit. He wanted more of it, all of it; he wasn't going to share. At least that was how he felt on April 1, 1996, when he climbed out of a C-130 at Sarajevo airport.

Wolfensohn's visit to Bosnia had precipitated the usual preparatory uproar. The country's chaotic sort-of government was unsure how to entertain this guest, and the Bank's local mission had insisted upon head-of-state treatment. As Wolfensohn emerged from the aircraft, the preparations appeared suitably high class: a delegation of top ministers had assembled to greet him at the airport. But then Wolfensohn's entourage emerged as well, and the ministers rushed forward to embrace the visitor they knew—not Wolfensohn but Dervis. Wolfensohn's body language said it all: He was the president! He wanted to be greeted! Heck, he had made Paul Volcker play second fiddle at his firm, and he was not about to be upstaged by some World Bank bureaucrat! Wolfensohn turned to Dervis and told him to fetch the luggage out of the plane. He wanted his staff to be close to the clients, but not closer than he was.

A little while later, Wolfensohn was riding the hotel elevator with Dervis and Eveline Herfkens, the Dutch member of the World Bank board who had championed the Bosnian cause from the outset. Because Herfkens's constituency included Bosnia, she had arrived in Sarajevo ahead of Wolfensohn to brief the Bosnians on his visit. Herfkens reported that her constituents were in an upbeat mood; she had told them about the board's recent approval of Bosnia's debt deal, and President Izetbegovic himself was positively delighted. At this, Wolfensohn let out a furious roar. How dare Herfkens tell the Bosnians that the deal had been approved? What was left for him to say? What was the point of his visit?

"This is my job, to inform my constituents," Herfkens protested.

"What's my job then?" Wolfensohn yelled.

"You can talk to them, too," Herfkens offered.

"I don't need this job anyway!" Wolfensohn screamed. Dervis tried to melt through the elevator wall. "I'm through!" he yelled at Herfkens.

Wolfensohn was ferried from the hotel to Sarajevo's presidency building. If he had let his imperious mood show, he would merely have conformed to the expectations of his hosts; he was a big man, and they'd been told to expect that. But Wolfensohn could be brutal to his own colleagues and quite another thing to his clients; he could switch from baffling temper to mysterious charm in the space of a few minutes. After the tense preparations for the visit, the Bosnians were astonished by the figure who arrived at the presidency building. The fearsome World Bank superboss was relaxed and unassuming; "an ordinary person, normal behavior, not demanding at all!" remembers one of them.[30]

Wolfensohn was escorted into the building, to a room where the hard work of Dervis and Wallich would bear fruit; the documents that would cement Bosnia's membership in the World Bank lay waiting for his signature. In the days before the meeting, the Bosnians had objected to some last details; they knew that the Bank needed a debt deal, and they had exploited their leverage. But as the Bank officials watched Wolfensohn weave among the guests, they felt as though the tables were turning; he radiated a glorious ease, and now the Bank had all the leverage. Wolfensohn moved from one Bosnian to another, talking and listening and talking; he was asking about the war, about the destruction and suffering and pain; and he never once glanced at the legal documents that awaited him. Some of the government officials were starting to appear nervous. They kept looking over toward the documents—This was a signing ceremony! So why wasn't he signing?—and Wolfensohn kept on chatting as though the whole debt business barely mattered to him. Who could now remember the eight-hour dinner outside Davos, when the Bank had nailed Yugoslavia's debt to Bosnia? The Bank in this moment was Jim Wolfensohn: charming, friendly, and insouciant.

The signing finally took place, and Wolfensohn emerged from the presidency building and set off on a tour of Sarajevo, accompanied by Prime Minister Muratovic. He visited a school that the Bank had rehabilitated, a housing project where the Bank had bought the materials for the roofs, and a kitchen where a man who'd lost a leg was manufacturing chocolate box trays, pressing them out with the help of a machine financed by a World Bank microcredit. He visited the leaders of the four religious denominations in the city: the chief rabbi welcomed him to a place where, as he put it, his community had suffered as citizens rather than as Jews; the chief imam assured him that Bosnians could overcome their hatreds if the Bank could open economic opportunities. There were moving stories everywhere, and Wolfensohn listened and wept. He was extraordinarily open and natural: "So normal, so human," the rabbi remembers; "only really great personalities can behave normally, and Wolfensohn is such a person."[31]

Wolfensohn and Muratovic were bonding famously, and the two set off in their car to visit the source of the river Bosna, a short drive from the city. The Bosnians' careful preparations laid down that Wolfensohn would view the river through the car window rather than walk up to it on foot; the Bank staff was terrified of land mines, which were still killing civilians with horrifying frequency. Not for the first time, the Bosnian planning went awry. When the car stopped at the appointed site, the back doors swung open, and Wolfensohn and the prime minister got out and plunged into the countryside, strolling across the grass, now in the sunlight, now over dark patches where the trees cast shadows, following a route that had been popular with weekenders in prewar times. Nobody moved, and nobody followed: This territory had seen intense fighting during the war, and land mines were surely buried all around the area. Wolfensohn and Muratovic arrived at the river source, where clean water bubbled innocently. They stood for a few moments talking and then returned to join their entourage.[32]

THE BRUSH WITH the land mines was an apt metaphor for the World Bank in Bosnia. Whatever the triumph of its quick arrival, the Bank faced enormous difficulties once there. Sarajevo was a dust bowl, with rags of dirty plastic drooping from windows; demobilization drove unemployment up to 75 percent, and clumps of resentful men roamed the streets of the capital. But the single biggest challenge was the split among Bosnia's still-warring entities. Dayton had declared peace, but it was up to the World Bankers to build it on the ground. And the ground was strewn with booby traps for the unsuspecting newcomer.

The Bank stepped on an early mine in Mostar, a beautiful city that had seen the worst Bosniak-Croat fighting. The Bank's European rivals, who had been administering Mostar since the Bosniak-Croat peace deal of 1994, had devised a careful strategy for bringing the two sides nearer: they had promised to pour millions into the wrecked electricity system, but only if Bosniak and Croat each gave up the idea of two ethnically run grids in the city. The Bosniaks had refused, but there was reason to hope that in the end they would relent; their people wanted the lights on. In the midst of this standoff, the Bank sprinted in: it promised to fix the Bosniak half of the system without bothering to demand reconciliation as a condition. There is no way to be certain that the European approach would ultimately have worked, but the Bank's intervention guaranteed that it would not. Mostar's rival grids remained stupidly separate, and a chance to reintegrate the city was squandered.[33]

If Bosniak-Croat tensions were bad, dealing with the Bosnian Serbs was even harder. They had emerged as pariahs from the war, and for much of 1996, they hunkered down in their village-sized capital, Pale, refusing most contact with foreigners. World Bank officials who made the trip to Pale wondered if it was worthwhile; they saw posters of Radovan Karadzic, the bootlegger and war criminal who ran the Serb enclave, but they were not permitted to see senior officials. Still, they had no choice but to keep talking to the Serbs, not least so that they might pay their share of the Bank's debt service. One time, after delivering an ultimatum on debt payment, Christine Wallich got a call in her Sarajevo hotel; a Serb official was summoning her to Pale. It was ten P.M. on a Saturday evening, but Wallich set off into the night with a colleague and a single bodyguard, winding along mountain roads to the cluster of low-slung chalets that passed for the Bosnian Serb capital. It was pitch-dark when she arrived, and she was shown into a room lined with Serb toughs. Before her stood the Serb minister of foreign affairs: "Your debt service," he said, indicating a leather briefcase on the table; "well, take it!" The case contained DM 17 million in banknotes, in other words, a death sentence; there was no way Wallich could drive that kind of cash through the lawless night and be sure to survive the experience. Wallich said that the World Bank could not accept briefcase payments, and the minister looked terrified; he had been ordered to hand over the money by midnight, and he didn't want anyone getting the idea that he had failed them. So Wallich wrote out a receipt, which saved the foreign minister's face and perhaps even his skin; and a few days later, the Bank received the money via wire transfer. For all Wallich knew, the minister had put the cash in the back of his VW and driven it to Belgrade; there were no banking services in Pale.[34]

Aside from Mostar, and the near impossibility of dealing with the Serbs, there were the usual problems with aid programs. The Bank designed projects and lent money, but it could not control everything; if the government was incompetent or corrupt, the Bank's efforts would suffer. Edhem Bicakcic, the likable head of the Bosniak electricity utility who gulled the Bank into the wrong project in Mostar, later misappropriated millions during his time as prime minister of the federation. The World Bank's Emergency Social Fund, worth $54 million, was partly used as patronage by mayors who controlled the expenditures; and the Bank's small business loans, worth $30 million, were distributed through Bosnian commercial banks that were controlled by ethnic nationalists.

From somewhere around late 1997, Bosnia started to bog down, but the Bank's performance early on amounts to a success story. In 1996, the economy grew 86 percent; the next year it grew another 37 percent; unemployment halved from about 70 to 80 percent at the start of 1996 to around 35 percent two years later.[35] Even allowing for the inevitable bounce after a war, this was a robust recovery, and there was no doubt that it owed much to the World Bank. In its first year in Bosnia, the Bank put together an astonishing sixteen loans and accounted for a quarter of all the reconstruction effort mounted by foreign donors. Even the projects that the Bank was not doing owed much to its presence, because the Bank had created the blueprint for all donor efforts and was doing more than any other agency to coordinate implementation. Later on, much of this coordination role was taken over by the Dayton-created Office of the High Representative. But in 1996, the high representative was "having enough trouble finding his ass with both hands," in the helpful image of one American official.

Years later, on a visit to Bosnia in 2003, the adulation for the Bank was almost embarrassing. Mirsad Kikanovic, Bosnian minister of finance in 1996, appeared for an interview with a glowing smile, and began to riff about how the Bank was a model organization. In the early days, the Bank left the European Union and the Office of the High Representative in the dust, Kikanovic maintained; the others were "slow, not very systematic, definitely inferior." The mere suggestion that not everybody regards the Bank as efficient drove Kikanovic into high gear; his big neck was busting out of his collar and his dark eyes were glowing. "The time from agreement [he brought his hand down, karate-chop style, onto the conference table] to completion [another karate chop] is much quicker than other donors," he insisted. "Quicker than the Europeans [chop!]. Quicker than the Saudis [chop!]. Turkey? We haven't even finished some deals with them!" How quick was the Bank? "We negotiate a loan in March 1996 [chop!]. We sign in May 1996 [swift chop!]. The project is done by the end of the year [the last chop crashed down on the table with a conclusive thud, and the interpreter was blushing]."[36]

Just about everybody said the same, though usually without the hand signals. Kasim Omićević, the national bank governor, emphasized that the Bank's importance extended far beyond its aid; it was a catalyst and intermediary for other donors. It hosted the donor conferences that followed the first one in Brussels; it would line everybody up, and coach the Bosnians on how best to address their backers. "If all other institutions had done as much as the World Bank, Bosnia would have made a lot more progress," Omićević declared. In contrast, the Europeans "delivered so slowly and in such a bureaucratic manner that by the time the money arrived you could hardly remember how or why you had applied for it."[37] With a handful of exceptions, it was hard to get a different perspective. You could ask a Bosniak, a Croat, and even a Serb, and you'd likely get the same response: The Bank had been magnificent.[38]

In Washington in 1996, the lessons of Bosnia were not lost on the key players. Faced with the spectacle of the Bank delivering rapid help to war-torn Bosnia, the NGO critics stayed quiet. Faced with the rescue of their Bosnia policy from the transatlantic rift, the U.S. government was delighted. Treasury officials even put a new post–cold war spin on the Bosnia experience. The end of the cold war had reduced the importance of heavy armaments, but it had boosted the world's economic interdependence, heightening the Western interest in stabilizing trouble spots. Development banks were to the new world order what security organizations were to the old, suggested Lawrence Summers.[39] Three years later, in Kosovo and East Timor, the Clinton administration turned to the Bank for reconstruction help again; and by 1998, reconstruction accounted for a sixth of total lending.[40] Like many presidents since 1944, Bill Clinton had learned to appreciate the potential of the World Bank as a tool of foreign policy.

To the Bank's new president, meanwhile, the experiment with speed had shown what his outfit could accomplish. The Bank was often excruciatingly slow, he admitted,[41] but Bosnia had shown that it was capable of moving fast; and this was at once a triumph and a source of yearning. Ever since his stop in Mali, Wolfensohn had wanted a Bank like Linda McGinnis, client-friendly and committed. After the success in Bosnia, he wanted the same thing, only more. If only he could banish the headquarters' slowness, and turn Bosnia into the rule rather than the exception. If only he could have a Bank like Christine Wallich, driving at top speed through the sniper intersections to a sandbagged presidency building, supported by a team at headquarters that trudged through Washington's snowstorms to get gas into Sarajevo.

If only, if only: but all this would take a revolution in the Bank's management.

CHAPTER SIX

NARCISSUS AND
THE OCTOPUS

THREE WEEKS BEFORE his flying visit to Sarajevo, and precisely one year after being selected to lead the Bank, Wolfensohn delivered a speech to the Bank's senior staff that summed up a fair chunk of his presidency. He marched up to the podium with his head slightly bowed, his hand clasping a white hanky that he used to wipe his mouth, his expression taut and nervous. "Well good afternoon," he began, the uneasiness cracking in his voice. "I've got a lot of papers which have been handed to me on subjects which I should perhaps cover." He waved a sheaf of documents above his head, and then he stepped off the stage and thrust them at two deputies sitting in the front row. This speech would be his speech. The officials who aspired to manage what he said would instead become his targets.[1]

Over the next hour and a half, the boss rammed home a dual message. On the positive side, the Bank's public image was improving fast. Wolfensohn had reached out to nongovernmental groups, turning the enemies of the Madrid summit into dinner companions. He had convened meetings with environmentalists and fellow development-bank chiefs, and forged new links with everyone from industrialists to charitable foundations. "I think that we are really making a major major change on the outside," Wolfensohn summed up, and it was clear that he was right: the boss was championing the cause of debt relief, changing the World Bank from despised money collector to dynamic ally of the NGOs; he was projecting a fresh image of the Bank on his incessant travels. "Now why have I thrown away the speech?" Wolfensohn asked. "Because I'm worried about the inside."

The inside, he said, was bureaucratic, cynical, distrustful; it was an affront to the nobility of the Bank's mission. Within the cathedral's headquarters, brilliant people seemed to shrivel at their desks; in far-off villages outside, misery was grinding on unnoticed. Wolfensohn had been to slums in Haiti and seen children with distended bellies and no hope; he had been to Africa and seen schools with ninety children per classroom and two children per pencil. Now he wanted to revitalize the Bank's capacity to fight this misery, so that the Bank's dynamism in Bosnia would be the rule rather than the exception. He had created a "change management group," launched a "change bulletin," and sent a batch of managers off to business courses at Stanford and Harvard. But he felt that he'd been met at every turn with carping and indifference. "I cannot have a situation where we as a group don't have that sense of excitement, commitment, and trust," Wolfensohn declared. By now his nervousness was gone. He was speaking naturally, confidently, the words sweeping him along. There was an invisible barrier, he felt, between his own enthusiasm and the "so what?" looks he encountered from the staff. "There is a need, somehow, to break through this glass wall, this unseen glass wall, to get enthusiasm, change, and commitment."

Wolfensohn stopped speaking and invited questions. Half a dozen managers took turns at the microphone while the rest listened impassively; they were getting to know their boss, and his sermons no longer surprised them. One questioner, a tall Sikh named I. J. Singh, echoed Wolfensohn's anger. The Bank's culture, he declared, is "overbred, inbred, and totally tied to process." But for the most part the managers hung on to the fence; they offered polite praise, but they also hinted at resistance. Wolfensohn stood at the podium and responded, always turning the conversation back to the staff's poisonous detachment. Finally a last question gave him the cue he had been waiting for, and he leaned forward and let loose: a silver stream of words that seemed to flow and flow forever.

The Bank's assembled managers, he said—and he looked them in the eyes—should be "talking about a new atmosphere of change, a new atmosphere of hope, and a new dream, and the reality that our institution by the year 2000 will be absolutely unique in terms of its development impact. Where we can say that we are affecting the lives of more people in the world positively than anybody else. We are doing it brilliantly. We are open. We are flexible. We want to listen. Where we can say that we care, that we can cry about poverty, that we can laugh when people have a good time, that we can embrace our clients, that we feel them, and that we feel part of them and their villages and towns and their environments. And that we are privileged to be in an institution where we serve four and a half billion people and where we can make a difference. And where we can tell our kids that we make a difference.

"I had two of my children at two of these recent meetings," Wolfensohn went on, holding the gaze of the audience, speaking slowly and naturally now that he had won their attention. "I had them there really because I want them to be proud of me. I want them to think that what I'm doing is different. And you all have that chance. You have that chance with the people who work for you. . . . That is something that involves your commitment and your heart and your body. And maybe that all sounds crazy to you. But it's what I wanted to say to you today before I headed off to the Middle East."

With that, Wolfensohn walked out of the room, leaving his audience of development veterans to ponder the meaning of his outburst.

. . .

AND IT WAS TRUE THAT the Bank Wolfensohn had taken over *was* a sprawling, messy empire of loosely linked programs, spread across nearly a hundred countries and a dozen different types of projects. In the year of Wolfensohn's speech to the senior managers, the Bank's biggest borrowers were China, Russia, and Argentina, which together accounted for about a quarter of its $22 billion in new loans; but the Bank's managerial complexity lay in the myriad of smaller accounts—$9 million for Congo, $11 million for Cape Verde, $5 million for Tajikistan. Each of the Bank's borrowers could theoretically sign up for each of the Bank's many categories of project: the most popular were energy, transportation, and agricultural development, but there was a long menu of other options, each of which involved teams of formidable specialists, ranging from country economists to procurement officers to legal advisers to engineers, public-health experts, and seed scientists. Tacked onto this core operation, which employed more than eight thousand full-time staff, the World Bank Group also included the International Finance Corporation, which employed nearly two thousand and lent money to the private sector rather than to governments, and the Multilateral Investment Guarantee Agency, whose one-hundred-strong team offered political-risk insurance to encourage private investment in poor countries. Managing this monster was, in Wolfensohn's own words, "like grappling with an octopus."

Jim Wolfensohn was not the first World Bank president to believe the institution needed shaking. His predecessors shared the sense that the Bank was less than the sum of its parts, that the brilliance of its individual staff did not translate into a brilliant institution. Relative to private companies, the Bank seemed slow off the mark. The average project took two years to prepare; elaborate proposal documents would go through an even more elaborate review process. At the start of a normal project, a Bank official would draw up an Initial Executive Project

Summary, followed by a Final Executive Project Summary, and then there would be a Pre-Appraisal Mission to the borrowing country. Next came reviews by the Regional Operations Committee and the Bank-wide Operations Committee. If those went well, the project manager would head off on an Appraisal Mission, and the report produced upon return would evolve through a series of stages: The "White Cover," circulated for departmental comment; the "Yellow Cover," circulated for wider comment; then the "Green Cover"; and finally the revered "Gray Cover," which was presented to the Bank's board at one of its biweekly meetings. The aim of this exhaustive process was to avoid the bad projects that gave the Bank's critics a chance to go on the attack. But it had a perverse consequence. World Bank officials often cared more about impressing their internal overseers than helping their clients. If you were preparing a health project in Peru, the opinion of the Norwegian director on the Bank's board mattered more than the opinion of Peru's health minister.[2]

Despite the multicolored bureaucratic hoops, the quality of the Bank's projects was often disappointing. Clinics got built, but there were no medicines to put in them. Roads were constructed, but were later not maintained properly. No matter how carefully you prepared your project, you could never foresee how things might change once it got under way, yet there were few incentives to adapt your strategy. So much effort had gone into the initial project design that you hated to tamper; besides, it would be years before the Bank's evaluation department reported on how the project had turned out, by which time you would probably have changed jobs and nobody would pin the blame on you. In 1992, the report commissioned by Lewis Preston to review the Bank's project portfolio suggested that quality had declined sharply in the course of the previous decade. In the early 1980s, the Bank's evaluators had judged just 11 percent of projects "unsatisfactory," meaning that they had failed to accomplish the goals laid down by the officials who designed them. By 1991, however, 37.5 percent were deemed unsatisfactory.

Frustrated by such criticism, both Barber Conable and Lewis Preston embarked on managerial reform, creating new departments, changing the Bank's mix of skills, trying to streamline its bureaucracy. Conable's reform had ended in hopeless confusion, which was why Preston had embarked on a successor effort; he eliminated one managerial layer and put the bureaucracy on a stern diet, banning first-class air travel on flights under twelve hours and cutting managers' administrative budgets. But Preston's efforts did not quell the sense that something was amiss. When Wolfensohn fumed that the Bank was an ungainly octopus, most commentators agreed with him.

To a newcomer with Wolfensohn's background, the solution seemed obvious. He should import the management techniques of dynamic private-sector firms, so that the children with distended bellies and women with no wells might be served as efficiently as the clients of a multinational. The Bank, after all, was not bigger or more complex than many private firms, which operated in dozens of countries and combined different lines of business. Daimler-Benz or IBM or the Hong Kong Shanghai bank all managed to appear nimble despite their enormous size, and all were run by Jim Wolfensohn's buddies. In his glittering career in banking, Wolfensohn had advised these corporate chieftains and sat on their boards. Now he would apply their methods to the World Bank, and the inspiring institution of the McNamara era would be conjured back into existence.

More than Wolfensohn appreciated at the outset, there were problems in his private-sector strategy. For one thing, the report commissioned by Preston exaggerated the Bank's decline: it was a decline relative to expectations, which had risen sharply as project managers had been required to write more and more goals into their projects—environmental goals, gender-equality goals, and so on. For another, the sense that private firms were brilliantly managed was overblown: The stock market bubble that was inflating at the time created a parallel bubble in executive reputations. But in the mid-1990s, the superiority of

the private sector was widely taken for granted. Newt Gingrich was citing the management theorists Peter Drucker and Alvin Toffler; Britain's
prime minister John Major was admitting that his government had
spent some $500 million on management consultants; and even Prin-
cess Diana of Britain was consulting a business-motivation guru.[3] Meanwhile Vice President Al Gore was busy "reinventing government," and
complaining that Americans endured "quill-pen government in the age
of Word Perfect";[4] and William Bratton, who ran the New York Police
Department from 1994 to 1996, was devolving power to precinct com-
manders and referring to New Yorkers as "clients." Astonishingly,
Gore's report on reinventing government reached the *New York Times*
bestseller list.

From the time that he arrived in office, Jim Wolfensohn was part of
this mid-1990s wave. He took the report on declining project quality at
face value, and concluded that a dose of private-sector discipline would
cure the problem. In his very first week on the job, he read a new internal
study that blasted the Bank all over again for its substandard projects;
arriving in the Bank's underground garage soon afterward, he saw the
head of the evaluation department and rushed toward him. "I've seen
your report! I want to shoot myself!" he said and demanded an immediate meeting in his office.[5] Right from the get-go, it didn't matter to Jim
Wolfensohn that both his immediate predecessors had tried reform with
limited success. There was no way he would accept the Bank as he had
found it.

The struggle that ensued was a classic saga of the times, mirroring
other attempts to apply private-sector thinking to public institutions.
But it was also a test of Wolfensohn's own character and style. Though
he had rubbed shoulders with the world's grandest chief executives, he
himself came from a boutique financial firm, and it was not at all clear
that he was up to the transition. As a public speaker, he had perfect
pitch; he could size up a dinner table or an auditorium of hundreds; he
could sense it, breathe it, and deliver just right, snatching phrases out of

thin air like a magician brandishing silk handkerchiefs. But he had never before managed an organization of thousands, and the culture of Wall Street had not prepared him for the rhythm of his new institution. For the World Bank was imbued with the spirit of an earlier era. As with Ford or Chrysler a few decades before, people who landed jobs at the Bank tended to remain there. The organization was steady, the pension scheme was plush; so people stuck around, rising gradually up the hierarchy. To borrow the expression of the 1950s, World Bank Man was "Organization Man"; but now here came Wolfensohn, a Disorganization Man if ever there was one.[6] The newcomer was determined to shake up the World Bank, even if he wasn't sure how it should look once he was done. Unsurprisingly, this wasn't popular.

BY THE TIME of Wolfensohn's speech to the senior managers in March 1996, his shake-up had proceeded quite a bit already. Soon after rushing at the Bank's chief evaluator in the parking lot, Wolfensohn told Gautam Kaji, one of the three senior barons who carried the title of managing director, that he wanted a top-to-bottom rethink of the Bank; and by August 1995, Kaji had dispatched two teams of his best people off on brainstorming retreats. One team focused on the Bank's personnel culture: it proposed that managers should be reviewed by their subordinates as well as their superiors; that there should be more training; and that the balance between technical experts and general managers should receive more focus.[7] The other team grappled with the Bank's structure. Here was an institution that delivered scores of different services in scores of countries. How should it be configured?[8]

The structural team assembled several of the men who were to dominate the Bank's reform efforts. It was led by Caio Koch-Weser, an exotic Brazilian German who had made his name as the Bank's country director in China; and by Jean-François Rischard, an elegant and eloquent Luxembourger with an MBA from Harvard, who could have persuaded a mom-and-pop corner store to do a bottom-up review of its managerial philosophy. The team brought in McKinsey, the top management consultancy, and holed up in the Watergate Hotel for a fortnight, mulling over the client surveys that painted the Bank as slow and unresponsive, juxtaposing those with the numerous reports on the declining quality of projects. The Bank, it appeared, faced a dual and in some ways contradictory problem. It needed to move faster, to deliver for its clients. But it must not allow haste to compromise its already dubious quality.

Rischard and Koch-Weser agreed on the outlines of a solution. To be closer to its clients, the Bank needed to create a new cadre of decentralized country directors—front-line Linda McGinnis figures, only a lot more senior, with the power to make decisions without burning up time in long consultations with Washington. To improve project quality, meanwhile, the Bank needed strong technical leaders to oversee its specialists: the water engineers should no longer be scattered among the regions; they should be part of a central department that pooled experiences from all over the world and applied the lessons to all countries. The dual imperative of faster response times and better quality suggested something called a management matrix. In future, the Bank's foot soldiers—water engineers and malaria experts and primary-education specialists—would report simultaneously to two bosses: a country director (who pressed you to deliver for the client fast), and a technical manager (who pressed you to deliver quality).

The brainstorming efforts had come up with complementary proposals: new training and hiring methods were part of boosting the Bank's quality, but the knowledge sharing of the matrix would promote the same objective. The consultants from McKinsey reassured the World Bankers that smart private-sector outfits were thinking along the same lines. Any multinational worth its salt had long since installed meritocratic personnel systems, and nearly every global service firm was married to a matrix. If the World Bank could embrace a similar reform program, it would rival the efficiency of the most driven multinational firms. The winners would be the 3 billion people in the world who lived on less than $2 daily.

Within three months of his arrival, therefore, Wolfensohn had what he had asked for: a plan to redraw the institution. But the quick start soon ran into trouble, because Wolfensohn had difficulty deciding whether the plan was good or not. The brainstormers got their first chance to brief the boss in the early autumn of 1995; they met him in secret at the offices of his old New York firm. Caio Koch-Weser remembers Wolfensohn sitting up there in his Park Avenue suite, looking at the PowerPoint slides, listening without giving much away, and then finally sounding doubtful; "I asked you for a Model T, and you delivered a Ferrari," Wolfensohn told his lieutenants.[9] Somehow Wolfensohn appeared to want reform in the abstract, but seemed less sure when confronted with a concrete plan to do it.[10]

A month or so later, the insurgents were invited to present their ideas again, this time at a meeting of the Bank's top managers at the Hay-Adams hotel in Washington. The secrecy of the New York rendezvous was gone, so presumably Wolfensohn was growing comfortable with their proposals. But again the boss hung back, asking questions in a tired and noncommittal way; he seemed to have cold feet; and if the reforms were going to trigger a revolution from the staff, he wanted someone else's neck under the guillotine. When managers at the retreat raised skeptical questions, Wolfensohn reassured them that no change was imminent. Wilfried Thalwitz, a Bank vice president and one of the old guard, drew the conclusion that the reform drive was over.

"He's leaving you hanging in the wind," Thalwitz said to Gautam Kaji.

"He's just disowned you," Thalwitz told Koch-Weser.[11]

As it turned out, Thalwitz was quite wrong: both the matrix reform and the new personnel system ultimately won Wolfensohn's blessing. But if the first rule of managerial reform is to exude a clear direction and purpose, Wolfensohn had flunked it.

. . .

THE CONFUSED SIGNALS on reform combined with confusion in Wolfensohn's immediate entourage. For much of the 1980s, the Bank had effectively been run by Ernie Stern, the formidable American who served as a sort of chief operating officer. But from the moment of his arrival, Wolfensohn was determined to do things differently: "You will not be my Ernie Stern," he told Gautam Kaji firmly. In December 1995, he promoted Caio Koch-Weser and one other official to the level of managing director, creating a cabinet of five barons immediately below him. On top of that, Wolfensohn had appointed Rachel Lomax, a powerhouse British civil servant, to act in a new chief-of-staff capacity; and he was busy hiring four "senior advisers" to advise him on what all the other advisers were advising. The consultants from McKinsey were wandering around the building, and Wolfensohn solicited yet more input by forming a buddy group of outside chief executives. Then there were Wolfensohn's meetings with NGOs and governments and foundations and development outfits. Everybody got a chance to hold forth on the World Bank's future.

With all these vast and varied egos in the mix, plots and fights and subplots were just about inevitable. Sometimes Rachel Lomax battled for preeminence with the managing directors and senior advisers, who did not want to take orders from her. Sometimes she battled with the boss, who couldn't seem to decide if she was his chief of staff or his chief secretary. One moment Lomax might dominate the president's morning meeting; the next moment Wolfensohn would send her out to fetch coffee. He would frequently explode at her, and she would explode back at him. After some of the worst bust-ups, she would storm into Gautam Kaji's office and bang the door closed; "that bastard!" she would yell, before calming down over a cigarette.[12] By June 1996, Lomax had had enough. Scarcely a year after taking up her post she announced that she would soon be leaving.

One morning in this early period, Wolfensohn lost his temper and demanded that the whole management team submit an undated resignation letter. Everybody blinked: Did he mean resignation from their senior management positions, in which they served at his pleasure anyway, or did he mean resignation from the World Bank, in which case they were not about to throw away their legal protection? Alone among the managers, Gautam Kaji did not hesitate. He was a proud figure, a bit contemptuous of this showboating newcomer. He went back to his office and dictated the letter and a cover note: "You wanted a letter, here it is, date it whenever you feel like it," Kaji remembers writing. Toward the end of that day, Kaji was chairing a meeting of the Bank's loan committee when his secretary appeared unexpectedly.

"Mr. Wolfensohn wants to speak to you urgently," the secretary informed him.

"I'm running a meeting," Kaji answered.

"He won't leave for home until he speaks to you," the secretary objected.

"He'll have to wait until I've finished the meeting," Kaji insisted.

After the loan committee wrapped up its work, Kaji called Wolfensohn. The heat was enough to melt the phone line.

"What are you trying to do to me?" Wolfensohn demanded.

"What do you mean?" Kaji shot back.

"Why did you send this letter?" Wolfensohn shouted.

"You just asked for it this morning!" Kaji snapped back. "Either I have the courage of my conviction and some level of self-respect, or I don't. And I do! So you have it. Accept it whenever you feel like it."[13]

THERE WERE MULTIPLE triggers for these outbursts and confusions. Sometimes Wolfensohn blew up because he was bone tired; when he exploded at Kemal Dervis in Sarajevo, he was on his way back from his seven-stop Middle East tour, and he was utterly exhausted.[14] Other times Wolfensohn's inexperience as a manager of big organizations showed through; when he sensed the senior managers' nervousness at the Hay-Adams retreat, he himself retreated.[15] On still other occasions, Wolfensohn did not trust the people around him, especially when he discovered that three of his five managing directors (Kaji, Koch-Weser, and an Organization Man called Sven Sandstrom) had been involved in the failed management reform under Barber Conable in 1987. For a personality like Wolfensohn, whose ability to inspire trust had always exceeded his ability to trust others, this discovery was poisonous. His managers had screwed up before! Now he was going to bet his presidency on them? They had to be joking!

The upshot was that the early management reforms were chaotic. There was never a clear moment when Wolfensohn sat down with his team, decided upon a reform strategy, and laid out a timetable to implement it. Later, Wolfensohn himself would concede some of these points.[16] And yet, even though he lost his nerve and his temper on too many occasions, the Bank was visibly changing. Wolfensohn's lieutenants understood that they could not expect the boss to bet his reputation on their plans. But they knew equally well that the boss wanted change, and if they didn't deliver, then a senior adviser or an outside adviser or some other advisory someone would emerge as the champion of the process. New faces were being promoted, and they all favored change. There was no overall strategy for reform, but reform was busting out all over.

In February 1996, Wolfensohn said good-bye to Kim Jaycox, the Africa vice president, and told his two replacements to make Africa a testing ground for the new management thinking. The personnel system was overhauled: managerial openings were now advertised; candidates were reviewed by a panel; incumbent managers had to submit to reviews of their performance, and the reviewers included their subordinates.

The Bank's clan system was being shaken by the hair: in the old days, a chief hired a favorite protégé, and the protégé hired another protégé, and nobody said anything nasty about anyone. In the new system, managers would owe their jobs to merit, not patronage. If they screwed up, there was at least a chance that they might be held accountable. Meanwhile, the reformers in the Africa region also embraced the matrix, and their lead soon caught the attention of others; in June 1996, Mexico became the first major borrower to get a decentralized country director. As the Bank's regional units reorganized, the technical groups began to form into new knowledge-sharing "networks," which pooled ideas from all around the world, the better to fight poverty. There was not much strategy involved in who went first or how you got there. "It was messy," recalls one of the reform mavens of the time. "Staff would ask you, 'What is this matrix?' and you couldn't give an answer."[17]

In this freewheeling atmosphere, change could spring from the most unlikely quarters. Steve Denning, a Jaycox deputy in the Africa region who had been deposed in the shake-up, hatched an idea for the Bank to embrace a new private-sector idea called "knowledge management." The computer revolution, he supposed, should spell a revolution in the Bank as well. The Bank needed to break out of the craft age, with artisan-loan officers designing each project according to their individual styles. It needed to jump into the Internet era, when every World Banker could access all the Bank's wisdom at the touch of a keyboard, and every Bank project would reflect state-of-the-art thinking.[18] Denning had no managerial position at the time, so he recruited support for his idea by buttonholing colleagues in the World Bank cafeteria. Eventually he was invited to give presentations on his knowledge-management ideas, and he told an inspiring story about a Zambian health worker who discovered a new way of fighting malaria by dialing up the Centers for Disease Control website. If the Bank created teams to distill its experience and make it available online, it could multiply that Zambian success across dozens of technical specialties and countries.

Little by little, Denning won followers, but the managing directors were not remotely keen; they were already steering a chaotic agenda, and they didn't need new initiatives bubbling up out of nowhere.[19] Sven Sandstrom, the Swedish managing director, told Denning to forget about this knowledge thing and find a worthwhile occupation. In Lew Preston's World Bank, that would have marked the end of the story. If a top manager turned you down, it was tough to dance around him.[20] But in Jim Wolfensohn's World Bank there was a free-for-all: ambitious managers grasped that reform could please the boss, and it was risky for a managing director to oppose reform too openly. Denning had by now recruited the support of several regional vice presidents who wanted to experiment with knowledge management in their departments, and Jean-François Rischard was talking about pitching the idea directly to Wolfensohn. One afternoon in mid-September 1996, Denning was in Rischard's office, and the two were strategizing and plotting: Should they approach Wolfensohn now? Should they wait until the calmer time after the Bank's annual meetings? Just then the phone rang. It was Wolfensohn, calling from a New York traffic jam. He was reading a draft of his speech for the annual meetings, and he was furious.

"There's not a single idea in this," Wolfensohn told Rischard. "Surely in this organization there is at least one good idea?"

"As a matter of fact there is," Rischard answered. "Let me tell you about it." As Denning sat watching, Rischard explained knowledge management: How the Bank should pool its expertise on everything from civil-service reform to electricity generation in central databases, multiplying the power of its ideas in the battle against poverty. Rischard talked for five minutes, then five more minutes, and presently he hit the fifteen-minute mark. Wolfensohn was saying it was intriguing, actually quite good, and maybe he would think about it. That Wednesday evening Wolfensohn tried the idea out on his dinner companions, and the next day he asked Rischard to draft a speech on the subject. Rischard and Denning worked until late that night, and on Friday

Wolfensohn laid out his brand-new vision for a "knowledge bank" to the Bank's board. A few days later the idea formed a key section of Wolfensohn's speech at the 1996 annual meetings.[21]

Within a year, a hundred "knowledge groups" sprang up across the Bank, each devoted to establishing global best practice in a technical specialty. Remarkably for a public institution, the World Bank had embraced a management fashion as quickly as its private-sector peers; and the Bank was soon being cited as a model by "knowledge gurus."[22] Whether this was altogether positive is a different question: The knowledge-sharing networks fostered a perfectionist culture rather than a speedy one, and it encouraged the powerful tendency in the Bank to focus on internal process rather than on outside clients. But the strangest lesson in the knowledge reform lay in the manner of its triumph. A management innovation hated by the management team had been adopted with gusto. What kind of an outfit was Wolfensohn running?

By early 1997, it wasn't just the Bank's old guard that was complaining. Many of Wolfensohn's new appointees were worried, too: the boss could grasp a hot new concept in the space of a single phone call from a traffic jam, but he had no sense of strategy. In the first months of his tenure, they had felt there might be an excuse; you needed a freewheeling period of uncertainty to break up the old order.[23] But after more than a year of charisma and chaos, that excuse no longer worked. There had to be other reasons why Wolfensohn avoided strategic planning.

Wolfensohn's lieutenants reckoned that it came down to two things: his thin-skinned determination to be loved, and his dislike for trade-offs. Wolfensohn would start meetings by asking, "What are people saying? What have you heard?"—he seemed more concerned about what others wanted than about thinking through his own position. He had built his banking career on his relationships, and he had managed from deal to deal, seizing every opportunity that chanced along and remaining friends with everybody. His personal life had been the same:

he had mastered fly-fishing and studied the cello and won the Gay Men's Health Crisis Award;[24] he had rebelled against the whole idea of trade-offs. In a strange way, Wolfensohn's great strength was simultaneously his great weakness. He was better than anybody at wooing outsiders. But if their often incompatible wishes drove the Bank, how could the Bank develop its own strategy?[25]

The answer was that it could not, but the trouble went deeper than Wolfensohn's personality. The central weakness in Wolfensohn's reform was catching up with him: the Bank is not a private firm, and importing corporate management techniques is problematic. The Bank's lack of strategy was a case in point. Private companies begin strategic-planning exercises by asking who their clients are; this helps to bring focus to their work and therefore to generate the profits that keep shareholders happy. But the World Bank cannot streamline itself that way: it must serve many "clients"—it cannot choose to ignore, say, Latin America— and the interests of these clients are not necessarily aligned with those of its shareholders. Instead, the Bank's shareholders want to be treated as a separate category of client as well: they aren't satisfied if it "merely" relieves poverty successfully. The shareholders want the Bank to serve their foreign-policy interests; they want it to promote a cleaner environment, human rights, and other values that their voters care about. This phenomenon of shareholders-cum-clients is common to most public bodies, and it frequently frustrates their efforts to emulate business. At the New York Police Department around the same time, William Bratton failed to take on corruption in the force, even though he could have served his "clients" the New Yorkers well by doing so. The reason was that Bratton's real client was New York's mayor, Rudy Giuliani, who was reluctant to offend the police unions.[26]

As well as wanting to be treated like clients, the World Bank's shareholders do not leave its managers to manage like private-sector boards do. Corporate boards tend to meet once a month at most; their officers are part-timers who seldom challenge the chief executive. But the

World Bank's board holds formal sessions twice a week and informal meetings on most other days; nearly all its twenty-four members devote themselves to the World Bank full time, and they are supported by busy teams of bright officials seconded from their various finance ministries. The board members, in turn, report to government departments in their home capitals, where further teams of mandarins labor, overseeing the Bank's overseers. This vast, far-flung machinery generates a constant flow of queries and directives, and the Bank's beleaguered staff is forced to respond with e-mails, briefings, phone calls back and forth, and sometimes with door-stop-sized reports to justify the Bank's activities. No private-sector chief executive is obliged to work with this sort of monster on his shoulder.

In short, presidents of the World Bank have little space for strategy. They have no choice but to spend much of their energy wooing outside NGOs and shareholders; if they fail to cover those bases, they will be besieged by demonstrators chanting Fifty Years Is Enough and they will be denied money for the soft-loan IDA kitty. In the early reform period, Wolfensohn was fielding pressure from the United States to support Russia's Boris Yeltsin with big loans; he was building bridges with the NGO movement by inviting them to review the Bank's record on structural adjustment; and he couldn't help the fact that neither of these moves would help the Bank to improve its speed and quality. When Wolfensohn did focus on management reform, he often found his path was strewn with obstacles by his shareholders-cum-customers. In the spring of 1997, Wolfensohn's frustrations came to a head in the fight over his so-called Strategic Compact.

IF YOU TALK TO Wolfensohn's critics, the Strategic Compact ranks among his worst abominations. It was vintage Wolfensohn—a deal that only a master deal maker could land—but it was less a strategy statement than a fund-raising maneuver.[27] In the spring of 1996, Wolfensohn had asked for permission to spend more of the Bank's profits on administrative costs—he needed the money for the Harvard management courses and various other schemes—but the board had insisted that he stick to the cost-cutting policies introduced by Preston. Over the next few months, Wolfensohn had brooded on this setback, and by the autumn he had come up with a plan. He wouldn't just ask for a few extra million dollars in the next budget cycle. He would raise the stakes and the rhetoric and transform the entire game. He would demand a quarter of a billion extra dollars.

Seen through Wolfensohn's private-sector spectacles, this was all quite reasonable. He was running an organization with a budget of $1.1 billion—not a small sum, to be sure, but modest when compared to its shareholders' ambitions. The rich countries that sat on the Bank's board thought nothing of making visionary pronouncements at their annual Group of Seven summits, and then calling on the Bank to deliver on their promises. Who wanted Bosnian reconstruction or loans to prop up Russia? Who wanted to promote gender equality or protect the environment? The answer was always the United States and its allies, so why wouldn't they invest in the instrument of their ambitions? All across the private sector, managers were leaping up in front of shareholders and demanding new cash; investors were happily reaching into their pockets, betting that companies would use their capital to grow more profitable than ever. The Bank's shareholders seemed every bit as expansionary in their vision as the average holder of a dot-com stock. Why wouldn't they support an ambitious proposal to invest in the institution?

This was not how the Bank's shareholders saw things. Private companies of that period may have been awash in funds; but in the public sector, austerity was ascendant. Schemes like Al Gore's reinventing government program involved cutting thousands of jobs; if management theory was in vogue, it was the theory of "downsizing" and "delayering," not some theory of expansion. Housed in its new headquarters, suffused with a notoriously laborious paper-shuffling style, the Bank seemed a prime candidate for belt tightening, or so the Bank's board members felt; they did not pause to wonder if the paper shuffling might reflect their own demands for documents and information. Yet under Wolfensohn's Strategic Compact, the Bank was proposing to spend $420 million on new priorities over the next two years, and would pay for only $170 million of that by cutting existing spending. The balance—a quarter of a billion dollars—would be taken out of the Bank's profits, which could otherwise have been used to help Bosnia or Russia or any other cause that the shareholders deemed deserving.

Wolfensohn did not give up in the face of this skepticism. Ignoring the hostility of the Clinton Treasury, he shoved ahead with the Strategic Compact, outflanking his foes much as he had done during his campaign to win the World Bank presidency. Neither Rubin nor Summers liked what he proposed, but they were too distracted to resist; when the Wolfensohn tornado was blowing at full blast it demanded too much energy to fight him.[28] Board members from other countries dragged their feet, but it didn't last long; Wolfensohn threatened to call up their finance ministries back home, and he knew how to make life unpleasant for them. During one board meeting, Peter Nicholl, the representative from New Zealand, accused the Bank of trying to frustrate shareholders' reasonable desire for cost savings. When the meeting broke up, Wolfensohn bore down on him.

"Fuck you!" he shouted at his shareholder, trembling with rage. How dare Nicholl suggest that the Bank was acting in bad faith? Who was he to insinuate that Wolfensohn was a liar? Wolfensohn was roaring and shaking, and the other shareholders were scuttling away, longing for this nasty budget fight to end, nervously registering that it really didn't pay to confront Wolfensohn on this issue. Showing some physical courage, Nicholl put his arm around Wolfensohn and managed to calm him down. But Wolfensohn had made his point, and with almost exquisite force. If his outbursts frequently reflected exhaustion, nervousness, or mistrust of his staff, this one was different. Wolfensohn knew that fury could be effective.

The wrangling carried on for a few weeks, but at the end of March 1997, the compact was voted through unanimously. Almost nobody on the board liked it, but that didn't matter in the end; Wolfensohn had beaten all of them. His critics resented it forever. [29]

THE MONEY THAT Wolfensohn extracted from the board was spread around the Bank, but the most visible consequences consisted of technology and training. Over the next two and a half years, the Bank spent $59 million on integrating the Bank's disparate and incompatible software, plus another $20 million on video and data links between the Bank's field offices.[30] Hundreds of World Bankers went off on six-week courses at Harvard or Stanford, followed by a seventh week in a village somewhere in a developing country; the aim was to revitalize the Bank's "marshmallow middle," as Wolfensohn put it, untactfully. For the critics of the Strategic Compact, this was all ridiculous: Why did the Bank need video conference links? What about picking up the telephone? To Mark Malloch Brown, the Bank's external relations chief, the idea of remaking the Bank's culture by sending people off to villages bordered on the absurd: "Mao and Pol Pot were the only people with similar ambitions, but even they thought reeducation would take more than a week," he observed dryly.[31] And yet the Bank's behavior was quite normal by the standards of big private companies, which routinely blew millions on technology and wacky training courses—and which were generally admired for it. Once again the disagreement came down to the question at the heart of Wolfensohn's reform efforts. Should public-sector institutions take their cues from private firms? Or did an entirely different set of rules apply to them?

Years later, when I visited Wolfensohn in Jackson Hole, there was a book lying on his desk that contained his defense of the path that he had taken. The book was by Lou Gerstner, the outgoing boss of IBM; "Who Says Elephants Can't Dance?" the title asked, a little smugly. Wolfensohn was reading this book because he saw in it a parallel to his own efforts at the Bank. Starting a year earlier than him, Gerstner had shaken up an entrenched and unsuccessful corporate culture; "It was like an isolated tropical ecosystem that had been cut off from the world," as Gerstner puts it in his book; it had "a preoccupation with internal politics"; it had "a management class that presided rather than acted."[32] In a nearly exact echo of Wolfensohn's language, Gerstner writes that he wanted to shake his managers out "of their depressed stupor, remind them of who they were—you're IBM, damn it!"[33] To the man who gave the glass-wall speech at the World Bank, this sounded strikingly familiar.

After eight years at IBM, Gerstner had emerged a hero. He was celebrated as one of the great managers of the age, a turnaround artist whose oracular sayings became the subject of a hundred business manuals. If Gerstner was so great, why shouldn't Wolfensohn have modeled his own efforts on him? And if Wolfensohn was right to take cues from IBM, surely the Strategic Compact was right also? Yes, Wolfensohn had thrown millions at technology, but IBM had done that, too: Gerstner regarded e-business as IBM's "moon shot," its "galvanizing mission."[34] Many of the Bank's board members had agreed with Wolfensohn's premise that the Bank was sluggish compared to private firms. How could they now complain when he copied dynamic corporations?

Wolfensohn was right that the critics could be hypocritical. But the test of his reform lay in its outcome. Not surprisingly, perhaps, the Bank's official data make the outcome look good: in the next few years, the two key measures of the Bank improved—speed on the one hand, quality on the other. In 2000, the average Bank project took fifteen months to prepare, down from twenty-four months in the year before the Strategic Compact; 77 percent of projects had satisfactory outcomes, up from 66 percent four years earlier. The precision of these measures is debatable, and one hesitates to put much weight on them, especially since, in the wake of the battle over the compact, Wolfensohn's lieutenants were under extraordinary pressure to come up with proof that the quarter of a billion had been spent well.[35] But, despite the lack of definitive data to assess Wolfensohn's reforms, one can suggest some rough conclusions.

Some of Wolfensohn's private-sector ideas succeeded. The decentralization of country directors, inspired by private-sector jargon about "flatter systems," and facilitated by the technology investments that linked the head office to the field, greatly improved the Bank by moving its decision makers closer to poor countries. By 2003, two-thirds of the Bank's country directors had moved out of Washington, and the country offices accounted for half of the Bank's staff, up from just over a third in the year before the launch of the Strategic Compact. Equally, the creation of a new Quality Assurance Group (QAG) seems to have made a real impact on Bank staff. Unlike the long-standing evaluation department, whose reports appeared belatedly, the new QAG vetted projects in real time, spreading a healthy terror among project managers.[36]

Other private-sector ideas translated less perfectly. Wolfensohn's new personnel system loosened the clan system in the Bank; in theory, at least, a boss can no longer hire a protégé without going through a formal procedure to find the best candidate.[37] But the change did not bring the revolution that Wolfensohn had hoped for, because the basic structure of the Bank made that impossible. A World Bank president can't fire people at will, so he lacks one tool for enforcing standards. He faces pressure to hire people from a politically acceptable balance of countries; at the senior levels, especially, Wolfensohn would sometimes promote inexperienced managers to appease a powerful shareholder, mocking his own talk of meritocracy. Moreover, World Bank managers can't even be sure which staff have performed best. At many big companies, each department has a bottom line, and if the profits are good, the team gets rewarded. At the World Bank, the amount of poverty you've tackled won't be clear until years after your projects are done—indeed, it probably won't be clear ever. Measuring poverty is notoriously hard, and statisticians fight over the numbers;[38] it's even harder to estimate how much a certain project contributed to a supposed reduction in the poverty rate. Did the new clinic drive down the rate of child mortality? Or was it the new access to clean water? Or was it that economic growth accelerated, allowing mothers enough money to buy nutritious food? It's impossible to be certain.[39]

The matrix reform was another private-sector idea whose translation worked imperfectly. Encouraged by the management consultants from McKinsey, the Bank set up an "internal market" for its technical specialists. Country directors were given a budget, and told to bid for the services of engineers or health experts who were now grouped into knowledge-pooling central teams. In the private sector, this system allocates the best specialists to the most important clients: if Boeing is paying a consultancy top dollar for advice, the account manager for Boeing can bid top dollar as well to get the brightest of his colleagues. In the World Bank's case, however, the countries with the most money are not necessarily the most important, so the premise of the internal market was faulty. On top of that basic problem, the Bank's internal market was poorly designed. After a period of protracted pain, the notion that specialists would be housed in central units and move around all regions of the Bank was more or less abandoned.

In sum, the personnel change and the matrix system delivered less than Wolfensohn expected. The exceptional dynamism of the Bank's Bosnia effort was not something that could be spread across the institution by a dose of private-sector medicine. The Bosnia experience reflected the adrenaline of the post-Dayton circumstances, the lack of obstructionism from shareholders, and the absence of criticism from NGOs, whose vigilance often forces project managers to proceed with extreme caution. In the absence of these special circumstances, private-sector methods could improve the Bank a bit, but they could not break through the encumbrances that are hardwired into its structure: meddling shareholders, a caution in the face of NGOs, and a poverty-fighting mission more complicated by far than the pursuit of profit.

If Wolfensohn had paused to consider these limitations, or if he had studied the thwarted reform efforts of his predecessors at the outset, he might have proceeded more cautiously. For, although his efforts did yield incremental improvements, they came at a huge price. The process of transition threw the Bank into uproar, distracting the staff from its core job of serving its poor borrowers. Project managers and economists were off having coffee, speculating about office politics; missions to the field were put on hold; and the Bank's lending fell by a tenth that year for the period up to June 1997. Even the Bosnia program lost precious momentum. Christine Wallich fell foul of the new-style personnel review—her subordinates believed she was too tough—and several members of her team drifted off to new positions.[40]

Because of Wolfensohn's pugnacious style, these transition costs were larger than they had to be. His tendency to blow up at his subordinates, to circumvent and undermine them, to demand reform urgently while refusing to specify precisely what he meant damaged his reasonable ideas about the Bank's direction. The resulting tensions among Wolfensohn's managing directors was disruptive, as Wolfensohn confessed in 2003, by which time he had finally gotten around to putting one managing director in charge of the whole lending operation.[41] Moreover, Wolfensohn's relationship with his board of directors went from bad to worse. The credit that he had garnered by his fast move into Bosnia was undone by the fight over the Strategic Compact. And to many members of the World Bank's board, Wolfensohn's obsession with "change management," "360-degree peer reviews," and all the rest showed he had no feel for public institutions, and no sense of the Bank's history.

. . .

ON NOVEMBER 25, 1997, Wolfensohn bade farewell to Marc-Antoine Autheman, the departing French representative on the Bank's board of directors. The other board members were seated around the conference table, and staff members crowded into the alcoves at the edges of the room, listening to Wolfensohn make a few remarks, watching him present the ornamental clock that is always given to leaving directors. Once the ceremony was over, Autheman regained his seat and prepared to deliver his valedictory comments. The speech that followed stands as the classic statement of Wolfensohn's critics—and the perfect counterpoint to Wolfensohn's glass-wall attack on the Bank's octopus bureaucracy.

Autheman began by saying what board members had muttered quietly a thousand times but had seldom said to Wolfensohn. The old Bank, he conceded, had been "boring and fearful," "arrogant and self-centered"; and yet it had not been quite the exhausted carcass that Wolfensohn believed it was. Wolfensohn's predecessors had possessed the rare virtues of humility and judgment; they had been "practical and realistic." As to the Strategic Compact, Autheman saw little to justify the vast energy it had consumed. "Why should the reform of the Bank itself be the central issue?" he inquired, before ridiculing the jargon of the management shake-up. "I reject the cultural revolution myth and all its geometric avatars," he drawled, referring to the Harvard training programs and the matrix. He had only contempt for "the obsessive reference to the exclusive and irrelevant model of the American private sector."

Autheman was speaking slowly and deliberately, and he looked over at Wolfensohn; Wolfensohn was rigid. During the interminable board meetings that he chaired, Wolfensohn would often parade his contempt for the process; he would be reading through files while a board director droned on tediously, or he'd be writing a note to one of his colleagues, asking how long this torture would continue. By sheer force of intellect, Autheman had always commanded different treatment; and now he was saying out loud what other board members had dreamed of saying, if only they had found the courage or the opportunity. For more than two years, it seemed to many board members, a spellbinding, silver-tongued, and self-infatuated maniac had been hacking away at this venerable pillar of the Bretton Woods system, declaring that anything that had been built up before his own arrival had to be knocked down, promising to save the World Bank, not to mention the entire planet. For many of these board members, who had known Wolfensohn's predecessors and respected them, this was all preposterous; "it was the hand-grenade theory of change," recalls one official on the board; "you blow everything up and start again." The World Bank, for all its flaws, was the product of the best minds in development. It did not deserve a leader whose theory of reform was Me! Me! Me! It did not deserve a leader who shared credit with no one.

If Autheman had stopped after his first elliptical attacks, his speech would not have unleashed the flood of messages that poured into his office the next day, and it would not have been photocopied and passed furtively around the Bank for the remainder of Wolfensohn's tenure. As it happened, however, Autheman did not stop. Instead he posed a question.

"Could we think of a better allegory of the Bank than Narcissus, the handsome, self-infatuated, and doomed hero of Greek mythology, who drowned himself while kissing his own image reflected in the water?" he inquired, and he looked around at his colleagues. Then he recited a brief poem:

> *Narcissus, you complain and praise your image*
> *Which the mainstream mirrors*

Only Echo Echo responds
But who would care for you,
If you only care for yourself
Who would follow you but Echo
If your motto remains
Follow me, Support me, and Repeat after me.

Autheman left his poem hanging out there in the air, without saying what he meant by it. The figures around the table seemed to freeze. Was Autheman calling Wolfensohn a Narcissus to his face? He hadn't quite said that, but what else could he be suggesting? The board members were sitting there, trying to fathom what had just happened, and Autheman was moving on; he was still needling Wolfensohn, but the strange poem had been left behind him. "I say yes, Jim, when you care for Africa; listen to the civil society; ask for a new, unprecedented debt relief. . . . But, I say no when you respond to dissent by the threats to resign—just kidding?; criticize staff to the point where they feel humiliated; try to reflate a fat Bank which required sustained downsizing." The audience in the boardroom was settling down; Autheman was not pulling his punches, but the inflammatory allusion to Narcissus seemed to have faded like a plume of smoke; it was hard to be sure that it had ever been there. But then Autheman changed gears again.

"Let me call on Narcissus to conclude," he said, still in his measured, low-key way. "When he died, the Oreads came to the pool. You know who Narcissus is. If I tell you that the Oreads are the Board, you should find who the pool is. Listen now to Oscar Wilde.

"But was Narcissus beautiful?" said the pool.

"Who should know better than you?" answered the Oreads. "Us did he ever pass by, but you he sought for, and would lie on your banks and look down at you, and in the mirror of your waters he would mirror his own beauty."

And the pool answered, "But I loved Narcissus because, as he lay on my banks and looked down at me, in the mirror of his eyes I saw ever my own beauty mirrored."

Autheman stopped reading and looked up.

"Thank you, then, to the unknown staffers who see and act that way," he said. And with that he rose and bowed slightly to Wolfensohn before walking out of the boardroom.

CHAPTER SEVEN
THE CANCER
OF CORRUPTION

WOLFENSOHN'S CRITICS were right that he had no sense of strategy. He had vision—in fact, he could have three visions a week—but his visions were arrived at less by sustained planning than by a native intuition. He loved surrounding himself with people and hearing their views; his staff would send him to his desk to focus on an urgent document, but soon the phone in the outer office would light up and he'd be yakking with his buddies. His appetite for human contact knew no bounds: he would explode at his staff, yelling that they had scheduled him to death; but then he would say yes to two black-tie dinners in New York and three meetings with acquaintances, including with such hitherto unheralded partners in the struggle against poverty as Anna Wintour, the editor of *Vogue.*

Somehow, in this crowd of influences, Wolfensohn made his way. If you had asked him ahead of time, he would have had no idea which way he was going to run; he had a set of instincts, an innate feel for the play, but he had no time for prechoreographed offensives. It was no coincidence that Wolfensohn's management reforms began without ever being properly announced, progressed without anybody really knowing where they would end up, and infuriated people deeply. If Wolfensohn had thought out his strategy at the start, he would have made fewer enemies. He would have seemed less impetuous, less reckless. He might even have avoided the comparison to Narcissus.

Wolfensohn had joined an institution that generated shelves full of development studies; indeed, it had taken over a disused mine in Pennsylvania to archive all its learning. Wolfensohn was not about to read much of this stuff, but neither was he willing to accept that he was never going to become a development expert; he had too little time for the first option and too little humility for the second. Instead, off he sprinted, and before he knew it, he was copying the theoreticians' moves and thinking he could compete with them. Heck, he hadn't chaired Carnegie Hall without performing on its stage. He wasn't going to be president of the World Bank without being the chief thinker in the institution. He took great satisfaction in coauthoring articles with Amartya Sen and Joseph Stiglitz (the first was the winner of the 1998 Nobel Prize in economics and a friend of many years, the second was a World Bank chief economist who won the Nobel Prize three years later). Reflecting on his relationship with Stiglitz, Wolfensohn said, "He would translate in many cases some of the ideas that I had intuitively and put it all into economic language. . . . I had the same with Amartya. So I was getting into the level of the Nobel development economists. They were my friends. I made a number of speeches with Amartya. We did joint editorials together and all sorts of things." Wolfensohn then added: "You've got to understand that I had none of the academic training that any of these guys had."[1]

Wolfensohn's basic instincts on development theory were pretty much on target. He arrived at a series of opinions that reflected the theoretical literature of his time, even without having read much of it. As a relationship banker, he instinctively believed that the World Bank should listen more to its clients; by 1998, with the appearance of a study called *Assessing Aid,* the Bank's research department had demonstrated that putting people in developing countries in control was indeed the key to more successful projects. As the product of a business school,

Wolfensohn instinctively believed that traditional economists have fewer answers than they claim. Again, the economists themselves were headed Wolfensohn's way, breaking with the macroeconomic focus of the 1980s and emphasizing the importance of the legal system, transparency, and other noneconomic factors.

Perhaps Wolfensohn's most instinctive move was to speak out against corruption. He had known that corruption harmed development since 1961, when he had tried to build air-conditioners in Nigeria. But what was obvious to him had been taboo at the World Bank; talking about corruption was thought to violate the Bank's apolitical charter.[2] Rather as with debt relief, dissenters from the Bank's official policy lurked in the shadows, referring opaquely to "sub-optimal procurement" or "implicit taxes." But at the Bank's annual meetings in October 1996, Wolfensohn denounced the "cancer of corruption" in front of the whole world, and a kind of intellectual dam was broken. Before long the Bank's research machine was gushing with new literature acknowledging the link between corruption and development.

The trouble, as with management, lay in implementation. Wolfensohn muscled up to the old development consensus and hit it with a hand grenade; he shoved and shouted for new structures to be built, not always pausing to explain how they would fit together. His speech about corruption signaled that the Bank might have to wade into judicial reform, civil-service training, and even efforts to foster investigative journalism; meanwhile, Wolfensohn was broadening the Bank's agenda in other areas as well. He wanted to do more on education and health, more in partnership with NGOs, more on postwar reconstruction in the Balkans; and pretty soon he was talking about new initiatives on subjects as far outside the Bank's traditional remit as religion and culture. In the period following the cancer of corruption speech, the Bank held seminars on the economic impact of corruption in several countries, and it designed a fuller anticorruption strategy for Latvia. But progress was halting, and meanwhile a new challenge to Wolfensohn's thinking emerged. A financial crisis was brewing in East Asia, which would prove his instincts both right and excruciatingly hard to implement.

THE CRUNCH for Wolfensohn's ideas on corruption came in Indonesia, which had done stunningly well by following the Bank's traditional macroeconomic prescriptions over the past three decades. In 1966, this huge and unwieldy nation—an archipelago of more than seventeen thousand islands stretched out over an area the width of the United States—had an annual income per person of $60, meaning that it was twice as poor as India. But in that year a military officer named Suharto came to power, and Indonesia's fortunes reversed themselves. Suharto put an end to the regional and ethnic conflict that had killed as many as five hundred thousand people, and he put in place a version of the Asian progrowth package: stable macroeconomic policy, a focus on exports rather than production for the domestic market, and investments in basic infrastructure, literacy, and health. In the ensuing decades, the economy took off, cutting the poverty rate from 60 percent to 11 percent. By 1996, Indonesia's 200 million people enjoyed an average income of around $1,000, triple India's level.

The World Bank assisted in this miracle, lending $25 billion to Indonesia during Suharto's reign, and maintaining a large office in Jakarta. The Bank's officials prided themselves on understanding the local language and culture; they sat through interminably polite meetings in government offices, eating fried snacks and inhaling the perfume of clove cigarettes, and showing their respect for local custom by avoiding confrontation.[3] There seemed little cause for confrontation anyhow, what with poverty receding by the year. True, Suharto was a dictator who rigged elections routinely; but he kept the lid on inconveniences like separatism, communism, and radical Islam; and his development policies were improving people's lives miraculously. Life expectancy had shot up from less than fifty years to around sixty-five; the rates of illiteracy and infant mortality had both halved. The Bank's annual meetings in Madrid in 1994 featured a special presentation on the Indonesian model, and around the same time the development agency Oxfam produced a glowing report on Indonesia's poverty-fighting achievements.

Wolfensohn's arrival at the Bank complicated this love affair. He visited Indonesia in May 1996, and gave an upbeat speech praising the country's leap from poverty, but he also went out of his way to meet nongovernmental leaders. Previous Bank presidents had breezed through Jakarta and talked to a dozen members of the "Berkeley mafia," the clique of impressive American-trained technocrats who presumed to speak for all 200 million Indonesians.[4] Wolfensohn pushed the Bank's Jakarta office to set up a different kind of program; and although its staff worried that courting independent leaders risked angering Suharto's government, the prospect of angering Wolfensohn was scarier by far, and he got the NGO meeting he wanted. The boss then added another meeting of his own: A friend's daughter worked for a local NGO, and she led a group of colleagues up the back stairs of Wolfensohn's hotel one evening.

There was a strange serendipity to these encounters. The Bank had acquired an NGO-friendly president who cared about corruption just when Indonesian NGOs were getting furious about the subject. Suharto's entourage had long been corrupt; his wife, Madame Tien, was unaffectionately known as Madame Tien Percent, and her children fought among themselves for opportunities to skim money. But after her health deteriorated in the early 1990s, the children ran amok, and the time when the ruling family would rake off only 10 percent soon became a pleasant memory. A son called Tommy ran a monopoly that bought the nation's clove crop at a fifth of its value, an arrangement that transferred poor farmers' rightful earnings into his own pocket; various siblings and family buddies organized other sections of the economy so as to embezzle millions. By the time of Wolfensohn's visit, Indonesia's NGOs were boiling with anger. The government had banned the largest magazine in the country; opposition leaders were being jailed; the nation's wealth was being ripped off by Suharto's cronies. Indonesia, according to these Indonesians anyway, was less a development miracle than a kleptocratic dictatorship.[5]

Wolfensohn also had an audience with Suharto during that brief trip in 1996, and it served only to underline the message from the dissidents. The two leaders each addressed a trade summit, along with a posse of regional big shots, including China's vice premier, Zhu Rongji, and in a gap in the proceedings the VIPs went off to have tea together. Suharto was talking to Zhu, and he summoned Wolfensohn over; and then he broached the subject of corruption. The latest corruption rankings produced by a watchdog group called Transparency International were most upsetting, Suharto declared, for they rated Indonesia as less corrupt than China; he had been happier with the previous year's results, which had recognized his own country as the more energetic embezzler. Zhu looked visibly annoyed, but Suharto carried on. "Don't you think we should tell the president of the World Bank about corruption in this part of the world?" he asked Zhu, who maintained a stony reticence. Then Suharto looked at Wolfensohn. "You know, what you regard as corruption in your part of the world, we regard as family values."[6]

Wolfensohn returned to Washington with strong feelings about Indonesia.[7] The World Bank's star client, its favorite model of poverty-fighting success, was led by a defiantly corrupt dictator who was hated by many articulate Indonesians. The Bank, Wolfensohn told several colleagues, needed to distance itself from Suharto, and his cancer of corruption speech to the annual meetings later the same year reinforced his message. And yet, though the message reached the Bank's office in Jakarta, it was not exactly heard. The reasons speak volumes about the conundrum of development.

. . .

WOLFENSOHN'S TWO MAIN INSTINCTS on development—that the Bank should listen to its clients, and that development depended upon noneconomic factors such as corruption—were in some ways in tension with each other. The first instinct cast the Bank as an understanding outsider: it should ask a client government what its objectives were and figure out a way to help, partly by offering expert advice and partly by offering money. The second instinct placed the Bank in the role of demanding advocate: it knew that sound governance mattered to development, so it should press its clients to train judges, improve government transparency, and generally combat corruption. The first instinct required a listening Bank that trusted developing countries; the second required a lecturing Bank that trusted its own prescriptions. You could never quite tell which instinct would win out. But after that trip to Jakarta in May 1996, it was clear that the corruption-fighting side of Wolfensohn was dominant when it came to Indonesia.

The same war of instincts raged within the Bank's Indonesia team. A faction that embodied the Wolfensohnian inclination to trust the client fought a quiet war against a group that stood for his corruption-fighting tendency. The trusting faction was led by macroeconomists who looked at the big picture of Indonesia's development miracle, and regarded corruption as an acceptable blemish on a rosy picture. The corruption fighters, who were fewer, tended to be more in touch with the Bank's project side, which was where corruption was encountered. In the years before Wolfensohn's visit to Jakarta, the corruption fighters had been gaining ground. They had delayed a big telecommunications project that would have profited the Suharto clan, and they were documenting the costs of lower-grade corruption, too. Schools were collapsing and irrigation channels were flooding, because the money to pay for decent workmanship had disappeared into unseen pockets.[8]

Three months after Wolfensohn's visit, in August 1996, the corruption fighters discovered a nightmare in Indonesia's vast state-owned banking system. Rather like those schools and irrigation channels, the state banks were about ready to collapse. They had accepted World Bank money to strengthen their balance sheets, but they had passed most of it out the back door to undeserving borrowers, doubtless including the regime's cronies. The World Bank's loan to the state banks was large—$300 million—and the corruption fighters pressed the case for freezing it. But, despite Wolfensohn's recent visit, they lost. The Bank's old Indonesia hands refused to alienate their star client. This was Indonesia, they pleaded; foreign institutions like the World Bank had to adapt to local ways of doing business.[9] Anyway, they added, the state banks' cronyism was old news—and was precisely the reason why the World Bank had to stay engaged in sorting out the problem.

This setback for Wolfensohn's ideas said much about his failures as a manager. Before his visit to Indonesia, the corruption fighters had been advancing because of the leadership of a tough country director. After his visit, he told his lieutenants that the Bank was too indifferent to Suharto's corruption. But somehow there was no connection between his convictions and the personnel decisions that went on underneath him; the lieutenants undercut the Indonesia director's authority, even though her views on corruption fitted with the boss's.[10] Moreover, the outcome of the argument over Indonesia's state banks reflected Wolfensohn's intellectual limits as well as managerial ones. By speaking out against the cancer of corruption, he had scored a brilliant rhetorical coup, but what was the World Bank supposed to do about it? Wolfensohn did not have an answer to that question, and so it was debated by and large without him.

The question of what the Bank should do about corruption was admittedly difficult. In an ideal world, you would tell the government that corruption harms the level playing field on which prosperity depends, and in that same ideal world the government would agree to fight it. But what if the government refused? Should you impose anticorruption measures by making loans conditional upon them? The experience of structural adjustment in the 1980s suggested that conditions seldom worked; if a government did not accept a policy voluntarily, its signature on a loan document would usually prove worthless. Between 1970 and 1997, to cite one celebrated example, the World Bank and the International Monetary Fund made twenty-two loans to Pakistan that were tied to reductions in the country's budget deficit, yet the deficit failed to budge throughout the period.

If lecturing and conditionality were unlikely to work, what were the Bank's options on corruption? One answer, as the tough faction in the Bank argued, was to cut lending to corrupt borrowers like Indonesia. But most Bank officials dismissed that as a kind of nuclear option. Almost by definition, they maintained, a developing country is likely to have bad policies: a budget deficit that risks hyperinflation; an education policy that ignores girls; a health policy that pours money into urban hospitals rather than cost-effective rural clinics. If the World Bank cut off lending to all countries that had self-defeating policies, it would lend very little; the challenge is to decide which policy mistakes are so grievous as to warrant disengagement. Hyperinflation wrecks everything in an economy, so it justifies a pullout. Ignoring girls' education or skewing the health budget to hospitals is not so pervasively destructive, so the Bank should soldier on in countries that commit these errors.

Where does corruption rank in this hierarchy of bad policy? Not very high, most people at the Bank argued. Indonesia's policies were lifting perhaps a million people out of poverty each year; how could you argue that Indonesia's corruption was debilitating? If a quarter of the value of a public-works contract was ripped off, that was certainly bad; but at least the road or bridge got built, and a lot faster than the equivalent project in, say, India. In some cases, moreover, the rip-offs even served a semilegitimate purpose; they maintained middle-ranking bureaucrats who got paid absurdly low salaries. This kind of corruption (as distinct from the Suharto cronies' grand scams) amounted to hidden taxation, a way of paying for a civil service that would otherwise have had to be financed by formal taxes. Hidden taxes, actual taxes—what really was the difference?

In the months after Wolfensohn's cancer of corruption speech, the accommodating majority within the Indonesia team basically won this argument. It was not a rosy verdict on Wolfensohn's capacity for leadership. The boss had attempted to change the development agenda; he had stood up at the annual meetings and stunned people with his bold language. But then the Bank staff "at the coal face" had listened, considered, and formed their conclusion: His pronouncements were irrelevant. The majority of the Bank's Jakarta office could see no good way of turning anticorruption rhetoric into actual policies. The most they would do was to talk more openly about corruption, but in a patient, Indonesian kind of way. They were not willing to resort to the nuclear option of canceling big projects.

In the maelstrom of the Bank's management reorganization, the corruption-fighting Indonesia country director was squeezed out of her job. Nobody was surprised about the identity of her replacement. It was the Bank's resident representative in Jakarta, who had mollified the Indonesians after the fight over the state banks. Little did he imagine what the next year had in store for him.

THAT MOMENT, in the summer of 1997, has a certain retrospective poignancy. Dennis de Tray, an intense, gauntly handsome Chicago-trained economist, had been awarded a dream job: as a new-style decentralized country director, he had the power over budgets and projects that used to exist only at headquarters, yet he was out there in the field, presiding over a World Bank office with more than a hundred staff members, advising a developing country that was a model for all others. But on July 2, the day after de Tray took up his new position, Thailand abandoned its long-standing policy of pegging its currency to the dollar; and people started to wonder whether the free fall of the Thai baht might spread trouble throughout Asia. The following week de Tray appeared before the Bank's board in Washington and put a brave face on the outlook. He batted away a few questions about Indonesia's corruption, saying that his team was paying due attention to the issue, and he insisted that Thailand's currency turmoil would not harm his client. Unlike Thailand, Indonesia had a flexible currency regime, rather than a fixed rate. Besides, Indonesia's macroeconomic vital signs looked excellent.[11]

It was one of the worst predictions ever made by a World Bank economist. By the end of 1997, Indonesia was falling like a stone, and de Tray was grappling with the loss of his intellectual moorings. A country that the Bank had long regarded as a star client was plummeting further than any of the other countries caught up in Asia's financial crisis. The economy shrank by 13 percent in the course of 1998, and unemployment jumped tenfold, compared with threefold in Thailand. This collapse transpired, moreover, at least partly for the reasons that the corruption fighters had urged over the past year, and that de Tray had resisted: Indonesia's cronyism was worse than that of its neighbors, and economics is not the whole key to development. Because of corruption, the country's macroeconomic miracle had rotted from within. Once financial trouble hit, the national institutions that might have tried to reassert control proved too feeble to do so.

De Tray's troubles began almost immediately. A fortnight after his appearance before the Bank's board, an American academic named Jeffrey Winters showed up at a press conference in a trendy Jakarta art gallery and alleged that around 30 percent of the Bank's Indonesia loans were lost to corruption. The number was based on casual chats with people from the Bank, none of whom expected their guesstimates to be used this way,[12] but the assertion played into the rising fury about corruption felt by Indonesia's NGOs and journalists. That night, the "revelation" of World Bank corruption led the television news, and a debate that had simmered quietly within the Bank suddenly went public.

From its headquarters in Washington, the Bank responded quickly. It was one thing to discuss corruption among colleagues and say it wasn't a big deal: that it was a kind of tax, an acceptable blemish on a star performer. But when somebody accused the Bank of allowing a third of its money to be ripped off, it couldn't just say, oh well, never mind, the macro numbers are lovely. Within twelve hours of the Winters press conference, the Bank put out a categorical statement: "We know exactly where our money is going," it declared; "we do not tolerate corruption in our programs." The trouble was that this was false: corruption permeated everything in Indonesia. Before long, articles appeared in the *Jakarta Post* supporting Winters's assertion; and meanwhile, the Bank's own project managers greeted the claim that their operations were clean with ill-concealed astonishment. De Tray soon found a mini-revolution brewing in his office.[13] The allegations of corruption needed to be taken seriously, not brushed off with a ludicrous denial— and that meant going pretty much where Wolfensohn's instincts had pointed after his visit to Indonesia a year earlier.

In the first week of August 1997, de Tray headed off in that direction. He went to visit Suharto's planning minister and raised the issue of corruption with new force; the Bank could not carry on supporting Indonesia indefinitely unless something was done about it. The minister listened earnestly, and asked how this alleged corruption occurred; it was a curious query given the questioner's known skill in the dark arts of embezzlement. De Tray replied that he would prepare a memo on corruption that the minister could take to Suharto; then he returned to his office and asked his staff to get to work on it.[14] The Bank's foot soldiers were at last grappling with the issue raised by their boss in his cancer of corruption speech. A single press conference by a junior professor had achieved what had eluded Wolfensohn.

The corruption memo arrived on de Tray's desk in early October. Its content was ominous. The Bank's staff had told the memo writer roughly what they had already told Winters: around 20 to 30 percent of loans to Indonesia were probably being stolen. If circumstances had been normal, the question of what de Tray would have done with this memo is a matter for debate: Did corruption on this kind of scale merit the confrontation with the government that the Bank's macroteam had earlier resisted? But circumstances were far from normal in the first week of October. Indonesia's currency had lost around 30 percent of its value against the dollar since de Tray's upbeat appearance before the Bank's board, and the government had taken the precaution of calling in help from the International Monetary Fund. De Tray set the corruption issue aside in favor of more urgent challenges.

Indonesia's currency slide began as a leisurely affair, and at first nobody was bothered. It was ascribed to mindless money managers in Boston or London, who didn't know the difference between Thailand's economic fundamentals and Indonesia's; and then it was ascribed to greedy speculators out for a killing; and then it was noticed that Indonesian companies had insane volumes of dollar debt, and were rushing to buy dollars to cover themselves. Up until October, however, the Bank's economists reckoned that the problem was containable, and one of them even moved his own money into Indonesian rupiah, figuring that the currency had bottomed.[15] The arrival of the IMF's mission signaled that the rupiah's troubles had at last reached the top of the agenda, and in the last week of October nervous investors dumped stocks in markets as far afield as Latin America and the United States, triggering a crisis meeting on October 27 at the Treasury in Washington.[16] Yet the more de Tray grappled with the financial issues, the more the question of corruption kept on coming back. Graft and cronyism were undermining Indonesia's efforts to control the crisis, rendering the IMF's medicine powerless.

Dennis de Tray had argued in favor of calling the IMF into the country. Ever since the founding of the two institutions at Bretton Woods, the IMF had played the lead role in currency crises. The Bank had been created to deal with longer-term issues, and its brain trust originally focused as much on engineering as on economics. Over the years, and especially since the structural adjustment of the 1980s, the Bank had come to be dominated by economists such as de Tray, blurring the original division of responsibility. But when it came to financial turmoil, the IMF remained the expert. It could parachute into a country and come up with a prescription in a week or two; the Bank took months mulling over its analysis. Yet although de Tray had been in favor of inviting in the IMF, he was less pleased when it arrived. The commandoes barged into Jakarta and moved all big decisions to their suite at the Grand Hyatt hotel, scarcely bothering to consult the Bank officials who actually lived in the country. At times the IMF would deign to ask a Bank economist to write a memo, and when the memo was handed over it was promptly declared secret; the Bank could not expect to have it back again.[17]

The IMF spent much of October in Jakarta, and came up with two prescriptions. The first was to stabilize the banking system, whose potential collapse threatened to deepen Indonesia's crisis. It was no secret why the banks were vulnerable: years of lending to cronies had left them in a parlous state, as the Bank's corruption hawks had documented. But cronyism was not merely the cause of the problem; it undermined the remedy. The IMF tried to close down rotten banks in order to leave only viable ones open, but it failed to close many rotters because they were politically connected. The sixteen banks that the IMF closed did include one owned by a Suharto son, but this achievement did not last. Within a month the son had risen up again, taking over a new bank and stuffing it with assets from the old one.

Not surprisingly, this halfhearted effort to excise the cancer in the banking system failed to instill confidence. Coupled with a fatal IMF miscalculation, it proved disastrous. Toward the end of its mission, the

IMF had debated whether to shore up the remaining banks by announcing a guarantee on deposits. One side insisted that a guarantee
was essential to prevent a bank run; the other side objected that a blanket guarantee would rescue rich depositors who had made millions
from Indonesia's corrupt system, and who had entrusted their money to
sleazy banks with their eyes wide open. In the end, the fear of rewarding
crony depositors won out, and only the smallest deposits were guaranteed. Within days of the IMF's departure, Indonesians panicked and
began pulling their money out of local banks. Partly because of cronyism again, the IMF had exacerbated the problem that it was supposed
to be treating.

The IMF's second goal was to stabilize the rupiah. It promised
Indonesia $33 billion in loans, hoping to persuade speculators that the
central bank would have ample ammunition to defend its currency. But
Indonesia's corruption undermined this policy, too. Any effort to defend
a currency has to include tight monetary policy; but Indonesia's central
bank was pumping out loans to Suharto cronies, and the money supply
was ballooning. As a result, the rupiah slid steadily until early December, and then the elderly Suharto fell ill. The panic engendered by this
political development swamped anything the economists could do. The
rupiah fell to less than half its precrisis value, and though Suharto re-
appeared in public after ten days, ordinary Indonesians never recovered
faith in him. In early January the rupiah plummeted by another 50 percent in the space of four days, and on January 8 the citizens of Jakarta
rushed out into the streets, buying up all the food supplies that they
could lay their hands on.[18]

Years later, when de Tray looked back on that moment, he saw it as a
kind of turning point for his understanding of development. In good
times, corruption and governance seemed like secondary problems; but
crises brought out their true importance. In a political transition, only
strong institutions stand as a bulwark against chaos, and corruption had
rotted every institution in Indonesia—from the courts to the bureau-

cracy to the banking system. It was no wonder that people panicked at the news of Suharto's sickness and scrambled to buy all the food they could find; the real shock was that the World Bank was unprepared for this moment. The Bank had been engaged for years in Indonesia, but its economists' worldview had left no room for the idea that if you don't get the politics roughly right a lot of development progress may be wiped out in a few weeks.[19] Perhaps corruption did rank right up there with hyperinflation on the list of systemic development problems?

In the immediate turmoil of January 1998, de Tray had no time to grapple with this question. Three days after the panic buying in Jakarta, the International Monetary Fund returned, and this time its team was led neither by its top Indonesia person nor even by the top person for Asia. The country's crisis had become a full-blown global threat, and the IMF showed up in the person of Stanley Fischer, the number two in the whole organization. The bailout package that he crafted was as remarkable as his attendance there, and it reflected his long friendship with de Tray, who pressed his newfound conviction that the crisis was political at bottom. In return for the IMF's seal of approval, Suharto was forced to promise a broad attack on the cronies. He would reform the timber monopoly run by his golfing buddy, Bob Hasan; he would reform the car monopoly run by his son Tommy; he would go after the clove monopoly (Tommy again); he would tackle the garlic monopoly, and the flour, and the palm oil—the thing read like a cookbook.[20] The IMF's goal was not just to change financial sentiment, as most bailouts try to do, but to change the political outlook, too: Suharto was being offered a chance to show that he would put crisis management ahead of crony maintenance.

It was, like any IMF package, a sizable gamble: Suharto might promise everything and carry on regardless. To reduce the chances of an empty signature, the IMF sent out its boss, Michel Camdessus, to ask Suharto whether he really was sincere; and as Suharto drew his pen to sign the agreement, Camdessus stood over him, arms folded, eyes cold, in an angry-father pose that was later to appear on the pages of a thousand newspapers. At a packed press conference, the IMF announced the new measures: It proclaimed an end to the garlic monopoly, an end to the cloves, and so on. When the list was completed, the audience sat in stunned silence for a moment, then applause broke out across the conference room.

As it turned out, Suharto was not sincere. The old man broke his promises within days, and the second IMF package failed just like the one before it. But Dennis de Tray soon had other problems on his mind. On February 3, Wolfensohn arrived for his second visit to Jakarta, and de Tray went out to meet him at the airport: the short, barrel-chested man emerged from the plane; the tall, waspish man waited there to greet him. Wolfensohn advanced toward de Tray and got straight to the point.

"You've really fucked this country up," he told him.[21]

THE PAST FEW MONTHS had been terrible for Wolfensohn. The chaos of his management style was catching up with him, driving senior lieutenants to desert and alienating the Bank's shareholders. Marc-Antoine Autheman delivered his Narcissus speech in November 1997, and a week later Gautam Kaji left the Bank; Wolfensohn had by now lost his chief of staff and two out of five managing directors. The management maelstrom was hurting the Bank's response to the turmoil in Asia: having failed to promote the corruption-fighting Indonesia country director, Wolfensohn had anointed a Frenchman as vice president for East Asia in order to mollify the French government. The Frenchman was called Jean-Michel Severino, and he was certainly clever; but his inexperience of Asia mocked Wolfensohn's loud talk about a meritocratic personnel system. As the Indonesian crisis deepened, the price of this political appointment became clear. Severino was treated brusquely by Sven Sandstrom, the managing director above him. He relieved the pressure from above by dumping on de Tray in Indonesia.

Partly because of this managerial dysfunction, the Bank was embarrassingly slow at the start of the Asian crisis. Everyone expected the IMF to take the lead, but it seemed reasonable for the Bank to play a strong supporting role; after all, Dennis de Tray headed a large resident office in Jakarta, whereas the IMF had no permanent presence. But the Bank could not turn its expert knowledge into timely policy. Under the new matrix system, the experts in de Tray's office owed part of their allegiance to sectoral bosses back in Washington, so they felt free to disregard his demands for immediate one-page memos on aspects of the crisis. The contrast between the fast Fund and the slow Bank was not entirely the Bank's fault. The IMF basically does just one thing in the world, which is to fight currency crises; being a single-product organization, it has no need for a matrix. But in the midst of Asia's crisis nobody cared about management theory. The name of the game was fixing the chaos, and it was clear that the Bank was ponderous.

If the result was painful for de Tray, it was excruciating for Wolfensohn. The boss wanted a seat at the world's top table, and he didn't like playing second fiddle to his Bretton Woods sister.[22] In the first year of his presidency, he had shown Sister who was dominant. He had championed the cause of debt relief, despite the IMF's initial objections, and he had impressed the Bank's chief shareholder by charging into Bosnia. But now that financial crisis topped the international agenda, the IMF was in the lead; and the crisis was not confined to Thailand and Indonesia. By November 1997, it was engulfing South Korea, too, and the more it spread the more it threatened to spread further. Having made fortunes by betting correctly against the Thai and Indonesian currencies, speculators were looking for other countries with similar Achilles' heels: a dependence on foreign-capital inflows, a large pile of debt denominated in dollars. Once speculators began attacking a currency, it was hard to hold them back. Other foreign investors would panic and start selling, too, and the sheer volume of money traded on private capital markets was likely to overwhelm official resistance. The

IMF itself was overwhelmed in late November, when it announced a huge package of loans to South Korea to stabilize the currency. The investor panic carried on, and by December a second rescue was needed.

The effect of these crises was to push the Bank to the sidelines, and simultaneously to exert unwelcome pressure on its finances. In Bangkok and Jakarta and Seoul, IMF missions were designing huge bailouts, treating the Bank's experts as research assistants; and then Larry Summers would call Wolfensohn from the U.S. Treasury at all hours of the day and night, demanding that the Bank contribute billions to these IMF-designed rescues. Summers was consulting the IMF's Stan Fischer, and Summers was consulting the Federal Reserve's Alan Greenspan, and Summers and Fischer and Greenspan were all saving the world together, and they were treating Wolfensohn like an ATM machine. The World Bank—Wolfensohn's Bank—was not going to take this quietly.

Wolfensohn could hardly refuse to contribute to the bailouts. The IMF clearly lacked the resources to stem investor panic by itself, and the World Bank was needed to provide reinforcement. When the Treasury demanded $2 billion for Korea in December, Wolfensohn fumed that this was "the wrong way to go about dealing with the Bank," and that if he was asked for another $2 billion he would "have to fight it." But he knew he had to come up with the cash anyway, since "otherwise we will be blamed for the crisis."[23] To assuage his sense of helplessness, Wolfensohn created a special financial task force that operated outside the matrix; it was given a large budget and a hierarchical command, in the hope that it could match the IMF's performance. At a management retreat in early January 1998, Wolfensohn berated his staff for allocating just $10 million to the new financial team; he wanted to spend double that, triple that, but he damn well wanted excellence; "I'm entitled to be a bastard," he proclaimed viciously.[24] But the lavishly financed SWAT team turned out to be a failure. It was resented by the rest of the Bank; it was assembled too quickly to be good; and it failed to throw off the

Bank's ponderous culture. At one point David Lipton, the U.S. Treasury official who had adored the Bank on Bosnia, asked the SWAT team to come up with a plan for South Korea's foundering financial sector. He was told that this would take half a year, so he barely bothered to consult the Bank thereafter.

As a result, Wolfensohn increasingly fell back on the opposite strategy. Rather than seek a serious role in the crisis, he sought distance from the whole business. If the IMF wanted to play economic cop in Asia, well it was most welcome; the Bank had done more than enough of that sort of work during the structural adjustment of the 1980s. The new Bank—Wolfensohn's Bank—was a kinder, gentler outfit, beloved of NGOs. It cared about poverty, not bailouts.

The first weapon in this distancing strategy came in the form of Joe Stiglitz, the brilliant and mischievous future Nobel laureate who had joined the Bank as chief economist at the start of 1997. Stiglitz had helped to create a branch of economics that explained the failure of standard market assumptions; he was like a boy who discovers a hole in the floor of an exquisite house and keeps shouting and pointing at it. Never mind that the rest of the house is beautiful—that in nine out of ten cases, the usual laws of supply and demand *do* work; Stiglitz had found a hole, a real hole, and he had built his career on it. Naturally, this had consequences for the way he viewed the world. There is nothing more satisfying for the discoverers of holes than to watch ordinary fools tumble down them.

When the Asian crisis got under way, there was a lot of tumbling. The IMF, which had always annoyed Stiglitz by failing to incorporate his economic theory into its models, made a series of errors in the design of its bailouts. In Thailand the IMF mistakenly urged high interest rates and cuts in government spending, on the theory that tough anti-inflation policies were needed to keep yet more investors from dumping the currency; as a result, Thailand's subsequent recession was worse than it needed to be. In Indonesia the IMF had embarrassed

itself again when its attempt to stabilize the banks had instead precipitated a bank run. In South Korea the IMF had put together a bailout
that was too small to turn investor sentiment around, so that a second
rescue had to be thrown together three weeks later.

Stiglitz could not contain his glee. He lambasted the IMF, focusing
particularly on two errors that resonated with the veterans of the Fifty
Years Is Enough campaign, who regarded both the IMF and the World
Bank as pushers of free-market dogma that harmed poor people. He
made much of the fact that IMF-prescribed austerity in Thailand had
bankrupted local companies, throwing people out of work, and he frequently implied that the IMF economists were too blinkered to realize
that this might happen. This last insinuation was utterly preposterous.
The IMF had indeed pressed too much austerity on Thailand and then
later reversed course, but it was slanderous to suggest that the IMF's
policy makers didn't know that raising interest rates could lead to bankruptcies. The point was that *not* raising interest rates could accelerate
capital flight and deepen a currency's collapse—and therefore trigger
even more bankruptcies.

Stiglitz's second target was the removal of capital controls, which he
presented as an IMF-prescribed free-market doctrine that laid countries open to speculative attack and made financial crisis possible. Again,
Stiglitz was mixing a reasonable point with unreasonable hyperbole. It
was true that currency speculators could be a destabilizing force, and that
the IMF had advocated the liberalization of the capital account with
the backing of the U.S. Treasury. But open capital flows often enabled
countries to grow faster than they could when relying solely on domestic
savings to finance investment, and the idea that all capital liberalization
reflected recent IMF advice was wrong: Indonesia, for instance, had
opened up at the start of the 1970s. Besides, speculative capital flows
were not the cause of economic crises; they were merely the trigger. In
the Indonesian case, the root cause of the collapse lay in large piles of
dollar debt coupled with rotten banks and a cronyistic government.

Nevertheless, Stiglitz talked as though the IMF was run by idiots. Wolfensohn allowed him to sound off to the press, blackening the IMF's name just when its crisis-fighting reputation was most precious. From time to time Wolfensohn would rein him in, but then Stiglitz would charge off again, and it was hard to avoid the conclusion that Wolfensohn was quite pleased about his pugilistic rudeness. The boss couldn't say those things himself, of course; and he found it upsetting when his underling got more media coverage than he did; but he privately relished the humiliation of the Bank's humiliators. Larry Summers and Stan Fischer were acting all superior; they were costing him altitude on the vast ladder that is Washington. Well, these white-hat, wise-guy, world savers weren't doing all that well! Let Stiglitz whack them off their pedestals![25]

The second part of Wolfensohn's distancing strategy was the one that animated his visit to Jakarta in February 1998. After the IMF's mission the previous October, the Treasury had strong-armed him into contributing to the bailout, and Wolfensohn had been in no position to prevent the World Bank from being treated like a piggy bank. But he soon came up with a rhetorical counterpunch: the Bank's billions, he proclaimed, would not be used merely to prop up Indonesia's currency; they would be used to fight the jump in poverty that accompanied the crisis. There was not much substance to this rhetoric, since all money flowing to the Indonesian government would help to prop up the exchange rate, and all money (even money from the cold-eyed IMF) would mitigate cuts in social spending.[26] But as a public-relations strategy, the Bank's poverty-fighting line sounded just right. Wolfensohn would go to Indonesia and show how much he cared about the poor. He would not stand over Suharto, his arms folded and his look frosty.[27]

For the purposes of this positioning, Dennis de Tray was a problem. It was one thing when de Tray's thinking had lagged Wolfensohn's anticorruption pronouncements in 1996; the boss was too distracted to care much. Now, by an irony, de Tray's view of corruption had caught up; but his eagerness to help design the IMF's bailouts did not fit with the distancing tactic. The way de Tray and his colleagues saw it, the world's fourth-most-populous nation was collapsing before their eyes, and they were working seven days a week to help; the question of the Bank's image, let alone Wolfensohn's standing, seemed of secondary importance. They soon had to adjust their glasses. On Wolfensohn's first evening in Jakarta, after that devastating greeting to de Tray at the airport, a few of the Bank's Jakarta staff gathered with him and Elaine in their hotel room.

"What shall I tell the press?" the boss demanded. He wanted to know which loans he could point to that were tackling poverty.

His staff answered that the Bank's lending was largely directed at macroeconomic stabilization, even though no such stabilization had materialized. There was a loan to promote trade liberalization, they ventured. There was another to reform the banking sector.

"I can't tell the bloody press that these reforms are being financed by our money!" Wolfensohn shouted. "I've got to tell them we're buying medicines, food for the poor, that's what I need to say!"

However terrifying his style, Wolfensohn's instincts were right. Jakarta's press—not to mention Jakarta's nongovernmental organizations—was ready to go after him, and he needed the best talking points possible. The World Bank had lent $25 billion to Suharto, and a chunk of that had found its way into the pockets of cronies; now a multiplying band of Indonesians wanted the Bank to answer for its record. The Bank's Jakarta office had arranged an NGO meeting for Wolfensohn the following morning, and it was expecting a large crowd; a chance to sock it to the World Bank president was irresistible, and the whole of dissident Jakarta would be in attendance. Wolfensohn demanded to know how the meeting room would be laid out, and the chief organizer told him that he had planned a cocktail-party format. The visitors would be free to mill about the reception room and greet him in person.

"You fucking idiot!" Wolfensohn bellowed.

The next morning the organizers rose early. They set out chairs in rows, replacing the cocktail concept with an auditorium-style layout, and erected a rope cordon to separate their boss from his critics. There were not enough seats for everyone, so some of the press was sent off to an overflow room down the corridor that was equipped with a video hookup.

Wolfensohn appeared on the safe side of the cordon at eight o'clock that morning, fighting a head cold but looking grimly determined. He'd lived by a principle since his years in investment banking: if you have enemies out there, talk to them.[28] There was a standard recipe for these encounters: Acknowledge your adversary's grievance, offer some plea in mitigation, and then get him above all to focus on a happier future, in which deals could be done and progress could be made if old grievances were buried. Wolfensohn stood up there behind his cordon and conceded the Bank's errors. The Bank had "got it wrong," he said; it had been too impressed by Indonesia's apparent miracle and too quiet about its corruption. Wolfensohn then pointed to the Bank's concern for poverty amid the collapse of the rupiah. The Bank had prepared one loan, he declared, to address potential food shortages. Finally Wolfensohn switched the focus to Indonesia's prospects. "You can whip me later and say I'm a fool," he concluded, "but let's find a solution to the crisis."

Wolfensohn was doing well, considering the challenge he'd been given. On earlier stops during this trip, in Thailand and Malaysia, he and his entourage had been charged by aggressive audiences and then photographed; their faces would appear in the papers the next day, looking fearful and hostile. But now the last-minute rope cordon was performing its function, and Wolfensohn looked sympathetic. After an hour and a half or so, the meeting drew to a finish. Wolfensohn said good-bye, walked off the podium and out into the hotel corridor accompanied by Elaine, the two of them thinking the worst was behind him. But the worst turned out to be ahead of them; in fact, it was coming straight at them. The press pack from the overflow room was crashing down the passageway, cutting off the route to the exit. Ben Fisher, the number two in the Jakarta office, who had played football in college, moved in front of the Wolfensohns to block the attackers; Mark Malloch Brown, Wolfensohn's giant communications supremo, got into position; and the hotel manager appeared from somewhere. The gang pushed ahead into the press pack, ducking to avoid the heavy cameras that threatened bodily damage. In the next few minutes, Ben Fisher was knocked over, but the Wolfensohns made it through the scrum. It was still not yet ten in the morning.[29]

For the next few hours, Wolfensohn made the rounds of the technocrats in the government and the business community. The program went tolerably, and the trip organizers were regaining some of their composure, and then the Wolfensohns climbed into a bus with freezing air-conditioning, an exhausting contrast with the heat outside. The bus headed off toward a slum on the northern edge of Jakarta, and the Wolfensohns sat with a deputy mayor, who was urging them in faltering English to appreciate the city sites as they drove by them. The Indonesians had arranged, in their fashion, for a supply of fried snacks, and the Bank staff was trying to keep them from being pressed on the Wolfensohns too insistently; the heavy food and freezing air-conditioning and enervating tour guide were all mixing together. The Wolfensohns wanted to know what this trip's purpose was. Well, it was to visit a public-works project, the staff explained; but the Wolfensohns wanted to know more. How could they be sure that the project was not corrupt? Did its beneficiaries include women? The deputy mayor was saying "yes, yes, yes," and not answering the questions, and in the end somebody confessed that this was an Islamic community, and hiring women to do manual labor had proved problematic.

The bus squeezed over a bridge into the slum, and Wolfensohn's party climbed out into the steamy sunlight. They inspected the canal, where people were digging noxious black sludge out of the channel, and the mayor gave a speech, and the World Bankers noticed that he had invited the press to be there. Ben Fisher, the old football player who had been knocked over earlier that morning, eyed the TV cameras warily, but no disasters happened; the speech finished, and Wolfensohn had his chance to showcase the Bank's efforts for the poor of Indonesia, and then he headed into the adjacent shanty. The paths were muddy, and they were thronged with curious people, and Wolfensohn visited two homes and got talking to the people there, and then he emerged into the shanty's narrow alleyways. Again the press stampeded him, and again Ben Fisher got shoved over, and this time Elaine was knocked off her feet into the mud, and Dennis de Tray got pushed about also.

Despite the muddy suits, the trip to the canal project served its purpose. The boss had been photographed handing out a living wage to slum dwellers; he had distinguished himself vividly from the International Monetary Fund. But the trip to the slum also brought home another point. Indonesia's security forces, which had once controlled the press ferociously, were now nowhere to be seen; the regime's grip was failing. You could sense the exuberance among the dissidents as they filed into the anonymous hotel banquet hall that morning; you could feel the amazement of these slum dwellers, who had never before witnessed a media circus like this one.[30] Indonesia was on the verge of an unfamiliar freedom. The World Bank, which for years had cultivated Suharto, was entering uncharted territory.

THE CHAOS THAT had confronted Wolfensohn continued for weeks after his visit, culminating in Indonesia's strange semirevolution. In March and April, student protests spread gradually through the country; in early May, Suharto raised fuel prices by two-thirds; and a few days later the protests reached the sort of critical mass that can topple a regime that is already shaky. On the morning of May 14, Dennis de Tray and his colleagues were up in their offices on the twelfth floor of

Jakarta's stock exchange building, with a picture view of the city; they could see a plume of smoke rising in the distance. Twenty minutes later there was another plume, and pretty soon there were fires all across the skyline, although the golfers in the nearby driving range played on, oblivious. The World Bankers carried on answering e-mails and poring over spread sheets, but the noise of chanting began to rise from the streets twelve stories below them. Demonstrators were waving flags and shouting, and there were tanks out in the streets and shots coming from the nearby university. By early afternoon the golfers had vanished. When one World Banker heard that his son's school was encircled by rioters, de Tray gave the order that people should go home if home was safe. That night one of the Bank's Indonesian secretaries called her boss: a mob was burning her neighbor's house down.[31]

Two days later the World Bankers evacuated Jakarta, and on May 21, 1998, Suharto announced his resignation. There was a certain symbolism to this. When it came time for its star client to leave office, the World Bank had itself left Indonesia. But there was also symbolism in the whereabouts of de Tray, who refused to abandon the country despite screamed orders from his French vice president in Washington. De Tray was not a man for the distancing tactic, and in the months after Suharto's departure he stuck to his guns, determined to help a country in which one in four citizens—fully 50 million people—risked falling back into poverty. As soon as Suharto's successor appointed a new economic team, de Tray got on the radio to praise it, again risking the Bank's reputation for the sake of an Indonesian government. But Suharto's successor was B. J. Habibie, a prize crony who had been vice president before, and it was not at all clear whether his arrival would reduce corruption. De Tray's outspokenness got him called back to Washington for a stern lecture.

The Bank, of course, was vilified from all sides for having backed Suharto. In July the *Wall Street Journal* published a long attack on the Bank's collaboration with the dictator, charging that the Asian crisis was just as much a crisis for the Bank as for Indonesia.[32] In August, the Bank's memo on corruption, which de Tray had commissioned one year earlier, was leaked to the *Journal*, which flailed the Bank all over again;[33] the staff in Jakarta felt they were suffering "death by *Wall Street Journal*," in the words of one rueful official.[34] Meanwhile 112 NGOs from thirty-one countries seized upon the leaked corruption memo to fire off a joint letter to Wolfensohn, demanding more details about corruption in Bank projects. The top managers in Washington were furious; de Tray had never told them what was in the memo, and his relations with headquarters grew even more disastrous. Still he did not change his methods. In September, he had an audience with President Habibie and reported back to Washington: "The meeting was fascinating. An hour and a half, a quarter of a kilo of chocolates, only the two of us," he wrote, apparently unaware that there would be demonstrations three days later calling for Habibie's resignation.[35]

The World Bank limped on, and Wolfensohn was apoplectic. If the Bank's octopus bureaucracy had only paid attention to his cancer of corruption speech, it could have corrected its stance before the financial crisis overtook it. Now, because nobody had listened to him, the Bank looked sleazy; how could this happen, after he had vowed to be the leading sleaze buster? Even more galling, the IMF was getting all the credit for tackling Suharto's cronies by busting up the garlic and clove monopolies; the cold-eyed cops had stolen the Bank's idea—Wolfensohn's idea—and the kinder, gentler Bank wasn't getting love from anyone.[36] Women in Islamic dress had staged pro-IMF demonstrations; they had been out there with placards reading, IMPLEMENT THE IMF PACKAGE![37] In the weeks after Suharto's fall, the IMF mission chief would sometimes go to a coffee shop in the shopping center that adjoined his hotel. There'd be a hush as people recognized him, and then strangers would approach shyly and shower him with thanks. The Bank, by contrast, was forced to send out two teams from Washington with orders to get the corruption stance right; but the NGOs in Jakarta and Washington could smell a damage-control exercise, and the Bank's reputation did not recover. On the final day of one mission, a Bank official was ferried to the wrap-up meeting by an Indonesian driver. When the driver learned that the purpose of the trip was to discuss fighting corruption with a corrupt Habibie official, he had to pull over: he was so convulsed with laughter that he could no longer drive straight.[38]

It took three things to rescue the Bank from the corruption quicksand. By early 1999, Indonesia's financial storm had calmed, ending the pressure to pump money into the country no matter how corrupt it might be. Then at the end of March, Dennis de Tray left, and his successor had no compunction about distancing the Bank from this country.[39] But the third factor in the Bank's recovery was the most interesting, and it said much about the direction of the institution under Wolfensohn. An anthropologist in the Jakarta office had grappled with the tension between those dual development instincts—the urge to cede "ownership" to the client on the one hand, and the urge to advance cleaner government on the other—and he had figured out a way to do both at once.

THE ANTHROPOLOGIST was called Scott Guggenheim, and his premise was simple: The client need not be the government. The Bank's real clients are the poor people of a country; it should be close to them and cede "ownership" to them; and there is no tension between that and fighting government corruption. On the contrary, corruption hurts the poor, and the poor are the real clients, so the Bank has a duty to push for cleaner government. In fact, Guggenheim argued, fighting corruption is not merely something the Bank should do. It is *the* thing the Bank should do, since responsibility for most other aspects of development can be handed over to the borrowers. It is villagers who should decide if they need a bridge or a clinic or an irrigation channel; once they have decided, they can hire contractors to deliver. The Bank's role is not to ponder what to build or how to build it. It is to create the institutions that allow poor clients to choose for themselves, without having their money ripped off by a crony-ridden system.

Guggenheim's views were more radical than anything Wolfensohn said about corruption. The boss had rightly shattered a taboo, ending the fear of violating the Bank's charter by straying into politics. But Guggenheim wasn't just straying into politics; he was marching right into the forbidden territory, and saying that politics was all that mattered. After arriving in Indonesia in 1994, he had studied the country's local government system, and concluded that it was designed to prevent the poor from getting the development projects they needed. Power in the village resided with the village chief, whose job depended on the approval of a district chief, who in turn reported to the center; given this top-down government machinery, it was not surprising that powerless people at the bottom got ripped off by corrupt district officials and their crony contractors. The key to real development, Guggenheim concluded, lay in changing Indonesia's system of local government—in building grassroots democratic institutions under the feet of a dictator.[40]

In ordinary circumstances, an anthropologist's ideas might have gone nowhere. But these were not ordinary circumstances, and Guggenheim himself was not ordinary either. From the moment that he arrived in Indonesia, he had doubted the macroeconomists' talk of a development miracle, observing that the villages that he visited across the Indonesian archipelago looked little different from the ones he had studied in Latin America. If the macroeconomists would not believe him, well they could come and trek the countryside with him; he once hauled Dennis de Tray off on a tour of West Java, and every village they visited had a schoolhouse that was falling down because corrupt contractors had pocketed the cash that had been meant for durable materials. If the macrofolks still failed to get the message, well then Guggenheim was willing to go public. He freely admitted that he was one of the people who had told Jeffrey Winters that around 30 percent of Bank loans were being lost to corruption; and a year later he was quoted in the *Wall Street Journal* saying that the Bank had never conducted a proper study of corruption for fear that it might leak. Not long afterward, the Bank's corruption memo did leak—and most people assumed that Guggenheim was part of the reason.

With the fall of Suharto, Guggenheim's difficulty in getting the Bank to face up to corruption was effectively over. For the sake of Indonesians and for the sake of its own reputation, the Bank needed a way of getting money into the country without going through the rotten government, and by this time Guggenheim had turned his field research into a project that did exactly that. Starting in 1998, Guggenheim had begun making grants of up to $110,000 (small sums, by World Bank standards) to subdistrict councils, choosing this level of government precisely because it was unencumbered by an existing budget system that was inevitably corrupt. Villages in each subdistrict were invited to propose uses for the money; it could be for anything they thought would promote development. But although Guggenheim did not mind *what* they spent the money on, he cared passionately about *how* they spent it. They had to get competitive bids from at least three suppliers, and read them out in public at a village meeting; then when the supplies were delivered, a monitoring committee had to count the planks or bricks as they were unloaded, thereby eliminating a venerable method of ripping people off. Of course, corruption is hard to root out in a society with no strong independent media. So Guggenheim's scheme included a grant to the Independent Journalists' Association (even though this group was formally banned under Suharto), and the association used the money to send reporters to the villages that received World Bank money.

In its first year, in 1998, Guggenheim's project involved thirty-five hundred villages. Three years later, after the Bank had seized on Guggenheim as its guide out of the quicksand, fifteen thousand villages were included, and the project accounted for fully half the Bank's lending to Indonesia. The Kecamatan Development Project, as Guggenheim's creation was formally entitled, became the largest community development project in Southeast Asia, and an important sign of the World Bank's transformation. The Bank had started out in the 1940s and 1950s by building physical capital. Then in the 1960s, it had latched onto the new idea of "human capital." Now in the 1990s, the Bank was building "social capital"—it was teaching the poor how to hold meetings, make decisions, and have their voices heard. This latest thrust was not without its troubles, as we shall presently discover. But the conundrum of Indonesia's corruption had pushed Wolfensohn's institution to a surprising new frontier.

In February 2000, when Guggenheim's project was expanding at full throttle, Wolfensohn returned for a third time to Indonesia. The Bank's stance had been transformed by the new country director, who had slashed traditional lending to the government, and the Bank's reputation was starting to recover. Wolfensohn could feel the difference; at last the cancer of corruption speech was being taken seriously, and his meeting with Indonesian NGOs this time was spirited but not bitter. A few demonstrators threw eggs at him, but this was nothing compared to the experience of the previous visit; they had kindly soft-boiled the eggs beforehand and they lobbed them underarm. After the NGO meeting, Wolfensohn set off out into the countryside and visited a village; he spent a couple of hours chatting in the home of a local dignitary, eating glutinous snacks and showing an interest in the local weaving; then he and Elaine went off to another house right there in the village to spend the night. It was the weekend home of a member of Parliament, but still pretty simple, and the villagers brought bedding and a basic meal before the Wolfensohns retired. After three visits to Indonesia, Wolfensohn was at last connecting. He was right out there in the countryside, staying with the local people, rubbing shoulders with the Bank's true clients. He was spending a night in a village, surrounded by the real Indonesia.

The World Bank's Jakarta staff, which remembered the disasters of the previous visit, had not taken any chances. The "villagers" who looked after the Wolfensohns had been hired from the local Sheraton hotel. The sheets that they slept in had been brought in specially. And the meal that they ate had been prepared for them with carefully boiled water.[41]

CHAPTER EIGHT

UGANDA'S MYTH
AND MIRACLE

IN THE FIRST YEARS of his presidency, Wolfensohn had tried to fix the Bank's external reputation and its internal management structure. He had reached out to NGO critics; he had impressed his shareholders with a show of dynamism in the Balkans; he had launched the matrix-management reforms. From late 1997, however, Wolfensohn's attention shifted. The dialogue with NGOs was losing its novelty; the fast progress of Bosnia's early reconstruction was slowing; the management reforms were beset with frustrations. More to the point, the Asian financial crisis, which spread to Russia in the first half of 1998 and then to Brazil in the second half, forced Wolfensohn to fight for oxygen. So long as currency crises dominated the global agenda, the International Monetary Fund would keep shoving him under. It would design rescue packages in concert with the U.S. Treasury, then expect the World Bank to devote a large slice of its resources to supporting its bailouts.

In February 1998, when Wolfensohn embarked on his trip to Indonesia and the region's other crisis countries, he thought he had figured out the right response. He would position the Bank as the fighter against poverty, leaving the IMF to worry about exchange rates and other technocratic stuff. But as the crisis spread beyond Asia into Russia, the pressure grew relentless. Having strong-armed the Bank into promising $1.5 billion for Thailand, $4.5 billion for Indonesia, and an extraordinary $10 billion for South Korea, in July 1998, the IMF demanded a further $6 billion for Russia. It was an "outrageous thing for Camdessus to do," Wolfensohn exploded at one management meeting; the IMF's chief had simply informed the Bank of the sum that would be needed, intimating that if Wolfensohn refused he would be assuming the responsibility for Russia's implosion. "The simple fact is that we didn't have a choice," Wolfensohn fumed bitterly. His whole agenda seemed at risk of suffocation. The Bank was supposed to be focusing on long-term development, but it was being used as a provider of short-term rescue funds. "It is a lunatic position for us to be put in," Wolfensohn declared.[1]

From the summer of 1998, Wolfensohn began to plot a whole different level of counterattack. He would not merely assert the Bank's poverty-fighting role in Indonesia and the other crisis countries; he would make a global case for it. He had arrived in his job against the background of the Madrid annual meetings, and he was convinced that the Bank had to distance itself from structural-adjustment-style macroeconomic prescriptions if it was ever to make peace with its critics. All his instincts told him that a narrow macroeconomic focus was a mistake in any case; noneconomic factors like corruption were essential to development. Moreover, if Wolfensohn did not resist the IMF's endless demands for bailout money, the Bank would soon be lending beyond its prudential limits; "I'm not going to be the one who endangers the AAA credit rating of the Bank," he vowed grimly at one point. All these factors pointed in the same direction. Financial crises were pushing Wolfensohn away from his poverty-fighting mission. Everything depended on his ability to fight back.

And so Wolfensohn conceived an extraordinary ambition. If financial crises were dominating the world's agenda, the world's agenda would have to be altered. Presidents and prime ministers would have to be told that financial contagion was not the only thing that mattered; the structural and social causes of poverty—corruption, illiteracy, broken-down health systems—mattered just as much. The IMF was welcome to its role of macroeconomic policeman; but equally the Bank should be allowed to play *its* role of long-term development strategist. Two decades earlier, the onset of the second oil shock had buried McNamara's poverty agenda and dragged the Bank into structural adjustment. In 1998, facing a similarly hostile environment, Wolfensohn was determined to change the environment before the environment changed him.

In a conversation in September, Wolfensohn told Michel Camdessus that he planned to use the October annual meetings to assert the relevance of long-term development. The IMF's boss was dismissive; the world's presidents and finance ministers would never care about such issues, Camdessus insisted.[2] But in the period leading up to the annual meetings, Wolfensohn and his team read the political winds differently. The IMF's track record in policing the financial crisis was studded with failures, and the pressure on the institution was mounting.

"There is gathering momentum for fundamental change at the Fund," observed Mark Malloch Brown, Wolfensohn's communications supremo, at a meeting with Wolfensohn in September. He cited that morning's *Washington Post* column by Jim Hoagland, which called for a rethinking of the IMF in light of its failures in East Asia and Russia. If there was a broad push for a restructuring of the Bretton Woods institutions, Malloch Brown suggested, the Bank stood a good chance of emerging on top.

Wolfensohn seemed to like this possibility. "Michel is becoming incredibly difficult," he responded. "He is very uptight, on a very short fuse."

Joe Stiglitz, the Bank's chief economist who had spent much of the past year lambasting the IMF, chimed in that the Fund had compounded its difficulties by refusing to admit its obvious errors.

"Like Bill Clinton," said Wolfensohn, referring to the president's denials of the Monica Lewinsky affair.

"Stan Fischer doesn't accept the fundamental political point that they have to admit that they are wrong, engage their critics, and fundamentally change," Malloch Brown added, referring to the IMF's deputy managing director. The implied contrast with Wolfensohn's determination to go out and embrace the Bank's critics could not have been more obvious, and nobody in that meeting doubted that the IMF was making a mistake.[3] Perhaps this meant an opportunity? If Wolfensohn stood up and proclaimed the Bank's poverty-fighting mandate, the contrast with the IMF's austerity prescriptions might win the Bank some sympathy. And sympathy—if it went broad enough or high enough—might make it harder for the IMF and the U.S. Treasury to treat the World Bank like an ATM machine.

As the annual meetings approached, Brazil's currency came under attack from financial speculators, and there was talk of yet another IMF bailout. Wolfensohn's fears over the Bank's stretched lending capacity were rekindled, and a week before the annual meetings he told his senior managers that he was prepared for "war" with the IMF. At the same time, however, Wolfensohn insisted that not a word of this rivalry should leak to the newspapers.[4] Direct attacks on the fund were straining the patience of the Clinton Treasury, which was not surprising: financial bailouts work only if they instill confidence, and Stiglitz's loud carping about the IMF's prescriptions was a confidence killer. The fight with the fund should therefore be kept private. Wolfensohn would use his setpiece address to the annual meetings to emphasize the Bank's antipoverty role in crises; and he would draw the link to his larger view of human progress. Swipes against the IMF would be confined to the subtext.

For anyone who knew Wolfensohn's mind-set, however, the subtext was obvious. "While we talk of financial crisis, 17 million Indonesians have fallen back into poverty," Wolfensohn lectured, mischievously implying that the IMF's focus on Asian exchange rates came at the expense of focusing on real people; "while we talk of financial crisis, an estimated 40 percent of the Russian population now lives in poverty." Across the world, Wolfensohn continued, 3 billion live on under $2 a day; 1.3 billion have no access to clean water; 2 billion have no access to power. "We talk of financial crisis while in Jakarta, in Moscow, in sub-Saharan Africa, in the slums of India, and the barrios of Latin America, the human pain of poverty is all around us," Wolfensohn declared.

What to do about this? Well, Wolfensohn continued, IMF-style macroeconomic stabilization was not enough. The world needed to confront inequality and social exclusion, to think about corruption and institutions and governance. Without social justice there could be no political stability, and without political stability no financial rescue package could succeed. The IMF's bailouts depended—indeed, global stability depended—on the World Bank's efforts to keep school attendance from falling, to keep medicines in the clinics. "We must learn to have a debate where mathematics will not dominate humanity," said Wolfensohn, sounding remarkably like a structural-adjustment critic from the Fifty Years Is Enough campaign. Only then would the world arrive at a solution that served not just the denizens of Wall Street but the poor as well.

If macroeconomics was only part of the answer, what was the other part? Wolfensohn gave an answer that reflected the lessons from the failure of structural adjustment, and his preoccupation with political processes in countries from Mali to Indonesia. Development would be sustainable only if it included political and institutional progress; and it must advance on all fronts. Roads, education, legal reform, women's emancipation, corruption fighting, a sound banking system, environmental protection, child inoculation: all were essential. In the absence of a silver bullet, only a broad war on poverty could help the Ugandan woman he remembered, who baked green banana skins into charcoal briquettes. "Mr. Chairman," Wolfensohn declared portentously, "we need a new development framework."

Wolfensohn's speech attracted modest attention in the following day's headlines. The world was understandably more interested in Brazil's immediate instability than in Wolfensohn's musings about long-run "holistic" development. But Wolfensohn did not give up quietly. He recruited a special adviser to assist him in fleshing out this new development framework that he had announced so boldly,[5] and on December 16, he convened a meeting of country directors who had agreed to experiment with new approaches. Then he left for Jackson Hole a few days later, saying he would commit his latest thinking to paper.

Wolfensohn's lieutenants never expected him to sit still long enough to write anything, but the boss surprised them. That winter in Wyoming, he found time for the usual skiing and socializing, time to enjoy the wine cellar and the breakfast pancakes, time to gaze out at the mountains on the far side of the Snake River, which rise out of the flat valley like the teeth of a dinosaur. But his mind was whirring, and by the end of his vacation he had filled the yellow pages of a legal pad with a six-thousand-word essay.[6] Over the past three and a half years as World Bank president, he had visited eighty-four countries and had seen hundreds of projects, and now he was putting it all together, laying out the grand challenge for the Bank and saying how it should be tackled, imposing an intellectual order on this bewildering mission. At the start of January 1999, when Wolfensohn returned to Washington, he handed the sheaves of yellow paper to his staff for typing. The new development framework, announced as a rhetorical flourish in his speech at the World Bank's annual meetings, had become a formal, capitalized New Development Framework. Selling it became his central passion over the course of the next year.

The battle that ensued took Wolfensohn through a series of unexpected showdowns. The framework was derided, ignored, and then ultimately embraced by all the world's big aid givers. How this happened—how Wolfensohn got his way, as he had done on debt relief and the Strategic Compact—is the subject of the next chapter. But it would be hard to understand this outcome without first considering Uganda, the most influential development model of the 1990s.

UP UNTIL THE PREVIOUS DECADE, Uganda had symbolized all Africa's disasters. It had gained independence from Britain in 1962, the year after Wolfensohn's visit to Nigeria, and its mix of vibrant Asian businesses and natural agricultural potential promised a bright future. But politics soon stifled that. In 1966, Prime Minister Milton Obote abolished the country's liberal constitution, and five years later Obote was ousted in a coup by Idi Amin, the high priest of bad African dictators, who was said to store the heads of enemies in a freezer at his residence and place them round his dinner table periodically for an evening chat. Amin expelled Uganda's Asians, and with them much of its economy; he unleashed a reign of terror in which anywhere from one hundred thousand to five hundred thousand people died. After Amin's fall in 1979, three short-lived governments imploded quickly, and then Milton Obote returned and presided over more dictatorial mayhem. In the years from Amin's arrival to Obote's second departure—years when the income of the average Indonesian doubled—Uganda suffered an economic, social, and spiritual collapse.

Uganda's fortunes changed with the arrival of Yoweri Museveni, an army officer who seized power in 1986. At first he looked no more promising than his predecessors; he had learned his economics in socialist Tanzania, and he had come to power by force. But after his early economic policies backfired, he changed course abruptly, and from the late 1980s onward he pursued a market-based agenda with increasing conviction. The absurdly high official exchange rate was abolished in favor of the black-market-driven one; coffee prices were liberalized; the president declared that "inflation is indiscipline," and from 1992 onward inflation was duly tamed. Uganda changed from an economy with few incentives to produce much to quite the opposite environment; and through thousands of small decisions taken in hundreds of different towns and villages, the result was a burst of economic energy. Coffee was the most dramatic example. By liberalizing coffee marketing, Museveni made it possible for poor farmers to retain as much as 65 to 80 percent of export proceeds, compared with 30 percent previously. Not surprisingly, coffee output blossomed, and the newly liberalized system had the effect of transferring nearly $100 million directly into poor farmers' pockets between 1991 and 1997.[7] By 1997, moreover, the average income of Uganda's 20 million people had shot up by two-fifths in the decade since Museveni's policy reversal. In 2000, the results of a new household survey showed that the share of Uganda's population living in poverty had plummeted from 56 percent to 35 percent in the space of eight years.

This success alone would have been enough to instate Uganda as a development role model. Around the world, one could point to plenty of success stories: in the decade following Museveni's policy reversal, China lifted some 90 million people out of poverty, and the rest of East Asia reduced poverty by another 50 million. But this kind of success, indeed any success, was rare in Africa, where poverty rose by 70 million over the same period.[8] Uganda's achievement—Asian Tiger growth rates that cut poverty by two-fifths in less than a decade—suggested that it had some kind of magic potion. If the magic could be analyzed and replicated, perhaps Africa's postindependence misery could be relieved at last.

The truth was that, in the early 1990s, there was nothing very exotic about Uganda's supposed magic potion. Museveni's government had followed the standard structural-adjustment prescription of controlling public spending in order to tame inflation and devaluing the exchange rate in order to boost exports. But by the mid-1990s, when potion seekers started to show up in Uganda, the potion had started to evolve. The very fact of Uganda's success was attracting development types from all over: aid missions from rich northern governments, big NGOs like World Vision and Oxfam, development professors from the famous universities, not to mention the UN agencies and the Bretton Woods sisters. Each visitor brought a flagon of his own potion: Oxfam wanted to turn Uganda into a showcase for debt relief; the World Bank pressed privatization; the United Nations Development Program sponsored an experiment to decentralize government. Pretty soon, everybody's potion was mixing with everybody else's, and Uganda became a blend of all the fashionable ideas about development. Of course, this made it still more fashionable. If there is one thing that the development experts love more than a success, it is a success that reflects their own brilliant advice.

In June 1995, when Wolfensohn visited Uganda on his first trip as World Bank president, he brought some of his own potion along. He believed that the Bank should listen to its clients, like Linda McGinnis did in Mali, and so he went out and visited President Museveni on his cattle ranch, and Museveni wowed him by grabbing one beast by the horns and declaring that this was the great-great-granddaughter of a cow he had tended as a child.[9] Wolfensohn also believed that the Bank should listen to civil-society groups, so he held a meeting with Oxfam and its colleagues in the local NGO movement, sending a signal to the Bank's Kampala office that it should do more listening in future. And he believed that the Bank should focus directly on poverty, so he visited the industrial slum of Katwe. A year later, when an Oxfam worker was touring that same shantytown, steeling herself against the smell of human excrement and the sight of wasting AIDS patients, she walked into a home and saw a large photo of the World Bank president stuck up on the filthy wall.[10]

Wolfensohn's instincts amounted to a novel deference: a willingness to listen to Africa's governments and NGOs and slum dwellers. It was the reverse of his instincts on Indonesia, where the Bank's deference was excessive and Wolfensohn's lecturing side came through. Just as

Indonesia's growth had prompted the Bank's fawning, so Africa's failures had bred the opposite: as the continent racked up one disappointment after another, the Bank responded by attaching ever more conditions to its lending—injunctions to cut spending, free prices, devalue the currency. As we have seen already, there wasn't much wrong with the economics of these structural-adjustment conditions, but the politics were awful: African governments were too weak to implement the tough policies that the conditions demanded. By the time Wolfensohn arrived, it was clear to him that the Bank needed to stop lecturing and start listening: to understand what was politically feasible, and to help bring it about.

If Wolfensohn's instincts had been shocking or original, they might not have altered anything, much as his views on corruption failed to change the Bank's stance on Indonesia until the financial crisis proved him right. But, in the case of Uganda, Wolfensohn's instincts matched those of the man who was about to become the Bank's key front-line operator, a laid-back natural listener whose name was Jim Adams. The way Adams conducted himself did not scream "PhD" or "expert" at you; he seemed cozy and approachable; he looked like an average American baseball fan, which indeed he was. Once or twice during his years in Uganda, he lost his temper with Museveni and started yelling and banging on the table about excess military spending, and Museveni roared back at him, shouting that he would not take advice on national security from a mere cook—a reference to Adams's position as a reservist in the U.S. Army. But Adams could have these fights because he had spent a long time listening. Museveni knew this cook respected him, and that they would discuss everything rationally when they both calmed down.[11]

Adams became the Bank's director for East Africa on July 1, 1995, a few days after Wolfensohn's visit to Uganda; later that same month he flew to Paris to host a Uganda donors' conference. The fact that the donors chose to convene in Paris was scarcely remarked upon—this was the standard venue for discussing aid programs—but it was nonetheless revealing. The gathering would set the conditions for Uganda's aid over the next year or so, but it would not take place in the country whose policies were under discussion. Each time one of these "Consultative Group" meetings was scheduled, a small government delegation would make the journey from Kampala, but its members felt like visitors at their own party; and the Ugandan NGOs that mustered the travel budget to get there were allowed in only as observers.[12] In the early years after Museveni's takeover, the Consultative Group meetings involved just about no consultation with Ugandans. The brief statements from the government delegation were drafted by the World Bank.[13]

The big topic at that 1995 gathering in Paris was the extent of Uganda's poverty reduction. The long years of Amin and Obote had destroyed the country's statistical services as well as most of its infrastructure, so there were no data on whether Museveni's market reformism was relieving the misery of ordinary people.[14] The World Bank and the IMF believed that poverty must be receding, given Uganda's growth numbers; other people at the conference doubted that the tide was lifting everyone. The Dutch delegate suggested that there be a conference in her country to debate the issue, and Jim Adams saw an opening. There should certainly be a poverty conference, he responded. But it should be held not in Holland or any other first-world capital. It should be convened in Uganda; and it should be hosted not by the donors but by the Ugandan government.[15]

INTELLECTUAL HISTORY oozes forward, defying the search for precise chronological markers, but that moment in Paris was surely an inflection point. Just a few years earlier, at one of the Paris gatherings in the late 1980s, a Ugandan official had been taken aside by a World Bank counterpart and told he would be getting a foreign "adviser"—actually, an overseer who would ensure he followed the Bank's policies; when the Ugandan suggested that he didn't need such nannying, he was told he had no choice.[16] But now the Bank's new country director wanted Ugandans to take charge of their own poverty conference; and he wanted them to hold it in their country, so that NGOs and parliamentarians and village leaders could participate. The conference that followed began a shift in Uganda that culminated four years later in the paradoxical triumph of the ideas in Wolfensohn's participatory New Development Framework.

For both Wolfensohn and Adams, the idea that you should give Africans control and encourage NGO participation arose from the bitter experience with structural adjustment. The failure of weak governments to implement structural adjustment showed that the key blockage to development was not an absence of good policy prescriptions, but a lack of the political will needed to put good policy in place. At the same time, East Asia's leap from poverty had shown that somewhat unorthodox economic prescriptions could spur miraculous progress, provided that they were implemented skillfully; again, economic policies sometimes mattered less than the quality of the political institutions that delivered them. The fate of postcommunist Europe reinforced this message. When communism collapsed, better economic policy did not always bring quick benefits, because the institutional vacuum undermined reforms like privatization, allowing kleptocratic oligarchs to run off with national wealth. Again, the Bank was forced to learn the same lesson. Good policies are meaningless without good governments to implement them.

For development types like Adams, this conclusion raised a question—how to build good government? The more you pondered, the more you hurled Bank orthodoxies overboard, starting with the emphasis on aid conditionality. It was not merely that conditions were not working; it was that they undermined a government's sense of responsibility and therefore risked weakening it—the very *opposite* of the government building that development ought to be about.[17] The next orthodoxy to be discarded was the traditional wisdom on inclusive development planning. A large literature insisted that broad participation in the formation of policy reduced the odds of launching virtuous reforms, because groups with a vested interest in opposing change would freeze the system. But by the mid-1990s, the mere launching of virtuous reform no longer seemed to mean much. The real battle was to implement it, and anticipating opposition through broad consultation increased the chances of success.[18]

These were the intellectual factors behind Adams's radical impulse to hold a Ugandan poverty conference in Uganda, so that Ugandans would get the chance to form their own consensus on the way ahead. But there was also a personal factor—a hulking, hard-drinking hammer of a person, actually. Emmanuel Tumusiime-Mutebile, to give the hammer his full name, was the chief architect of Uganda's success story, and hence arguably the greatest contributor to Africa's struggle against poverty in his generation. He had grown up poor, the son of a school cook; and as a student leader in the early 1970s he had stood up and denounced Idi Amin's expulsion of Uganda's Asians, risking his life as he did so. He fled Uganda—disguised, legend has it, as an Asian—and was lucky enough to meet a British development economist in Kenya who recognized his intellect.[19] The economist arranged for Tumusiime to study under him at Durham University, and then after graduating to attend Balliol College, Oxford; and then in the late 1970s, Tumusiime moved to Tanzania, a center for Ugandan exiles. The combination of Balliol's drawing-room Marxism and Tanzania's self-destructive socialism drove Tumusiime to drop his youthful leftism and embrace the market.[20] After the fall of Amin he returned to Uganda, and by the time Jim Adams became the Bank's country director he was Uganda's reigning technocrat.

Adams was temperamentally a listener; but Tumusiime's character only reinforced that tendency. Tumusiime was tough and forthright and unafraid of donors; he frequently scolded the IMF's mission chief for the holes in his advice. At the periodic Consultative Group meetings in Paris, Tumusiime was sometimes the sole Ugandan leader to remain awake through the proceedings; he did not mind telling foreigners that their ideas were "stupid," and often he was right.[21] But even more important, by the mid-1990s Tumusiime had achieved the very thing that the Bank had come to crave most powerfully. He had taken a chaotic mess of a bureaucracy and created a machine that could drive good policy forward. The reforms that Uganda had undertaken—notably the liberalization of coffee prices, which had transformed the lives of many poor farmers—had sometimes begun as World Bank proposals. But none would have gone anywhere without Tumusiime's clout.[22]

There were two secrets to Tumusiime's achievement, besides his intellect. The first was his relationship with President Museveni, which had got off to a rough start. In Museveni's first year in office, when he believed he could command the economy as he had commanded his insurgent army, Tumusiime told him bluntly that his policies would backfire, and further that he was going to draw up a sane economic program for the president to implement when he saw the light.[23] Sure enough, Museveni's efforts to control the allocation of everything from foreign exchange to salt and sodas did backfire, and he did come to his senses, and he never forgot that Tumusiime had been right. From then on, Tumusiime generally won the big arguments on Uganda's economic direction. In 1992, after a period of rivalry between Tumusiime's Planning Ministry and the Ministry of Finance, Museveni merged the two departments and told the hammer to run the whole shebang.

Tumusiime's second secret was his lack of racial hang-ups. He knew he could hold his own in any argument, so he felt secure enough to welcome foreign economists into the country. Distinguished development professors visited Uganda regularly and had audiences with the president, and Tumusiime would sit back happily while the visitors gave tutorials to Museveni that reinforced his promarket advice.[24] Within

his own office, Tumusiime always had a team of young British economists working for him, even though Ugandan colleagues chided him:
"How can you open up the ministry to these foreigners?" they asked.
Tumusiime just laughed at them. What were the foreigners going to do
with the ministry? Walk off with the furniture?[25] On the contrary, it
was in the national interest to harness these hardworking outsiders,
whose salaries were paid by the World Bank and other donors. Indeed,
with the help of these foreigners, Tumusiime was training a cadre of
Ugandan technocrats—and the ones who showed promise were sent
off to the United States for training courses, often courtesy of the
World Bank. Little by little, Team Tumusiime grew in stature. Uganda
was at last acquiring competent government, the key ingredient of
development.

The character of Tumusiime's battles told you how profound this
change was. Until the early 1990s, Uganda had no real budget process;
government made promises and spent money in all directions without
adding up what it was doing or asking where the money might come
from. It took Team Tumusiime to fix this. By the mid-1990s public-
spending priorities were being weighed against projected revenues; the
tough choices were being hashed out by Museveni's cabinet; and the
technocrats even began to project expenditure several years ahead. Until
the 1990s, similarly, Uganda had no way to implement its budget
because it had no measure of its cash flow. Again, Tumusiime's technicians conquered chaos: They tracked monthly expenditures by monitoring the government's check-printing machine in the bowels of the
finance ministry, then they logged those numbers against revenues from
taxes and donors. Now, for the first time, the government could tell if it
was about to spend money it didn't have, forcing the central bank to
print it. For the first time, therefore, spending could be reined in to
forestall sudden inflation.[26] This was not a theoretical danger: in 1992,
before Team Tumusiime got a grip on Uganda's cash flow, inflation hit
an annualized rate of 200 percent.

These technical battles laid the foundations for development. If you don't know where your money's going, you can't even begin to discuss whether you should do more for clinics or for schooling or for rural transport. If you don't know how much you're spending, you can't hope to prevent triple-digit inflation. Thanks to Tumusiime's technicians, Uganda was transformed from a place where there was no hope of implementing good policy to a place where smart ideas could make a difference. And the architects of this miracle were still flying off to Paris to sit as junior partners with the donors? It took the World Bank of Jim Wolfensohn and Jim Adams to recognize how ridiculous this was.[27]

AFTER ADAMS'S DECISION to push for a poverty conference in Kampala, the Bank's relationship with Uganda began to change quickly. Museveni had been pestering the Bank for extra road-construction money, and the Bank had been protesting that the cash should go to education; but now Adams got his staff around the table and demanded to know why they were second-guessing the client. Hadn't the Bank learned that foisting unwanted loans upon borrowers was unlikely to produce development? How could the Bank expect African governments to implement reforms if they were not allowed to share responsibility for forming them? And what was wrong with Museveni's suggestion anyway? There was a good case to be made for rural road building, which would link poor farmers to markets, boosting their incomes and therefore their ability to pay school fees. If the Ugandans did not want money for education, was it wise to jam it down their throats?

One member of Adams's team pushed back at him. Just a few months ago, he noted, Uganda's finance minister had declared that he didn't want nine-tenths of the things in the Bank's lending program. It would take a mini-revolution to start delivering what the client wanted.

"How have we got into this situation?" Adams demanded. In just a few days, Museveni was due to meet Wolfensohn in New York, and

Museveni would complain that he'd been asking for roads for two years now, and Adams would have to explain why he hadn't got them. "I'll be sitting there with my boss Mr. Wolfensohn, who thinks most of us in the Bank need some educating, and he is going to say to me, 'Why the hell aren't you going to do what this obviously intelligent man is asking?'"

"So what are you going to say?" Adams's colleague demanded.

"I'm going to sit there, and I'm going to have to take it. I'm going to get my head clobbered!" Adams retorted. "I'm not going to say, I've got a bunch of jerks working for me who won't listen," he went on. "But I don't want to be in a situation twelve months from now where Mr. Museveni comes to me and says, 'Where the hell are my roads?'"[28]

A few days later President Museveni was sitting in a New York meeting room, a small man with a shiny pate who seemed lost in his huge leather armchair. Museveni began to make his case for road construction, and Adams and Wolfensohn listened. Soon Wolfensohn was promising that he personally needed no convincing on the importance of transport. The intelligent man started quoting "our friend" Mao Tse Tung, who taught that warriors must not dissipate their strength by punching in two directions simultaneously, and he was thrusting his fist into an imaginary adversary by way of emphasis. "In my previous job of fighting, I was used to prioritization," Museveni lectured. Roads and schools? Mao counseled otherwise. Roads and roads only? That would be better, because roads reduce poverty and then education follows. At the end of Museveni's lecture, Wolfensohn just grinned at him.

"My guess is you'll get your way," he said. The new Bank would no longer ignore what the client wanted and presume that it knew better. Within a few weeks Adams went out to visit Museveni on his cattle ranch and delivered the good news to him. The Bank had rethought its position. It would now be delighted to finance a road-construction program.[29]

In November 1995, on that same trip out from Washington, Jim Adams attended the promised poverty conference. He brought along one of the top people from the Bank's research department,[30] and Tumusiime assembled his team, and President Museveni himself arrived to give a speech. Uganda's NGOs also participated, a big shift considering their long record of complaining that Tumusiime's market-based reforms were not reducing poverty, and that the Bank was morally culpable for its failure to forgive debt.[31]

The conference ended with a promise of more inclusive action. The delegates divided the battle against poverty into its various components—economic policy, health policy, education policy, and so on—and created a working group to deal with each one. The economics group spent some time studying local taxes, which were enforced in a medieval manner; poor people who failed to pay them were tied up with ropes and left by the road until a relative could bail them out. The education group looked at the burden caused by school fees, which was keeping poor children out of classrooms; since the World Bank had sometimes advocated school fees, the NGOs viewed this as a turnaround.[32] But more remarkable than the working groups' findings was the fact of their existence. The World Bank and Team Tumusiime and feisty NGO types were collaborating as partners: whatever they agreed together stood a reasonable chance of avoiding sabotage during implementation. The Poverty Eradication Action Plan that the working groups produced in 1997 turned out to have a significance way beyond anything its leaders dreamed of. Uganda's experiment was to change the fate of Wolfensohn's New Development Framework.

In 1996, as Uganda's working groups plowed onward, other changes were afoot. The Bank had supported the government's efforts to get a grip on public spending; and now it wanted to measure what the spending accomplished. What, for example, had happened to spending on primary schools, which had tripled in the past half decade without producing any increase in reported enrollment? The Bank teamed up with a Ugandan consultant and spent days poring over the government's

data on school spending; they figured out what each school was theoretically getting, then they dispatched an army of surveyors to 250 primary schools to find out what was going on. As the results trickled in, a
spreadsheet wizard from Bank headquarters arrived to help the effort;
she hunkered down in the consultant's dingy office in the run-down
national theater building, converting the scrappy reports from field
workers into elegant statistics.[33] The results, when they emerged, were
terrifying. Only a fifth of the central government's grants for schools'
nonsalary expenses actually made it to the classrooms. In two-thirds of
the schools covered by the survey, fully 100 percent of the money was
being ripped off by middlemen in the district government.

    This finding shed a new light on the Bank's arguments with Muse-
veni. The Bank had been urging the Ugandans to borrow money to
boost education, yet (if the results of the survey were true for the whole
country) 80 percent of the money going into the school system was
being stolen by district bureaucrats. This was yet another proof that
good policies are useless without competent institutions to deliver them:
the chief challenge of development is getting the political system to
work right. But how to make that happen? In Indonesia, Scott Guggenheim empowered villagers by requiring that competitive bids to construct roads or bridges be read out in public meetings so that everybody
would know who had made the fairest offer. In Uganda, something
similar happened. The government began to announce its education
transfers in the newspapers and on radio so that parent associations all
around the country knew what their schools were owed. The Ministry
of Education ordered primary schools to display the information on
their public-notice boards, and pretty soon the middlemen in the local
government bureaucracy were too scared to swallow all the money. Ordinary people now knew how much was supposed to be arriving in their
children's classrooms, and they might kick up an almighty rumpus
if the money went astray. Four years later, the Bank and its Ugandan

partner conducted a follow-up survey of school spending. The share of schools receiving zero had plummeted—from almost 70 percent to less than 10 percent.[34]

Years later, when it became clear that a single statistical survey had greatly reduced corruption in the school system, the Bank did what it is best at: it broadcast this new development tool to its clients the world over. But the survey's immediate results in Uganda were just as important. After ten years in office, Museveni had agreed to subject himself to an election; and as the school data were coming together in the run-down national theater building, Museveni was out touring the country for his first presidential campaign. As he spoke in village after village, the candidate began to notice something: the campaign pledge that got people excited was the promise of free primary education. The pledge began to expand within his stump speech, and pretty soon his campaign aides were calling back to Team Tumusiime, warning them that the candidate was making a promise that would prove exorbitant to fund.

It was one of those moments when a country's progress hangs in the balance. Tumusiime had spent a decade building up a sound budget system, and now an election campaign was driving his boss to make promises that could destroy his achievement. In lucky rich democracies, governments can pay for rash election promises by selling bonds to investors; but countries like Uganda have no access to the capital markets, and overgenerous spending promises can only be paid for by printing money, and printing money means runaway inflation and an end to economic growth. Tumusiime's technocrats started crunching numbers, figuring how much it would take to pay for the president's promise of universal primary education, and when they took the results to Tumusiime he knew whom to contact. Jim Adams would soon be making one of his trips out from Washington, and when he arrived in Kampala one day in early 1997, he got a message from Tumusiime: Be in his office at nine the next morning.

When Adams showed up for the appointment, Tumusiime put his

cards on the table. He needed well over $100 million to fund the presidential promise, a sum that would dwarf the Bank's usual project loans in Africa. What was more, Tumusiime had to get this money quickly; the president's pledge was in effect already and children were flooding to the classrooms; there was no time for the Bank to study the issue from six angles and run a pilot project. In the old Bank, there was no way that Tumusiime would have got what he was asking for. But Adams was different. He asked for an assurance that Tumusiime would parachute one of his smart technocrats into the education ministry, and then he agreed to find the money. By June 1998, the World Bank came up with $155 million for education, and enrollment in the primary schools practically doubled.

Uganda's school initiative was not all perfect. While enrollment shot up, the quality of education lagged behind. Still, the near doubling of attendance was truly remarkable, and it reflected the distance traveled by Uganda in the 1990s. Tumusiime had created a budget process that could take in money from the Bank and spend it as intended, a considerable achievement given that money is fungible. In many developing countries, aid simply results in the government diverting its own resources from the aided area to some other one, so that the area targeted by donors is no better off. For every dollar aimed at rural development, according to one multicountry study, rural spending rises by just 11 cents or so;[35] and indeed when nearby Malawi promised free primary education three years before Uganda, actual spending on primary schools failed to rise at all. But Tumusiime's Uganda was different. In the three years after Museveni's promise, spending on primary education jumped from 20 percent of the government's budget to 26 percent.[36]

The success of Uganda's education effort also reflected the changed relationship with the World Bank. If it had not been for a cooperative venture between Bank economists, a Ugandan consultant, and Team Tumusiime, the local government's rip-off of school funds would have continued, and the millions spent on the education drive would have been wasted. Moreover, if it had not been for the trust between the World Bank and its client, Tumusiime would never have received the fast support he needed. But Jim Adams, and more distantly Jim Wolfensohn, stood for a new style in Africa. They were willing to give up the illusion of control that you get when you study a question from six angles and run a careful pilot project. They were willing to accept that real control over the success of development rests not with the Bank or any donor. It rests with the Africans themselves.

FOR THE NEXT TWO YEARS, Uganda refined its approach to development. Ugandans rather than aid donors were gaining power over the agenda—the country was "in the driver's seat," as the development jargon had it—and in 1998 the Consultative Group meeting was held in Kampala rather than Paris for the first time.[37] Moreover, it was not just the Ugandan government that had climbed into the driver's seat; it was Ugandans more broadly. The first participatory poverty plan, completed in 1997, was soon followed by a second one; and at the same time Uganda created a new kind of public-expenditure review, through which NGOs and parliamentarians were invited to comment directly on the government's budget. In 1998, Team Tumusiime extended the idea of participation by seeking direct input from poor people. Squads of surveyors were sent out to interview villagers: Did they feel better or worse off than previously? What would make them happier? When the results of this "participatory poverty assessment" arrived, several policies were adjusted. The survey showed, for example, that villagers wanted money to construct homes for schoolteachers rather than money for school buildings. Acquiring a teacher was more important than acquiring a classroom, and in order to acquire a teacher you had to build his family a house.[38]

Uganda's development model—consisting of country "ownership" of development planning plus broad popular participation—was bound to attract attention, given Uganda's dramatic progress.[39] The new model did not displace the orthodox economics of structural adjustment, which Uganda embraced enthusiastically; but it was a change in the process by which those policies were implemented—old-style conditionality would now be abandoned. The long list of people who favored a new conception of development, a break with the tired formula of structural adjustment, now had the ammunition they needed: a country that had thrown off donor conditionality and had yanked 4 million people out of poverty in a few short years. For NGOs and development gurus and even some World Bankers, Uganda was no longer just Uganda. It was a shorthand for a new view of development.

There was something a bit strange about Uganda's new status, for the lessons that the world drew from the country were sometimes too simple. Were donor conditions inimical to development? If you considered the full stretch of Uganda's success story, starting in the late 1980s, the answer was not so clear. Although Tumusiime had asserted Ugandan "ownership" of development in the second half of the 1990s, he believed that Bank-imposed conditions had been crucial in the first half of the decade, when antireformers in the cabinet opposed his promarket program. The liberalization of coffee, for example, had been opposed by traditionalists in the agriculture ministry, so Tumusiime had encouraged the Bank to make coffee liberalization a condition of its lending. In the same way, controlling government spending had involved constant battles with the cabinet, so Tumusiime was delighted to have the Bank and the IMF mandate spending discipline. In sum, the lesson from Uganda was quite subtle. It might be true that conditionality cannot force reform upon an unwilling country. But that did not make all conditionality useless. Where you have strong reformers, conditions can make them even stronger.[40]

Similar qualifications applied to other lessons from Uganda. Was broad participation essential to development? Uganda had indeed used participation skillfully, especially after the poverty conference in

November 1995. But the reforms of the early 1990s had been done mostly without participation, and in the second half of the decade participation sometimes yielded only argument. Likewise, some of Uganda's admirers asserted that the country demonstrated the virtues of a direct focus on poverty. But nearly all Uganda's poverty reduction reflected economic growth,[41] which in turn reflected orthodox economic prescriptions that dominated the agenda before the mid-1990s;[42] the liberalization of coffee prices accounted for half of the fall of the national poverty rate over the period.[43] Even in the second half of the 1990s, Uganda's Poverty Eradication Action Plans contained many measures—to attract foreign investment, to boost exports—that amounted to structural adjustment in a new guise.

Besides, insofar as ownership and participation did help Uganda, it was not really clear that you could bottle this potion and market it worldwide. How do you create "ownership"? In Uganda, Adams had been smart enough to cede leadership to Tumusiime; but the more important point was that Tumusiime himself had claimed it, partly through the force of his own character, and partly through the wise backing he enjoyed from an equally forceful president. How far was this replicable in other countries? Foisting ownership on reluctant leaders seemed contradictory: it was like ordering people not to take orders. Equally, was it smart to press participation in countries that lacked a Tumusiime? The Bank could send squads of participation experts off to some client country, and orchestrate a participatory poverty reduction plan modeled on Uganda's example. But if there was no Tumusiime-style machinery to translate the resulting poverty plan into real action, this seemed a little pointless. You were inviting civil society into the driver's seat before connecting the steering wheel to the engine.[44]

In short, Uganda's real miracle was subtly different from the mythical version. The country had prospered thanks to the huge hammering personality of Tumusiime and the good sense of a president who backed him; it stood out not for its policies, which were taken from the structural-adjustment textbook, but for its success in implementing them. Part of that implementation success reflected "ownership," but this was more a product of Tumusiime's efforts than a cause of them; part of the success reflected participation, but the less fashionable truth was that part of it reflected the influence of an enlightened autocrat. It was a troubling irony, indeed, that the new development consensus in favor of strong institutions depended so much on strong individuals. Yet as 1998 ended, these distinctions scarcely mattered to the wider debate about development, nor to the reception that awaited Wolfensohn's New Development Framework.

CHAPTER NINE

A FRAMEWORK
FOR DEVELOPMENT

IF YOU READ the New Development Framework with a feel for Wolfensohn's passions, it's clear where most of it comes from. As he mused at his desk with the view of the Wyoming mountains, brooding over the effect of the financial crises on his agenda, Wolfensohn began with a swipe at the International Monetary Fund. A country's development strategy, he wrote, is a two-sided balance sheet. On the left are the macroeconomic issues that the IMF deals in; on the right—and equally important—are the structural and social challenges of development that are the province of the Bank. Next, Wolfensohn elaborated on the contents of the right side of this balance sheet, starting with the governance issues that he cared most about. The first priority, Wolfensohn contended, is "an absolute commitment to clean government," since "corruption is the single most corrosive aspect of development." The second priority is an effective justice system, essential for corruption fighters. The third is a properly supervised financial system, another thing that crony countries lack. Wolfensohn went on to list ten more development ingredients, and then he described the players that deliver them: governments, multilateral donors, civil society, and the private sector. It was up to developing countries, Wolfensohn suggested, to come up with a long-term, comprehensive strategy, parceling out the thirteen challenges among the various development actors.

Wolfensohn's idea was an abstract version of Uganda's success story, and it had a lot in common with Scott Guggenheim's village-development project in Indonesia. It was less about *what* countries should invest their aid in, since Wolfensohn's list of thirteen development ingredients was so long as to legitimize all choices. It was really about *how* aid should be spent. Poor countries needed to draw up plans that covered all development challenges; they needed to coordinate donors, who otherwise had a tendency to pile into trendy areas while ignoring necessary ones; they needed to take charge of the process, to "own" their development programs. Moreover, these programs needed to enjoy broad political legitimacy, since otherwise they would prove impossible to implement. Just as Uganda achieved that legitimacy by inviting a broad range of groups to take part in its development planning, and just as Scott Guggenheim insisted that villagers agree upon projects at public meetings, so Wolfensohn's framework insisted on "participatory" development. Just as Uganda rooted out corruption in the school system by posting central government payments on the walls of village school buildings, and just as Guggenheim required that contractors' bids be read out in public, so Wolfensohn's framework insisted that development planning be "transparent" and "accountable."

The New Development Framework built on Wolfensohn's instincts since his first days at the Bank. His call for participatory development put an intellectual frame on his outreach to nongovernmental organizations, a central feature of his presidency since his first visit to Africa. His call for countries to take charge of their own development implied a break with the donor-imposed conditions of structural adjustment, which he had disliked from the outset. At the same time, the framework deepened Wolfensohn's break with the Bank's apolitical traditions. His belief in a comprehensive approach to development—encompassing all of those thirteen various challenges—would stand or fall on the quality of a country's political process, since it would take strong institutions to assert control of a complex agenda in the way that he proposed.

For anyone who knew Wolfensohn—for anyone who knew the trends in the Bank's thinking—the New Development Framework should not have come as a surprise. From the sea of influences around him, Wolfensohn had come to a position that blended his own instincts with the intellectual fashions of the moment. And yet the New Development Framework caused consternation.

ON JANUARY 1, 1999, Wolfensohn circulated his framework to a handful of his senior managers. When the group discussed it at a meeting a few days later, the conversation quickly soured. The problem lay partly in the Bank's constant fear of overstretch, which went back to the arguments on Bosnia; Wolfensohn's broad framework, with its thirteen categories of development challenge, seemed like a recipe for doing even more. But the main cause of the tension lay in the way that Wolfensohn presented his creation. The text was peppered with self-aggrandizing Renaissance-man phrases—"I could write volumes on the subject of environment," the author boasted at one point—and rather than introducing his idea as an effort to distill other people's thinking, Wolfensohn unveiled his framework with the proud look of an inventor: He had created a new paradigm! He had changed development theory! He was practically shouting *eureka!*[1]

At that first meeting in early January, the lieutenants struggled to grasp Wolfensohn's abstractions, and then they were struck by the idea's apparent banality. By itself, the insight that development was complex was not exactly novel—it had animated the fix-everything integrated rural-development projects of the McNamara period—so surely the Bank wasn't going to build a new initiative out of that? The emphasis on political institutions was no longer revolutionary either. The Bank's senior barons did not need to be told about the Uganda experiment, nor of similar developments elsewhere. Undeterred, Wolfensohn sent out a second draft of his framework to a wider circle of Bank managers on January 20; and he sent it to the World Bank's board the next day; and the day after that, unbeknownst to his senior managers, he mailed his new development paradigm to his Rolodex of friendly world leaders. Before long, reactions were rolling in from presidents and finance ministers. The managers realized that this was indeed a new World Bank initiative, whether they liked it or not.

Wolfensohn did not take kindly to criticisms of his framework, and the managers tiptoed around his ego like men in a minefield. They ventured that he might rethink the title—perhaps "New Development Framework" might give out the, um, unfortunate impression that he was, ah, overlooking certain previous theories of development. But they could not bring themselves to declare bluntly that parts of his theory were old hat.[2] Wolfensohn agreed to rename his proposal the "Comprehensive Development Framework"; he abandoned a postscript that would have provoked the IMF unduly; and he added material about macroeconomics to avoid the impression that he had no regard for its significance. But the boss rebuffed attempts to edit his manuscript or to add a Bank-written executive summary to it. He had written this thing personally, and he wanted the world to know that it was his and nobody else's; he frequently showed off the yellow sheaves of legal paper to his visitors. Besides, Wolfensohn was out to change the world's agenda with this document. He wanted to fight back against the IMF's claims to preeminence, and he did not need the Bank's defensive bureaucrats to advise him on that.

At the end of January 1999, Wolfensohn flew off to a conference in Côte d'Ivoire, where he met the heads of other development agencies. For the umpteenth time, Wolfensohn explained his framework: how it was essential to recognize the comprehensive nature of development, and how countries needed to take control of the process, sharing out the various challenges among their development partners. Wolfensohn spoke with a persuasive passion, and the audience seemed to be warming to him, but then an IMF official who was standing in for Michel Camdessus spoke up. Wolfensohn's proposal was certainly welcome, the IMF man offered. But the group should not ignore the PFP and its history. Other people round the table nodded knowingly. Wolfensohn looked deeply unhappy for a moment, and the discussion moved on.[3]

Wolfensohn flew from Côte d'Ivoire to Munich, where he was met by Javed Burki, the Bank's vice president for Latin America and the Caribbean. The two men got into a car together, and then Wolfensohn turned to Burki.

"What's a PFP?" he demanded.

"It's a Policy Framework Paper," Burki replied.

"Why hasn't anybody ever told me about it?" Wolfensohn said bitterly.

"Did you ask anybody?" Burki responded. "And why are you asking anyway?"[4]

Wolfensohn related the encounter in West Africa. Burki explained to him that the PFP was a joint IMF–World Bank document that laid out a country's development strategy. It wasn't exactly the same as Wolfensohn's concept: it did not cover the role of other donors, and it did not emphasize transparency or participatory planning. But Wolfensohn was mortified. He was angry that he had appeared ignorant at the meeting with the IMF man, angry that nobody had warned him of the trap that lay in store for him, and angry at his own failings. The whole episode showed how distant the staff had grown from him; how his tantrums and explosions cut him off from good advice. Several of the forthright figures in his entourage—Gautam Kaji, Rachel Lomax—had long since left the Bank after too many furious clashes; and those who were left were mostly masters of long-suffering tact. There were stories about Mark Malloch Brown, the Bank's communications chief, losing his temper over Wolfensohn's behavior, but he was usually too smart to do so while the boss was present. "Yes Jim, absolutely, Jim," he purred into the phone on one occasion, before ripping the phone out of its socket and flinging it at the nearest window once Wolfensohn was safely off the line. When it came to the Comprehensive Development Framework, however, neither Malloch Brown nor any of the other senior managers had flung the full truth at Wolfensohn. At least not in a manner that the boss could hear.

There was a tragic element to this. Wolfensohn's instincts—that there is more to poverty reduction than macroeconomics, that there are no silver bullets in this struggle, that institutions underpin development—were generally accepted by his colleagues at the Bank. But Wolfensohn's Renaissance-man vanity, his tendency to blow up at the first sign of criticism, made it hard for his lieutenants to help him develop his ideas. Only a few months earlier Caroline Anstey, Wolfensohn's tough speechwriter, had told him bluntly that if he continued to bawl people out, his presidency would be finished; although Wolfensohn had promised to reform himself, the reform was taking time. The explosive vigor of the Salomon Brothers management meetings lived on within him; he believed in yelling and cursing and banging the table, and then forgetting the whole argument as soon as it was done. "The smoke was flying from cigars and the language was terrible, and what the fuck are you doing here, and what is this over there," Wolfensohn remembers fondly; but the partner who called you an ignorant son of a bitch in the morning meeting would defend you to the death when a client appeared later. The problem was that the World Bank is not Salomon Brothers. You cannot scream at a World Banker at breakfast and expect to be forgiven by the time you go to lunch.[5]

At the end of January 1999, when Wolfensohn arrived in Munich, it was not yet clear how much this mattered. Wolfensohn had the agility to reinvent his own invention: he could drop all claims to novelty, while reasonably pointing out that even if other theorists had proposed similar ideas before him, development practitioners appeared to have ignored them. After all, his suggestion that development challenges should be parceled out among aid donors in a coordinated manner touched on a well-recognized problem. Many poor countries were overrun by aid agencies, pursuing pet projects in a go-it-alone fashion. There might be seventeen outfits trying to erect school buildings and nobody paying attention to rural electricity or roads. This invasion of aid agencies could undermine the institutions on which development depended: Tanzania was required to produce twenty-four hundred reports each quarter for its many foreign benefactors, and to host a thousand visiting aid missions per year.[6] Equally, many countries had indeed followed the orthodox macroeconomic prescriptions on the left side of their balance sheets, yet they remained as poor as ever because they had failed to grapple with the structural and social issues on their balance sheets' right side. The Comprehensive Development Framework, Wolfensohn could argue, was a salutary reminder of these obstacles. It was a call to action, and action was urgent.

As it turned out, Wolfensohn's efforts to reinvent his framework were doomed to trouble. It was partly that deep down he could not quite bring himself to drop his eureka attitude to his creation; he was proud of what he'd done. But it was more than that: by early 1999, the dysfunction of the Bank was swirling and howling all around him, frustrating his efforts to get his ideas out. The sour relationship with his top staff, which had prevented them from warning him of the PFP booby trap, was one sign of this dysfunction. But at the time of the birth of Wolfensohn's new framework, the most furious gales were coming from a small Latin American client.

THAT SMALL CLIENT was Bolivia, an achingly beautiful and poor country on the Andean plateau. In 1999, Bolivia's 8 million people had an average income of $1,000, making them one-third richer than

Ugandans but still the poorest nation in South America. As in many Latin countries, Bolivia's development challenges were worse than the average-income numbers suggested, because inequality was dramatic. The bottom fifth of the population did only 5.6 percent of the consuming, a smaller share than in Uganda; four out of five Bolivians in the countryside lived in poverty.[7] But Bolivia had for a while been blessed with reformist democratic governments, and after the 1997 election Bolivia's hopes centered on a young and appealing vice president called Jorge Quiroga.

For new-wave development types searching for hope in a bleak landscape, Quiroga seemed wonderful. He had begun his career working for IBM in Texas, and he exuded the can-do confidence of an American executive. He had returned home and become the technocrat responsible for coordinating Bolivia's aid flows, and the experience had left him with big ideas about foreign assistance. He liked to tell the story of his visit to a meeting of donors in Paris, held in 1992. Quiroga had shown up with a cartoon that depicted international aid givers— the World Bank, the Inter-American Development Bank, bilateral donors—pouring sacks of money into a vast network of pipes that looped and joined together and separated and fed into new pipes labeled "consultants"; and then passed through a series of stages labeled "pre-orientation mission," "orientation mission," "observation mission," "loan definition mission," "board approval," "no objection"; until finally it reached a small bucket labeled Bolivia into which two meager coins emerged. The cartoon was Quiroga's way of saying that the whole aid business was rotten. The donors had spent a decade preaching structural adjustment for poor countries. It was time to turn the tables and impose structural adjustment on the donors for a change.

Quiroga's ideas echoed Wolfensohn's impatience with draconian aid conditionality, and his managerial effort to streamline the Bank. But they also fitted Wolfensohn's belief in participatory development planning.

In September 1997, a month after his administration took office, Quiroga launched a national development dialogue: people from NGOs, trade unions, academia, and the media were invited, and over the course of three weeks together they came up with a plan that organized Bolivia's aspirations under four headings—stronger institutions, greater social equity, a growing economy, and progress in the war on drugs. Quiroga took this plan to the next donors' conference in Paris and demanded that they back it. He was the vice president; he had a fresh democratic mandate; he had consulted all the nation's stakeholders and forged a development consensus. Did the donors believe in backing progress? Or did they believe in spending aid dollars on preorientation missions and consultants? They had to decide.

One donor who responded warmly was the country director from the World Bank. Her name was Isabel Guerrero, a highflyer with a woolly-sweater soccer mom's demeanor. Guerrero had recently been promoted; she was a beneficiary of the Wolfensohn shake-up; and she was ready for Quiroga's radical ideas. Indeed, she had encouraged them; right after his election, she had approached him with the idea of creating a participatory development plan. Once the plan had been formulated, Guerrero made sure that the Bank's programs in Bolivia fitted under Quiroga's four headings. The country's priorities should be the Bank's priorities, especially since those priorities had been arrived at in an open, participatory style. Guerrero's approach won the approval of Caio Koch-Weser, the managing director who oversaw Latin America, and pretty soon Koch-Weser was adding his own potion to the mixture. The buzz from Bolivia was all over the Bank.

Koch-Weser's excitement reflected the management maelstrom of the times. Cohorts of World Bankers were zipping off to Harvard as part of Wolfensohn's reeducation program, seeking inspiration in case studies of corporate triumph. Among the most triumphant cases was AES, a go-go power company that took the principles of delegation and decentralization to extremes. By the late 1990s, AES had more than twenty-five thousand employees, but it had no central personnel department, no public-relations department, no legal department, no environmental department, and certainly no time wasters doing "corporate planning." Front-line AES employees performed all these functions themselves, dammit; they were not treated like children, to be overseen by head-office nannies; they were "empowered"; they had "ownership." The echoes of fashionable aid jargon were no coincidence. This was the Internet era, in which everyone could access knowledge; if the people on the front line now knew as much as managers in the head office, well then firms and development agencies and every other institution should obviously empower them.

Isabel Guerrero read the AES case study up at Harvard, and regarded it as a manifesto for decentralization that the Bank would never match. But Caio Koch-Weser thought differently. He liked schmoozing with business executives, and he cultivated AES's two founders, especially Dennis Bakke, the charismatic chief executive.[8] Some time in 1998, Koch-Weser arranged a dinner with the AES duo and Wolfensohn; and when Wolfensohn began to push his new development framework after the annual meetings speech that October, Koch-Weser spied an opening. The boss wanted countries to pilot his new aid framework? Clearly Bolivia was suitable. The boss wanted to decentralize the Bank's development professionals? Apply the AES model to Bolivia, and he would get all the decentralization anyone could want.

The wedding of AES to Bolivia took place in the first week of January 1999. With Caio Koch-Weser's blessing, the Bank's Bolivia team staged a two-day "workout"[9]—they bonded with Quiroga and his top advisers, and Dennis Bakke was brought in specially to give a sizzling pep talk. Bakke's father was a Christian minister, and two of his brothers were ministers. He kept a bronze statue of Jesus washing St. Peter's feet in his office, and he knew how to put on a humdinger of an evangelical performance that would make everybody's juices flow. Parents educate their children by allowing them freedom, Bakke preached to the audience; development institutions need to trust developing countries as well. If you could only stop infantilizing people—infantilizing poor governments, infantilizing Bank task managers who labor under layers of oversight—you could unleash a magic power within us; you could work a miracle.

The way Bakke spoke, people actually believed him, and pretty soon the room was full of born-again World Bankers, their faith in their mission newly restored. They would tear up the Bank's rules and procedures! They would walk free into a new world of spontaneous lending! They would discover the idealistic adventurers that hid within their bureaucratic selves! Looking around the room, Isabel Guerrero saw tears in the eyes of colleagues. On the second day of the workout, one World Bank veteran told her that for the first time in a long time he had looked forward to coming to work in the morning.[10]

It was not just Dennis Bakke who preached revolution. The workout took place, fortuitously, just as Wolfensohn came back from the Wyoming mountains bearing his yellow tablets of wisdom. The long-running management ferment was now compounded by a new intellectual ferment at the top echelons of the Bank. In the days before the session, Isabel Guerrero read the New Development Framework and told Quiroga about it: this was a time for business as *un*usual, each of them agreed. The new rules were that there were no rules, or at least none that were unchangeable. The workout would imagine that no World Bank existed, and then it would design the perfect institution for supporting Bolivia's progress. "What would I do if God let me be the owner of the world for a week?" Quiroga asked the assembled brainstormers, somewhat ambitiously. "I wouldn't waste my time trying to fix Europe or America, that would be way too complicated. But I would certainly try to work on different ways to get multilateral lending agencies working better."[11]

What would better look like? Well, it would mean cutting the red tape that made the Bank slow and costly to deal with; it would mean creating an institution that was less inclined to lecture and more inclined to help. The Bank would take the leap of trusting in Bolivia's procedures, rather than imposing its own rules on procurement, financial oversight, and so on; it would give Bolivia the space to "own" its development, and then judge Bolivia by its results. In the old days, Quiroga continued, it had been okay to impose World Bank procedures, because development was thought to be about creating infrastructure or getting economic policies right. But now development theory had moved on a step. Development was about creating institutions, according to the new understanding; and telling a country to create institutions while starving those institutions of responsibility was self-contradictory and futile.

The workout continued, with more excited voices taking turns at the microphone. Caio Koch-Weser arrived to give a pep talk. The Bank's Bolivia country team produced slides proclaiming the Bank's red-tape rigmarole to be "time-consuming," "costly," and "confusing"; countries that came up with democratically legitimate development plans were not getting the fast support that they deserved. The Bank's procurement officers, who had been invited along in an attempt to win a relaxation of procedures, took exception to this criticism; they had a responsibility to prevent corruption, a big problem in Bolivia. But for the most part people were swept up in the moment. In keeping with AES decentralization principles, Isabel Guerrero agreed to relocate from Washington, even though her family would not be able to move with her; and the whole group agreed on a new and streamlined relationship with the Bank's board. Rather than seeking board approval for each project, a process that required endless honing and polishing of loan documents, the Bolivia team would ask for a pot of money that could be allocated flexibly in support of Quiroga's national plan. Bolivia would at last be spared the endless red tape that reduced the Bank's effectiveness; and the Bank's task managers would be freed to do the real work of development rather than preparing nonstop updates for their overseers. As Dennis Bakke liked to put it, every decentralized employee should be a mini-CEO.

At the end of the workout, Quiroga was taken to see Wolfensohn. The boss was slightly irked to meet another inventor of paradigms,[12] but he could see that the Bolivia experiment was useful. Quiroga had come up with a participatory development plan; he wanted to take charge of the process and break free from burdensome donor conditions; he had created just about the perfect pilot for Wolfensohn's framework. A few days later, Isabel Guerrero was invited to speak about Bolivia at the senior managers' annual strategy meeting, and she was hailed as a sort of incarnation of the times. By backing a model development plan, the Bank was shifting its sights from its own inputs (mere projects) to Bolivia's outputs (the targets on child immunization and so on laid down in Quiroga's national strategy); it was moving from rules to results, from centralization to empowered teams. The managerial and intellectual ferment that had bubbled up under Wolfensohn were now fused in one experiment.

UNFORTUNATELY FOR WOLFENSOHN, the Bolivia experiment was indeed an expression of his leadership, but not just of the good parts. His appetite for change—management change, development-theory change—was certainly invigorating; but it had encouraged the Bolivia team to think so far out of normal World Bank boxes that they wound up in la-la land. The team had dreamed up a new relationship with the Bank's board of directors, and there was certainly a case for that. No private corporation could work efficiently if its board members met twice weekly and demanded the right to vet every management decision, as the World Bank's board does. But the Bolivia team had not paused to wonder how the board would react to its proposal. The subsidized IDA credits that Isabel Guerrero would be funneling to Bolivia were financed by grants from the Bank's shareholders, and the shareholders might object to having their oversight diluted. In the maelstrom of the moment, nobody considered that. This was a time for business as *un*usual! The yellow tablets brought down from the Wyoming mountains promised a whole new paradigm!

Toward the end of February, five of the World Bank's twenty-four board directors visited Bolivia. They went in cheerful innocence; nobody had told them of the grand experiment that was afoot. They were shepherded around the government ministries in the capital, puffing a bit on account of the altitude, catching the occasional glimpse of the majestic mountains in the distance. One of the people who received them was Vice President Quiroga. What they heard astonished them. Quiroga was talking about this brave new paradigm he had cooked up with the Bank's Bolivia country team; Caio Koch-Weser had blessed it; and Wolfensohn himself had anointed this experiment as a pilot for his new framework. The board members returned to Washington in a fury. Around the same time two years before, Wolfensohn had come up with his quarter-billion-dollar Strategic Compact, and somehow he had put that past them. Now he was talking about a Comprehensive Development Framework and Bolivia was set to implement it—all before the board had really grasped what "it" really was.

On March 11, 1999, a week after the five directors returned to Washington, the board assembled for its first formal discussion of Wolfensohn's framework. The boss had circulated his manifesto to the board in January, and a subcommittee of the board had met to discuss the document in February, but the board had yet to pronounce officially on Wolfensohn's brainchild. Nobody expected this to be an easy meeting. The first time Wolfensohn had described his idea to the Bank's directors, it was over a dinner. He had just flown into Washington and he was jet-lagged; and when his audience started to come back at him with the standard this-ain't-new objections, Wolfensohn flew into a temper. Naturally, this did not endear the board members to his new framework. The U.S. director was driven to insist that the boss never again convene a dinner meeting when he was jet-lagged. The French director, successor to the orator who had made the Narcissus leaving speech, was so incensed by Wolfensohn's eureka attitude that, at another meeting a bit later, he circulated an old article by Joe Stiglitz, the Bank's chief economist, which floated pretty much the same ideas.[13] Still, in early March, it did not seem too late for Wolfensohn to bring the board round to his position. Precisely because the proposals in his framework were not entirely original, it was surely not impossible to have the board rally behind these familiar ideas.

The meeting that transpired was one of the worst of Wolfensohn's presidency. The boss arrived in a testy mood, evidently unhappy at subjecting his creation to nitpicking directors. The directors arrived in an equally tough mood, particularly those who had been to Bolivia. The Italian director, who served as spokesman for the Bolivia group, declared that Quiroga's big ideas could not possibly be tried out without the board's prior say-so: How could anyone talk about the board preauthorizing money for Bolivia's national development plan without consulting the board? Wolfensohn tried to brush this off, but the Italian persisted.[14] Pretty soon, Wolfensohn was sputtering and boiling. He was the Bank's president! He was on first-name terms with heads of states and finance ministers! Who was this career bureaucrat to question him? Not very tactfully, Wolfensohn announced that he would be visiting Berlin shortly, and would present his new framework to a group of European development ministers. This was more than the board directors could stomach. How dare he circumvent the Bank's governance structure and go over their heads to their bosses?[15]

The squabbling grew so bitter that consideration of the framework became just about impossible. Wolfensohn ordered staff members and other observers to leave the room, and when he was alone with the directors, he suggested he might quit if that was what they wanted. His good-faith effort to rethink development was not being taken seriously; the board was making his life impossible; and he was of two minds whether it was worth the heartache to go on. Several board members felt that Wolfensohn's departure would be welcome, for the Bank and for development, but none was fool enough to say so. It was true that Wolfensohn knew their bosses and got along with many of them; and when he raised the stakes this high it was not prudent to call him. For the rest of the day, Wolfensohn brooded in his office, where the ledge along the back wall is forested with trophy photographs. The directors met in small groups, wondering how to calm him down. That evening the directors went in ones and twos to see him, and a wary peace was reestablished. When the board reconvened the next day, Wolfensohn invoked the memory of Yehudi Menuhin, the master violinist who had just died, and he declared that he had a similar artistic vision that deserved better than pettifogging objections.[16]

The Bank's Bolivia country team never got the full delegation of authority it had hoped for. The board eventually approved loans of $57 million to support two of Quiroga's objectives—institutional reform and an extension of health services—and the Bank stationed project managers in La Paz to oversee these, with more autonomy from headquarters than was usual. But the high hopes fizzled. The acceleration of Bank lending that the workout had called for failed to materialize; indeed, in September 2000, the Bolivians realized that the rate of Bank disbursements had actually gone down. Moreover, the idea that authority was decentralized to locally based Bank managers was not really true in practice; the Bank's vice president for Latin America was closely involved in the Bolivia program, so decisions tended to flow up to his office in Washington.[17] The vision of a streamlined Bank that got behind a politically legitimate, nationally owned development plan had been inspiring. But the wariness of the board and the naïve ebullience of the visionaries had combined to undermine a good idea. A little while later there was a fitting epilogue to the Bolivia story. Dennis Bakke vacated the executive suite with the statue of Jesus and St. Peter. His faith in radical decentralization had helped to land his firm in trouble, and his shareholders decided that head-office oversight is not so evil after all.

The Bolivia fight almost buried Wolfensohn's Comprehensive Development Framework, but Wolfensohn fought on. He flew off to Berlin the week after the disastrous board meeting and sold his idea directly to Europe's development ministers. He proposed that a network of officials in European aid ministries be formed to promote his framework, and the network duly assembled for its first meeting a month later, during the World Bank's spring meetings of April 1999. The following month Wolfensohn coauthored a newspaper column with Amartya Sen, the recently anointed Nobel laureate, which served to keep his brainchild in the limelight; and all the while he was pressing for more countries to draw up broad, participatory development plans, and soon a dozen such pilots were identified.

Yet the most powerful locomotive for Wolfensohn's new paradigm was gathering steam elsewhere. Rather unusually, Wolfensohn's antennae failed him. He did not sense the locomotive coming until after it arrived.

THE LOCOMOTIVE was debt relief, one of the signature issues of Wolfensohn's first year. After his early trip to Africa, Wolfensohn had outflanked the resistance to multilateral debt write-offs, and a scheme to forgive debts of the poorest countries was finalized at the annual meetings of 1996. Now, by a strange symmetry, the debt issue would return the favor: it would outflank the resistance to the Comprehensive Development Framework.

The first debt-relief campaign had been a political victory for Wolfensohn, and it won him the valuable affection of nongovernmental groups such as Oxfam. But the financial fruits were disappointing. To qualify for relief, poor countries had to jump through hoops that seemed cruelly exacting: They were eligible only after they had managed their economies diligently under IMF-approved programs for six consecutive years. By 1998, only two of the forty Highly Indebted Poor Countries supposedly covered by the "HIPC" initiative, Uganda and Bolivia, had actually had debt canceled; and even their rewards were modest. Naturally frustrated, the NGOs that had campaigned originally for debt relief took up the cause again, only this time they were better organized. They added a network of churches to their alliance, and they seized upon the calendar to create a sense of urgency: Debt should be forgiven now, quickly, before the new millennium arrived. Jubilee 2000, as the debt campaign called itself, soon claimed affiliates in more than fifty countries.

In the first debt-relief campaign, Wolfensohn had taken on powerful opponents, notably the Japanese and Germans, who thought forgiving debt would send a pernicious signal to borrowers worldwide. But the second time around there was no need to bang the table. The world's rich democracies had seen how effective the debt campaigners could be in mobilizing popular opinion, and few Western leaders wanted to get on their bad side. That was especially true of the new Third Way governments in Britain and Germany; both Tony Blair and Gerhard Schröder had repudiated the blue-collar socialism of their parties, but they retained the progressive urge to help the disadvantaged, and the plight of developing countries offered a good outlet for their compassion.[18] The Third Way Clinton administration soon joined the Brits and the Germans, though it faced the usual problems in persuading Congress to spend money on debt relief rather than on domestic programs.[19] Development spending pitted "Ghana versus grandma," in the words of one powerbroker in the House of Representatives.[20]

Wolfensohn should have been delighted: Blair and Schröder and Clinton were following a trail that he had blazed three years before. The new debt campaign was asking for essentially the same thing as the first campaign, but with relaxed eligibility criteria; it was building on Wolfensohn's platform. But now that Wolfensohn was no longer driving this issue, he was strangely cold to it. In October 1998, he attended a meeting with Catholic leaders in New Jersey, and when the Vatican's representative made an impassioned plea for greater debt relief, Wolfensohn demanded to know whether the Vatican bank was in the business of forgiving its debtors.[21] He resented this pressure from these Catholics; and he suspected that the IMF's boss, himself a Catholic, had special ties to these people, something that a Jew could never match.[22] He complained that the Jubilee campaigners were failing to appreciate the debt relief that he had already delivered for them.[23] And he worried that a new debt write-off, which would be paid for in part by drawing from the Bank's income, would weaken the institution's finances, compounding the pressure from successive IMF-led bailouts.

Over the next six months or so, Wolfensohn's misgivings persisted. He pointed out that more resources for debt relief would mean fewer resources for new aid flows. He worried that the Bank's capital adequacy had already been battered by the Asian, Russian, and Brazilian crises, and that further strain could prove too much. To his old allies in the debt-relief movement, it seemed that pique was also driving him. Some demon inside him resented a campaign for a debt scheme that might eclipse his own; he wanted to be best at everything. It was a familiar complaint about Wolfensohn. Was there anything good about the Bank before he had arrived there? It seemed he could see little. Had others understood the comprehensive nature of development before him? It seemed he could not accept this possibility. But despite Wolfensohn's apprehensions, the debt-relief movement pushed ahead anyway, and for a brief moment during the April 1999 spring meetings, Wolfensohn allowed his frustration to boil over. He called a U.S. Treasury official at home at around ten-thirty one evening and started venting to him. The Bank was being left out of all the talks on debt relief, he shouted. If the Third Way types weren't careful, they would jeopardize the Bank's AAA rating.

Perhaps because Wolfensohn resented the new drive for debt relief, he also missed the broader importance of the Jubilee campaign. The Jubilee people were insisting not merely that debts be canceled, but that the newly freed money must finance direct efforts against poverty. And to show what they intended, they cited Uganda.

THE FIRST SIGNS of the debt campaigners' strategy had been clear at the time of Wolfensohn's Uganda visit in 1995. Here, said the NGOs, was a good government in a dirt-poor country, struggling under an impossible debt burden, two-thirds of which was owed to multilateral development lenders. But Uganda had come a long way since then. The more Team Tumusiime strengthened its grip on the country's budget process, the more you could be sure that the money freed by debt relief would be spent responsibly. The more Tumusiime opened up to broad participation, the more you could be confident that debt relief would finance spending with wide popular appeal. Uganda's dramatic achievement in enrolling all primary school students made the point most eloquently. If you wanted to persuade aid skeptics that debt relief would not be money down a rat hole, Uganda was your poster child.

Tony Burdon, the Oxfam representative in Uganda whom Wolfensohn had met on his early visit, had come a long way, too. He had taken part in the 1995 poverty conference in Kampala and in the subsequent working groups that created Uganda's participatory development plan. In March 1997, he had grown frustrated at the slow pace of debt relief under the deal forced by Wolfensohn, and he'd prompted the Ugandan finance minister to write to the *Financial Times* of London, protesting that the delay might undercut his country's push for universal education.[24] That letter made a pledge that Tumusiime had rendered possible. If donors doubted that money freed by debt relief would be spent on poverty reduction, Uganda would be happy to direct the proceeds into a special poverty-action fund that donors could audit. Toward the end of 1997, Burdon left Uganda to lead Oxfam's debt campaign in Britain. Over the next couple of years, as Oxfam and its partners in the new Jubilee 2000 movement gradually cranked up the pressure for faster debt relief, every Oxfam paper on the issue cited Uganda's example.[25]

Despite Wolfensohn's misgivings about a second round of debt relief, the Bank could not avoid being at the center of the discussions forced by the Jubilee campaign: Along with the IMF, it housed the technical experts on the subject. The leading finance ministries, particularly the United States and Britain, weighed in on the argument, and the Jubilee campaigners were invited to say what they wanted—given their popular following, any new debt deal would require their endorsement. Presented with this opportunity, Burdon and his colleagues pointed to Uganda's Poverty Action Fund—the realization of the idea in the *Financial Times* letter. The NGO campaigners suggested that all countries should set up special funds to collect the proceeds of debt relief, and that the money should be spent on education, health, and other services for the poor.

To the economists at the World Bank, the Poverty Action Fund was a gimmick. It ignored the elementary point that money is fungible. If the proceeds from debt relief went to health or education, the government might simply cut other flows of money to those sectors and spend the savings on palaces or guns. To get out of this hole, the Bank and the finance ministries and the Jubilee campaigners borrowed a bit more from Uganda. Candidates for debt relief should come up with development strategies that covered the waterfront of public spending, so that observers could see whether total spending on education was heading upward and avoid the fungibility trap. The model for this broad strategy was Uganda's Poverty Eradication Action Plan—the one that had grown out of the 1995 poverty conference.[26]

Meanwhile the debt negotiators saw a chance to promote other development ideas. Britain's government was Uganda's largest bilateral donor, and like the World Bank and Oxfam, it was impressed by the results of participatory planning. Indeed, in 1998, the British development ministry and Oxfam had seconded experts to run Tumusiime's participatory poverty assessments; and the Bank had begun work on *Voices of the Poor,* a gigantic, worldwide version of Tumusiime's project, which canvassed the views of sixty thousand poor people in sixty countries. The enthusiasm for participatory methods was shared by Masood Ahmed, the Bank's chief debt negotiator; the vice-presidential unit that he headed had produced a stream of research suggesting that projects were better implemented if they solicited broad input in the design phase. Indeed, the Bank's researchers were coming to the view that a failure to promote farmers' participation explained the disappointments of McNamara's Integrated Rural Development Projects in the 1970s. And so, as well as requiring that poor countries come up with broad development plans in order to avoid the trap of fungibility, the debt negotiators required that these plans be drawn up in a participatory fashion.

The support for broad planning and participation blurred into the other big idea that was then brewing in the World Bank's brain trust. At the end of 1998, the Bank had published *Assessing Aid,* a devastating multicountry study of the failures of donor conditionality, which showed that aid given to countries that don't voluntarily pursue good policies is ineffective. To illustrate the fruitlessness of aid to places with poor policies, *Assessing Aid* cited Tanzania, where donors had poured $2 billion into road building over a twenty-year period, but where roads often deteriorated faster than they could be built.[27] To illustrate the hopelessness of changing bad policies by imposing conditions, the study cited countries such as Zambia, where policies grew steadily worse during the 1970s and 1980s despite a steady increase in aid throughout the period. But to show how aid could be productive in countries that drew up good, politically legitimate development plans, the study cited success stories including (yes, again) Uganda. It helped perhaps that Paul Collier, the Bank's head of economic research, had frequently advised Uganda's president, Museveni.

By the middle of 1999, therefore, three strands of development thinking were coming together: countries should draw up broad development plans so that donors could be confident that their aid was really boosting direct attacks on poverty; they should do this in a participatory fashion; and since donor conditions were fruitless, they had to "own" their development. And so, at the World Bank's 1999 annual meetings, the rich world's donors declared a profound change in policy. To qualify for the enhanced debt relief now offered—indeed, to qualify for aid more generally—all poor countries should draw up a Poverty Reduction Strategy Paper modeled on Uganda's development plan. The new poverty paper should lay out all the country's development challenges; it should explain which donors were expected to help solve each one of them; and it should arrive at its conclusions through a broad, participatory process. Although donors were ordaining this, the intention was to put poor countries in the driver's seat. A successor strategy to authoritarian aid conditionality had finally emerged.

There could scarcely have been a clearer vindication of Wolfensohn's development instincts. The boss had issued a call for comprehensive, participatory, country-owned development strategies. He had been blocked and ridiculed because he had made the mistake of claiming novelty, because his style had encouraged his staff to get too far ahead in Bolivia, and because the Bank's board mistrusted and resented him. But by the annual meetings in September 1999, his instincts had become the rich world's policy, and the communiqué made his victory official. The Development Committee, the group of ministers that assembles at the Bank's annual and spring meetings, laid down that countries hoping not just for debt relief but also for IDA assistance must draw up their new poverty papers in the spirit of Wolfensohn's Comprehensive Development Framework.

. . .

IN A SENSE, Wolfensohn's roundabout triumph was not really surprising. His framework had reflected the same intellectual currents that had animated the debt-relief negotiators; and not for the first time, development fashion was responding to the spirit of the era. At the start of the 1960s, the new IDA-equipped Bank reflected the expansive spirit of John F. Kennedy's "development decade." In the late 1960s and early 1970s, McNamara's focus on poverty reflected the contemporary concern with inequality, expressed in happy talk about the "dethronement of GNP." In the 1980s, the Bank's agenda mirrored the Reagan-Thatcher faith in radical free-market reformism. Now, in the Internet age, a new faith was rising: it was skeptical of hierarchy, and it preached "empowerment." The bottom-up participatory philosophy of Wolfensohn's Comprehensive Development Framework and the debt negotiators' Poverty Reduction Strategy Papers reflected the popular assumptions of the times.

You could see the rise of bottom-up thinking in many fields and disciplines, but it was especially evident among the modish cohorts of American business. In corporations all over the country, the top-down authoritarianism of Henry Ford's production lines (workers are stupid, so give them simple jobs that they can repeat mindlessly) was giving way to a Dennis Bakke–style grassrootsy optimism (workers are creative, so give them full decentralized authority); in 1999, the *Harvard Business Review* reported that thirty thousand articles on managerial empowerment had appeared in the business press over the previous four years.[28] Bill Clinton, Tony Blair, and other Third Way leaders had absorbed much of this writing, and so they found participatory development intuitively attractive.[29] For discredited top-down Fordism, substitute authoritarian aid conditionality. For decentralized "network" businesses, substitute participatory development plans.

Participation was also attractive to Third Way types for another reason, and therein lay great hope for the World Bank. The Third Way faith was that the old conflict between the Left and the Right reflected a failure of imagination; if you consulted widely and heard everybody's voices, you could chart a course down the center. For the missionaries of this faith, the obligations were onerous: you had to get out there and bond with people; you had to hear everybody, poll everybody, feel everybody's pain. But the rewards were potentially enormous. You could heal the divisions that caused societies to work at cross-purposes; you could turn cynical bystanders into allies in the struggle for progress. To differing degrees, Clinton, Blair, and Schröder shared this healer's ambition. They refused to play to the class divisions of the old politics, and they aspired to bring everyone together. It was a new path to consensual national progress. It was a marvelous strategy for winning elections.

For the World Bank and for Wolfensohn, the attractions of participatory consensus were at least as strong. Few institutions had suffered more from the left-right polarization of the old politics: The Right had lambasted the Bank because it was a public-sector institution; the Left had assailed it because it preached free-market nostrums. What if Third Way balm could heal these old divisions? Wolfensohn's first term in office was a Third Way attempt to prove healing was possible. The new Left—the Third Way Left—was not knee-jerk antimarket, so the Bank might catch a break for once, particularly if Wolfensohn cranked up the Bank's rhetorical focus on poverty and social justice. The new Right—or at least the electable Right—was not against public institutions if they made an effort to learn from the efficient private sector; and Wolfensohn had launched a campaign to do just that. The old Bank had been surrounded and embattled. The new Bank would reach out to everybody and participate with everybody, and end its debilitating encirclement.

In sum, there were many good reasons why participation came to dominate development in the late 1990s. The spirit of the Internet pushed in that direction. Third Way governments were setting the agenda. The World Bank was fighting its long battle against its numerous critics. If the Madrid annual meetings of 1994 had marked a low point in the Bank's fortunes, the Washington annual meetings that ratified the new participatory approach in 1999 marked the completion of the Bank's comeback strategy. The Bank had listened to its critics and changed radically. It had abandoned an economics-first approach in favor of a comprehensive one. It had abandoned top-down conditions in favor of bottom-up participation. It would meet everybody, hear everybody, appreciate every last problem. It would banish the gentlemanly reserve of Lewis Preston or the senior George Bush. It would reflect the empathetic personality of a new generation of leaders: leaders like Bill Clinton and Jim Wolfensohn.

NONE OF THIS MEANT that the Bank was set for calmer waters, not by a long shot. Third Way exponents had a knack for busting up the quiet created by their policies with unquiet personal behavior, as the Clinton scandals demonstrated. In the last part of 1999, Wolfensohn fumed and fizzed about the fate of his Comprehensive Development Framework, compounding the bitter relations with his top managers and the board. His ideas had won out, but not in the way that he had planned, and this made him furious. The CDF network, the CDF pilots, the innumerable CDF speeches and one-on-one sales efforts— none in the end mattered as much as an entirely separate debt-reduction process that Wolfensohn neither initiated nor led. All through that time, the demon inside Wolfensohn regarded the Poverty Reduction Strategy Papers as an evil rival, a plot to bury his Comprehensive Development Framework with someone else's paradigm. Masood Ahmed, the Bank's debt negotiator who had played a lead role in the creation of the new poverty-reduction papers, quit the institution shortly afterward. Wolfensohn had made his life impossible.

But it was not just personal demons that overshadowed the Third Way. The strategy's basic premise—that by hearing everybody you can build a warm consensus—is unfortunately too hopeful. A year after the excitement of the Bolivia workout, the country discovered the limits to participation. Despite Jorge Quiroga's efforts to promote national dialogue, there remained no real national consensus, and a botched water privatization provoked violent riots in the city of Cochabamba in 2000. Three years later, Bolivia's persistent social divisions welled up again. Opponents of World Bank–backed reform staged protests around the country, upsetting the government that succeeded Quiroga's and forcing the president's resignation.

Uganda's progress proved a bit more durable. If you visited the country in 2003, you could see Kampala's prosperity in its dense traffic; in the bustle of the light-industrial workshops in Katwe, the slum that Wolfensohn had visited; and even in the window of a real estate agent opposite the Kampala Casino and the Goldfinger Forex Bureau, which advertised a spacious three-bedroom bungalow for $250,000. Perhaps just as tellingly, you could marvel at the physical security that Uganda had accomplished, at least in the southern part of the country: Ugandans were now worried about such mundane risks as dangerous drivers, and a prosperous lawyer explained that visiting Canada was just too perilous because of a recent SARS outbreak. And yet, by 2003, Uganda combined worrying signs with good ones, and new data suggested that the decline in poverty had halted and even reversed slightly. Museveni had spent too much on his army and launched a military adventure in Congo; he had neglected the poor north of his country; and corruption was on the rise. Donors faced a mild version of the Suharto problem. A strongman and a gifted technocrat had created a development role model, and a tide of enthusiastic aid money was buoying the country. But the strongman was by no means perfect, and there would be no substitute for independently strong institutions when it was time for him to go.

In the years after 1999, as the Bank tried to replicate Uganda's success story the world over, the participatory approach proved hard to implement. The Bank's better clients drew up Poverty Reduction Strategy Papers just as they were told to, and in a handful of cases the Bank rewarded this effort with a promising innovation known as the Poverty Reduction Strategy Credit. This new kind of loan was a tame version of the Bolivia experiment. The Bank cut its red tape, streamlined its lending, and left it to the government to figure out the best way to reach agreed development targets. But in most developing countries, the new approach proved hard to implement. Governments resented the Bank's efforts to get civil society around a table; or civil society was suspicious and disruptive; or there was no Tumusiime-style budget machinery for translating a participatory development plan into real shifts in spending. By late 2003, when Bolivia's government was falling, only forty or so countries had completed Poverty Reduction Strategy Papers, and fewer than a dozen were deemed good enough to be rewarded with the new Bolivia-style credit.

In sum, Wolfensohn's Comprehensive Development Framework was a compelling vision of the way the Bank might work in ideal conditions—handing control over to poor countries, supporting their development plans in a new and streamlined fashion—but the unfortunate truth was that many of the Bank's client countries lacked the institutions and conditions to assume this responsibility. There was an answer to this conundrum, and the Bank duly moved toward it: it should direct most of its loans to countries with good policies and institutions; elsewhere it should concentrate on dialogue and technical assistance, in the hope of fostering a promising environment that could absorb aid usefully. But the next three years were to show repeatedly how hard it was for the World Bank to stick to this playbook. Rich-country NGOs and rich-country shareholders would constantly disrupt its efforts, ruining Wolfensohn's hopes to put poor countries in the driver's seat, and raising questions about the viability of big multilateral institutions.

Wolfensohn scarcely had to wait to feel the limits of his Third Way strategy. In December 1999, just two months after the victory of his participatory ideas at the Bank's annual meetings, a summit of the World Trade Organization in Seattle collapsed in violent confusion. Unannounced and unexpected, the era of antiglobalization protests had started.

CHAPTER TEN

FROM SEATTLE TO TIBET

NOBODY SAW WHAT WAS COMING in Seattle. Perched on the Pacific Rim, and home to global corporations like Boeing and Microsoft, the city seemed a natural place to hold a trade summit. The local business establishment gladly coughed up nearly $10 million to host the gathering: the summit would be a boon to the city's merchants, they reasoned, and besides, trade accounted for one in three jobs in the city. Sure, labor unions would stage a protest, but they had a right to express their opinion, and the city fathers obligingly renamed a downtown avenue Union Way to welcome them. Sure, environmentalists would dress up in turtle costumes, in reference to a trade dispute involving turtle-safe shrimp nets, but there would be no harm in such street theater. Nobody predicted that the summit would end in a mess of smashed shop windows and tear gas. Nobody anticipated the placards proclaiming, FUCK THE CIVIL, LET'S GET DISOBEDIENT.

It did not take long, however, for the message to sink in. The battle in Seattle announced a new kind of public protest, as international and as militant as the brigades that stormed the Madrid annual meetings five years earlier, but newly agile and spontaneous. The Fifty Years Is Enough campaign had spent months working up to the Madrid spectacular, and the World Bank's strategists knew that they were in for trouble. But the Seattle phenomenon had come almost out of nowhere. With the help of the Internet and cell phones, a thousand disparate groups could coalesce in a matter of a few days or so; they could swarm against a target and paralyze it with stings. And their ranks had multiplied dramatically. According to one count, the number of international NGOs had leapt from six thousand in 1990 to twenty-six thousand in 1999.[1] The environmental movement had grown especially quickly, and the headquarters of groups like the World Wildlife Fund in Washington were as large and imposing as fancy corporate offices. In his State of the Union speech three years earlier, Bill Clinton had famously proclaimed that the era of big government was over. Now the era of big nongovernment was dawning.

The new era promised trouble for all established institutions: a fresh player had muscled up to the world's top table and was challenging the veterans. After the assault on the World Trade Organization in Seattle, a flood of newspaper commentary predicted a new world disorder, with other multilateral bodies like the International Monetary Fund likely to be assailed in the same way. Yet the World Bank was expected to escape this treatment. Jim Wolfensohn, noted *The Economist,* had spent the past four years building bridges to big nongovernment. He had made "dialogue" with NGOs one of the Bank's central priorities. More than seventy NGO specialists worked in the Bank's field offices. More than half of World Bank projects involved NGOs as implementing partners.[2]

This was if anything an understatement of Wolfensohn's efforts. On scores of occasions, he had sat down with the Bank's most vociferous critics and invited them to have at him; he would preside at the head of the table, writing notes in order to contain his temper; and then after forty-five minutes or so he would suggest that he had understood. "Why don't we stipulate you think we're all a bunch of shits," he'd say, and then he would come back at them. The World Bank's people, he would tell them, are just as concerned about poverty as anyone; they don't get up in the morning and wonder how to entrench poverty; they work in a development institution because they believe in development. And who are NGOs to criticize? NGOs are not democratically accountable, whereas the World Bank answers to mostly democratic governments. NGOs are capable of screwing up development projects; the difference is that World Bank screwups get attention, because the Bank is more open to scrutiny. Neither side could claim a monopoly on virtue. Surely it was time to quit pointing fingers and unite against the common enemy of global poverty.[3]

Wolfensohn was a master of this kind of meeting. The NGOs were used to walking into sessions with World Bank officials and seizing the moral high ground; they would talk emotionally about poverty, and about their own struggles to relieve suffering. But now they confronted a World Bank president who was more missionary than they were, who could talk longer and more passionately about shantytowns and villages.[4] More than that, Wolfensohn combined this passion with other techniques of seduction. He would flatter NGOs with his intense listening. He would talk eagerly of partnership. He would use his intellect to enlarge their ideas rather than merely to belittle them. Bruce Rich, perhaps the leading anti-Bank environmentalist, had been treated as a mortal enemy by the Bank's spin doctors until Wolfensohn's arrival. But then Wolfensohn had him over to his home for dinner, and the Bank vice presidents in attendance treated him with unfamiliar deference. They respected his views; they wanted to learn from him. At the end of the evening, one of the vice presidents declared that after such a friendly interchange they could no longer possibly be enemies. "I guess we are frenemies," he said.[5]

There was more to Wolfensohn's outreach than personal diplomacy. He was changing the substance of the Bank's policies in ways the NGOs wanted. He broke the taboo on debt relief; he canceled the controversial Nepali dam project that had been decried at the Madrid annual meetings; and when the Bank announced in 1999 that all IDA borrowers must prepare participatory Poverty Reduction Strategy Papers, it was effectively giving NGOs a say in the Bank's choice of projects. Meanwhile, Wolfensohn invited NGOs into the Bank's global strategizing, setting up a variety of commissions to consider, for example, the record on structural adjustment or best practice on dams. Mark Malloch Brown, the Wolfensohn adviser who did as much as anyone to forge this inclusive strategy, later compared this phase in the Bank's history to the time when the British East India Company allowed missionaries into its territory. The nineteenth-century missionary societies were the NGOs of yesteryear; in 1813 they swarmed the British Parliament with no fewer than 837 petitions, urging that the East India Company end its practice of excluding evangelical preachers. Nearly two centuries later, the World Bank found itself in a similar position. The Fifty Years Is Enough campaign had swarmed all over it, making further effort to exclude NGOs seem futile, and Wolfensohn was duly summoning them into his dominion.[6]

Letting in the missionaries did not solve India's problems, and it did not solve Wolfensohn's either. Less than five months after the Seattle protests, the hope that Wolfensohn's outreach would protect the Bank from the new antiglobalization movement proved unfounded. At the Bank's spring meetings in April 2000, the globophobes laid siege to it. Meanwhile the Bank's NGO-friendly positioning got it into trouble with the U.S. administration.

THREE WEEKS BEFORE that year's spring meetings, the self-styled Mobilization for Global Justice descended upon Washington. It was a motley alliance of odd groups, ranging from the Forum of Indian Leftists to the Progressive Librarians Guild to the splendidly named Quixote Center. The mobilizers set about organizing protest workshops, complete with instructions on how to cope with tear gas, and there was not much evidence that they had even heard of Wolfensohn's half decade of

bridge building with the more responsible portions of the NGO movement. When the spring meetings began, the protesters kicked off with a
piece of street theater designed to dramatize the debt issue, and never
mind that the World Bank had approved deeper debt relief six months
previously. They held up placards reading, IMF PLUS WORLD BANK
EQUALS HUNDREDS RICH, BILLIONS POOR, oblivious to Wolfensohn's
efforts to distance the Bank from the IMF's prescriptions. Other placards attacked the Bank's dam-building program, even though Wolfensohn had allowed almost no large dam projects to go forward in the past
half decade.[7]

The unfairness of these attacks was obvious. "Blaming the World
Bank for poverty is a bit like blaming the Red Cross for starting World
Wars I and II," lamented the head of the World Trade Organization.
But there was no point in looking for logic: the international technocratic and commercial elite, untutored in the rough arts of street politics,
was facing off against an angry and amorphous adversary, untutored in
economics.[8] Few of the protesters paused to consider that the Bank had
transferred nearly $1 billion a year to sub-Saharan Africa during the
1990s, even after you subtracted African repayments on old loans. They
felt good beating up a bogeyman called globalization. Big international
organizations were presumed to be the bogeyman's henchmen.

Looking back on the confusion of those protests, they seem like a
sort of parody of the NGO movement a decade earlier. In the 1980s,
environmental groups had assailed the Bank with mostly reasonable
criticisms. The Bank was indeed insensitive to the environment, often
unwilling to consult local communities about the impact of its projects,
and secretive. By the late 1990s, however, the Bank had changed substantially: the shift had begun under Lew Preston, who created a strong
environmental department despite his fear of institutional overstretch,
and had been vastly accelerated by Wolfensohn's outreach campaign.
Some groups like Oxfam recognized the change, and turned from
adversaries to allies; other NGOs such as Care were more interested in

delivering aid than in anti-Bank campaigning. But another portion of
the NGO movement kept pounding on the Bank, and never mind that
it had changed; they always found new things to hate, even if they
found them by imagining them. And yet, in the spring of 2000, not
everyone saw that. The halo effect from the early NGO campaigns
against the Bank remained. Hadn't the critics been right about the
Bank's destruction of the Brazilian rain forest in the 1980s? Hadn't they
driven the Bank to take the environment seriously and to become more
transparent? And didn't the research literature now show that NGO
participation improved projects? Besides, the turmoil of the Asian
financial crisis seemed to prove that arrogant Washington institutions
still needed to be held to account. Whatever the confusion of the protesters' placards, they were widely presumed to be onto something.

One person who credited the demonstrators with more logic than
they exhibited was the World Bank's sometime chief economist. During the course of 1999, Joe Stiglitz's continuing attacks on the IMF had
infuriated both his target and the U.S. Treasury, until finally in November Wolfensohn had removed him; there were rumors that Larry Summers, who by then had become treasury secretary, had demanded
Stiglitz's dismissal as the price for Wolfensohn's second five-year term,
which would start in June 2000. Whether Summers really did this
seems doubtful[9]—"I'd have told him to fuck himself," Wolfensohn said,
upon hearing this charge—but there is no doubt that Summers was
annoyed at what happened next. Even after his dismissal, Stiglitz stayed
on at the Bank as a senior adviser; and in the run-up to the April 2000
spring meetings, when the demonstrators' workshops around Washington were already humming, Stiglitz published a cover story in the *New
Republic* that tipped Summers from annoyance into fury.

From Wolfensohn's point of view, keeping Stiglitz on the payroll
helped to distance the Bank from the IMF and mollify NGO critics.
But Stiglitz's *New Republic* article took the principle of siding with the
NGOs to new and extraordinary lengths. Stiglitz began by noting that

the demonstrators would decry the International Monetary Fund, though he conveniently overlooked the fact that they would decry the Bank also; he went on to assert that the demonstrators would "have a point." Stiglitz then repeated his critique of the IMF's record in Asia and Russia: the fund had got its prescriptions wrong; it was obsessed with macroeconomics and ignorant of microeconomics; it handed out too much shock and too little therapy. Stretching to connect his critique to the street protests that would dominate the headlines, Stiglitz concluded: "This is what the demonstrators shouting outside the IMF next week will try to say."[10]

As it turned out, there were no reported sightings of placards proclaiming, "We agree with Stiglitz." Indeed, for anyone who actually went to the protest workshops or waded in among the demonstrators, the idea that the mobilizers were animated by excessive fiscal tightening in Thailand was ludicrous. It was clear, in fact, that the throng was jubilantly muddled—especially when a mini-protest broke out over a fictional Bulgarian pastry chef who rejoiced in the name of Stanko. A low-budget-film maker had needed a crowd scene for his movie about Stanko, so he had rigged up a few placards and sent his friends to wave them in front of the demonstrators. Soon there was a buzz of interest. Was Stanko a hero of the antiglobalization movement, the nearby protesters were asking? Nobody could say, but what the heck, he must be! Before long several had quit denouncing turtle-killing fishing nets and sundry other enemies. "Stanko!" they screamed happily.

The carnival of craziness continued, with some people stripping off their clothes and some people charging the police with bits of broken fencing, and the demonstrators, perhaps having missed the nuances of Stiglitz's *New Republic* article, were linking arms outside the World Bank's headquarters, blocking delegates who wanted to get in. Amid the tear gas and pepper spray, some six hundred people were arrested. But Stiglitz was not daunted. On April 17, the second day of the protests, he appeared on television.[11]

The protesters were saying that the IMF and the World Bank were unjust, observed the interviewer. Did they have a point?

"I think they do," Stiglitz answered, sticking to his *New Republic* argument. And then the television audience was treated to the spectacle of a World Bank senior adviser savaging the International Monetary Fund. Stan Fischer, the IMF's number two, got home that evening after a long day of dodging the demonstrations and heard Stiglitz's comments. What could have possessed this man? The TV interviewer had asked Stiglitz to choose sides between Stankoist crazies and the International Monetary Fund, and Stiglitz was with the Stankoists! For both Fischer and Summers, this was a low point in their regard for Stiglitz— and by extension Wolfensohn. Why had Wolfensohn allowed this rabble-rouser to stay on as his adviser? Either he was too cowardly to fire him, or he agreed with his message.[12]

Meanwhile, Wolfensohn's standing at the IMF and the U.S. Treasury was suffering another blow, also stemming from the drive to bring the NGO missionaries inside the Bank's tent. The Bank's global version of Uganda's participatory poverty assessment was coming to a climax in early 2000, with the finalization of the Bank's World Development Report on poverty. The report's lead author was Ravi Kanbur, the economist who had written a pro-debt-relief memo to Wolfensohn when he first arrived at the World Bank five years earlier, and Kanbur had gone about preparing his poverty study in the same iconoclastic spirit. Having used participatory assessments to understand and define poverty, Kanbur used participation to write his report about it. He traveled about the world consulting NGOs on the report's content, and in February and March 2000, hundreds of organizations took part in an Internet conference to comment on a draft version. Not surprisingly, this participatory process yielded a document that stressed participation's virtues: the poor must be allowed to participate in the planning of development; they must be given "voice," Kanbur insisted. The early draft also made concessions to NGO complaints about structural adjustment. Liberalization of trade and capital flows is not always good for poor people, the report contended.

All this fitted Wolfensohn's agenda. It reinforced the idea that "voice," "empowerment," and other noneconomic challenges lay at the heart of development; and it built bridges to big nongovernment. But, just as in the case of Stiglitz, what suited the Wolfensohn agenda did not necessarily impress others. Larry Summers and the U.S. Treasury were appalled by Kanbur's first draft, and Summers didn't shrink from attacking Wolfensohn in front of all the international bigwigs on the Bank's governing Development Committee. To write a report about poverty without putting economic growth front and center was like staging a performance of *Hamlet* without the prince, Summers suggested; besides, dwelling on the wrinkles in the case for trade would merely encourage the protectionist backlash that had loomed since Seattle. Summers's views were echoed by several academic heavyweights,[13] who agreed that Kanbur's exposition of voicelessness would distract the Bank from the basic challenge of getting economic policy right in poor countries; and even the Bank's own research department came out with a report arguing that the best way to tackle poverty was to promote growth.[14] Kanbur was told he had to revise his first draft in ways inimical to big nongovernment. In May 2000, Kanbur resigned his position, and NGOs cried out that Wolfensohn's failure to protect the poverty report's original thesis reflected U.S. bullying, again.[15]

And so, in the space of just a month or two, the illusion of a Third Way escape from left-right confrontation had been shattered three times. The demonstrations during the spring meetings showed that Wolfensohn's five years of NGO outreach had not insulated the Bank from noisy adversaries. The fight over Joe Stiglitz showed how siding with NGOs in public arguments could bring down the wrath of the U.S. Treasury. The row over Ravi Kanbur taught the same lesson again. Meanwhile the Bank was stumbling through a fourth firestorm, more serious by far than any of the others. It was disrupting the Bank's relations with its biggest client, and demonstrating that the Bank's political encirclement was more than merely disagreeable. Encirclement could undermine the Bank's poverty-fighting mission.

THE BIG CLIENT WAS CHINA, which borrowed more from the Bank during the 1990s than any other country.[16] There was an extremely good reason for this: not only was China the world's most populous nation, it was also the most spectacularly efficient at eliminating poverty. Indeed, China's performance was so strong that it transformed the global picture, rescuing the Bank from some embarrassment. In the rest of the developing world, according to the Bank's own statistics, the number of people living below the dollar-per-day line actually increased between 1987 and 1998, and not by a small number: 100 million extra people were living in abject poverty despite all the efforts of the world's development agencies. But, fortunately for the aid folk, China lifted the same number of people out of poverty over this period. So if you added China into the picture, the embarrassment vanished.[17]

Because the Chinese were so successful, the Bank was eager to lend them as much as possible. Projects in China nearly always succeeded: they reduced poverty; they won terrific grades from the Bank's internal evaluation department; and the government had no difficulty repaying the money. The intellectual currents of the late 1990s only reinforced the case for shoveling money into China. *Assessing Aid,* the 1998 study that had discredited conditionality, offered two central conclusions. First, since conditions were generally powerless to reform laggards, the Bank should lend to countries with a track record of successful development; second, the Bank should lend to countries with large amounts of poverty. China fitted both conditions. Indeed, the Bank could arguably maximize its effect on human suffering if it pulled out of every other country and did business exclusively with the Chinese.

In early 1999, one year before the Stankoist Mobilization, the Bank
had some forty China projects in various stages of preparation. One of
these schemes, which was nearly ready to go forward to the board,
involved moving fifty-eight thousand farmers from a hopelessly
parched hillside in the western province of Qinghai. The farmers would
go to an irrigated area in another part of the province; a small dam
would be built to collect melting snow for them; their resettlement
would be voluntary. A few years earlier, a Bank study had noted that
similar relocation projects in China had been—yes—hugely successful
in reducing poverty, and there was no reason to suppose that this one
would be different. In April 1999, when a Chinese team visited Washington to conclude project negotiations, everything went smoothly. The
work finished faster than expected, and the World Bank's task manager
returned to his office with a sense of achievement.[18]

Back at his desk, the task manager found a message from the Tibet
Information Network in London. He returned the call and answered a
few questions.[19] The province of Qinghai borders on the Tibet Autonomous Region, and 1 million of Qinghai's 5 million inhabitants are
Tibetan, so the interest of Tibet watchers was not surprising. The task
manager put down the phone and forgot about the conversation. But
later that month, during the 1999 spring meetings, it became clear that
trouble was brewing. The Tibet Information Network had a story in its
newsletter about a "controversial" Bank project that would "dramatically affect the demography" of Qinghai by moving ethnic Chinese into
an area that was culturally Tibetan. This was an explosive accusation.
"Population transfer of Chinese into traditional Tibetan areas has become a major concern for Tibetans in terms of the ongoing viability of
their civilization, identity and land," the newsletter said ominously.[20]

There was no denying that China's Tibet policy was abominable, but
the Bank's relocation plan presented no obvious threat to Tibetan
rights. On the contrary, it would benefit the thirty-five hundred

Tibetans who were part of the group that would move to newly irrigated farmland; and it would benefit those who stayed behind also, since it would reduce population pressure on their land. To be sure, most of the farmers who moved would be Muslim or Han Chinese rather than Tibetan; but it was not as though these settlers would disrupt a Tibetan community, because no Tibetans lived in the immediate settlement area. The nearest Tibetans were 276 nomadic herders—the Bank had counted them carefully—who wintered in a place sixty kilometers south of the project.[21] Indeed, the whole notion that Qinghai was "traditionally Tibetan" was debatable. Qinghai Province had been settled by Tibetan nomads in the seventh century and by Mongolian nomads in the thirteenth century, and its eastern fringe, where the majority of its people lived, had been under Chinese rule for most of the past two thousand years, stretching back to the Han dynasty. For the past two hundred years, moreover, the Chinese had ruled over the entire territory. In short, Qinghai had been part of China for as long as the United States had been independent. It was no more Tibetan than Texas is Mexican.[22]

The Bank's first response to the Tibet Information Network was to put out a polite press release, explaining that the project was neither located in Tibet nor bad for Tibetans. This did not impress anybody. The Tibet Information Network in London was in touch with Tibet campaigners in Washington, and they had received some protest letters from Tibetans in Qinghai—evidence that no matter how good a development project, it will always make somebody unhappy. The Tibet campaigners linked up with veterans of the Fifty Years Is Enough campaign: environmental groups that opposed anything with a dam in it, human rights groups that opposed anything involving relocation, still other groups that opposed pretty much anything the Bank did. Within a month, this coalition had dispatched a long letter to Wolfensohn blasting the Qinghai project. It warned of "a social and ecological disaster." It protested the transfer of "Chinese farmers into a traditionally

Tibetan area." And it was signed by representatives of fifty-nine organizations, an astonishing worldwide network stretching from Mexico to Thailand.[23]

In May and June 1999, the NGOs swarmed frantically. The campaigners organized a deluge of e-mails and faxes, which clogged up the Bank's hardware; they organized rock concerts and handed out prewritten protest postcards. They quickly won allies in Hollywood and allies in the U.S. Congress, notably Nancy Pelosi, a prominent California Democrat. On June 15, a press release announcing a joint appearance by Pelosi and a pro-Tibet musician stated bluntly that the Bank planned to move "60,000 ethnic Chinese" into Qinghai, even though Han Chinese constituted only 40 percent of the settlers, and even though they were not moving *into* Qinghai, just moving to a different part of it.[24] Two days later, sixty members of Congress fired off a letter to Wolfensohn, protesting the project. When a World Bank delegation went up to the Hill to mollify the lawmakers, it was confronted with a map that did not even show Qinghai. The entire province had been labeled Tibetan, and never mind that Tibetans accounted for only one in five people living there.

Anti-Chinese sentiment—which united legitimate hatred of dictators with self-interested hatred of low-wage competition gave the Qinghai campaign its impetus. But the NGO swarm was as diverse in its arguments as in its membership. The traditional anti-Bank groups poured through the Qinghai project documents and seized upon possible infringements of the Bank's own policies—policies that had been written mostly because of NGO pressure. The Bank, for example, had a guideline requiring "special action" to protect ethnic minorities, and the critics suggested that this had been violated. It had a guideline on resettlement, and the critics charged that the Bank was wrong to call the Qinghai resettlement "voluntary" given that China is a police state. Finally, the critics made hay out of the Bank's environmental guidelines. The Bank had classified Qinghai as a medium-risk "Category B" project rather than a high-risk "Category A" one, and had commissioned an environmental impact study that was correspondingly less searching. The critics declared that anything involving a dam was supposed to be an "A."

The June letter from the sixty members of Congress combined all these criticisms, and added that there was a danger that the Qinghai irrigation scheme would be constructed with prison labor. This was a particularly low blow. The Bank had extracted written assurances from the Chinese that no prison labor would be involved in the project, and Bank documents stated clearly that it would monitor the issue. The same went for the question of "voluntary" resettlement: China was clearly a police state, but the Bank's China veterans were confident that in the case of the Qinghai project, the relocation was genuinely voluntary because farmers wanted better land; indeed, three times more farmers wanted to move than the project could accommodate.[25] The idea that the project had ignored the needs of ethnic minorities was wrong also: own-language schooling and other provisions were built into the project. The accusation on which the Bank proved most vulnerable was the "B" grade environmental categorization. The project involved a dam, albeit a small one. Perhaps "A" would have been appropriate.

In the confusion of June 1999, however, it was hard to sort out the reasonable criticisms from the unreasonable ones. The Clinton administration announced it would vote against the project when it came up for board approval; it had no desire to face down the Tibet lobby in Congress. Most journalists accepted the NGOs' view of the project; there is a tendency to assume that small, underdog groups must be the good guys, whereas big outfits like the World Bank are presumed to be malign. Anti-Bank posters started going up around Washington, and body-pierced Tibet activists set up camp outside the Bank's headquarters. A rap star from the Beastie Boys showed up to address the campers, and declared that the Bank's loan would lead to "the destruction of the Tibetan peoples"; "I want to think there are human beings running this establishment," he growled. Bhuchung Tsering, director of the International Campaign for Tibet, was more passive but no less aggressive: Bank officials, in his view, needed only enlightenment to change their minds. Jesse Helms, a far-right senator from North Carolina, seized the opportunity to condemn China and the development business in a single press release. The Bank was simultaneously up against students with body piercings and the right wing of the Republican Party. It was on a highway to nowhere.

As the pace of this campaign mounted, so did Wolfensohn's fury. He counted himself a friend of the NGOs, a friend of the Dalai Lama, a friend of Congresswoman Pelosi, and certainly a friend of China; he hated the idea that it was impossible to be friends with everyone. He fretted that this screwup might cost him his chance of winning a Nobel Peace Prize, and he fretted that his Hollywood connections would turn on him; Harrison Ford's wife was close to the Tibetans.[26] He had been put in an impossible situation, he fumed bitterly: if he pulled the Qinghai project, he would alienate the Bank's biggest borrower; but if he pressed ahead he would alienate the Bank's biggest shareholder. Either way, the penalty could be significant. The Chinese were threatening to cut off borrowing from the Bank, which would deprive the institution of the strongest part of its portfolio and maybe weaken the long term flow of profits from the Bank's market-based lending. On the other hand, the U.S. Congress was threatening to cut payments to the next replenishment of IDA, which would weaken the Bank even more surely.

In his frustration and fury, Wolfensohn lashed out. He railed that the whole mess reflected the political blindness of World Bankers— Didn't they ever read the newspapers? Didn't they know that Tibet was supersensitive?—and he would summon people to his office and demand whose arse he should kick first. It was not an edifying spectacle, since Wolfensohn shared responsibility for failing to predict the wrath of the Tibet lobby; Lodi Gyari, the Dalai Lama's representative in Washington, had raised the project with him early on and warned him of potential trouble. And yet, in the days after the June letter from the sixty congressional opponents, Wolfensohn devised an exit strategy. Little did he realize what that strategy would bring.

WOLFENSOHN'S EXIT STRATEGY involved the Bank's Inspection Panel, a sort of internal tribunal set up in 1993. Having lobbied the Bank to create safeguard procedures on the environment, resettlement, and so on, NGOs had lobbied for a mechanism to enforce this quasi-legislation; they had persuaded the U.S. Congress to block money for IDA until the Bank gave in to them. The result was the Inspection Panel. If a project appeared to violate one of the Bank's prudential guidelines, NGOs could complain to this new panel and have the project investigated.

On June 18, 1999, the day after the letter from the sixty members of Congress was sent, the International Campaign for Tibet duly filed an Inspection Panel complaint. There were questions as to whether the filing was valid: The panel's rules stipulated that the filer generally had to be a member of the Bank's board or an outside group affected by the project, and an NGO based in the United States hardly seemed to qualify. But Wolfensohn saw an opportunity. The Inspection Panel offered a way out of his dilemma—alienate the United States or alienate China—since it would take the fate of the Qinghai project out of his hands. He therefore looked about for another way to activate the panel; and when the American director indicated that she might do so on her own authority, Wolfensohn moved fast. A board meeting on June 24 formally approved the project but simultaneously suspended it pending an Inspection Panel investigation. Wolfensohn calculated that a political fight over Tibet would now become a technical inquiry into Category A and B environmental risk factors. Tempers would cool gradually, and a compromise would become possible.

Wolfensohn's strategy was paradoxical. To escape an NGO swarm he had embraced an NGO demand for an Inspection Panel inquiry. It was the same paradox that ran all through the Bank's approach to post-Madrid encirclement: to placate your missionary critics, allow them into your dominion. But the flaw in this strategy is that some NGOs cannot be placated; their whole reason for existence is to be implacable. Campaigning NGOs, as distinct from those with programs in the field, almost have to be radical; if they stop denouncing big organizations, nobody will send them cash or quote them in the newspapers. Partly for this reason, and partly out of a likable conviction that the status quo is never good enough, most NGOs do not have an off switch. You can grant their demand that you abandon structural adjustment or call in the Inspection Panel, but they will still demonstrate outside your building. Of course, there will be grown-up groups like Oxfam that do accept your olive branch. But they will be the exceptions, and they may cooperate only cautiously. They don't want to be the next target for the radicals.[27]

Unfortunately for Wolfensohn, the Qinghai episode illustrated this lack of an NGO off switch. The Inspection Panel exit strategy was a clever compromise; it promised the project's critics ample chance to prove their grievances. And yet, two days after the board meeting, a pair of student activists clambered up the face of the Bank's headquarters and unfurled a banner proclaiming, WORLD BANK APPROVES CHINA'S GENOCIDE IN TIBET. Privately, other Tibet groups disapproved of these tactics—after all, there was no evidence of "genocide"—but they were unwilling to speak out publicly against their fellow activists.[28] As always, the most extreme voices boomed loudest. From the U.S. Congress, Senator Connie Mack and Representative Benjamin Gilman accused the Bank of "cultural genocide." And despite Wolfensohn's efforts at compromise, the House of Representatives voted to cut IDA funding by $200 million.

The tension with Congress continued on into the autumn, with the introduction of a House bill accusing the Bank of providing "$160 million to build a large dam in Tibet."[29] Yet this was by no means Wolfensohn's sole worry. In an attempt to build international acceptance for the Qinghai project, the Bank had persuaded the Chinese to allow journalists and researchers access to the region; but when an Australian and an American took advantage of this access, they were promptly arrested. After three days of vicious interrogation, the American attempted to escape by jumping from a window; he fell and shattered several of his vertebrae.[30] The premise for the Qinghai project was in danger of shattering simultaneously. The Bank's decision to go ahead depended on the credibility of Chinese promises not to use prison labor and so on; if the promise on researchers' access had turned out to be empty, why believe the rest of them? The American Tibet lobby redoubled its calls for the project to be canceled and summoned its legions for another demonstration outside the Bank's headquarters.

In Jackson Hole that summer, Wolfensohn had assembled his top managers for a bonding session. There were several new faces in his entourage, and he wanted to build team spirit. There were fishing outings during the day and great wine in the evenings, but the shadow of Qinghai loomed over the group. During one bull session when the managers were assembled near the fireplace in the living room, the discussion turned to China and Wolfensohn exploded.

"Goddamn it!" he roared, according to one of the managers who was in the meeting. "I still want to find out who approved this project! And I'm not getting any names!" Wolfensohn rounded upon Sven Sandstrom, the Swedish managing director who oversaw East Asia. "You don't travel at all!" he yelled at him. "You didn't even go to China!"

Very very quietly, Sandstrom answered, "I've been there."

"Well, when did you go?"

"I went there three months ago," Sandstrom replied evenly.

For a moment Wolfensohn looked deflated, but only for a moment. "Did you go to Qinghai?" he demanded. "Any idiot would know, if you went out there, that there were Tibetans. Why would you do a project when the Tibetans were there?"[31]

In the midst of this recrimination, the Inspection Panel inquiry got under way. It did not exert the calming influence that Wolfensohn had anticipated. The head of the Inspection Panel, Jim MacNeill, was a Canadian environmentalist; he maintained excellent relations with the NGOs that had campaigned on Qinghai, but he treated the Bank's staff with prosecutorial vigor. He summoned the Bank people in for questioning, which took place without any kind of defense counsel; then he published allegations of staff misconduct without publishing the evidence on which his claims were founded. Robert Wade, a political scientist from the London School of Economics, was hired by MacNeill to serve as a consultant to the panel; he arrived in October to find an atmosphere of fear and loathing. The Bank's staff described MacNeill as a "know-all," "patronizing," "nonlistener," "curmudgeonly"; he was prone to phrases like "only an idiot could say that." It felt, as Wade recalled later, like a court-martial—with the slight difference that in most courts-martial you have a right to an attorney.[32]

The court-martial took its toll on the morale of the East Asia region, which had already been punctured by the financial crisis and Wolfensohn's chaotic management reforms. In October 1999, the regional vice president announced his resignation; his deputy announced his departure soon afterward; and by March 2000, more than half of the East Asia department's twenty-seven managers had declared plans to move on.[33] Somebody was said to be spying on the managers of the Qinghai project—a surveillance camera was fitted in one office to deter snoopers—and it didn't help that the staff felt they were the object of a witch hunt not only from MacNeill and the Inspection Panel but also from Wolfensohn. The panel itself grew steadily more paranoid. In the first three months of 2000, MacNeill prepared the panel's report on a deliberately unnetworked computer to minimize the risk of hacking.[34]

On April 28, 2000, a fortnight after the Stankoist spring meetings, the Inspection Panel delivered a 160-page indictment of the Qinghai project. It insisted that the scheme should have been rated Category A for environmental riskiness; that insufficient attention had been paid to the impact on Mongolian and Tibetan nomads; that the recruitment of "volunteers" for resettlement had been compromised because the interviews had not been confidential. The complaints went on, echoing the assertions that the NGOs had made from the outset. In an attempt to leave no stone unthrown, as Robert Wade later put it, the report even objected that the settlers' new houses featured no power points for domestic appliances. This was an odd complaint considering that the settlers had incomes of under $60 a year.

A Qinghai crisis team, headed by the managing director, Sven Sandstrom, began to hold long and fractious daily sessions. It had to concede that some of the panel's points were true, yet they were blown out of proportion. The Bank's environmental assessors had failed to list all the local animals that might be affected by the project; some of the project documentation had been skimpy. The question of Category A versus Category B was something on which the Bank's experts had an honest disagreement; and although it might be true that the consultation exercise had not been properly confidential, there was no real doubt that these impoverished farmers were genuinely desperate to relocate. Perhaps it was right that the settlement would have some spillover impact on local nomads, but why had the panel ignored the compensating benefits, such as access to new clinics? All in all, the panel was quibbling with details but not asking the big questions. Would this project reduce poverty? The answer was yes, but the panel seemed indifferent. Would it cause environmental damage? The bottom line was no, and yet the panel insisted on poking holes in the Bank's methods and procedures.

In early May 2000, Sandstrom's group began to prepare a point-by-point rebuttal of the Inspection Panel's conclusions. But during the course of that month, while the fight over Ravi Kanbur's World Development Report was boiling, the group came to a painful conclusion. There was no realistic prospect of victory. The point-by-point rebuttal would only escalate the battle with the Inspection Panel; escalation would bring another NGO swarm down on them; and Congress and the U.S. board director and several other directors from countries with Tibet lobbies would side with the NGOs again. The argument had reached the point where the project would have to be 100 percent flawless in order to win tolerance, and no development project can attain that standard. The more the issue was drawn out, the more it spread its poison. By May 2000, thirteen other China projects had been frozen while the Bank double-checked their vulnerability to NGO attack.[35]

On June 21, 2000, the Bank's management finally delivered a muted response to its tormentor. It proposed that much of the project preparation be repeated. Another year's worth of studies, costing an estimated $2 million, would be undertaken to satisfy the Inspection Panel's objections. Even then, there would be no guarantee that the project would ultimately go forward; once the new studies had been digested, the Bank would consider its options. This was, from the Chinese point of view, an absurdly expensive and cumbersome proposal. They had already carried out thirty or so similar relocation projects in other parts of China, and all had been shown to reduce poverty. Why another expensive year of studies? The answer, of course, was that this project was different; it involved Tibetans, an NGO swarm of global proportions, and the U.S. Congress. But if that was the case, then no amount of preparation could render it acceptable. Why blow another $2 million on environmental and social assessments that would ultimately prove irrelevant?

Wolfensohn and his lieutenants knew the Chinese might withdraw the project,[36] but they insisted they would fight for it. They did not want to be the ones to kill it; it would be better for the Bank's relationship with China if the Chinese withdrew it themselves. Meanwhile the NGOs carried on swarming. They called for the Inspection Panel report to be made public; they called for the project to be canceled; and for a while the Bank's main entrance was partially obstructed by Tibetan monks brandishing a loudspeaker. On July 6, the Bank's board finally assembled to vote on the management's compromise proposal, and the meeting spilled over into the next day. On July 7, after seven hours of deliberation, the compromise was rejected. Despite the promise of an extra year of evaluation, the board would only give the go-ahead if it— and not just the Bank's management—retained the right to review the project yet again once the studies had been completed. That was the last straw for China. The Chinese representative on the Bank's board delivered the message that many had long expected.[37] His government was withdrawing its request for World Bank assistance in Qinghai.

THIS WAS NOT quite the Indian mutiny, in which a colonized people rebelled against the missionary imposition of alien values, slaughtering the British wherever they were found. But it was something a bit like that. The missionaries in India had turned an amoral British order into a crusading one; the natives were now to be taught that practices like widow burning and female infanticide were barbaric and unacceptable. Nearly two centuries later, the modern missionaries of the NGO movement aimed to turn the World Bank into a crusader; the Chinese were now to be taught that their Tibet policy and their dictatorial system were evil. In both cases, to be sure, the missionaries were on the side of virtue; neither infanticide nor dictatorship is good. But the Indian rebellion, like the Chinese one in 2000, showed that the missionary agenda was too ambitious. After the 1857 mutiny, the British order in India was reconstructed on secular foundations. The old policy of turning a blind eye to practices like widow burning was reestablished, and the missionaries were sidelined. After the Chinese withdrew the Qinghai project, something similar happened. The World Bank was forced to rethink its own relationship with missionary groups.

The rethink began with the Bank's prudential guidelines—the "safeguards" and "operational directives" that mandated caution with indigenous people, environmental risks, relocation, and so on. These regulations were the fruits of NGO lobbying; they contained the missionaries' commandments. For developing countries, they were a burden. They laid down that, as a condition of World Bank assistance, poor nations should meet environmental and social standards that they could ill afford. According to one Bank study, safeguard policies of one kind or another inflated the institution's project preparation costs by $83 million annually. On top of that, the Bank's borrowers spent anywhere from $118 million to $215 million a year on complying with the safeguards, so that the direct and indirect costs to developing countries came to as much as $300 million.[38] Then there was the sheer frustration of dealing with this red-tape rigmarole. It was hardly surprising that borrowers with the option of going to private capital markets were increasingly doing so.

This desertion was troubling, whatever point of view you took. From the NGO perspective, the goal of higher development standards was rendered more elusive: once the Bank pulled out of Qinghai, the Chinese felt free to go ahead with the relocation while ignoring the social and environmental safeguards that the Bank had built into the project; they moved nearly double the number of people that the Bank would have allowed.[39] From the point of view of the Bank, the consequences of the safeguards were still more worrying: if the Bank lost its strongest borrowers—the ones with the option of tapping private capital—its own finances would suffer. This was the worry that Wolfensohn had encountered in his first month as World Bank president, when he visited South Africa. From the point of view of the Bank's staff, meanwhile, working in a Bank dominated by safeguards was enough to drive you nuts.

It was partly the way that they were written. It was hard to anticipate all the challenges that could crop up in the Bank's many projects, so the safeguards were often loosely drafted; interpreting them was hard. This might not have mattered if project managers had been free to exercise reasonable judgment. But the Qinghai experience ended any illusion of freedom; if you put a foot wrong, the Inspection Panel might swoop down and chop it off. In order to protect themselves, project managers had to seek guidance from their bosses on interpreting the safeguards, and the bosses would confer with the Bank's legal department, and if you multiplied that process a dozen times or so per project it was hardly surprising that work advanced at a snail's pace. In December 1998, one project manager wrote a description of the red-tape hassles she'd encountered in the course of preparing a small loan for Poland: "It doesn't have to be that way," the e-mail was entitled, and it went on for six pages, describing how weeks had been lost to an argument over who was entitled to sign some of the loan documents, and how procurement officials changed their explanation of their rules on a regular basis.[40]

In short, the NGO encirclement, visible in the streets around the Bank's headquarters in Washington, existed invisibly inside the Bank. To placate the missionaries, the Bank had allowed them into its dominion; it had written rules reflecting missionary values and promised to live by them. The result was a development organization that was losing touch with developing countries, an organization that reflected the agenda of northern activists, not the hard circumstances of its poor clients. For all Wolfensohn's desire to put borrowing countries "in the driver's seat," the safeguards limited his ability to do that. Small wonder that stronger developing countries like South Africa regarded the Bank as unacceptably high maintenance and preferred to borrow elsewhere.

In the wake of the Qinghai battle, Wolfensohn acknowledged the danger that the Bank's strong clients would desert it.[41] But it was quite another thing to know how to fix this problem. The missionaries encircled the Bank because they encircled the Parliaments of aid-giving governments, and especially the U.S. Congress. Time and again, they had got their way—over the creation of the safeguards, and then over the creation of the Inspection Panel—by lobbying the World Bank's shareholders; time after time, the Bank had to give in to pressure in order to secure the triennial IDA replenishment. Breaking out of the NGO encirclement meant breaking the grip of the Bank's IDA donors, and there seemed no way to do that. Indeed, the more that lending in middle-income countries stagnated, the more the Bank needed its IDA operations in order to justify its staff levels. The IDA donors were growing more powerful, not less so. NGO influence seemed set to grow as well.

Two or three years later, the Bank started to push its way out of this encirclement; and the push was led, quite fittingly, by a Chinese managing director named Shengman Zhang. But in mid-2000, the prospect of escape seemed minimal. The Bank was being shoved about by its shareholders, and especially by the NGO-friendly Americans. And the pressure that Wolfensohn felt from the Larry Summers Treasury was just the tip of the iceberg. The Bank had to contend with American conservatives as well.

CHAPTER ELEVEN

WAKING UP TO TERROR

THE TWO ACTIVIST ASSAULTS on the World Bank—in Madrid in 1994 and in Washington in 2000—served as bookends for Wolfensohn's first term as president. He arrived at the Bank against the background of protest; he spent five years trying to build bridges to big nongovernment; then he was battered by a fresh barrage of protests despite all his efforts. It was a depressing sequence. Wolfensohn could hardly have done more to reach out to NGO critics, and he had indeed built good relations with some groups like Oxfam, Care, and World Vision. But a large section of civil society remained uncivil—and this section included not just flamboyant protest outfits like the Ruckus Society but groups that your mom might support, like Friends of the Earth and the Environmental Defense Fund. The Third Way hope that by consulting everybody, hearing everybody, you could chart a centrist escape from left-right confrontation had been rudely shattered. It was only fitting that, in the U.S. presidential election at the end of 2000, the Third Way grip on American politics was broken.

Wolfensohn seemed ill equipped to deal with the passing of the Third Way era. His affinity with Bill Clinton had been powerful. The two men shared a liberal social conscience, an instinctive internationalism, an intellectual fluency, a talent for empathetic listening, a hot vanity, a hotter temper, a nagging weight problem, a marriage to a strong woman, a taste for Hollywood glamour—it was no coincidence that Clinton had twice celebrated his birthday in Wolfensohn's Wyoming "cabin." The new president, however, was made of different stuff. George W. Bush came to the White House with conservative social instincts, an indifference to international issues, a suspicion of intellectuals, and a Texan disdain for the cultures of the coasts—for Hollywood and Wall Street. Vice President Dick Cheney had a home in Jackson Hole and so had socialized with Wolfensohn. But there was no getting around the fact that the new American president did not know the World Bank president, and did not particularly want to know him either.

Like the activist assault on the World Bank, the shift of power in Washington strained the Bank's ability to stick to its development principles. All through 2001, Wolfensohn was pushing the Bank to implement his Comprehensive Development Framework. He wanted to defer to poor countries, to put them "in the driver's seat." Yet there was no way that the Bank's leadership could focus completely on this task. However much Wolfensohn might want to put poor countries first, he was obliged to reckon with the transformation of his chief shareholder, and generally with the shifting appetites of his rich political masters. Rather like the NGOs, these masters did not always have an off switch: they imposed demand after demand upon the Bank, unbothered by the fact that today's instructions often conflicted with the ones they had urged earlier. As with the battles against the NGOs, the Bank's poor clients were the losers.

In the transition from the Clinton era to the Bush era, the Bank experienced this perverse sequence on the issue of education. In 1999, as we have seen, the Clinton administration had endorsed the concept of Wolfensohn's framework, including the idea that poor countries should come up with national plans covering the whole waterfront of development challenges. The following year, however, the Clintonites departed from that broad vision, launching a campaign for one single development goal: universal primary education. This was a good cause, to be sure—an estimated 113 million children were not enrolled—but it was not a better cause than clean water or a dozen other challenges. Indeed, one way to get kids into school is to provide their parents with nearby sources of water so that they don't need child labor to fetch it. Development does need to proceed on many fronts, which is why Wolfensohn pressed comprehensiveness. Nevertheless, the Clinton team encouraged the World Bank to lead the primary-school drive, and in 2001, the British, the Canadians, and the Dutch stepped up the pressure, and the Bank duly spent more than a year working up a global education initiative. Poor countries were invited to submit plans showing how they would drive primary-school enrollment to 100 percent, on the understanding that good plans would be rewarded with generous assistance. But by 2002, when the Bank had collected dozens of education plans and announced a short list of good ones, the shareholders' interests had moved on. The Bank—and, more important, the overstretched governments of the poor world—had labored for months to respond to the donors' education call. But the promise of generous funding had evaporated.

This made a mockery of Wolfensohn's idea that poor countries should determine their development agendas. But there was no way he could ignore the pressure to act as the rich world's education campaigner. He could not afford to position the Bank as being indifferent to primary schooling, particularly since Oxfam's effective campaign machine was backing the initiative. He could not afford to alienate rich governments, since he needed their money every three years to replenish the Bank's soft-loan IDA kitty. Moreover, in the first year or so of the Bush administration, Wolfensohn was especially vulnerable. His chief shareholder had changed political color, and staff morale within the Bank was at a low point.

At the start of 2001, Wolfensohn's most immediate challenge was to get along with the Bush team at the Treasury. But the new treasury secretary was no more congenial than Bush was. His name was Paul O'Neill, and his rise to international prominence was as remarkable as Wolfensohn's. He had begun life in a house without running water and had earned multimillions; he had gone to Fresno State College in California and outsmarted nearly all his Ivy League contemporaries. But his style could not have been more different. O'Neill was as buttoned-down and blunt as Wolfensohn was loose and charming. His hair was neat, his frame was trim, and his promptness was legendary. His proudest achievement at Alcoa, the aluminum giant he had revived brilliantly, was to instill a manic attention to detail that had virtually eliminated worker accidents. Alcoa's aluminum operation was, as O'Neill frequently boasted, a safer place to work than the U.S. Treasury.

Everything that O'Neill had heard about Wolfensohn's World Bank made him feel impatient. He divided the world into two categories—logical thinkers who made things happen and lazy minds content with drift—and he lumped the Bank and the whole aid industry under the second heading. He often declared that the world had spent "trillions of dollars" on development, "and there's damn little to show for it," implying that if somebody would only run the Bank as he had run Alcoa, poverty would be plummeting. To his way of thinking, it was a scandal that the aid people aimed merely to lift the world's poor over the $2 per day line. "We're letting ourselves off too easily," he once told me; we should be aiming for success on the scale of South Korea, which jumped from poverty to middle-class comfort in the space of four decades.[1] In his own life, O'Neill had made that size of jump himself. He saw no reason why the rest of the world should not jump right up after him.

O'Neill's hostility to the Bank reflected the conventional thinking among Republicans. A year before he had arrived in Washington, a congressional commission led by an owlish economics professor named Allan Meltzer had offered the latest version of the conservative critique: that the explosion in private capital flows rendered much of the Bank obsolete. Meltzer recommended that the Bank should close down its market-based lending to middle-income countries like Brazil, which could finance development by tapping private capital; the Bank should remain active only in the poorest nations, where it should stop providing loans that piled up debt and switch instead to making grants. The Bank, in other words, should destroy its own financial foundations. It should abandon all its strongest clients and confine itself to making grants, and so risk becoming as dependent upon donor largesse as UN institutions.[2]

It was strange that this line of thinking had survived the emerging-market crisis. By 1999, private capital transfers to the developing world had fallen by nearly a third from their peak; and the Bank had played a reluctant but important role in coping with the instability. Although it was true that countries like Brazil had been able to resume private borrowing soon after the crisis, the interest rates they paid were often punitive.[3] Besides, Meltzer never really explained the harm he saw in the Bank's continued involvement in stronger developing countries. To the extent that Brazil or South Africa borrowed from the Bank, they presumably found the arrangement useful. And because the Bank's market-based lending generated a small profit, the cost to the Bank's rich shareholders was zero.[4] If there was no obvious harm in the Bank's continued presence in middle-income countries, it was worth considering the benefits. Brazil's government—or India's government or China's—is stuffed full of first-rate technocrats who know their country far better than any foreigner. But there is still a role for a friendly outside institution that can distill global experience and provide technical advice—an analysis of rival models of pension privatization, for example, or of malaria control or high-altitude road construction.[5]

Despite the weaknesses in Meltzer's case, it was the dominant view in the Bush economics team. Meltzer hailed from O'Neill's home city of Pittsburgh, and he knew the treasury secretary slightly; he had a long friendship with John Taylor, O'Neill's international point man at the Treasury.[6] Meltzer also knew the two key economists at the White House—Larry Lindsay and Glenn Hubbard—since both had been scholars at the American Enterprise Institute, a conservative Washington think tank to which Meltzer was affiliated. By the time he arrived at the Treasury, Paul O'Neill had absorbed Meltzer's thinking on the Bank in direct and indirect ways, and so had most of the policy makers around him.

Moreover, O'Neill was appalled by the Bank's management problems. He found it incomprehensible that Wolfensohn lacked a second in command, preferring instead to delegate haphazardly to a chaotic caste of favorites. He found it astonishing that the Clinton Treasury had put up with this mediocrity, even though it had resented Wolfensohn's management record since the fight over the $250 million Strategic Compact. In March 2001, when Wolfensohn invited him over to his home, O'Neill pointedly refused to go. He said he would prefer a "neutral" venue, and the location was switched hurriedly to the Four Seasons hotel.[7] Over dinner that evening, Wolfensohn fought valiantly to establish a rapport. He did his best to entertain O'Neill with tales of Krome George, one of O'Neill's predecessors as chairman of Alcoa; then he and two lieutenants talked about the Bank's achievements, doing their best to get the treasury secretary to buy into their way of thinking. But O'Neill was not impressed. Perhaps at that dinner or perhaps sometime afterward, the treasury secretary made up his mind. He didn't want to get to know Wolfensohn. He wanted to get rid of him.[8]

O'NEILL WAS RIGHT that the Bank's management was chaotic. It was true that Wolfensohn had no clear deputy, and deep down he knew this was a problem. On at least one occasion, he resolved to fill the gap by elevating Sven Sandstrom, the Swedish managing director. He told Sandstrom he was going to do it, and he told several members of the board that he was going to do it; but then he chickened out and withdrew his announcement. Because Wolfensohn could not bring himself to delegate, the managerial confusion persisted. Lines of authority looped and curled and petered out in odd dead ends. You could never quite be sure who was empowered to make what happen.

And yet a lot of stuff *was* happening: stuff that upset the massed ranks of World Bankers. The new matrix system bred little efficiency and much grumbling. In the name of the new meritocratic personnel system, old managers were being turfed out in favor of a new gang, but the new lot wasn't always better. Meanwhile, the Bank's project managers felt overworked and underloved.[9] In mid-1999 the staff received a modest 2 percent pay rise, which was widely considered an insult, and two days later the Bank rolled out its new computerized management system, which rendered routine tasks excruciating. The result was that the Bank lost track of its spending, and a painful crunch ensued. In the year beginning July 2000, the Bank was forced to cut five hundred staff members, and many more felt threatened.[10]

In December 2000, when the fate of the Third Way was being decided by Florida's chaotic election recount, the staff's unhappiness bubbled up into overt rebellion. Wolfensohn returned from a visit to India and delivered one of his pep talks. He complained that staff was "bitchy." Gripes leaked to the press, and he demanded an explanation for this corrosive disaffection. The response exceeded anything that he had bargained for. Manuel Conthe, a Spanish vice president who ran the financial-sector department, collected a vast list of grumblings from his staff and forwarded them to Wolfensohn. The boss was forever embracing fresh challenges with no thought to the staff's capacity to deliver, according to the memo; the result was a constant internal battle for resources and equally constant backstabbing. But this attack was soon eclipsed by the response from the Middle East and North Africa department, which identified the Bank's chief problem as the "president's management and leadership style." Wolfensohn embraced too many new fads, according to the Middle East people. He surrounded himself with yes-men; his abusive temper wore people down and deterred honest discussion.

By January 2001, just as Team Bush was taking over Washington, this frontal attack on Wolfensohn's record was being passed around the Bank in anonymous brown envelopes. It appeared mysteriously in people's mailboxes, and a copy soon leaked to the *Financial Times*. On January 23, about forty-five randomly selected staff and managers from the Middle East department were invited to meet Wolfensohn. The boss listened to the complaints and knew there was some truth to them: He had campaigned against the cynicism of the Bank, but his own style had deepened that same cynicism. A few days later Wolfensohn sent out a letter to the staff. He regretted the computer glitches and the redundancies, and he acknowledged that the broadening of the Bank's agenda had made everybody's job harder. Then he appealed for a fresh push to fix the Bank. "We owe it to the world's poor people whom we serve," he pleaded.

IT WAS SCARCELY SURPRISING, given all the grumbling within the Bank, that the new Republican administration would take a dim view of Wolfensohn. The standard conservative critique of public institutions—that they are unfocused and inefficient—was believed by many of the Bank's own people. To be sure, the Bank's morale problems predated Wolfensohn, and some of his innovations were a clear success, notably the decentralization of staff to field offices. But this was small consolation at the start of 2001. "Almost all bureaucracies in the world are much better organized than we are," one of the complaining memos had stated. Never mind that this was an exaggeration; it came directly from the Bank's own staff, and the *Financial Times* had quoted it.

In the first months of 2001, Wolfensohn knew he had a problem. Paul O'Neill showed no interest in meeting him, and the first dinner at the Four Seasons hotel in March happened only after Wolfensohn pulled out all the stops to arrange one.[11] In April, O'Neill attended the Development Committee get-together during the Bank's spring meetings, and though he made a show of modesty, telling his fellow ministers that he was the new kid on the block, his comments also betrayed Meltzerite impatience with the Bank's performance. The gossips were starting to report that O'Neill was canvassing candidates to take over the Bank, and the Treasury was looking into the option of appointing a board director who would block Wolfensohn's initiatives and force his resignation. In May, Wolfensohn invited Ken Dam, the Treasury's number two, over for lunch at the World Bank. He had known Dam slightly in business circles and had condescended to him in the past, but now he revealed his insecurity by bending low in a mock-serious bow as Dam walked in to greet him.

There was no precedent for pushing out a World Bank president midway through his term in office. But Wolfensohn still braced for the worst. He spent hours plotting and strategizing with his lieutenants, wondering how to get through to the new treasury secretary. On June 1, 2001, O'Neill summoned him to lunch. Wolfensohn was nervous: if there was going to be a time when O'Neill tried to push him out, this might well be it. On the day of the encounter, Elaine was sufficiently anxious to come into the World Bank building; she waited upstairs by her husband's office for his return, ready to administer comfort and counseling. But when Wolfensohn appeared, he had no drama to report. O'Neill was scheming, casting the occasional stone, but he was not ready to declare war yet.

Fortunately for Wolfensohn, O'Neill turned out to be a clumsy adversary. If he had gone after Wolfensohn for his managerial failings, or for his lack of development priorities, he might have won allies among the Bank's other big shareholders. But he chose instead to press a crude version of Meltzer's critique. He declared at every opportunity that the Bank made no impact on poverty, and that it was uninterested in measuring the performance of its projects. This put him on weak territory. The Bank's research department quickly produced numbers showing that the past generation had yielded more development progress than any since the Industrial Revolution. Since 1960, life expectancy in poor countries had risen from forty-five to sixty-four. Since 1970, the illiteracy rate had fallen from 47 percent to 25 percent. And since 1980, the number of poor people had fallen by about 200 million—this at a time when world population had increased by 1.6 billion.[12] Of course, one could not be sure how much of the credit the Bank deserved for this advance. The Bank's efforts are mingled with countries' efforts, as the story of Uganda demonstrated.[13] But O'Neill baldly asserted that there had been next to no progress against poverty. The Bank duly stomped all over him.

The claim that the Bank made no effort to measure its performance was just as easily demolished. The Bank made many such efforts: it maintained a whole department to evaluate loans after completion; it had set up a new unit to check projects' quality in real time; and some of the best work on measuring aid effectiveness came from the Bank's researchers. To be sure, these measures were imperfect. Measuring efforts to train government officials or spread awareness of AIDS is a subjective business. But O'Neill was wrong to imply that the Bank was uninterested in assessing results, and he was unable to suggest better ways of doing it. As Wolfensohn would occasionally point out, the U.S. government itself had no great tools for gauging the impact of its own domestic spending.[14]

Through the spring and summer of 2001, as O'Neill plotted his removal, Wolfensohn began to elaborate his counterattack. It was a routine he knew instinctively. First, subject your adversary to a large dose of charm. Second, confront him with tough argument. Third, if he still isn't yielding, prepare your flanking maneuver: keep him talking, hold his gaze, and build a series of relationships that loop around his back until eventually you dance right past him. Wolfensohn had pulled off this sort of end run a hundred times in business, and he had pulled it off when he had won the World Bank presidency despite the misgivings of the Clinton Treasury; he wasn't going to be cowed now by

O'Neill and his simplistic hectoring. Bit by bit, Wolfensohn forged ties with other Bush administration figures—notably the national security adviser, Condoleezza Rice, and Secretary of State Colin Powell. He capitalized on his relationship with Alan Greenspan, the Fed chairman and a confidante of the Bush team, who stayed on Wolfensohn's estate in Jackson Hole each year in August. And he made the most of his multitude of foreign contacts, who served as his last line of defense.[15] After all, if the United States were to unseat a World Bank president in midterm, it would set a precedent that the Europeans would regret. All future presidents of the Bank would feel they served at America's pleasure, and the sway of other shareholders would diminish.

As Wolfensohn worked on outflanking O'Neill, the atmosphere inside the Bank was mending. Some staff had been shocked when the institution's dirty linen was aired in the *Financial Times;* others rallied to the Bank because O'Neill was attacking it.[16] Still others experienced a kind of hate fatigue: after months of bitching and moaning, they were finally beginning to see that nothing good would come of it. Besides, the annoying new computer system had started to work right; the fear of layoffs had subsided; and in the summer of 2001, the staff was pleasantly surprised by a 6.8 percent pay increase.[17] There were still setbacks, as when the April edition of *Bank Swirled,* the anonymously written satirical in-house magazine, portrayed Wolfensohn and his top staff playing "eeny meeny miney mo" to determine the Bank's lending priorities. But the internal challenge to Wolfensohn's leadership was burning out. It seemed reasonable to hope that the clumsy external attacks from the Treasury would soon burn out also.

Unfortunately for Wolfensohn, a third kind of attack was brewing. Between May and August 2001, he suffered three consecutive blows from ex-Bank veterans: for his embrace of the participatory NGO agenda, for his failure to set priorities, and for his erratic style of management. It was a bruising triple punch. Unlike Paul O'Neill, these attackers were not ill informed. Unlike the internal grumblers on the staff, they could not be dismissed as grasping whiners. By the time the third blow landed, the question of whether O'Neill would attempt to replace Wolfensohn seemed almost beside the point. Wolfensohn was on the verge of quitting.

THE FIRST OF the three blows came from Larry Summers, the former World Bank chief economist who had been Clinton's last treasury secretary. On May 2, 2001, Summers addressed the Bank's country directors, and he used the occasion to let off steam about the sort of development thinking that had flourished under Wolfensohn. He attacked the Bank's rhetoric of "empowerment," saying that inviting the participation of local groups would not improve decision making. He pointed out that NGOs had no special claim to speak for the poor; they could claim less legitimacy in this regard than the elected governments of many developing countries. Rather than deferring to these unelected groups, the Bank should defer to its own technical experts. The best route to successful development lay in rigorous analysis, not participatory waffle. The Bank, for example, should promote environmental standards when hardheaded cost-benefit analysis suggested this made sense; it should not pursue environmentalism in the blanket, NGO-appeasing way laid down by the safeguards. Striving to be politically correct would only strengthen the forces of political correctness.

The second blow came from Jessica Einhorn, one of Wolfensohn's early managing directors. In the September issue of *Foreign Affairs*, which began to circulate in August, Einhorn laid out the case against the Bank's lack of priorities. Having evolved through successive development fashions, and having finally arrived at an all-encompassing "Comprehensive Development Framework," the Bank had lost its way, Einhorn argued: "Its mission has become so complex that it strains credulity to portray the Bank as a manageable organization." Yes, development itself was multifaceted and complex. But that did not mean that everything from postconflict reconstruction to cultural heritage should be handled by one institution. Rather like Meltzer, Einhorn recommended that the Bank be shrunk—not by withdrawing from middle-income countries but by handing off some of its functions to other organizations.

The Summers and Einhorn critiques signaled that mainstream heavyweights had misgivings about Wolfensohn. Yet there were counterarguments to both. It was ironic that Summers was attacking the participatory development approach that his own Treasury had endorsed in 1999, and if one wanted examples of capitulation to politically correct NGOs, the Clinton administration's capitulation to the Tibet lobby was an obvious candidate. Moreover, even if it was true that participatory development planning risked blunting the Bank's analytical edge, eschewing participation carried an equally big risk: that the Bank and its projects would fail for lack of popular support, as had often been the case with structural adjustment. As to Jessica Einhorn's criticisms, one could point out that the Bank's mission creep was in part a symptom of its strength—the Bank had taken on challenges from Bosnia to universal primary education because other institutions were not up to carrying the burden. Indeed, the education campaign had been a case in point. In theory, the lead agency on this issue was the UN outfit UNESCO. But the Clinton administration and other shareholders knew that UNESCO could never mount a multibillion-dollar fundraising effort, so they insisted that the Bank take on the challenge.[18]

It was the third blow that made the mainstream attack on Wolfensohn so painful. At the start of August 2001, when the boss retreated from Washington to Jackson Hole, he took with him an offprint of an article in *Foreign Policy* magazine. The cover of the new issue carried a picture of Wolfensohn, his eyes creased in concentration, his mouth obscured behind his hand. The caption was no more flattering. "The Man Who Broke the Bank?" it asked, ominously.

The article was by Stephen Fidler, the respected *Financial Times* journalist who had broken the story about the Bank's internal malaise earlier in the year; and it bore the imprint of Moisés Naím, *Foreign Policy*'s editor. Naím had been one of the four senior advisers hired by Wolfensohn at the start of his tenure; he had spent a year devising a strategy for the Bank and had ultimately left in despair, believing that Wolfensohn was incapable of setting priorities. After scores of interviews with past and present World Bankers, Stephen Fidler took the same line. He began by asserting that Wolfensohn's "personal failings and misguided policies have muddled the bank's mission and pushed its best staff out the door"; then he quoted a chorus of critics who denounced just about everything Wolfensohn had done, from the Comprehensive Development Framework (a "cruel joke") to a more recent strategy paper ("confusing, meaningless and stuffed with every cliché," according to one informant). Wolfensohn's personal outbursts had cost him the affection of his managers, the article observed. "Loyalty, the thing he craves so much, is precisely the thing that has eluded him."

The *Foreign Policy* article hit Wolfensohn like a huge kick in the stomach. It laid him lower than he'd been at any point during his tenure at the Bank, and for the first time he thought seriously of quitting.[19] Some of his lieutenants flew out from Washington to coax him out of his black mood. Nobody resigns over a magazine article, they told him. But the mood lasted through most of August, and Elaine spent hours talking to him about whether he should soldier on. The summer was ruined. Wolfensohn found the attack monstrously unfair. Since the bleak days of December and January, when he had been assailed by the two grumbling staff memos, he had felt he was turning the corner: The dissatisfaction with his management, which was partly a dissatisfaction with computer screwups for which he was only distantly to blame, seemed to be abating. But now this article had blackened his reputation in the most personal terms; it was being handed out free on the shuttle between Washington and New York. Even his own quotes were hurting him. "Put me aside for the moment and say I'm useless, egocentric, insecure, all the things you want to say," Wolfensohn had told Fidler in an interview. His intention had been to disprove the accusation of insecurity by absorbing it calmly. But the way it sounded on the page, he was acceding to his critics' view of him.

Humiliations of this sort are a hazard of public life, and the best advice is to press on as though nothing particular has happened. In 1996, *The Washington Post* made a laughingstock of Hillary Clinton by breaking the news that she had communed with Eleanor Roosevelt via a spirit medium.[20] The next morning Clinton appeared before a conference and declared that Eleanor Roosevelt thought the discussion topic wonderful; the laughter from the audience immediately dispelled the shadow cast by the *Post* article. But Wolfensohn does not bounce back that fast: he takes criticism to heart, and despite his remarkable success he can be remarkably fragile.[21] However unfair he thought the *Foreign Policy* article, he spent days wondering if it was right. "Am I a perfect shit? Am I screwing up?" he asked himself.[22] It was not until the end of August that he started to regain confidence. But when he finally recovered, he came back tougher than he'd been before, just as he had done after setbacks early in his career, in Sydney and in London. "Screw it!" he told himself. "I'm doing the right thing, I'm trying hard, I don't think many people could do better. And goddamn it, I'm going to go for it."[23]

The question was whether he would be allowed to do that. The simultaneous attacks on Wolfensohn in two leading foreign-policy journals, coming on top of the Bush administration's known animosity toward the Bank, set many tongues wagging. Bank officials who disliked Wolfensohn sensed he might be on the skids; Treasury officials got used to being asked, "When are you going to get rid of him?" For a while there was a rumor that the administration wanted James Baker, the former treasury secretary and secretary of state, to take over the

Bank. Wolfensohn checked into this story, and Baker assured him that it was unfounded.[24] Somewhere around this time, O'Neill began to interview other pretenders to the throne. He spoke to Peter McPherson, the president of Michigan State University, but decided he lacked charisma; he interviewed John Reed, the former boss of Citibank, and decided to support him for the job, though the White House blocked his candidacy.[25] Meanwhile, O'Neill was pressing on other fronts as well. His anti-Bank rhetoric did not abate, even though most mainstream commentators robustly disagreed with him. The new American director on the Bank's board, Carole Brookins, took office in August, and the Bank's staff found her difficult to work with.

At the end of the summer, Wolfensohn returned from Jackson Hole, determined to fight on but unsure of his prospects. Just a few days later, hijackers slammed into the World Trade Center towers and the Pentagon building. The world around Wolfensohn was transformed, and so was his battle with his chief shareholder.

A FEW MINUTES before nine A.M. on September 11, Elaine Wolfensohn got a call from her oldest daughter, Sara, a pianist who lived in Manhattan. Sara had been out walking when she had heard a terrible noise up above, and then she'd seen smoke billowing from the north tower of the World Trade Center. Elaine talked briefly to her daughter, then called her husband's office. She reached him as he was preparing for the biweekly senior management meeting. Wolfensohn flicked on the TV and saw the surreal images: the twin towers, a plane gliding over the Manhattan skyline, a billowing of black smoke and a flash of orange flame as the plane collided with its target. Wolfensohn asked his secretary to alert him if anything more happened, and then he walked into the adjoining conference room, where his senior managers also had the TV on. At nine oh-three A.M., the Bank's top brass looked on in horror as a second plane appeared out of the brilliant blue of a September morning. There was another burst of orange, angrier even than the first, and flames started to consume the south tower of the World Trade Center.

The meeting broke up after a few minutes, and Wolfensohn emerged from the conference room. A CNN camera crew had come to film his office for a documentary, and Wolfensohn submitted to an interview. Then at nine forty-three A.M. there was a judder in the distance, and the television news was announcing that a fire had broken out in the Pentagon, a few metro stops away from the World Bank on the far side of the Potomac River. From Wolfensohn's twelfth-floor office, you could see smoke rising in the distance, and the TV news was announcing that a fourth plane had been hijacked. The CNN cameraman remarked that it might be smart to get out of the building. Wolfensohn realized he must now decide whether to send people home or not.[26] If the fourth plane were headed for the World Bank, a distant possibility but one he needed to entertain, he should evacuate everyone immediately. On the other hand, if the terrorists had targeted the White House, three blocks away from the Bank's complex, going outside could be perilous.

The Bank was no better prepared for terrorism than anybody else was in America. Wolfensohn hedged his bets on the decision to evacuate: he consulted the Bank's security staff, then told people they were free to leave if they felt safer doing so. The staff who chose to go went down to the garage and got into their cars as usual, then spent the next hour in hot-tempered subterranean honking. But by the end of that day, Wolfensohn had put his initial confusion behind him. He sensed the scale of what had happened, and he knew where he should head. He must seize this moment, much as Tony Blair seized the moment of Princess Diana's death or Bill Clinton seized the moment of the Oklahoma bombing. He must pull everyone together, make them feel a sense of purposeful outrage; and he must tap into the special affinities between the Bank and the burning towers in Manhattan. As a financial institution, the Bank had many employees who knew people at the World Trade Center. As an international institution, it was vulnerable to any upsurge of tension between the United States and other countries. And as a development institution, the Bank's central mission was to fight the misery and alienation that bred this horrific violence.

Three days later Wolfensohn convened a ceremony in the Bank's atrium, which coincided with President Bush's prayer service at Washington's National Cathedral. Wolfensohn stood up on the stage next to Carole Brookins, the U.S. board member, and he looked down at the multicultural throng that filled the vast hall before him. "It's a time for us to tell our host country, and its citizens, that we are with them, that we share their grief," Wolfensohn announced emotionally; "we need each other. We need to join together." Brookins responded briefly on behalf of the U.S. government, and her message was no less warm. She thanked the Bank's employees for the outpouring of sympathy that had flowed into the U.S. office since the terrorist attacks; and she declared that the Bank and its mission represented "what is good and true, and the best in mankind." Then Wolfensohn asked everybody to join hands, and he reached out and took Carole Brookins's hand, and everyone observed a minute of silence. It was a moment of unity in the face of a new terror, a moment of reconciliation between Wolfensohn and the Bank's unhappy staff, and a moment of peace between the Bank and its chief shareholder.

Wolfensohn did not let go, long after that ceremonial silence ended. He seized the opportunity to reassert the Bank's mission, harkening back to the security thinking that had led to the Bank's creation fifty-seven years earlier. He told audience after audience that "there is no wall": that the troubles of poor and distant countries could affect the lives of people in Toulouse and Tampa. The message was largely a recasting of speeches he had given since his first months at the Bank. Ever since his inaugural trip to Africa, when he sat under a tree in Mali with a wizened village chief, he had fought for words to grab the attention of the rich world, to make the affluent wake up to poverty. The terrorist attacks gave him a new chance. Now surely public opinion in the West would understand development's importance.

In the weeks after the terrorist attacks, not everyone accepted Wolfensohn's claim that the Bank's antipoverty mission mattered to the war on terror. Many observers, some of them high up in the Bush team, pointed out that fifteen out of the nineteen hijackers came from rich Saudi Arabia. But there was a larger logic to Wolfensohn's preaching. For one thing, there were counterexamples to the Saudi Arabian one: in parts of the Muslim world, poverty drove children into the free religious schools known as *madrassas,* and some of these served more or less as terror training camps.[27] For another, failed states like Sudan and Afghanistan had served as havens for the terrorists; helping poor countries to grow was the best way to prevent more state failures from creating more terrorist bases. Besides, even if it was true that terrorists were predominantly middle class, it was worth asking what fueled their violent resentment. Were they driven by a sense of global injustice? If so, World Bank development programs might help to assuage their grievances. Or was their anger rooted in their own rotten political systems? In that case, the Bank's new drive to promote cleaner governance around the world should be at the center of the struggle against terror.

Soon after September 11, Wolfensohn spoke to Condoleezza Rice, President Bush's national security adviser. He offered the Bank's support against terror, and whatever skepticism Rice might have felt about the Bank's ability to make a real difference, she saw nothing to be gained from spurning the offer. From that moment on, the Bank's relations with the Bush administration proceeded on a dual track. To the delight of the White House and the State Department, Wolfensohn pressed his staff to get involved in countries that were newly strategic— notably the Central Asian states that bordered on Afghanistan—and the budget for Bank missions to that sensitive region was increased in short order. But the new alliance between the Bush team and the World Bank did not encompass the O'Neill Treasury. Indeed, O'Neill remained as hostile as ever.

The Bank's annual meetings that autumn were canceled, partly for fear of violent antiglobalization protests and partly for fear of terrorism. Instead, the Bank's policy-setting Development Committee gathered in November for a low-key meeting in Canada. O'Neill used this occasion to deliver his stock speech about the Bank's incompetence. He laid it on thicker than usual this time, and other members of the committee were appalled. Here was this businessman, whose knowledge of development was based on a few visits to aluminum factories in the third world, lecturing an institution with half a century of development experience. Here he was, claiming that nothing the Bank did ever worked, and that the Bank made no effort to measure its performance. The Europeans in particular were incensed. Eveline Herfkens, the Dutch development minister who had served on the Bank's board, rounded on O'Neill; and the British, who had just come out with a bold proposal to double annual flows of aid, also dissented vigorously. Other Europeans spoke up indignantly, and at the end of the session, Wolfensohn could not resist piling on as well. The Bank, he said, was already doing much of what O'Neill said he wanted. Perhaps the treasury secretary would like to pay the Bank a visit?

Two weeks later, on November 29, 2001, O'Neill did visit; but it was not in order to learn or listen. He came to address the Bank's board, and many of the Bank's top managers turned out to hear him. He began by portraying himself as a great supporter of development, and then launched into a riff on mankind's limitless ingenuity. He had seen how progress could happen when he had run Alcoa. The firm's workforce had multiplied, its accident rate had shrunk, and lives had been made happier. It was his ambition, he declared, to unlock this human potential all around the world. He knew this must be possible. And then he made a speech about how all nations must aspire to issue investment-grade debt. What was that supposed to mean? Surely he could see that strong credit ratings would be the result of strong development rather than its cause? But O'Neill clearly thought he had come up with a brilliant innovation.

Throughout that winter, O'Neill kept beating on the Bank. He insisted that aid should boost developing countries' productivity, but it was hard to see how this helped to define the Bank's mission. Everything from roads to health systems to schools can promote a country's productivity, and there are no general rules about which promotes it most—the answer depends upon a country's circumstances. O'Neill also protested that the Bank should cut back on cheap IDA credits to poor countries and make grants instead—a reasonable idea, given that IDA was already so concessional as to be two-thirds or more grant, but one that depended upon the Bank's rich shareholders to pay for this extra generosity. Meanwhile, O'Neill resisted the British call to double international aid flows, saying that the development types must first demonstrate that they could put the money to good use. In February 2002, the British Treasury produced a paper suggesting that extra money would indeed be used productively. According to the British, who got their numbers from the Bank, every $1 billion of aid given in 1997 had raised 284,000 people permanently out of poverty. But O'Neill was not impressed. He continued to insist that the whole aid business was hopeless. It deserved no extra cash until it overhauled itself.

Over at the Bank, Wolfensohn's internal motor was accelerating. He had been pounded by O'Neill for a whole year, and now he sensed a chance to struggle off the ropes and begin to pound right back at him. The Bank's morale problems were on the mend; the damning *Foreign Policy* article was a receding memory; and in the post–September 11 climate, his arguments for extra aid were winning. Wolfensohn's British ally, the finance minister Gordon Brown, was calling for a new Marshall Plan. Several other European states were following, and Mexico's former president, Ernesto Zedillo, had recently headed a blue-ribbon commission that echoed Wolfensohn's call for a big jump in aid funding.[28] The veterans of the debt-relief campaign were on the move, most notably Bono, the Irish rock star who had branched out from performing songs like "Bullet the Blue Sky" and "I Threw a Brick Through a Window" to become an articulate development advocate. In January 2002, the annual Davos shmoozathon convened in New York, its traditional Swiss hosts having bowed out for fear of antiglobalization protests, and Wolfensohn's team lined up a series of big hitters to call for extra aid. Bono spoke out, and Bill Gates spoke out, and Senator Patrick Leahy joined in, and so did the superstar ex–treasury secretary Bob Rubin.

The push for extra aid was boosted by the approach of a summit in Monterrey, Mexico. The summit had been called to raise money for the United Nations' new Millennium Development Goals, which laid out poverty-reduction targets for the world: extreme poverty and hunger were to be halved; there should be universal enrollment in primary education; and so on. Some of these goals were almost as ambitious and unattainable as those in McNamara's famous Nairobi declaration, which had called for the elimination of absolute poverty; and while McNamara had set a deadline twenty-seven years off, the notional deadline for the Millennium Development Goals was 2015. Still, in the new climate after September 11, bold poverty-eradication goals had a fresh and powerful appeal, and more than fifty heads of state had promised to attend the Monterrey summit on financing them. After some hesitation, President Bush announced that he would attend, too, and Wolfensohn sensed the wind was at his back. The Europeans would arrive at the summit with promises of extra aid, and the United States risked looking mean-spirited if it failed to follow. In the run-up to the summit, Wolfensohn was speaking to Gordon Brown in London and to Bono wherever he might be, and calls for extra aid were echoing from all corners. "We will not create a safer world with bombs or brigades alone," Wolfensohn told an audience in early March.[29] Slowly but surely, his argument was winning.

Five days later, on March 11, 2002, Wolfensohn went over to see O'Neill at the Treasury. It was their first encounter since the treasury secretary had addressed the World Bank board three months before, and its tenor was no better. O'Neill came into the meeting with his jacket off, clearly spoiling for a fight; he hit Wolfensohn with all his gripes about the Bank, and demanded that he get serious about responding. Wolfensohn's lieutenants, who had accompanied him to the meeting, shifted in their seats a bit and wondered how he might respond. O'Neill's aggression was so raw, and so infuriatingly ill informed, that even a calm man might have exploded. Indeed, it seemed that an explosion might be O'Neill's desired outcome. If he could bait Wolfensohn into losing his temper, he might gain the pretext to get rid of him. But Wolfensohn responded with surprising calm. Unbeknownst to the others in that room, he had met Condoleezza Rice at the White House that morning. O'Neill could rant as loud as he might please. Wolfensohn had outflanked him.

The meeting with Rice was about the Monterrey summit. Wolfensohn went over to the White House and gave his standard pitch for aid, but he added an extra twist to it. As an American citizen, he said, he did not want to see his president go to the summit empty-handed. The Europeans were already promising a big increase in aid, he noted, not mentioning that these were promises he had done much to encourage; and it was widely known that the Bush administration was resisting a British push to put numerical targets for aid into the Monterrey communiqué. "You cannot let the president go down there with empty words," Wolfensohn told Rice. The fact that the national security adviser was taking the time to listen to him seemed like a good omen.[30]

Three days later, Wolfensohn got a call from Bono, who was now a prized member of Wolfensohn's legendary Rolodex. Bono, like Wolfensohn, had been over to the White House, and he had seen the president himself. His access tells you that his band, U2, had considerably more fans among American voters than the World Bank would ever muster. Bono had been pressing the Bush administration for additional aid, often using talking points that the World Bank had supplied,[31] and now the president had come up with a response: he was offering a $5 billion increase, and he wanted Bono to appear with him onstage when he announced it.

Bono did not want to sell his photo op too cheaply. "Is $5 billion enough?" he asked Wolfensohn.

"I think $5 billion is enough to sit on a podium," Wolfensohn responded.[32]

The photo op took place later that day, at the Inter-American Development Bank in Washington. Half an hour before the ceremony, Wolfensohn got another call. It was Condoleezza Rice, inviting Wolfensohn to sit up on the stage with Bush and Bono and Paul O'Neill and Cardinal McCarrick of Washington. Wolfensohn duly accepted, and took his place on this surprising team; as the U.S. president announced $5 billion in extra aid over three years, the World Bank president grinned a victorious grin, and the treasury secretary listened stiffly. After months of rejecting entreaties to increase aid, the Bush administration was performing a U-turn. Wolfensohn's post–September 11 pitch to link poverty to security had triumphed. He had squared off against a skeptical adversary at the U.S. Treasury; he had kept him talking, held his gaze; and in the end he had cut a path around his back so that President Bush himself was singing out the World Bank line, and O'Neill was looking on powerlessly. "We work for prosperity and opportunity because they're right; it's the right thing to do," Bush was declaring, though the words might have been Wolfensohn's. "We also work for prosperity and opportunity because they help defeat terror."

In the weeks after that photo op, the full extent of Wolfensohn's victory became apparent. First, the White House "clarified" the amount of money in the pledge: rather than offering an extra $5 billion over three years, it was making an indefinite promise of $5 billion *per* year—and never mind that O'Neill's Treasury had earlier circulated briefing papers stating the opposite. Second, it became clear how far the White House thinking had been influenced by the Bank. Bush's announcement speech had been peppered with arguments that originated with World Bank researchers, notably that aid was highly effective in countries with good policies. Indeed, the president's proposal to allocate the new U.S. assistance to a select group of high-performing developing countries could have been taken straight out of *Assessing Aid,* the Bank's 1998 study of development effectiveness. Over the next year or so, as administration officials fleshed out the president's proposal, the Bank's influence became steadily clearer. To define "high performers," the administration settled on sixteen benchmarks of good governance and policy: seven had been created by the Bank, and several others were widely known because they were tracked and disseminated by World Bankers.[33] In its effort to measure performance, the U.S. government relied heavily on the very institution that O'Neill lampooned for its ignorance of performance measurement.

At the Monterrey summit at the end of March 2002, Wolfensohn savored his victory. He had staged a remarkable comeback over the past year, and he felt as he had felt when he pulled off the Chrysler bailout after the top job at Schroders had eluded him. And yet his victory was fragile. Ever since its founding, the Bank had periodically ramped up its messianic rhetoric to grab the attention of its shareholders: It had preached about "absolute poverty" in order to shame rich governments into supporting development; it had stressed the threat that poverty posed to the rich world's interests. "There is no wall," Wolfensohn declared after the terrorist attacks; "the plight of the developing peoples . . . is *the* central drama of our times," George Woods had insisted, some thirty-four years earlier. But there was a risk in all this rhetoric. By promising more than it could deliver, the Bank would fuel another cycle of recrimination in the years to come. Sooner or later, the new sympathy for the Bank's mission would fade; the old skepticism would return; and the Bank would be asked all over again to explain the gap between promises and accomplishments.

The extent of the Bank's overpromising soon became apparent. Wolfensohn had pledged to step up the Bank's engagement with the newly strategic region around Afghanistan, and the Bank duly mounted missions and conferences in Central Asia, consuming weeks of staff time. There was some value in this exercise. By spreading its ideas in the region, the Bank was supporting Central Asia's modest crop of enlightened reformers. But the truth was that the Bank could not lend much in these places. Having learned the lesson that aid tends to fail in corrupt environments, the missions returned from the region without loan recommendations. The same went for the Millennium Development Goals, which cropped up with increasing frequency in World Bank speeches after the Monterrey summit. By becoming one of the chief cheerleaders for the millennium goals, the Bank encouraged the idea that it was responsible for making them happen. This was fine in the case of the first goal—to halve the proportion of people living under the $1-a-day line between 1990 and 2015—because spectacular growth in China and India put that goal within reach. But several of the other goals were not attainable. One was to reduce by two-thirds the mortality rate for children under five; but between 1990 and 2000 the rate fell by just one-tenth, a creditable performance but nowhere near what the Millennium Development Goals promised.[34] Another goal was to halve the proportion of people without access to sanitation; but between 1990 and 2000 the proportion without such access fell from 55 percent to 45 percent—a rate of improvement way below the millennium target.[35] A third goal was to achieve universal primary-school enrollment. But economic conditions and slow-changing parental education levels tend to influence school attendance, making the idea of universal enrollment utopian.[36]

The strident ambition of these goals ignored the spirit of the Comprehensive Development Framework. The World Bank is not some kind of all-powerful world government; the reality is poor countries must draw up development plans and make such goals happen. The Bank can advise countries and finance them; and no other development institution is better at this vital task, but the Bank cannot wish away the problems of child mortality or scarce water, and it cannot make every country embrace its agenda. As the Bank's own research had shown for several years, aid works only in countries with good policies—which is to say that *global* targets may often be unrealistic. You can stand up in front of the world's television cameras and vow to get all children into schools. But you'll only ever reach the ones whose governments are competent.

From the time of his first trip to Africa, Wolfensohn had imagined a Bank that respected its clients, that served them with the same devoted excellence he had lavished on his Wall Street customers. He had built upon this instinct, turning against the donor-imposed conditions of structural adjustment and calling upon poor countries to take charge of their own development. But this vision of a development agenda led by developing countries was hard to sustain. Northern NGOs were forever muscling up to the table, disrupting the Bank's efforts to build hydro-electric power in Uganda or move Chinese farmers off degraded land; and the Bush administration was pounding on the Bank as well, driving it to seek refuge in extravagant promises that ignored the eminent good sense of Wolfensohn's initial instincts. For all its money and brainpower and influence, the World Bank can't wish away the poverty of its clients. It has to work slowly, in partnership with the people of the world's developing nations, people like Yoweri Museveni and Emmanuel Tumusiime-Mutebile, who brought about Uganda's progress in the 1990s.

CHAPTER TWELVE

A PLAGUE UPON DEVELOPMENT

ACTIVISTS WITHOUT AN OFF SWITCH, demanding shareholders: both complicated Wolfensohn's instinct to defer to the Bank's clients in poor countries. But there was a third complication, too. On some issues, deference was the wrong strategy. The case for deference, after all, is practical. It starts from the fact that there are no silver bullets in development. Everything matters, from corruption to reliable power supplies. The key thing is that, whichever projects you embark on, you've got to implement them competently. Because implementation is so important, it makes sense to defer to poor countries' priorities. They are the ones who do most of the implementing, after all, so their commitment is crucial. But when a priority of truly extraordinary moment is ignored, this logic breaks down. The Bank needs to insist that poor countries wake up, and never mind the usual talk of deference.

In Jim Wolfensohn's time at the World Bank, the truly extraordinary priority was AIDS: a plague that had killed 19 million people by the year 2000; a plague that had infected another 34 million by that time; a plague that is set to kill more people than World War I, World War II, and the Korean and Vietnam Wars combined, nearly all of them in developing countries.[1] A calamity on this scale demands a rewrite of the normal rules. The Bank needs to do everything it can to put AIDS on poor countries' agendas. And yet the Bank has been slow to treat AIDS with the desperate urgency that it merited.

There are several reasons for this failure, as we shall presently explore. But it's worth noting at the outset that they reflect poorly on the World Bank's shareholders. If you were bending over to be generous to the Bank's overlords, you might argue that, for all their hopscotching from issue to issue, they are at least attuned to big strategic challenges. They might trumpet universal primary education one year and something else the next, but at least they will yell out if the Bank is missing the big picture. But neither the Bank's board nor its governing Development Committee goaded the institution to fight AIDS.[2] The goading had to come from within—from a handful of enraged staff, supported belatedly by Wolfensohn.

THE FIRST CASES OF AIDS were diagnosed in the early 1980s, and from the start the world's response was insipid. The HIV virus hid within its human carriers and wrapped itself in layers of taboo that served to stave off action. At first it was said to be a gay disease, and conservative preachers called it God's retribution. Then evidence from Congo showed that AIDS could kill heterosexuals, too, but this finding was shrugged off at international conferences. It was not until 1986, three years after the first Congo diagnoses, that a charismatic American doctor named Jonathan Mann shook the World Health Organization awake, and the WHO's boss held a press conference in New York: "We stand nakedly in front of a pandemic as mortal as any pandemic there has ever been," he declared, and he put Mann in charge of WHO's AIDS strategy. But even this breakthrough was not quite what it appeared. In 1988, WHO's director general changed, and the fight against the plague suffered. The new boss crippled the WHO's AIDS efforts because he resented the resources and prestige Jonathan Mann had amassed.[3] Mann quit in 1990.

In other institutions, too, the rare individuals who sounded the alarm heard mainly their own echo. The health division of UNICEF fought to avoid involvement in AIDS, and the senior health administrator's secretary resigned because she objected to handling letters about condoms. In the American government, meanwhile, it took an intelligence officer three years to get permission to study the virus; when her report finally appeared in 1991, virtually nobody in the U.S. government reacted.[4] This was not for lack of an arresting story line: the study projected 45 million infections by the end of the decade, twice as many as died from the Black Death in fourteenth-century Europe. Yet during the early 1990s, U.S. government spending on AIDS control abroad ran at around $125 million a year—half of what Americans spend on baldness therapy—and other governments came up with even less than that.[5]

The World Bank in the early 1990s was not very different. From time to time its officials would raise the issue of AIDS with borrowing countries, but they found countries resistant.[6] The clients did not want to hear the message; they refused even to collect statistics on AIDS-related deaths, much less borrow money to combat the virus. In 1990, Nigeria's respected health minister visited the Bank to negotiate a loan, and was treated to a separate presentation on AIDS, complete with projections of the disease's reach and the importance of early prevention. To press home their argument, the Bank officials noted that Nigeria had a high prevalence of sexually transmitted diseases, well-traveled truck routes, and a large military establishment—all factors known to spread the virus; they even pulled out a copy of *The Washington Post* and turned to the obituaries, to show how people in the United States were having to face up to the new killer. It was all to no avail; the minister made it clear that he had other priorities.[7] A little while later, Peter Piot, the Belgian virologist who had led the first diagnoses in Congo, gave a speech on AIDS to the Bank's staff. The director of the Bank's Sahel department was inspired to invite Piot to deliver a second talk at a special gathering of her team, and she wrote letters about AIDS to the ten heads of state in her region. But none of these efforts greatly changed the content of the Sahel department's lending.[8]

Elsewhere the Bank did lend, but with varying effectiveness. Its best project was in Brazil, where the political culture was remarkably open to confronting AIDS, and where the Bank helped to put in place a system for HIV testing and treatment, laying the foundation for what was later to become the model for antiretroviral therapy in a developing country. The Bank also persuaded India to accept a loan for AIDS in 1992, apparently breaking down a wall of denial; the Indians had wanted to borrow money only to upgrade their blood safety equipment, but the Bank insisted that they invest in a broader strategy against the virus. But after that loan was approved, India's reluctance persisted. Three years into the project, the government had fixed the blood supply but refused to draw down the Bank's money for other AIDS-fighting activities. The authorities regarded AIDS as a low priority—there were only two thousand cases of AIDS reported in India in 1995—and they suspected it might be an aliens' disease. The director of the Indian Council of Medical Research had once suggested that the remedy to AIDS lay in banning sex with foreigners.[9]

In 1993, the Bank finalized one of its few freestanding AIDS loans to Africa, in the promising setting of Zimbabwe.[10] The country's health minister, a white doctor called Tim Stamps, had spoken out about the plague as early as 1989,[11] and didn't mind telling audiences that, although he would not allow his twelve-year-old to drive his car, he wanted him to know about condoms. The Bank's AIDS loan to Zimbabwe was building on a sturdy base; the country's health system was strong, at least by African standards. But despite a supportive health minister and favorable conditions, the Bank's loan achieved little. Its project paid for drugs to treat sexually transmitted diseases and other medical supplies; it involved no effort to research the spread of the disease, and no attempt to change sexual behavior. There was a simple reason for this void: just about nobody outside the Ministry of Health wanted to confront AIDS honestly. If Bank officials tried to discuss the virus that had already infected one in five adult Zimbabweans, they were greeted with jokes about people having too much sex. Rather as in India, in other words, the borrower's reluctance to grapple with the plague set limits to the Bank's achievement.

What the Bank needed at that time was table-thumping leadership. It needed someone to energize the tentative struggles of the Bank's project managers: someone senior enough to call on a reluctant president and demand that he get serious about fighting the pandemic. But no such leadership materialized. Wolfensohn's predecessor, Lewis Preston, almost never mentioned AIDS,[12] and the executive directors on the Bank's board mounted no campaign on the subject. And so the efforts of middle managers were doomed, and AIDS lending amounted to less than half of 1 percent of the Bank's portfolio.[13]

Stronger leadership from the top might also have broken through the Bank's internal confusion. By no means everyone at the head office was convinced of the plague's importance. The Bank's World Development Report on health, published in 1993, acknowledged that by the year 2000 AIDS might be claiming 1.8 million lives a year, but it also noted that tobacco might kill 2 million annually.[14] Demographers insisted that AIDS would not make much impact on Africa's headlong population growth; health experts pointed out that malaria and diarrhea-related dehydration killed more children than HIV;[15] still others simply disbelieved the data.[16] In 1994, a math whiz in the Africa region worked out that, if the horrifying reports were accurate, a young African who expected to go through a number of sexual partners during the course of his lifetime had a more than 70 percent chance of contracting the virus. In fact he was precisely right—the Bank's AIDS experts were later to recognize that the odds for a young African in countries like Botswana were indeed within that range—but the calculation was too much to stomach. The math whiz walked into the office of a colleague who worked on AIDS, and told him the numbers must be screwy.

The upshot of these disparate views was a scattershot approach rather than determined action. Some in the Bank wanted to do more; others were not sure. The consensus was to talk a bit, but not to scream and yell that the world faced a pandemic equivalent to two world wars plus Vietnam and Korea. In the absence of such screaming, it was a sure bet that not much would happen. The Bank's loan officers get judged, inevitably, according to whether they make loans; nobody gets credit for working diligently on projects that the client doesn't want, even if the client *ought* to want them. To overcome the incentive to do easy, popular projects, you need a firm message from on high. But Preston was silent. The shareholders were silent. Nobody was yanking the Bank's project managers out of their grooves, yelling at them to wake up to this new enemy.

Other international agencies were no better at this time, but the Bank's failure on AIDS remains inexcusable. The evidence of the crisis was already to hand, which was why a dedicated minority inside the Bank had seen it. The World Health Organization had seen the light in 1986, though it had donned blinkers later; the CIA, in its report of 1991, had predicted African infection rates as high as 30 percent, and a fall in the region's life expectancy at birth of fifteen years or more, enough to reverse the development achievements of the previous generation. A public version of that CIA report appeared in 1992, but the Bank's leaders could have learned the facts in many different ways. They could have read *The Economist,* which in 1991 noted that the pandemic's reach knew almost no bounds, given that some 250 million people contracted sexually transmitted infections annually.[17] Or they could have skimmed the front page of *The Washington Post,* which announced in 1991 that AIDS was "virtually canceling out public health gains otherwise expected in Africa."[18] Or they could have read *The New York Times:* "In Deception and Denial, an Epidemic Looms" ran a front-page headline, some eighteen months later.[19]

Indeed, denial prevailed at the top of the World Bank. A plague threatened to wipe out everything the institution had achieved in some countries, but the Bank continued in its grooves, doing business pretty much as usual.

THE ARRIVAL OF Jim Wolfensohn did not end this scandal. Instead, AIDS carried on killing and the Bank plodded on indifferently. Around the time that Wolfensohn took office, in 1995, officials at the World Health Organization in Geneva were searching for a way to reinvigorate the fight; they set up a new campaign unit called UNAIDS, and badgered the Bank into joining it. The Bank acceded with bad grace; it emphasized that it would "assume no liability" for the new outfit and wished to have "as little involvement as possible."[20] The Bank's AIDS lending coasted along at a modest level in the next years,[21] and Wolfensohn ignored the plague.[22] In his first four annual meetings speeches, spanning 1995 to 1998, he made a total of just two fleeting references to AIDS, and by 1999, the Bank was funding only three substantial AIDS projects in Africa—in Kenya, Uganda, and Zimbabwe. All three of these African projects were winding down. Most astonishing of all, no new freestanding AIDS projects were under preparation in the region.[23]

In hindsight this is almost unbelievable. On so many other issues—on debt relief, NGO outreach, management practices, and corruption—Wolfensohn yanked the Bank out of its grooves and charged off across new territory: indeed, groove busting was something of a trademark. On AIDS, however, his instincts failed him.[24] Yet AIDS made Wolfensohn's efforts on corruption, for example, appear almost beside the point. Of course it was bad that Indonesia's government pocketed 20 or 30 percent of the Bank's loans, but one could debate how to weigh corruption against Indonesia's antipoverty advances. When it came to

AIDS, by contrast, there was not much to debate. In many parts of Africa, 20 or 30 percent of urban adults were infected with a virus that would almost certainly kill them; clearly this was a calamity that dwarfed other development challenges. Starting in the late 1980s, the Bank's highest priority in Africa should have been to fight this killer. Elsewhere in the world, the Bank should have pressed harder to save other regions from repeating Africa's experience.

It was not until 1999 that the Bank's leadership awoke from its long slumber. It was an awakening that spread simultaneously through U.S. government agencies—an example of how the Bank is sometimes almost unconsciously attuned to its main host and shareholder. On the American campaign trail, Al Gore got heckled by AIDS activists, who accused him of siding with U.S. pharmaceutical firms against South Africa's plans to treat HIV patients with cheap generic medicines. In New York America's ambassador to the United Nations, Richard Holbrooke, announced plans to use the U.S. presidency of the Security Council to convene a special session on AIDS—the first time ever that a health issue had achieved that level of UN attention. The U.S. government, like the Bank, was finally waking up to the pandemic because the evidence of its impact was now too stark to ignore—1999 was the year when AIDS finally surpassed all other causes of death in Africa. Yet the change at the Bank also owed something to an internal coincidence as well—to an unlikely partnership, in fact, between a huge Swiss champion of gay rights and a motherly Ethiopian doctor.

The Swiss was a man called Hans Binswanger. He was known at the Bank for two very different things: he had founded the Gay and Lesbian Organization of Bank Employees to campaign for domestic partner benefits, and he was also among the Bank's most oft-cited economists. In 1997, Binswanger transferred from the Mexico department to head rural development projects in Africa; he traveled around the continent with the fresh eyes of a newcomer, and one central fact seized him. Everywhere he went, people were dying. Meetings were often canceled because officials were attending funerals; businesses were forced to take on extra labor because workers were falling ill and not recovering. You could mount a rural development project, or train an extension specialist to go out and teach farmers how to plant better crops, but you'd be lucky if your new extension worker survived five or ten years, let alone a normal life of service. And the response to this vast challenge was vanishingly small. Everywhere Binswanger went, the Bank's AIDS programs were either nonexistent or just bad. It was a massive call to action.[25]

Toward the end of 1997, Binswanger was on a bus returning from a World Bank staff retreat, and he found himself sitting next to a doctor from the Bank's central health unit. The doctor was called Debrework Zewdie, and she had worked on AIDS for more than a decade; before coming to the Bank, she had shepherded AIDS projects all across Africa, including in her native Ethiopia. Binswanger mentioned that through his connections in the gay community, he had been invited to address the World AIDS Conference in Geneva the following year; and Zewdie said she would help him to figure out what he should say there. Binswanger then invited Zewdie to give a talk to his rural development team. During that presentation Zewdie brought up the subject of HIV treatment, and Binswanger made a comment about his own treatment, and pretty soon the people in the meeting were looking at him in a new light. Their chief had, in a roundabout way, announced that he was HIV positive. A decade and a half after its discovery, the plague had arrived inside the sanctuary of the World Bank headquarters.[26]

A little while later, in January 1998, Zewdie organized an AIDS workshop. The opportunity had arisen because an old controversy had flared up. A Bank demographer had returned from a trip to Namibia and circulated a memo saying that life expectancy in Africa would decline fifteen years or more, and the Bank had divided in its habitual way between those who saw this projection as a call to arms and others who suspected that the AIDS numbers were screwy. Zewdie used the controversy to convene the best academics in the field, and then she saw to it that the Africa region's vice president, a Zimbabwean called Callisto Madavo, would chair the last part of the workshop. A little while into the proceedings, one of the visiting experts displayed the numbers on a slide that had given rise to the meeting. It showed life expectancy in Africa, and the numbers were pointing inexorably downward.

"Are you telling me that life expectancy in my country now is what it used to be when I was an elementary school student?" Madavo demanded. He sounded shocked, horrified—which was horrifying in itself, since the evidence of the plague's impact had been around for a while by then. The next week Madavo asked Zewdie to speak about AIDS to the Africa region's top management. When Zewdie arrived, she switched on a cassette recorder, which was loaded with a tape of her workshop. Madavo's incredulous voice emerged from the loudspeaker.

"Are you telling me that life expectancy in my country now is what it used to be when I was an elementary school student?"[27]

From that moment in early 1998, Zewdie's job changed. She transferred from the Bank's central health unit, where she had next to no budget or influence, and began to lead the AIDS effort in the Africa region. She suddenly had staff, a special $1 million grant from Norway, and the support of a Bank vice president. In the summer of 1998, when Hans Binswanger went off to address the world AIDS conference in Geneva, Callisto Madavo went, too. For the first time ever, a top-level Bank official found the time to make a speech to a world AIDS conference.

The mood at the conference was grim. In the rich world, two years' experience with antiretroviral drugs had encouraged optimism; but that only highlighted the gap with the poor world, which could not afford such medicines. Moreover, the plague was spreading at a furious rate. In 1997, according to a UNAIDS report prepared for the Geneva gathering, 2.3 million people had died—considerably more than the Bank had expected back in 1993, when its World Development Report on health predicted 1.8 million or so AIDS-related deaths a year by the end of the decade. But the truly scary number concerned new infections. In 1997 alone, there had been nearly 6 million of these, meaning that, at some point a decade or so hence, 6 million people would be dying per year—a death rate far above the toll from malaria, tobacco, and diarrhea-related dehydration. The old argument from the early 1990s—that other diseases killed more people than AIDS—had been oddly static. It had failed to note that, whatever the relative death toll back then, AIDS was spreading faster than its rivals. Just in the three years running up to the Geneva conference—years in which Wolfensohn had run the Bank—twenty-seven countries had seen their HIV infections more than double.

All through the conference, Hans Binswanger was fuming.[28] Every session he attended contained terrifying prognoses. He used the time to cross-examine Bank colleagues about why they had been doing next to nothing. Toward the end of the conference, Binswanger had a conversation with Zewdie, and spilled out all his thoughts on what the Bank should do. The motherly doctor looked at the big bear of an economist. "Yes, but what are *you* going to do about it?"[29]

OVER THE NEXT NINE MONTHS, the Africa region hammered out a brand-new AIDS strategy. The brainstorming began in late 1998, when Uganda's successful model was near the zenith of its influence, and participation was widely held to be the key to development. Moreover, Hans Binswanger was a famed proponent of participation in his own right; he had devoted much of his career to something he called Community Driven Development, which had pumped money into villages in Mexico and left ordinary people to spend it. The Africa region's interest in Uganda-style development mingled with Binswanger's pride in community development, and both currents drove the Bank's AIDS team to pin their hopes on a broad participatory approach. Rather than tell Africans how to combat the plague, Zewdie and her team would get money out to village groups and NGOs. Some might perform sketches for schoolchildren about AIDS. Some might hold meetings to educate women. Some might arrange care for AIDS orphans.

The climate outside the Bank was pushing toward the same inclusive strategy. From the first stages of the AIDS crisis, the leading figures in the resistance called for a broad social mobilization, a response that would go far beyond the narrow medical approach that had failed in the Bank project in Zimbabwe. Jonathan Mann, the charismatic American doctor who had galvanized the World Health Organization, declared that the epidemic thrived on denial, silence, stigma, poverty, illiteracy, human rights abuses, and oppressive gender relations. You had to fight on all these fronts; you needed a comprehensive framework. Mann was a hero among the embattled medics who worked to contain AIDS, including many at the Bank; "AIDS is a mirror of who we are," Debrework Zewdie would say, echoing Mann's view that AIDS was a sort of proxy for all poverty's problems. Of course, Mann's philosophy resonated with Wolfensohn's comprehensive approach toward development. There was no way that the Bank could escape his influence.[30]

The comprehensive strategy against AIDS was not without its critics. In November 1997, around the time that Hans Binswanger encountered Debrework Zewdie, the Bank's economics research department published a formidable study of the pandemic.[31] The authors called for a stepped-up effort against the plague, but they dwelt on the question of which type of effort would work best, and they did not assume that grassroots groups necessarily knew the answer. To the contrary, those groups were quite likely to be wrong. The chances were that they represented the elite of the village rather than marginalized people who spread AIDS most actively. The way the Bank's research department saw it, these marginalized groups were key. African governments have scarce money and administrative oomph, so it was essential to focus their efforts on high-risk groups like truck drivers and prostitutes.

The economists' approach was an echo of the Larry Summers view: on many issues, as Summers told the Bank's country directors at their retreat in 2001, the Bank's own experts have a better handle on good policy than grassrootsy amateurs—top-down prescriptions beat bottom-up participation. But the participation enthusiasts in the Africa region were not swayed. The economists' prescriptions, they said, were based more on logic than experience. Admittedly, the argument for focusing on high-risk groups was bolstered by the successful AIDS-prevention effort in Thailand, which had indeed focused on brothels; but brothels in Thailand were formally organized, whereas the sex industry in Africa operated largely without rules or fixed locations. As Zewdie and her team argued, one of the few AIDS success stories in Africa—Uganda— had little if anything to do with focusing on high-risk groups. Instead, the government's leadership in speaking out about the epidemic was key; and even more important, ordinary Ugandans seemed to discuss AIDS more with one another. Somehow or other, there were more community groups and village meetings at which the subject was aired, and so AIDS-prevention messages filtered through to Ugandans via dozens of channels, much as a child growing up in the United States is dissuaded from smoking by a multitude of warnings. Thanks to Uganda's dense network of social groups, teenage sex began later than it did before the plague; and it seemed to be safer. A broad strategy of social mobilization had apparently been vindicated.

Even so, Zewdie's adversaries in the research department had a powerful argument. The empirical evidence might certainly be mixed, but logic clearly favored focusing on high-risk segments of the population. Zewdie and her team objected that, in countries with high prevalence rates, everybody is at risk; but this was misguided in two ways. Even if everybody is at risk, not everyone is at equal risk; and even more important, not everybody *poses* equal risks to others. African society is sometimes loosely said to be promiscuous, but this is an absurdly general claim. Some people there are monogamous; some people may have five partners a week; but the women who are forced into the commercial sex trade may have a dozen partners daily. Getting a safe-sex message to one sex worker is likely to prevent more new infections than getting that same message to fifteen members of the five-partner-a-week crowd. A woman in a village is no doubt at risk of infection from her truck-driver husband. But does it really make sense to focus your prevention effort on her? Couldn't you reduce new infections more by educating her husband?

The Bank's research department was right to press for a focus on high-risk groups, but its view was utterly at odds with the all-encompassing approach of the established AIDS-fighting community. The philosophy of Jonathan Mann—indeed the philosophy of the medical profession writ large—is to treasure every single life; it is not to make Sophie's Choice trade-offs between categories of patients.[32] If you ask the leading anti-AIDS campaigners whether they favor prevention strategies, treatment strategies, or community care, they will tell you that they favor all of them; if you object that resources are unfortunately scarce, they will retort that they shouldn't be. There is a moral logic in this position: if AIDS is more lethal than two world wars combined, why shouldn't resources be radically increased? And there is a political logic in it, too. The way to change the world is to proclaim a bold ideal and demand that necessary resources be found. You won't get anywhere with drab debates about trade-offs and cost-benefit analysis.

In November 1997, when the Bank's economists came out with their report, nobody in the AIDS-fighting establishment wanted to be slowed down by their sensible appeal for focusing on high-risk groups. In the Bank's central health unit, Zewdie reacted immediately against the report. It was too academic, she said, too unrealistic.[33] At UNAIDS in Geneva, Peter Piot was furious; he almost refused to allow the UNAIDS logo to appear on the report's cover, even though his staff had collaborated on the project, and even though he had previously coauthored a paper with one of the Bank authors. When the authors presented their findings at a conference in Côte d'Ivoire, the reaction was equally hostile, not least because President Jacques Chirac of France had used the occasion to promise antiretroviral therapy for Ivorians. At a press conference afterward, journalists hammered Zewdie for the Bank's supposedly callous position.[34] It was as though the Bank's economists were reliving the battles of structural adjustment. Their arguments were right, but also politically unpalatable.[35]

In March 1999, Zewdie's group in the Africa region produced its own report, which bore no hint of influence from the Bank's research department. Instead, it was a manifesto for action.[36] "Those who look back on this era will judge our institution in large measure by whether we recognized this wildfire that is raging across Africa," the foreword declared; "they will be right to do so." The report went on to catalogue reasons why AIDS is a threat to development. Unlike diarrhea or malaria, it kills people in the prime of life. It disrupts businesses; it interrupts farming; it destroys the incentive to invest in education and training. It creates millions of orphans who may grow up without adults, with consequences for society that boggle the imagination.

After the manifesto circulated in the Bank, Zewdie began to press for action. She wanted to create a freestanding AIDS department within the Africa region so that the cause would no longer be mired in trade-offs against other public-health crises. In meeting after meeting of the Africa region's management team, Zewdie made her pitch and Hans Binswanger would listen, waiting for strategic moments to support her. Another manager might say, well, Wolfensohn was just in Africa, and none of the African governments asked for AIDS projects; and Binswanger would seize his cue: "Goddamit, the African governments didn't ask for structural adjustment, did they? They didn't ask for environmental stuff, did they? These people are dying on your watch!" Nobody had the nerve to rebut that sort of assault. Binswanger stood well over six foot tall, and he had the particular moral authority that comes from being HIV positive.

In May 1999, two months after the manifesto appeared, Zewdie won her campaign for a new AIDS department in the Africa region. The breakthrough coincided with the shift in the world's awareness of the crisis: Later that same year, AIDS activists embarked on their tactic of heckling Al Gore, and Wolfensohn woke up to the enormity of the pandemic. At the annual meetings in September 1999—the very same meetings in which his deferential Comprehensive Development Framework triumphed—the boss walked into a meeting with finance and economy ministers from Africa, and waved Zewdie's AIDS manifesto in their faces: "Unless you read this book, I will not talk to you about development," he told them.[37] For the first time that year, his set-piece annual meeting speech mentioned AIDS in a substantial way: "In at least ten countries in Africa, the scourge of AIDS has reduced life expectancy by seventeen years," he said, noting the "more than 33 million cases of AIDS in the world, of which 22 million are in Africa." The next month Wolfensohn visited Nigeria, and told the traditionalist emir of Kano that he should allow public displays of condoms;[38] and from that moment on he made a habit of badgering reluctant clients into facing up to the crisis.

The tide was moving Zewdie's way, but she still needed to get the Bank's board to approve new lending. Far from pressing the Bank into confronting the world's largest development crisis, the shareholders had been silent; the hypothesis that the Bank's political overseers might be quick to spot the burning issues—that they might yank the technocrats out of their grooves—had been tested and found empty. At the Bank's spring meetings in April 2000, the policy-setting Development Committee got around to considering AIDS for the first time, but the pandemic was on the agenda only because the Bank's staff put it there.[39]

Faced with the possibility that foot-dragging shareholders might delay the rollout of projects, Zewdie pursued a version of the failed Bolivia idea. Rather than have the board approve each project one by one, she would submit two fully negotiated country programs and seek standing permission to replicate the same model across the rest of Africa. She dispatched one team to Kenya and one to Ethiopia, and financial managers and procurement specialists and health experts worked flat

out over the summer of 2000 to design two pilot loans; and at a preliminary briefing to the African board members around that time, Zewdie
explained her strategy. When the shareholders started to ask awkward
questions, Hans Binswanger reached into his pocket. He brought out
an envelope of brightly colored pills and laid them out on the table.

"This is how I live," he said. "Why are you not doing something
when your own brothers are dying in Africa?"[40]

The shareholders stared at the big Swiss economist and his small
colored tablets. From that moment on, there was no danger that Zewdie's strategy would suffer the same rejection as the previous year's ill-
fated Bolivia program.

The board approved Zewdie's Multi-Country HIV/AIDS Program
in September 2000. Her achievement completed the transformation of
the Bank's attitude to AIDS. No longer could the institution be accused
of neglecting the pandemic. Two weeks later, Wolfensohn used his
annual meetings address to speak out about the disease again, and he
dwelt on the specter of Africa's 10 million orphans at his closing press
conference. "This is not just another problem of health," he said. "This,
for many parts of the world, is a problem of existence."

IF THE FIRST LESSON in the AIDS story was that the Bank's busybody shareholders utterly failed to set the Bank on the right course, the
second lesson emerged over the next years as Zewdie implemented her
program. The original obstacle to AIDS programs persisted: borrowing
governments did not regard them as a priority. The consequent difficulties in the Bank's projects showed how crucial poor countries' attitudes
can be—even in a case where the Bank has resolved to go all out for
progress.

When the Bank's board embraced Zewdie's AIDS strategy, it set aside
$500 million in soft IDA credits and promised to commit another half
billion as soon as it proved necessary. Armed with this open checkbook,

the Bank's AIDS experts fanned out across the continent, urging countries to build the two main planks of their new strategy. The first was an adaptation of Hans Binswanger's Community Driven Development projects: countries should create financial pipes to funnel World Bank cash to community groups in countless villages so that people at the grass roots might be empowered to become allies in the fight against the virus. The second was an attempt to boost governments' effectiveness: countries should shift the lead role in the crisis from weak health ministries to new high-profile AIDS councils, which would operate out of the office of the president or the prime minister. If there was ever an opportunity to persuade governments to fight the virus seriously, surely this was it: AIDS was by now killing 2.5 million Africans a year, and any country that took the Bank's advice would get a lot of money. But by late 2002, two years after the board blessed Zewdie's program, at most $50 million had been disbursed for AIDS in Africa—a fraction of the $1 billion that the Bank had put on the table.[41] Six months later, in April 2003, disbursements still stood at less than $90 million.

Both planks of Zewdie's strategy proved extremely hard to implement. The idea of funneling money to community groups assumed you could build such a funnel; but in Ethiopia, the target of one of the two pilot projects that Zewdie had originally taken to the board, the government refused for a long time to let the Bank's cash leave the capital. One year after the government had received a commitment of $60 million from the Bank, only $1.5 million had been passed on to AIDS-fighting community groups. After two years the amount had risen to $12 million, still only a fifth of the total—and this in a country with 1 million AIDS orphans.[42] The efforts to build high-profile National AIDS Councils proved frustrating, too. It took protracted battles to set them up, and they were often no better than the health ministries that they displaced. In Kenya, the other pilot for Zewdie's strategy, the head of the new AIDS council was arrested for corruption. In Botswana, where other donors pressed for an AIDS council, the new body lacked cabinet status and hence was ineffectual. By 2004, the whole idea of creating National AIDS Councils looked like a mistake. Granted, Africa's health ministries had been hopelessly weak. But the Bank might have done better to build them up, enlisting the help of its traditional partners in the finance ministries.[43]

The slow rate of disbursement in Ethiopia and elsewhere was not for lack of trying. Since his trip to Nigeria in 1999, Wolfensohn had pounded on the AIDS issue, telling borrowers in country after country that they had to wake up to this challenge. On a trip to India in November 2000, his staff briefed him to raise AIDS with the prime minister—he should note India's welcome progress, but urge an accelerated pace—and Wolfensohn walked into the meeting and told his astonished host that he was doing nothing about the pandemic and he'd better get serious.[44] On a trip to Russia the following July, Wolfensohn pressed the issue of AIDS again. The Russians were dragging their feet in negotiations over a Bank project to address AIDS and tuberculosis. "I don't much care whether they take our money or somebody else's," Wolfensohn told one interviewer during his trip. "My only concern is that action is taken, and I will make a nuisance of myself until that happens." Meanwhile, Wolfensohn was a nuisance to his own staff, too. In December 2002, at a meeting of the senior management, Wolfensohn blasted his AIDS team for the slow pace of disbursement.[45]

Throughout this period, therefore, the message to the Bank was clear: AIDS was on the boss's mind, and they better do something about it. But there was not much the Bank could do in the absence of willing local partners. In Russia, for example, negotiations about a potential AIDS project had begun in 1998, but then the country was swept up in its financial crisis. After a while the crisis simmered down, but then the Russian authorities did not want to acknowledge a problem that involved drug users, a TB epidemic among prisoners, and gay sex. Then the health ministry said it might do a program, but it had qualms about borrowing money for it. Then Russian pharmaceutical makers went all out to block the World Bank's proposal, fearing that it would open the drug market to foreign competitors. The toughest resistance came from Russia's medical establishment; hospitals had a large and antiquated infrastructure for treating TB, which would be rendered redundant by the Bank's modernizations. Ultimately it took the Bank five years to persuade the Russians to accept its help—and never mind the fact that Russia had one of the highest rates of TB infection in the world, or that the Bank was projecting that HIV cases would jump more than fourfold between 2005 and 2020. At one point the Russian health minister interrupted a public seminar, pointed at the Bank's AIDS expert, and told him to get up and leave and never again to set foot in his ministry.[46]

In the end the Russians came around, and Zewdie's programs in Africa began to disburse more money.[47] Given the cataclysmic scale of the AIDS crisis, the prolonged effort to get programs up and running was clearly justified.[48] In India, where the government had initially refused to spend the Bank's money, the tide began to turn in the second half of the 1990s, showing that persistence could pay off eventually. India's progress remained halting, certainly: to promote condoms, for example, you had to find community teachers, train them, get them into the field, support them, measure their efforts—and repeat the exercise hundreds of thousands of times in this country of a billion people.[49] But in Tamil Nadu and Maharashtra, two states that used the Bank's resources more than most, the percentage of women reporting that they were aware of AIDS jumped more than threefold during the seven years of the project, spanning 1992 to 1999; condom usage among Tamil sex workers and truck drivers rose to the 80 to 90 percent range.[50] Admittedly, other states did much less well. Some fundamentalist Hindu provincial authorities objected to NGOs that counseled sex workers, and even locked them up; corrupt police officials harassed AIDS workers as well, extracting a mixture of bribes and sex from them.[51] But the Bank's perseverance probably needled India into responding to the pandemic earlier than it would otherwise have done—indeed, "several years" earlier, according to some Indian experts interviewed by the World Bank's evaluators.[52] If that was so, millions of lives were saved by the Bank's project.

In 2004, it was too early to know whether Zewdie's programs in the Africa region would yield similar results, or whether the Russian loan would prove successful. The design of the Africa projects made evaluation tricky—the disparate community groups to which much of the money flowed were hard to oversee, and Zewdie made little effort at the outset to build monitoring into her programs. In all likelihood, the projects did suffer from the failure to focus on high-risk groups. This was a case where the Larry Summers view was right: the Bank had gone too far toward a participatory approach and paid too little attention to technical experts. India's experience offered some warnings: the Indian authorities had hoped to reach high-risk groups via NGOs, but it proved difficult to find NGOs that had experience with society's most marginalized people.

And yet, however the Bank experiments turned out in Africa and Russia, the broader lesson was clear. There was no way that the Bank could spend five years negotiating every project in its portfolio, as it did in the case of the Russian AIDS loan. There was no way it could make a habit of strong-arming governments into accepting its projects, then wait for years for its money to be used—the experience with its AIDS project in India. In most areas of development, the Bank needed to do projects faster, to deliver for its clients. It needed to recall Wolfensohn's earliest instincts on his first trip to Africa.

THE SLOW PROGRESS on AIDS was yet another sign of the danger in overpromising. Even when the Bank went into top gear, and even when it was willing to mobilize almost limitless money, its success remained prisoner to the enthusiasm of its clients. If borrowers were uninterested, or incompetent, or perhaps plain corrupt, the Bank would not even get its money out the door, let alone save lives in poor countries. Wolfensohn's initial instinct had been right: the Bank needed to act as a partner to its clients, because this was pretty much the only way it could act. It took too long to shove policies on unwilling countries, as the slow progress on AIDS demonstrated.

The problem was that deferring to poor countries was difficult to sustain in practice. The Bank's embrace of the NGO agenda on the environment, relocation, and so on had alienated clients such as China, and its millenarian pronouncements were adding to the problem. Where, in the Millennium Development Goals, did it say anything about building a reliable power supply or decent roads? Where was there anything about economic growth, the emergence of a solid middle class, and social stability? To many governments in poor countries, these goals mattered more than the struggle against poverty; and yet the Bank, in its eagerness to forge a new pro-aid consensus in the wake of September 11, was proclaiming the poverty-fighting Millennium Development Goals anyway. By 2002, Wolfensohn was presiding over a Bank that had reached out to its nongovernmental critics and done much to build support in the rich world for aid. But he was also presiding over a Bank that was losing its own borrowers—especially the strongest ones. China, for example, had borrowed $3 billion from the Bank in each of the three years before Wolfensohn's arrival. But in the wake of the battle with the Tibet activists, its borrowing fell off to less than $1 billion annually.

In the end, Wolfensohn would have to face a trade-off between two visions of the Bank. The first vision cast the Bank as the partner of northern NGOs and northern governments, who steered the machinery of the international system. The Bank's role, in this conception, was to act as a sort of secretariat for the north's global ambitions. The second vision cast the Bank as the partner of poor countries, not of NGOs and shareholders. Its role, in this conception, was to fend off the demands of northern constituents as much as possible. In 2003, as he passed his eight-year mark, Wolfensohn began to push the Bank back toward the client interests he had started with. The Bank began to listen with new eagerness to borrowers, especially the larger ones; and this listening led it in a curious direction. Having graduated from physical capital to human capital, and from human capital to social capital, the Bank was now heading back in time: back toward its future.

CHAPTER THIRTEEN

BACK TO THE FUTURE

IN 1976, a young idealist called John Briscoe arrived in Bangladesh. He had left the oppressive atmosphere of his native South Africa; he had earned a PhD at Harvard; now he was coming to live in a village. He chose a place called Fatepur, which was perched upon an island that was surrounded by the tentacles of the world's second-largest river system. Life in Fatepur was miserable. For four months of each year, the village was under several meters of water. The houses were perched on mud plinths, and even in the dry season the nearest market was an hour away by boat. The people survived by working in the teams of human mules that pulled barges up the river; they planted a special breed of floating rice in their submerged paddy fields, which looked wonderfully exotic but which yielded little to eat. Malnutrition and disease were present constantly. The average person in Fatepur died before age fifty.[1]

For a young white South African, radicalized already by the abomination of apartheid, Fatepur was enough to confirm Marxist sympathies. Observing life in the village "was like reading Marx and Engels on nineteenth-century Europe," Briscoe wrote later; the dominant families practiced the "naked, shameless and direct exploitation of the market," forcing the poor to sell their meager plots of land at knifepoint, driving their families below the margin of subsistence. When Briscoe heard of a proposal to build an embankment around Fatepur, he was convinced no good would come of it. In theory, the wall would protect homes from the annual flood tide and capture water to supply an irrigation system. But Briscoe interviewed families from all social strata; he concluded that the rising value of land resulting from the embankment would merely encourage powerful families to grab it. In the absence of revolutionary political and social change, the project would entrench the misery of the majority.

Two decades later, Briscoe was working for the World Bank in Washington. The Bank, in a strange way, had caught up with his youthful radicalism. It no longer believed that infrastructure was the route to human betterment. In the 1960s and 1970s, it had moved from building physical capital to building human capital, and now it was moving from human capital to social capital—which was another way of saying that it was promoting the revolutionary political and social change that Briscoe had hoped for in his youth. In the new Bank of the 1990s, Scott Guggenheim was out in Indonesia working to change village power structures under the feet of a dictator; and Hans Binswanger was preaching the gospel of Community Driven Development, getting money into the hands of the humblest villagers in Mexico. Jim Wolfensohn himself spoke the language of solidarity with the least fortunate: he wanted the Bank to focus on the human aspects of development; he did not care about concrete. To promote a sense of identification with the poorest, Wolfensohn was sending his ivory-tower professionals off to spend a week in a village.

John Briscoe was glad to take this opportunity, and in 1998, he went to Fatepur again. What he saw amazed him. The villagers who had always struggled with disease now looked radiantly healthy. They wore clothes instead of rags, and their children were in school. Bustling markets had sprung up, and women were newly independent. Life expectancy had jumped by nearly two decades. It was a transformation that had taken centuries in many places; here it had happened in a single generation. Briscoe went back to the families he had known in the 1970s and asked them to explain their progress. They looked at him as though he might be soft in the head. "The embankment!" they exclaimed.

A bit of investigation confirmed how true this was. The embankment had been built, despite Briscoe's misgivings, during the 1980s; and the transformation had been wonderful. Moreover, the poor had shared in this progress, despite what the young Briscoe had predicted. As landowners had become richer, they had stopped working their land themselves and started running businesses. The poorest residents of Fatepur, who once had starved for lack of economic opportunity, now found jobs as farm laborers; compared to their peers in a nearby area outside the embankment, they felt themselves lucky. They had a third more income than their neighbors, according to the local government's statistics. They consumed 50 percent more calories. They enrolled three times as many of their children in school.

Before returning to his village, Briscoe had followed Bangladesh only from a distance. The country was known among World Bankers mainly for its impressive nongovernmental organizations. There was the Grameen Bank, which spawned the microcredit movement by pioneering small loans to poor women; there was the Bangladesh Rural Advancement Committee (BRAC), which has enriched the countryside with some fifty thousand teachers. When Briscoe went back to Fatepur, he asked the villagers about these NGO heroes. The way he recounts these conversations, they went something like this:

"So what made a difference to your life here?"

"Obviously the embankment!"

"Well yeah, anything else?"

"Yes, the bridges."

That made sense, since bridges had greatly cut the time it took to get to the local market town, but still Briscoe persisted.

"What about Grameen?"

"What?"

"The Grameen Bank. Microcredit."

"Oh, yes, that helps," the villagers responded, not wanting to seem ungrateful. Briscoe then asked about BRAC, the NGO famous for rural education. The response was again appreciative—BRAC's schools were part of the reason why enrollment had tripled—but it was clear that, in the minds of villagers anyway, having your kids in class mattered considerably less than having food to feed them.[2]

After his year in Fatepur in the 1970s, John Briscoe had emerged more radical than ever. He left Bangladesh to spend several years as a solidarity worker in the newly independent Marxist republic of Mozambique. After his second stay in Fatepur, Briscoe emerged no less indignant, but this time his wrath was directed at the politically correct nostrums of the development business. The good people of the North thought that health and education were what mattered; they favored universal schooling, not construction projects. But the people of the South had different priorities. If they lived knee-deep in water, they wanted an embankment to protect their homes and fields from flooding. If they lived eight hours from a market, they craved roads and bridges. Shortly before Briscoe's return to Fatepur, the Bank had produced a report on Bangladeshi poverty, and the executive summary mentioned education, health, microcredit, and NGOs thirty-seven times. Infrastructure had merited just one mention. To Briscoe's way of thinking, there could be no better illustration of his institution's identification with its northern stakeholders—nor of its deafness to its real clients.

The World Bank under Jim Wolfensohn had indeed moved away from infrastructure, continuing the long pilgrimage begun in the 1960s. Infrastructure-investment projects had accounted for 36 percent of the Bank's lending when Wolfensohn took office; five years later it accounted for 29 percent.[3] In the meantime, social-sector lending had grown over the same period, from under a fifth of the Bank's portfolio to fully a quarter.[4] The World Bank—Wolfensohn's Bank—wanted to focus directly on poor people. It did not want to be guilty of harming the environment, and it wanted to make peace with NGOs. Everything pushed it to stay out of controversial infrastructure projects, and it was incidentally convenient that a huge tide of private capital was headed for emerging markets, suggesting that the Bank no longer needed to finance water systems or telephones. Before Wolfensohn's arrival, the Bank had withdrawn from the Narmada dam project in India after NGOs denounced it.[5] Wolfensohn quickly built upon that precedent, withdrawing from Nepal's Arun III dam project in August 1995.

The way John Briscoe saw things, this was a mistake. Nepal had almost no resources apart from water and gravity; if you refused to build a dam there, you condemned its people. In other countries, where the Bank had stopped short of a flat refusal, its social and environmental requirements were prohibitive. In Laos, Briscoe reckoned, the environmental standards that the Bank proposed for a megadam project matched those of a country like Sweden; this was like telling the Laotians that they must not travel in motorized vehicles unless they purchased brand-new Volvos with passenger-side air bags. Laos, with a per capita income of $280 annually, had a hard time complying, and the intended dam had been delayed interminably; indeed, during Wolfensohn's first five years in office, no big new dam projects got off the ground. But the Bank appeared unbothered. It was encircled, after all, by NGO critics, who filed dams under the same heading as structural adjustment and torture. Delay in Laos was a public-relations bonanza. Us? Build dams? You must be mistaken!

If this was the tone of Wolfensohn's first five years in office, the pendulum swung back a little in his second term. The turning point came with the upsurge in antiglobalization radicalism in 2000, coinciding with the Bank's battle against the Tibet lobby over its project in Qinghai. These shocks showed that placating NGOs was just not possible. After five years of energetic outreach, the Bank remained a favorite object of attack. On the other hand, the attempt to placate NGOs rendered the Bank onerous to its borrowers. The Bank demanded too many conditions, both social and environmental, to the point that big clients preferred to borrow for infrastructure projects elsewhere.[6] You could see this in the decline of the Bank's infrastructure lending; and, even more worrying, you could see it in the decline of its overall lending. After a spike during the emerging-market crisis, the Bank suddenly found that demand for its market-based loans evaporated. In the year ending June 2000, the Bank's commercial operation lent less than half of what it had the year before.

It took the Bank a little while to react to that astonishing collapse. But over the next two years the Bank's commercial lending failed to recover, and the Bank's non-IDA clients seemed to have settled down to borrowing around 50 percent less than they had before the Asian crisis. There was no way the Bank could ignore this rebuke forever. The old specter that haunted the Bank—that it would become more and more an IDA institution, and that it would suffer a UN-type dependency on its rich donors—returned now with a vengeance. Clearly the Bank needed to shake itself. It must not allow NGO attacks to chase it out of areas like infrastructure. It must no longer shy away from risky projects.

By a curious coincidence, an extremely risky project was in the works just as the battle with the Tibet activists was raging. It was a project that involved infrastructure. It involved outraged NGOs and rain forests. And it involved one of the diciest countries in the Bank's portfolio.

THE DICEY COUNTRY was Chad, a vast landlocked slab of territory in central Africa. Nobody knows how many people live there—the World Bank says 7 million, the CIA says 9 million—but everyone agrees that Chad is among the poorest countries in the world. The life expectancy is less than fifty; the average daily income is two-thirds of a dollar; fully

80 percent of the people live in poverty. Most Chadians have no access to a banking system, or postal system, or electricity; in 1999, the country reportedly had ninety-seven thousand telephones, fewer than the World Bank Group. The one world-class institution in the country is the Gala brewery, which has consistently stayed open despite civil wars and Libyan invasions, heroically producing the best beer in the Sahel.

Chad, you may have guessed, is not much of a democracy. The country is divided between nomadic Arab northerners, whose political thinking resembles that of Afghan warlords, and Christian and animist Africans, who cultivate the South. In the French colonial period, the Jesuit teachers steered clear of warlike northerners, so southerners got most of the education, and the country's first independent government was drawn from the South. The northerners resented this, and not without reason: at one point the southern dictator executed members of his civil service who refused to undergo his tribe's initiation rites. In 1982, France switched its allegiance, and French soldiers installed a northern president, and then it was southerners' turn to feel left out. Chad's current northern strongman is a tall slim warrior called Idriss Deby, who reserves a remarkable number of key government positions for his own kinsmen.

The one thing Chad does having going for it is oil. There are reckoned to be about 900 million barrels of recoverable oil in the southern Doba Basin, a trifle by Saudi Arabian standards, but still a veritable treasure for a country with a per capita income of $230 a year. Western oil firms had been visiting Chad off and on since the 1970s: they were keen to start drilling, but they faced enormous obstacles. For one thing, you couldn't export the oil unless you built a pipeline, and the pipeline would have to travel through a wild stretch of Africa. It would begin near the southern towns of Doba and Moundou, scene of periodic uprisings against the northern government; and it would travel one thousand kilometers southwestward to the coast of Cameroon. On the way, it would pass through rain forests inhabited by Pygmies. The combination of rain forests, oil drilling, and Pygmies seemed sure to conjure up a furious swarm of NGOs.

Moreover, the oil companies faced another obstacle. Chad's government was neither reliable nor stable. A Western company might pour in millions of investment capital to drill the wells and build the pipeline, only to find itself the victim of nationalization, civil war, or other manmade shock. Because of these risks, the oil firms found that no bank wanted to finance a Chadian venture. And so they came up with a solution: persuade the World Bank to come into the project. The Bank could vet the developmental impact of the pipeline, and its seal of approval would protect the oil companies from NGO attackers. Moreover, the Bank's involvement would raise the cost to the Chadians of expropriating the oil firms, and so transform commercial lenders' attitude, even if the Bank's own financial stake in it was minimal.

The lead oil company in Chad was Exxon,[7] and its officials first broached the idea of a joint effort with the Bank in the early 1990s. From the Bank's point of view, there were good reasons to say no to the oilmen. The prospect of acting as their shield against NGO critics was not especially attractive, and the prospect of guaranteeing the good behavior of Chad's government was daunting, since the Bank had poured nearly $1 billion of IDA money into Chad since the 1960s and seen much of it wasted. Even so, it was hard to say no to Exxon. Oil might change Chad from a no-hope country into one that actually deserved the term "developing." How could the Bank denounce the evil of poverty, and then inform the Chadians that their oil must stay forever underground?[8]

If Exxon had approached the Bank early in the era of Jim Wolfensohn, perhaps it would have been rebuffed.[9] But this was the early 1990s—a time before the Fifty Years Is Enough campaign, and before the disastrous 1994 Madrid annual meetings, and before a new and energetic president set out to woo the NGOs. And so the Bank hedged its bets and told Exxon it would move forward, consoling itself in its nervous moments that a full-blown project was a long way off.[10] Once the Bank stepped aboard, however, it found the train was shoving forward. The usual obstacles that hold up tricky projects were being blown aside.

There are few things more awesome than the power of a vast company that alights in a small country. The constants of life there—that there are no roads to get about on, that the government is hopeless—melt suddenly away. Over the next few years, Exxon created its own private air service to link the oil field to the capital; it created its own electricity system, with six times as much generating capacity as existed for the rest of the country; it built a road that bisected the oil region, and surfaced it with molasses that baked hard in the sun. The compound that housed the oil workers came to resemble a small piece of Texas; it was as though porta-cabins and oil derricks and beefy men with twanging accents had been minding their business somewhere outside Houston, and then a magic carpet hidden underneath them had whisked them to another continent.[11] When it came to the development impact of its project, Exxon applied the same bulldozing determination. It was not going to allow the usual rules of Chad to stop it. It needed the World Bank's allegiance, and it was out to show NGOs from Berlin to Berkeley what a good citizen it was.

The spearhead of Exxon's development effort was a small and feisty American anthropologist named Ellen Brown. She had come to southern Chad in 1968, as a volunteer with the Peace Corps; she remained in the region to do fieldwork for a thesis, and later earned a doctorate in anthropology from Cambridge University. For much of the 1970s and 1980s, through Libyan incursions and French military interventions, Ellen Brown stayed on in the country, working as a consultant to various NGOs and aid agencies, deepening her knowledge of the people and customs. In 1995, Exxon officials heard of her and set their hearts on hiring her to run their community outreach efforts. A Peace Corps veteran who spoke Chad's southern dialects? That ought to impress the Bank!

Over the next few years, as Exxon's geologists scoped out the scrubby landscape, Brown was duly reaching out. She assembled a team of sixty people to work with her, and she began by making a baseline study of the area around the project site. She found that fully half the people had no access to wells or piped water, that nobody at all had electricity, that only one in ten had access to latrines. She surveyed the local farming techniques, which were astonishingly simple. Animal traction was a novelty, with humans doing much of the plowing unaided; almost no vegetables were cultivated; women fed their families with wild leaves and vegetables gathered in the bush. Farmers abandoned worn-out fields and cleared new ones; there was no effort to conserve soil. Having completed her survey, Brown calculated the likely disruption to this way of life as a result of the oil project, and weighed in on subjects like gravel, chicken, and land.

Exxon's first instinct had been to dig its gravel out of a quarry, which seemed like a reasonable way to get it, but Ellen Brown proposed a different route. By local tradition, widowed mothers earned their living by sifting gravel from the local rivers, so Exxon bought from them instead of quarrying it, boosting the income of a disadvantaged local group. Similarly, Exxon was planning to hire locals to do some of the less-skilled construction work, but it had not thought about the consequences for local prices. The new band of wage earners would drive up the price of luxuries like chickens, leaving the rest of the population worse off. Ellen Brown organized a team of villagers to check chicken prices in the markets weekly. If the Chicken Price Index—a variant on the CPI that American economists follow—spiked up a bit, Brown had chickens brought in from other parts of the country, so that supply balanced demand.

Brown's biggest challenge was to figure compensation for lost land. The farmers around the oil site were in some ways well placed to sustain losses. In the slash-and-burn system of the region, they were used to moving on. Still, moving was costly: a farmer might lose a year of crops in the transition, and clearing scrub from a new plot involved back-breaking labor. Ellen Brown calculated the value of the lost crops and the labor, and then she considered how to pay compensation for it. There were no banks in the villages, so nowhere for villagers to store cash. Brown stomped around the countryside, asking people what they might prefer instead of money: farm carts, bicycles, and sewing machines were the most popular choices.

Exxon was right to be proud of Ellen Brown's efforts; the World Bank itself was only beginning to embrace participatory development in the mid-1990s, and here was Exxon, doing something that looked rather like a participatory oil project. For Exxon, moreover, gestures of good citizenship were something of a novelty. The firm had sucked much of its oil out of offshore boreholes, where there were no local farmers to worry about; in places like Indonesia and Angola, its reputation was mixed, to be polite. But now here was Exxon being represented by this ex–Peace Corp aidnik, half outdoorswoman and half hippy in appearance, clad in tough boots and floppy tunics as she set off to consult villagers. On issue after issue, Ellen Brown challenged the oil company's usual way of doing business. And the company was usually prepared to listen. If the oil men did not do right by the local people, the World Bank might walk out.[12]

Brown's work in the oil region was matched up and down the route of the proposed pipeline. Exxon sought the advice of primate experts so that the pipeline could avoid gorillas; it consulted Cameroonian anthropologists about the Pygmies in the rain forests. The World Bank had said there must be a "Category A" environmental assessment—the meticulous sort that the Inspection Panel believed appropriate for Qinghai—and Exxon promptly commissioned one; the Bank said the assessment's verdict wasn't positive enough, and Exxon agreed to re-route the pipeline. The Bank also wanted the firm to invite NGO input, and Exxon assigned Miles Shaw, a perpetually sunny executive, to globe-trot around North America and Europe, visiting every outfit that might take an interest in a central African pipeline. However high the Bank set the bar, the oilmen jumped over it—even when the Bank repeatedly moved the bar higher as the project went ahead.[13] The tentative decision to keep options open was leading the Bank inexorably to a position that was unusual in the cautious mid-to-late 1990s. To its own surprise as well as everybody else's, the World Bank was supporting an audacious oil project in a dicey country. It was risk and risk combined.

JIM WOLFENSOHN was aware of this locomotive's gradual advance. In February 1996, he had dinner with the Bank's critics from the Environmental Defense Fund in Washington; they raised concerns about the Chad project, and he invited them to call him personally if things were going wrong. Wolfensohn also spoke occasionally to Lee Raymond, Exxon's chief executive; and from time to time the French government would pester him on behalf of Elf, the French oil company that was partnering with Exxon. So long as Wolfensohn could talk to both sides, he saw no great cause to worry. He could assure the Environmental Defense Fund that he would come down hard on abuses, and he could assure Exxon's chief executive of his support at the same time.

Yet there was no way that the Bank could escape controversy indefinitely. African oil projects had an appalling record—from Congo-Brazzaville and Equatorial Guinea to Gabon and Angola, oil revenues have financed corrupt dictators, bringing no perceptible benefits to their people—and in October 1997 the Chadian adventure started heating up. Ellen Brown went with Miles Shaw, Exxon's sunny community-relations expert, to discuss their firm's environmental and social impact assessment with local-government officials in Moundou, the main town in Chad's south. A few days later, however, this outreach effort was buried by Chad's government, which attacked a southern rebel group that was hiding out in Moundou, killing forty of its fighters.[14]

Pretty soon northern NGOs were putting out the theory that oil was fueling human rights abuses by the northern military. Although there was no proof of a connection, it was a plausible thesis. Chad's military did indeed have an appalling human rights record, and oil gave the northern government new reason to subjugate the South.

This pattern was repeated the following summer. In June 1998, Exxon released a lengthy plan showing how it would mitigate the project's environmental and social impact; it was a monument to the company's determination to placate the World Bank. But the following month the government's behavior raised fresh questions about any project that might bolster it. Chad's most prominent southern leader was jailed after accusing a minister of corruption, and two journalists who had reported on his allegations were jailed as well.[15] Meanwhile reports of another skirmish trickled in from Moundou. Was this sort of country really going to translate oil revenues into development?

The fighting and imprisonments brought down the wrath of NGOs. German activists circulated a resolution in the Bundestag, demanding that human rights abuses cease before the oil project went forward. Soon there was a similar resolution in the European Parliament, and Miles Shaw was scampering around Western capitals, greeting people with his cheery handshake, often passing NGO adversaries who were tracking down the same officials in the hallways of the European Parliament. In the United States, the Environmental Defense Fund was getting other NGOs fired up about the Chad issue, and the Sierra Club and Amnesty International joined it, and this coalition printed up some prewritten protest postcards, and pretty soon Exxon fielded letters from a thousand outraged citizens. At the Bank's annual meetings in the fall of 1998, the activists signaled their displeasure in typical fashion. The iniquities of Chad's oil scheme became the subject of a protest puppet show.

If China's Qinghai project was defeated at the hands of activists, there was no way the Chad project should have made it through. The

Qinghai scheme came after a series of relocation projects in China, all of which had reduced poverty; the Chad scheme came after a series of oil projects in Africa, all of which had failed to do so. But the Chad scheme did have one large advantage. The World Bank's most visible partner in this instance was not a mistrusted communist government but an astute American multinational. In late 1998 and 1999, as the project's moment in front of the Bank's board grew nearer, Exxon was lobbying assiduously. Its boss was checking in with Wolfensohn, and President Chirac called to lobby on behalf of the consortium, and Exxon was rolling out its secret weapon: a small and feisty anthropologist.

In July 1999, Ellen Brown made the pilgrimage from southern Chad to Washington, where she briefed officials from the World Bank's board representing half a dozen or so of the big shareholders. One of the board members had heard from NGOs that Chad's government was moving thousands of northerners to displace local people in the oil region. Ellen Brown had demographic data to disprove that. The board members were worried that land compensation might be inadequate. Ellen Brown explained the underlying math. The board members were especially exercised about mangoes. Well, Ellen Brown had calculated the average yield of a mango tree, multiplied it by the average price of mangoes in the market, and multiplied the result by eight. It could take eight years, she explained, for a mango seed to grow into a mature fruit bearer, so Exxon was paying out enough to compensate the farmers for all fruit lost in those years.

The more Exxon focused the discussion on the environmental and social aspects of its project, the stronger its position looked. In June 1999, the company released the final version of its plan to mitigate the impact of the pipeline, and by now any reasonable critic had to admit it was impressive. It was fully six years since Exxon first set out to do a Category A environmental assessment, and the latest compendium of good-guy promises ran to an extraordinary nineteen volumes; it did everything imaginable to comply with the World Bank's Volvo-style safeguards. Experts from the company, the Bank, and the Chadian and Cameroonian governments had walked the thousand-kilometer route of the pipeline, double-checking data from aerial surveys. They had agreed that, for the whole thousand kilometers, the pipeline would be buried, reducing the risk that sabotage would spill black waste on the ground. For most of its length, it would follow existing infrastructure, so minimizing the disruption to virgin territory. Only about fifteen square kilometers of rain forest would be destroyed; and by way of compensation Exxon promised to help establish two nature reserves many times larger.

Two years later, in 2001, the Bank's fearsome Inspection Panel came to Chad and raked through the project. It toured the region and took testimony from the project's critics; and in the end it found rather little to complain about, proving that Exxon had been better at complying with the Bank's environmental and social safeguards than most of the Bank's partners. But the diciest part of the project actually lay elsewhere, beyond the scope of the Inspection Panel's remit. It lay in a revolutionary attempt to rescue Africa from its sorry experience with oil.

THE CURSE OF OIL in Africa is a subset of a wider problem, diagnosed originally in a small country that has contributed unselfishly to economics textbooks. The small country is Holland, which in the seventeenth century succumbed to speculation in tulip bulbs, providing a colorful case study in financial mania for economics students ever since.[16] Three centuries later, Holland succumbed to a malady that came to be known as Dutch disease. In 1959, the discovery of gas in Holland's territorial waters seemed to promise national riches. But gas exports drove up the value of the Dutch currency, rendering other Dutch enterprises uncompetitive and destroying thousands of jobs.

There is nothing inevitable about Dutch disease: having learned from Holland's experience, countries like Norway pretty much avoided it. The defenses are commonsensical. You relieve the upward pressure on your currency by saving part of the windfall in a foreign-currency account for future generations; you invest your petrodollars in things that boost productivity so that firms remain competitive despite a stronger exchange rate. But Dutch disease, although avoidable, strikes countries with compromised immune systems—countries where the government is corrupt and unaccountable and where institutions are weak. Iran, Nigeria, and Venezuela have seen their GNP per person fall since the mid-1970s, despite enormous oil riches. Chad's government is a family enterprise run by a warlord. It seemed almost guaranteed to waste its petrodollars.

Early in its Chad adventure, the World Bank began to struggle with the Dutch disease problem. It could hardly regard it as unbeatable, since that would be embarrassing. Foreign aid is a bit like an oil windfall—it can push up the exchange rate and therefore harm exporters—so the Bank is almost bound to argue that this problem can be solved. And yet it had to admit that Chad's lousy government rendered the challenge enormous. In the studies leading up to its famous *Assessing Aid* volume, the Bank's research department demonstrated that aid in poorly managed countries achieved nothing, and that imposing conditions on bad governments could not be expected to alter their behavior.[17] If this was true for aid, it had to be true for oil windfalls. In poorly managed countries, oil money would be damaging: it would provide fresh incentives for corruption, and would weaken governance. There was no use pretending that a few World Bank conditions could save Chad from this fate.

Confronted with this probability, the World Bank's Chad team came up with a novel trick. In philosophical moments, they waxed almost Hegelian about it. The Bank's old-style conditionality was Thesis; the anticonditionality findings of *Assessing Aid* constituted Antithesis; and now the Chad model had brought the Bank to Synthesis. The synthesis consisted of accepting the insight of the 1990s—that institutions rather than donor conditions determine a country's policies—and then col-lapsing the dichotomy: What if the donor condition was that good institutions should be built? Instead of merely asking countries to put their names to promises, the Bank would ask countries to build govern-ment departments to implement those promises. A promise was just a piece of paper with a signature. An institution was a posse of living, breathing officials.

The shift to institutions-as-conditions was not confined to Chad. The AIDS group in the Africa region demanded that countries set up high-level National AIDS Councils, though with limited success. But the Chad effort was perhaps the most elaborate. To save Chad from the errors of its neighbors, the Bank devised an oil-revenue plan: a propor-tion of the revenue would be kept offshore in a fund for future genera-tions, and the balance would be spent on health, education, and other areas that would have a poverty-fighting impact. There would be pub-lished audits of the petroleum accounts to deter corruption, and regular checks to ensure that the money was going to the approved areas of health, education, and so on. All of this would be enshrined in a law, endorsed by both president and Parliament. And, most ambitiously, there would be a new institution to oversee this regimen. A special over-sight committee—consisting of representatives from Chadian NGOs as well as the supreme court, the government, and Parliament—would be created, with powers to enforce audits and transparency and to veto inappropriate disbursements of oil funds.

At the end of 1998, Chad's Parliament duly embraced the Bank's Hegelian synthesis. The Bank set about planning the new oversight committee and lined up an IDA credit to pay for the training of com-mittee members, which was approved by the Bank's board in January 2000.[18] And yet, however readily Chad went along with the Bank's formula, there was no denying this was risky. Can strong institutions be created by external donors, without the benefit of an insider like Uganda's Tumusiime? What if Chad's ruler set up the oversight college and equipped it with offices and secretaries and fancy new computers, and then, once the oil money was safely flowing, dispatched a handful of soldiers to close the whole operation?

In the fall of 1999, as the battle over the project grew heated, the critics seized this argument. The Environmental Defense Fund produced a pamphlet that cunningly quoted Wolfensohn saying that development was impossible in a corrupt environment and then drew attention to Chad's lousy human rights record. Yet the Environmental Defense Fund, like many of the Bank's most vociferous critics, is first and foremost an environmental outfit, and so the pamphlet muddied its powerful governance objection with weaker ones. It claimed that the project threatened the rain forests, despite Exxon's nineteen-volume environmental management plan; it feared the worst for the Pygmies; it raised the specter of spilled oil. The flamboyant Rainforest Action Network was no different. In August, it took out a full-page ad in *The New York Times* attacking the project, and posted WANTED signs in Jackson Hole with Wolfensohn's face on them; in September, it stuck a pipeline-protest banner to the façade of the Bank's headquarters; and in November, it staged a protest outside Shell's offices in Washington, because the Anglo-Dutch company was part of Exxon's consortium. Much like the Environmental Defense Fund, the Rainforest Action Network emphasized the environmental risks in the Chad project. It denounced the "rain forest pipeline," charging that it would destroy pristine habitats that were home to threatened species and disturb native tribes.

The muddying of the critics' message gave the Bank and Exxon an easy out. They rebutted the social and environmental charges easily: they had the facts, they had Ellen Brown and all her data, and many of the NGO screamers had never been to Chad. Winning on those points made it easier to slide past the tougher question about Chad's governance. The project was, according to the Bank's press chief, not an oil project but a poverty project—but that only begged the question of whether poverty would go down. To be sure, the Bank's revenue-management scheme was impressive, but who knew whether the transplant of a new institution into a rotten body politic was possible? If you believed Wolfensohn's past pronouncements on corruption and governance, optimism on Chad was difficult. And yet, with a few exceptions like the Environmental Defense Fund's pamphlet, his critics often failed to point this out.

Despite the critics' intellectual clumsiness, the fate of the project remained uncertain.[19] After all, utter intellectual flakiness had not prevented the Tibet activists from burying the Qinghai loan. When the WANTED posters appeared in Jackson Hole, Wolfensohn's latent suspicions of his staff—his tendency to believe what outside critics said of them—bubbled to the surface, and he demanded that the Chad project team double-check its compliance with the Bank's safeguards. His skittishness was compounded by the pressure he was feeling on Qinghai, and his feeling that the China team had let him down by ordering up a Category B environmental assessment instead of a Category A one. Then, toward the end of 1999, Exxon's two partners, Shell and Elf, pulled out of the consortium, possibly because of NGO pressure.[20] Some Bank officials greeted this news eagerly. Perhaps this risky venture would now die of natural causes?

The withdrawal of Shell and Elf had a paradoxical effect on Wolfensohn. The boss insisted on yet another review of the project's soundness, this time conducted by managers with no previous involvement, and later a war-room meeting took place at nine o'clock each morning to examine the project's potential pitfalls from every angle.[21] But at the same time Wolfensohn rallied behind the venture. The collapse of Exxon's consortium brought out his investment banking instincts: a deal was falling through and it had to be rescued. Wolfensohn got on the phone with Exxon's boss, Lee Raymond, and urged him to go out and find new partners, assuring him that the Bank would not back out of the deal if he could assemble a new consortium; then he followed up with calls to oil firms that Exxon was courting. By early 2000, Exxon had lined up Malaysia's Petronas and America's Chevron, and the project had been saved.[22] Just as important, Wolfensohn had assumed a personal stake in it. In a way that mirrored his broader transformation around this time—the time of antiglobalization attacks on the Bank and the battle with the Tibet activists—the boss's allegiances shifted. He was now aligned firmly with his staff, and against the outside critics.

There was one remaining obstacle, however. The Bank's board of directors needed to approve the $190 million in loans to the pipeline.[23] The Environmental Defense Fund was pulling out all the stops to block the Bank's participation; it flew an elegant Chadian human rights leader to Washington and introduced her to people who might rally Congress against the project.[24] For a while Nancy Pelosi, the California congresswoman who had sunk the Qinghai project, looked as though she would fight the Chad one also.[25] For a while, too, the Congressional Black Caucus seemed hostile, and Wolfensohn took the extraordinary step of asking the Bank's African staff members to press black Congressmen to change their minds, a request that breached the Bank's rules against lobbying.[26] The African staff duly produced a position paper railing that the continent would be left in a "state of nature" if the environmentalists got their way; eventually the Black Caucus came out in favor of the pipeline. The situation was so tense that Wolfensohn refused to submit the project to a board vote on the appointed date, much to the fury of his project team. Instead, the board was invited merely to discuss the project, and the argument boiled on for eight and a half hours. After two more weeks of consensus building, on June 6, 2000, Wolfensohn finally presented the Chad venture to his shareholders. The project team was anxious: if the board members raised tough questions, perhaps Wolfensohn would desert them. But the boss defended the project through more than four hours of debate and argument. When the vote was finally taken, not a single board member opposed the project, and only Italy abstained from voting.

It was a strange contrast with the fate of the Qinghai project. But the Bank had shown that, with some help from the might and muscle of an oil company, it could stand up to its critics; it could defy the Rain-foresters and the Environmental Defense Fund and all the other antis, and it could do so despite the rising tide of antiglobalization protests. Having been branded an environmental criminal by the Rainforest Action Network's WANTED posters, Wolfensohn derived some satisfaction from this victory. "I think it's important that we have a proper balance between the Berkeley mafia and the Chadians," he observed a few weeks later. "And I, for my part, am more interested in the Chadians."

WOLFENSOHN'S PRONOUNCEMENT could have been a manifesto for that second vision of the Bank: the vision that placed the Bank on the side of its poor borrowers rather than its northern stakeholders. It could have been a manifesto, too, for John Briscoe, who argued that the Bank needed to deliver infrastructure if it wanted to fight poverty, and that it should not let NGOs dissuade it; or a manifesto for the Bank's big non-IDA borrowers, who argued that the Bank needed to take risks—to abandon Volvo-style perfectionism—if it was going to remain relevant. To be sure, the Chad project was an anomaly that fitted some of these arguments imperfectly. It involved an oil pipeline rather than a dam or water system, and so the effect on poverty was less certain; Chad was a poor IDA borrower, rather than a big middle-income client.[27] But the Bank's withdrawal from dams in places like Brazil or China was so complete that Chad acquired a special status. If you wanted to cite a case where the Bank had taken risks in defiance of the NGO chorus, Chad was your best candidate.

In the years after Chad made it through the board battle, the Bank grew hungry for examples of this kind. The fall in the Bank's market-based lending was becoming alarming, threatening the Bank's financial stability and political independence. At the same time, big middle-income clients were growing more assertive in the wake of the Qinghai experience, and were demanding that the Bank pay more attention to their interests. The push from the middle-income group was backed by rich shareholders that had been reluctant members of the pro-NGO consensus. Japan had long believed that infrastructure was a key part of development, and besides, its ruling party depended upon campaign cash from big construction firms, which stood to win a lot of World Bank contracts. The French favored infrastructure, too, not least because their powerful water companies also stood to profit. All these forces came together, affording proponents of infrastructure within the Bank's bureaucracy a new chance to push their arguments. One of these proponents, needless to say, was none other than John Briscoe.

Briscoe's sense of mission had steadily grown stronger since his trip to Bangladesh. In the two years or so that followed, he had been involved in a body called the World Commission on Dams, which published a set of guidelines on how dam building should be done. Because the commission appeared broad-based and respectable, the recommendations were greeted as a sane compromise by polite commentators.[28] But the truth was that the guidelines were appalling: they demanded so many precautions and perambulations that they amounted to a virtual ban. Some time later, the chief antidam campaigner published an article explaining how he had secured this outcome. Because the World Bank had been anxious to include his group in the commission, he had enjoyed enormous leverage; he had used this to ensure that developing-country governments were kept out of the deliberations. The upshot was that a self-appointed activist from Berkeley had more say than the elected government of India. No wonder that the Berkeley mafia triumphed.[29]

This was the perfect illustration of Briscoe's contention: in an effort to reach out to NGO critics, the Bank had accorded them excessive influence at the expense of real clients. But by late 2000, Briscoe was working on his counterpunch. He was preparing a new version of the Bank's official water strategy. He was traveling the world, visiting the governments that the Berkeley mafia had pointedly excluded, and figuring out what they most wanted from the Bank. The answer was much as he expected. Countries like Brazil or India did not particularly need the Bank's assistance to perform simple tasks like building schools; but when it came to complex infrastructure, they wanted the Bank's input. Indeed, big infrastructure projects seemed almost tailor-made to fit the Bank's comparative advantage. They involved tough judgments across a range of subjects—engineering, finance, social impact, and the environment—which suited the Bank's multidisciplinary nature; they often involved more than one country, which suited the Bank's international makeup; they were the sort of capital-intensive, long-term ventures for which long-term World Bank loans were designed in the first place. Countries like Brazil and India would be delighted to have the Bank as a partner—provided it stopped pressing Volvo-style standards.

By January 2002, Briscoe had completed a first draft of his water strategy. It pointed out that 1.3 billion people lacked access to clean drinking water, and that some of the world's poorest people were farmers whose lives could be transformed by irrigation. The strategy duly called for a renewed push into water infrastructure. Briscoe circulated it to board members, taking care to reach out to developing-country shareholders; he visited the Chinese, the Brazilian, the African, and the Indian directors, and encouraged them to work together. Outside the Bank, the antidam radicals were denouncing him, but Briscoe responded firmly. He had consulted them at the outset, and promised that their views would be considered; but he never promised them the effective veto that they had enjoyed over the World Commission on Dams. To defend his tough line with the activists, Briscoe produced a document analyzing what everybody thought of his water proposals. This showed that governments, the private sector, and academics in developing countries all liked them; and that, rather revealingly, NGOs in developing countries were broadly onboard as well. The two groups that bitterly opposed Briscoe were the international donors and international NGOs.[30] In the first vision of the Bank, these were the groups that Wolfensohn should be responding to. But in the second vision—Briscoe's vision—neither NGOs nor fellow donors had a special entitlement to be heard.

In the first part of 2002, Briscoe waged a lonely battle. There was little enthusiasm for his approach among his superiors, so Briscoe cobbled together a committee of allies, people who had battled to mount big projects in the field and shared his impatience with excessive safeguards. The chair of his group was called Praful Patel, a manager who played an important role in the Chad project; and Patel and Briscoe and their friends brainstormed about the bind the Bank found itself in. More and more, the Bank was fleeing projects that involved high risk, yet some high-risk projects offer high rewards as well. If the balance of risk and reward was attractive, the Bank should go forward. The Laotian economy, for example, could be transformed by a big dam, and Laotians had few other routes out of backbreaking poverty. The brainstorming sessions came up with a way to make risk taking more possible—they proposed a mechanism for taking high-risk, high-reward projects to the Bank's top management early on, so that people lower down would not be left to stick their necks out by themselves—and the mechanism was duly incorporated into Briscoe's water strategy.

Toward the end of 2002, the reformers' fortunes started to look up. Praful Patel's efforts had started to win people over, and the rising star in Wolfensohn's entourage was a deft operator called Shengman Zhang, who had learned the art of bureaucratic infighting in China's Ministry of Finance. Perhaps because he was Chinese, Zhang had a keen sense of what big clients wanted; and he could see the threat to the Bank's own balance sheet from its declining market-based lending. At a management retreat in November 2002, Zhang gave the floor to Jim Adams, the former country director for Uganda who was now a headquarters vice president, and Adams presented a set of slides on the Bank's sorry outlook.[31] Project-based investment lending, as distinct from policy-linked program lending, was declining precipitously. In each of the three previous years it had been lower than in any of the previous twenty. Why was this happening? "Bank requirements that impose costs and delays on borrowers," Adams's slide declared. And why did it matter? Because policy-based lending was hugely volatile; it had run into the billions during the Asian crisis, then suddenly dried up. The Bank needed a steady flow of project loans to stay financially healthy.

Shengman Zhang's influence was formidable: with the departure of Sven Sandstrom, he had become the dominant figure among Wolfensohn's four managing directors. But Zhang's influence was reinforced by the shareholders with whom he was most in tune: the Chinese, most obviously, but also the Brazilians and Indians. Around the same time as Zhang and Jim Adams sounded the alarm on declining investment lending, big middle-income countries were starting to assert themselves in other international forums. In world trade talks, for example, the Indians and Brazilians and South Africans were protesting the absurd intellectual property rules imposed by rich countries, which restricted poor patients' access to AIDS drugs. It was only natural in this climate that middle-income countries should assert themselves within the World Bank.

At the end of 2002, all these forces came together: Shengman Zhang's emergence and Praful Patel's alliance with John Briscoe and the stirring of the Bank's big borrowers. In December, the board met again to consider Briscoe's water strategy, and the day before the meeting, the Nordic director called him. "This strategy is about doing away with safeguards, right?" he asked him.

"That depends," said Briscoe. "If you mean commitment to sensible environmental and social standards, then every borrower and every Bank staff member supports those. But if you mean an inflexible set of standards that nobody can meet, then yes, that is incompatible with what we're doing."[32]

At the board meeting the next day, the Nordic director was the first to take the floor. As in any meeting, the starting speaker sets the tone of the discussion, and Briscoe could feel his year-long effort crashing to defeat. But the Norseman delivered a surprising message. The Bank, he suggested, might consider moving to "materiality." Immaterial breaches of the Bank's safeguards would not trigger persecution; although the safeguards should not be watered down, there was a case for a sense of proportion. This was a sea change coming from a Scandinavian, and it signaled victory for Briscoe. He knew he could count on the support of the big borrowers: the Chinese director had come up to Briscoe and hugged him, declaring that his strategy was about far more than water, it was about changing the Bank's governance. But now the mood among rich countries seemed to be changing. They had received the usual mass e-mails from furious NGOs, but this time they seemed to take that in their stride. Briscoe's analysis earlier in the year had shown how northern NGOs did not speak for people in poor countries. A point that had been true in countless battles before now was finally being recognized.

Briscoe's water strategy was approved unanimously by the Bank's board that day, and more advances followed rapidly. The Chinese and Indian board directors built on the progress in the water sector by demanding that the Bank's staff prepare a reassessment of its standoffish posture toward all infrastructure. When the management presented a cautious response on February 13, 2003, the Chinese and Indian board members went ballistic. Together they issued their first-ever joint statement, denouncing the management's response for merely "tinkering at the margins," pointing out the contrast with the bold water strategy, and noting that between the two of them they spoke for more than 2 billion people, or one in three members of the human race. The Chinese and Indians e-mailed their joint rebuke of the Bank's managers to all staff members who worked on infrastructure. Soon the people in the trenches were replying to the board members, heartily agreeing that their sector needed to respond more energetically to their poor clients.[33]

IN THE SPRING OF 2003, when the Bank's big borrowers were finally making their views heard, Wolfensohn was distracted once again by relations with his rich shareholders. In March, the United States invaded Iraq, throwing the multilateral system into crisis. However much he may have wanted to focus on long-term development, Wolfensohn had no choice but to manage the immediate threat to his own institution.

The transatlantic rift caused by Iraq dwarfed the worst fights between Europe and the United States over the Balkans. At the Bosnia peace talks eight years earlier, Richard Holbrooke's strong-arm diplomacy had infuriated the French and even the British; but the Clintonites had gone out of their way to repair the damage, allowing the Dayton peace deal to be named the Treaty of Paris, and leaving the Bank and the European Union to cochair the fund-raising effort for reconstruction. But the Bush team was less interested in mollifying allies; some parts of the administration, notably the Pentagon and Vice President Dick Cheney, preferred to act alone in order to demonstrate American willpower, on the theory that this would force other countries to accept American objectives. Because of the Pentagon-Cheney preference, the Bush team was of two minds as to whether diplomacy was a good idea. It was divided on whether to seek the blessing of the United Nations Security Council in late 2002; then, after a first UN resolution was secured, it flipped and flopped over whether to seek a second and more explicit authorization for invasion.[34] In the end, it did try for a second resolution, but without success; and although this failure owed much to the unreasonable intransigence of the French, the administration's halfhearted efforts doomed its chances of winning over persuadable members of the Security Council. The contrast to the coalition building before the first Gulf War was stark. In the prelude to the war of 1991, the then secretary of state, James Baker, made forty-one international visits. But in the lead-up to the Gulf War of 2003, Secretary of State Colin Powell did not even visit Moscow, even though Russia's president, Vladimir Putin, could probably have been won over.[35]

Having tried and failed for a second resolution, the administration went to war with the implicit disapproval of the UN Security Council.[36] The resulting tension was bound to spill over into other multilateral institutions, including the World Bank. In the first week of the war, France, Germany, and other critics of the invasion let it be known that they would punish the United States diplomatically; Germany's development minister declared that "those that do the damage carry the main burden for reconstruction"—a statement that did not bode well for American attempts to enlist help from the World Bank and other potential contributors to reconstruction. Moreover, it was not even clear that the Bush administration wanted to enlist the Bank's advice. The task of postwar planning had been assigned to the Pentagon, and the planners sought no input from the Bank, despite its reconstruction experience in Afghanistan as well as in the Balkans. The contrast with the Clinton team's early alliance with Kemal Dervis and Christine Wallich on Bosnia was striking. The Clintonites had proved masterful at marshaling the Bank and the IMF as foreign-policy allies. On Bosnia and during the emerging-market crises, they had mined the Bretton Woods institutions for money, technical advice, and international legitimacy. But the Bank and the IMF do not supply these things spontaneously. They can be useful only to administrations that know how to use them.

By the time of the invasion of Iraq, the Bush administration's clumsy attitude toward international outfits was concentrated largely in the Pentagon. Paul O'Neill, Wolfensohn's old antagonist, had been fired from the Treasury at the end of 2002, not least for his incompetence in marshaling the IMF during currency crises in Brazil and Argentina.

His successor, John Snow, was cannier, and while the Pentagon persisted in planning for reconstruction without tapping into the World Bank's expertise, Snow made a belated push to compensate for this error. As American and British forces advanced into Iraqi territory, both the Treasury Department and the State Department began to round up international contributions for the postwar effort. They put out an appeal for peacekeepers, police officers, engineers, doctors, and nurses. And they let it be known that they expected the World Bank's assistance.

Iraq's capital fell to U.S. troops on April 9, three days before the Bank's spring meetings in Washington. In the run-up to the meetings, Snow announced that the World Bank should conduct an assessment of Iraq's postwar needs, much as it had done in Bosnia, and that it should prepare to lend for reconstruction. This put Wolfensohn in a nasty position. He hated to say no to his biggest shareholder, particularly since he was anxious to establish better relations with Bush's second treasury secretary than he had enjoyed with the previous one, and also because he wanted to hold open the possibility of a third term as World Bank president—a possibility that he floated in a *Washington Post* interview two months later. Yet there was no way Wolfensohn could send the World Bank into Iraq on the back of American tanks. He had to respect the feelings of his other board members.[37] Besides, big loans to Iraq might damage the Bank's finances. If the Bank lent soft IDA money, it would do so at the expense of other IDA borrowers. If it lent market-based money, it had to worry about Iraq's ability to repay. The Iraqis were already mired in debt, and they would need substantial relief before they could qualify as creditworthy.

As U.S. troops struggled to control looters in Baghdad, the Bank was in a quandary. If the Bush administration pressed its demand for help in Iraq, the Bank's board would be split; Wolfensohn would be forced to take sides; and he would alienate one of them. The Americans and British, who wanted the Bank's help, resented the fact that the

Bank's Middle East specialists leaned toward the Franco-German view that the invasion had been ill advised, and Wolfensohn himself did not always disguise his own reservations. When Wolfensohn declared that the Bank could not lend to Iraq until the country had a legitimate government, and that that would require a UN Security Council resolution, John Snow pronounced himself "baffled" at Wolfensohn's response— which was Washingtonspeak for "furious." "We are prepared to go in if we have an authorizing environment from our board," Wolfensohn told a press conference on April 10. "I hope he rethinks that," Snow retorted tartly.[38]

Luckily for the World Bank, Snow was better than O'Neill at knowing where to compromise. On the eve of the spring meetings, the Bank and its shareholders worked out a deal. The Americans accepted that the Bank could not lend to Iraq without a government that had been formally blessed by a UN resolution. But the Bank agreed that in the meantime it could begin to assess Iraq's reconstruction needs.[39] The understanding kept the fight over the legitimacy of the Iraq invasion squarely at the United Nations, sparing the Bank from a divisive row. Bank officials soon visited Iraq to begin work on the needs assessment.

Through the summer and early fall of 2003, Wolfensohn struggled to keep the tensions among his shareholders from flaring up again. He visited Baghdad at the end of July, flying in on a jet lent to him by Jordan's king; he visited the Bank's offices in the Canal Hotel, wanting to show solidarity with World Bankers working in harm's way; and he met Paul Bremer, the American proconsul, and Iraq's provisional governing council. At a press conference afterward Wolfensohn was asked when the Bank would begin lending to Iraq, and he repeated the understanding that there must be a recognized government to lend to. On his return he reaped a whirlwind. The *Wall Street Journal* editorial page, which was reliably hostile to the Bretton Woods sisters, accused him of gratuitous foot-dragging, and suggested he remove the Bank from Washington to a

capital that fitted his worldview, like Paris.[40] On the day of that broad-
side, Wolfensohn got a call from John Taylor, the international point
man at the Bush Treasury. Taylor demanded that the Bank pledge billions in loans to support Iraq's budget, undoing the deal reached at the
spring meetings four months earlier; when Wolfensohn demurred, Taylor grew angry. Pressure from Congress to raise money for reconstruction from sources other than the U.S. taxpayer was driving the Treasury
to change its position, and Wolfensohn suspected that Taylor had con-
spired with the *Journal* to soften his defenses.[41]

This time Wolfensohn was saved not by John Snow's tact but by
Iraqi tragedy. Two weeks after Taylor's call, a gleaming new cement
mixer drove up to the Canal Hotel, which housed the UN operation as
well as the World Bank's; it was packed full of explosives. The ensuing
blast destroyed the three-story building and killed seventeen people,
including the UN chief Sergio Vieira de Mello, my Council on Foreign
Relations colleague Arthur Helton, and a member of the World Bank
delegation.[42] The Bank, like the United Nations, withdrew its staff after
the attack, and the escalation of bombings over the next weeks deterred
both organizations from returning. The U.S. Treasury carried on pressing the Bank to pledge money even so, but it ultimately settled for a
commitment that was partly symbolic. In order to persuade Congress to
come up with reconstruction funds, the Bush team wanted the Bank to
announce an impressive-sounding headline number for its Iraq lending.
But it was content to let the lending be mainly in the far future, meaning that nobody could know whether it would ever happen.

In the end, the Bush administration also got the Bosnia-type needs
assessment that it wanted. The Bank's staff put a document together,
even though the work was conducted mostly from outside Iraq, and the
assessment was used to drum up pledges of financial aid at a donor conference in October. But the World Bank's potential as an arm of Western policy had not been fully realized: whereas it had funneled money
into Bosnia within three months of the Dayton accords, and had done

its early work there while the Serb part of Sarajevo was going up in flames, World Bank money had yet to reach Iraq a year after the fall of Baghdad. Development banks were to the new world order what security organizations were to the old, Lawrence Summers had remarked in the wake of the Bank's early work in Bosnia. But the Bush administration, even after the departure of Paul O'Neill, did not see things that way. It had gone into Iraq without many of America's traditional allies, and it had paid the price. Hobbled by the divisions on its board, the Bank has been slow to assist the reconstruction.

Meanwhile, inside the Bank, a new consensus was gelling. As he dodged the bullets from his major shareholders, Wolfensohn did not lose sight of the pressure from his borrowers. On April 22, 2003, in the wake of the Bank's spring meetings, he sent out an e-mail to all staff, finally addressing his need for a strong deputy by putting Shengman Zhang in charge of all the Bank's lending operations. The same e-mail confessed to a "need to sharpen our focus. . . . Infrastructure is a major example," and it announced the creation of a new vice presidency dedicated solely to infrastructure. In July, this department responded to the Indian and Chinese pressure by presenting the board with a brand-new Infrastructure Action Plan. Wolfensohn expanded the budget to support the development of infrastructure projects by $8 million, and Praful Patel, the champion of the high-risk, high-reward approach, was promoted to vice president for South Asia.

At the annual meetings in the fall of 2003, the Bank's governing Development Committee endorsed this march back to the Bank's origins in the 1950s, when the bread and butter of its business was roads and dams and other things involving tons of concrete. In many corners of the Bank, the call for "high-risk, high-reward projects" became the new mantra. The Bank must reengage with infrastructure, the mantra maintained; it must not allow itself to be deterred by NGO critics. And whenever that mantra was heard, you could bet that one model project would be cited in support. The model, of course, was Chad's oil pipeline.

. . .

IN OCTOBER 2003, soon after the Bank's annual meetings, I took a trip to Chad. My Air France jet touched down late on a Monday evening. There was just one other plane in the airport, and I walked across the tarmac into a scruffy low-slung building. Up in front there stood a wide table inviting Exxon staff to show their passports, but for everybody else the route to the passport officers lay through a crazy scrum of passengers, all heaving and shoving and mixing with the gray shadows cast by a low-watt neon light. I squeezed my way in, and a small man in a white robe confronted me.

"Your health form?" he demanded.

"What health form?"

"Give me that," he answered, grabbing my passport. "You pay two thousand."

I experimented with charm, aggression, and all the usual tricks of hapless travelers confronted with bald cons. It occurred to me that this might be a sign of the Bank's prospects in the country, and I protested loudly that Chad's representatives in Washington had said nothing about health forms. Then a U.S. embassy official happened to come by. We made eye contact, just long enough for my adversary to worry that I knew somebody important, and I snatched back my passport and bolted.

I had lived as a foreign correspondent in Zimbabwe and had traveled around Africa: I'd bribed my way onto planes in Nigeria and visited Mozambique's war-encircled capital and been deported from Sudan. But Chad still managed to shock me: the fact that big provincial towns had no electricity, that I could scour a commercial street for fruit stalls and find that no fruit was available, that I could see the road through a gaping hole in the floor of one of N'djamena's cabs. The sheer remoteness of the country was impressive. I spent part of the trip with journalists who had come in from Nairobi and Johannesburg. To get from Africa to Africa, they had been obliged to fly through France.

Three years had passed since the Bank's board had approved the oil project, and the pipeline was already done. There were modest signs of progress in the capital, albeit the sort that mainly affect visitors. An international hotel had recently been renovated, more foreigners were passing through, and there was a boom in the security-guard business. Strange electronic tunes chimed from the pockets of eminent people, signaling that cell phones were starting to make up for the near absence of fixed telephone lines; the cars in N'djamena may have been rickety, but at least there were cars, and Exxon's boss in Chad was proud to report that he had even spotted traffic jams. But none of this was going to be much help to ordinary Chadians. At the height of the construction, the pipeline had generated jobs for fewer than five thousand locals; now that the construction was completed, most of the new employment was gone. So it is with oil projects—big revenues, few jobs.

If the signs of progress were tentative, what of the project's downside? Throughout the pipeline's construction, the NGOs had maintained their critical chorus, but most of their objections looked empty. Exxon's new molasses-capped road, they said, was insufferably dusty. Actually, it was less dusty than a government road I also traveled on. Exxon was burning gas flares, creating air pollution. Well, there was one flare, and it was temporary, and Chadians seemed proud of it. The flare was a symbol of their new status as an oil state, and it was displayed prominently in the propaganda posters produced to celebrate the pipeline's completion. The pipeline construction, said the NGOs, had disturbed the people of the Cameroonian rain forest. But according to a Cameroon-based BBC journalist I talked to, the forest dwellers were pleased with the construction because it had brought new roads and bridges. Indeed, the one big disturbance had occurred when Exxon explained that, to comply with its environmental promises, it would dismantle some bridges once construction finished. The villagers threatened violent resistance. Like most people everywhere, they like access to transport.

Like the northern NGOs, the northern press coverage had tended to be critical. It was easy to see why. I made the rounds of various government officials and ministers, and they were mostly off-putting; the prize went to the prime minister, who convened a press conference at his residence and batted away questions arrogantly while a panoply of flunkies looked on obsequiously. In contrast, the Chadian nongovernmental groups were impressive and open, and they tended to oppose the pipeline. They were mostly southerners, and they disliked the idea of oil revenues in the hands of a northerner. Visiting the oil field, the negative press coverage grew even easier to understand. Exxon's pristine portacabins and oil derricks, deposited as if by magic carpet, cast the grim poverty just beyond the fortified perimeter in sharp relief.

One afternoon I went to Kome Atan, a village that had sprung up just outside the oil base. It was a standard stop for journalists looking for a graphic contrast: on one side of the high wire fence, a strange slice of Texas; on the other side, Africa. Kome Atan felt like a wild boomtown. Some people were drunk; some were aggressive; and my colleague Amelia Branczik got talking to some made-up women who probably were prostitutes. And yet you had to ask yourself: Had oil made people's lives here worse, as the NGOs and press coverage often insisted? Kome Atan looked more affluent than other villages in the region. People were dressed better, and the stalls sold a wider choice of products, and the tailor at the Atelier Couture Non-Violence was doing a brisk trade.

I chatted with a tall man lounging on a chair in the tailor's thatched cottage.

Did he resent the wealth behind the tall perimeter?

No, he responded. His people had been poor anyway before the oilmen came.

Did Exxon cause his community problems?

No again, came back the answer. The company had provided the village with water wells, and it was nice that the security floodlights allowed villagers to see their way around at night.

Above my companion's head, the thatched roof of the tailor's workshop had been lined with thick plastic discarded from the oil base. Disused Exxon packing cases had provided the tailor with the raw materials to make his furniture. Why did the workshop's name refer to non-violence? Well, the tailor said, looking up from behind his sewing machine, customers could be impatient sometimes, what with all the orders coming in these days. He didn't want fights breaking out when they discovered that there'd be a wait for their new clothes.

That evening I rejoined the press group I was traveling with and had dinner with some local NGOs.[43] The NGOs rolled out a string of grievances. They complained that the compensation price for mango trees had taken lengthy wrangling, even though a deal had eventually been agreed on before the trees had been cut down; they worried that villagers had wasted their compensation money, even though Exxon had offered in-kind compensation to those who wanted it. But questions of compensation or environmental damage were not their main message. Their chief concern was that oil money would flow into the hands of a northern government that had long mistreated southerners. Did the foreign journalists really suppose that northerners would help the people of the oil region?

This was indeed a reasonable question. I had a long conversation with Mahamat Mustapha, the head of the new institution for overseeing oil revenues that had been set up with the World Bank's help. He was certainly impressive: he had studied in France and the United States, and had worked at the IMF in Washington before returning home to Chad. He was clever and forthright and insisted that the president would back him. It was in Chad's interests to see that the oil money was spent right, and the president himself had said as much; besides, the whole international community was watching. The World Bank was in touch with Mustapha all the time, giving him whatever help he requested; he had seen Shengman Zhang in Washington not long ago, and Zhang had even come all the way to Chad to express his support for his revenue-monitoring mission. With that kind of backing, surely his new institution stood a good chance of succeeding? But then again, who knew really? The World Bank had embarked on a grand experiment in central Africa, a test case for its high-risk, high-reward mantra, and an attempt to operate in a new way, building institutions rather than proclaiming conditions that were ignored too easily. And yet the outcome of this experiment would not be determined by the Bank, or anyone it had control over. It would depend on the political culture of this slice of central Africa, and particularly on a tall, slim warrior called Idriss Deby.

On October 10, 2003, the warrior appeared at a ceremony to celebrate the completion of the pipeline. It was held inside Exxon's oil base, in a huge hangar equipped with powerful amplifiers and a big overhead screen. Some six hundred people sat on plastic chairs, a sea of military hats and Muslim skullcaps and brightly colored headscarves. The heads of Africa's oil states had been invited along, and a Ghanaian journalist summed up each of them: "Former soldier, instigator of civil war, killer, dictator." A warm-up speaker declared that Deby "provides rays of sun to light the way ahead for all the sons of Chad," and executives from Exxon and its consortium partners followed on in similar fashion; President Deby had "graciously consented to honor us with his presence here," according to the bootlicker from the Malaysian firm, Petronas. The heat in the hangar was throbbing, and the guests in the audience were sweating and fanning themselves, and after an uncomfortably long time the gracious Idriss Deby took his turn at the podium. He spoke pompously and emptily, and then he led his fellow statesmen outside, where a marching band struck up a tune and Deby accepted a ceremonial spanner. With some fumbling, the spanner was applied to a ceremonial valve on a ceremonial glass section of the pipeline; the president applied a presidential twist, and oil gushed into the glass pipe. The audience watching on a video hookup inside the hangar applauded dutifully.

Was this a triumph, or was this a disaster? The World Bank officials looking on honestly weren't sure.[44] They had shepherded the pipeline to its completion point, and defied the NGO predictions about its terrible social and environmental consequences. They had weighed the dangers that the oil money would be misspent. They had admitted openly that it might be, and they had rightly decided that if the Bank always shunned risks of this kind there would be no point in having it. Yet it was not enough in this game to be three-quarters successful. If the oil revenues were stolen and Chad's poverty persisted, the safe installation of a high-risk pipeline would count for nothing. And if the project went wrong, the world was sure to know about it. The critics were always out there, watching and waiting for the time when they could assail the Bank all over again.

Now it was time for lunch, though. The World Bankers followed their fellow guests out of the hangar and into the pounding heat of Africa. Then they boarded a yellow school bus that Exxon had trucked in for their convenience, all the way from Texas.

CHAPTER FOURTEEN

A LION AT CARNEGIE

ON DECEMBER 1, 2003, at six-thirty in the evening, vehicles on West Fifty-seventh Street in Manhattan faced more obstacles than usual. Outside the grand edifice of Carnegie Hall, the police had put up barriers that cut off one lane of the road; cabs and limousines were stopping in the middle of the traffic flow to disgorge distinguished passengers. The passengers proceeded in their tuxedos and furs up the steps of the Carnegie entrance, past paramilitary policemen holding stubby automatic guns, past the footmen in red livery who awaited them inside, and into a room filled with conversation and champagne and a busybody photographer. There, in that reception room, stood figures from Jim Wolfensohn's full life: Paul Volcker and Alan Greenspan, who between them had run the Fed for the past twenty-four years; Barbara Walters and Peter Jennings; Queen Beatrix of Holland and Queen Noor of Jordan. There, too, was Vernon Jordan, the old friend of Bill Clinton who had helped Wolfensohn get the World Bank job. Sandy Berger and Strobe Talbott, Clinton's national security adviser and deputy secretary of state, were exchanging views about Taiwan; Joe Stiglitz the Nobel laureate was holding court; Al Gore smiled a politician's smile; then Talbott was introduced to a small man with large guards, who turned out to be the president of the Kirgiz Republic.

Half an hour later, the guests filed out of the reception room and into the Isaac Stern concert hall. There was a murmuring and a whispering as the programs were opened: What would Wolfensohn play? How long would he go on for? The first piece was a Mozart quartet, and if you looked carefully at the lineup you noticed something strange: three pianists, all famous, would take turns at the piano, so that Wolfensohn would get a chance to play with all of them. The guests waited and whispered. One lady was asking how a World Bank president had time to practice the cello, and a man next to her was wondering how late dinner would be served, and up and down the auditorium there was a mute conspiracy of understanding. This extraordinary birthday party was at once so human and so monstrous. After seventy years of life and seven hundred achievements, Jim Wolfensohn still wanted to get up on the stage, to show off to five hundred friends, to lay himself open. There was something adorably brave in this, and something preposterously vain at the same time. *You gotta love Jim Wolfensohn*, the guests seemed to be laughing. *So absurdly exhibitionist. So humanly in need of adulation.*

Wolfensohn walked onto the stage and sat down with his cello. His unruly mane of hair had been tamed for the evening, and the creases on his heavy face were thrown into relief by the stage lights; he looked his full seventy years, but splendidly. When the first movement was finished, he smiled for the first time and wiped his bow hand on a handkerchief. The first pianist was replaced by a second one, and the quartet began to play again; and after three-quarters of an hour, the Mozart was finished and Wolfensohn stood up with a microphone.

"We'd like to welcome you to this rather exotic and egocentric birthday party," he declared, and you could almost feel the current of relief running through the audience. The slight squirming sensation—the queasy feeling that this whole evening was an egomaniac's folly—seemed to evaporate at Wolfensohn's remark, leaving only admiration and affection. So what if Jim Wolfensohn was egocentric? He admitted it quite openly! It was as though the guests had been given permission to acknowledge their friend's vanity and enjoy the evening anyway. And so they settled into their seats and drank in the music: the performances by Yo-Yo Ma, Pinchas Zukerman, and a special Peace Orchestra with members from ten countries. It was glittering and soothing all at the same time. *You gotta love Jim Wolfensohn!*

When the music was over, the stage was arranged with dinner tables, and the guests took their places. There was some eating and some schmoozing, and a soprano sang "Happy Birthday," and there were mini-cakes garnished with chocolate cellos, and Wolfensohn's son, Adam, called upon the most distinguished friends of Jim to say a few words. Vernon Jordan spoke, and Senator Edward Kennedy spoke, and UN Secretary General Kofi Annan spoke, and New York's mayor, Michael Bloomberg, spoke, and so did Queen Beatrix. But the best speech of the evening came from Wolfensohn's daughter Sara.

Not many people, Sara said, have a father who calls up and announces he's just met three presidents, two chiefs of staff, and a finance minister; and then sounds annoyingly surprised that you are not doing much yourself because it's eight-thirty in the morning. But then not many people have a father who calls in a wave of excitement to announce the selling of his firm, calling it a glorious chance to expand the family's philanthropy. Wolfensohn, said his daughter, never forgets where he comes from. The memory of little Jimmy, growing up in a modest apartment in Australia, has stayed with him always; and despite seventy years and seven hundred achievements, he remains surprised by what he has and is instinctively charitable.

PEOPLE ASK BIOGRAPHERS whether they like their subject, and my answer is two-sided. A friend who read parts of my manuscript said he couldn't figure out which character was dominant: the noble Wolfensohn or the manic one? Ben Kingsley or Danny DeVito? Well, Wolfensohn is both, as his daughter suggested; yet there is something delightful in a person who is so transparently honest about wanting to know everyone, outshine everyone, and be the best at everything, who is constantly reaching higher and frequently falling, only to leap up again. It is as though Jim Wolfensohn were born with a triple dose of all the contradictory energies that animate our lopsided progress: avarice and generosity, egocentricity and compassion, curiosity and insecurity, and most of all a roaring restless hunger to do all the things that man can do, and to succeed at all of them.

Is James Wolfensohn a good World Bank president? That is the more important and difficult question. He came to office with three connected goals: to sharpen the Bank's management, to escape from the dead end represented by structural adjustment, and to rebuild the Bank's relations with three key stakeholders—shareholders, NGOs, and borrowers. To judge Wolfensohn's presidency, one has to judge him against each of those goals in turn, and then to ask whether those goals were the right ones.

The managerial goal is the one that Wolfensohn scores worst on— not so much because of the ultimate result, but because of the costs of getting there. The Bank when he arrived was in need of a shake-up, but its troubles did not justify the hand-grenade treatment he administered. Wolfensohn formed an exaggerated view of the challenge partly because the demon inside him was blind to the accomplishments of those who came before, and partly because in the mid-to-late 1990s all public-sector institutions suffered from comparison with supposed private-sector excellence. To an extent that is clear perhaps only in hindsight, the stock market bubble of the times created a reputational bubble for corporate America as well, and Wolfensohn fell prey to it. He was right to look to the private sector for management ideas, but wrong to suppose that he could ever match the inflated managerial reputations of hot private-sector CEOs, many of whom were turfed out in disgrace when the bubble burst a few years later.

The truth is that the Bank will never match the managerial prowess of private firms, even postbubble deflated ones. The World Bank's management is not at liberty to fire people; it has to put up with a resident board that breathes down its neck at biweekly meetings; it has a complex set of stakeholders, ranging from shareholders to borrowers to advocacy NGOs, who muddle the Bank with contradictory objectives. To an extent that Wolfensohn did not appreciate at first, even hand-grenade reformism is not enough to blow away these shortcomings. They are imprinted on the Bank's DNA, and nothing can erase them. Consider, for example, the Bank's clannish nature, which Wolfensohn sought to change by imposing meritocratic personnel practices imported from the private sector. If you are a Pakistani or Nigerian water specialist with twenty years' experience at the Bank, losing your job means losing both your income and your U.S. visa, and uprooting your baseball-playing kids from the culture they grew up in. The DNA of the Bank is therefore fixed: people are desperate to protect their jobs, and clan structures that afford some measure of security will spring up almost inevitably.[1] Wolfensohn's meritocratic personnel system may have weakened the clans a bit, but it could not blow them clean away. A survey of the Bank in 2003 found that only 51 percent of the staff believed that promotions were made on an objective basis.[2]

Given the limits to what the management shake-up could achieve, Wolfensohn was wrong to burn up so much time and energy on it. He came to the Bank never having run a large outfit, and he was in awe of those who had; he convened buddy groups of CEOs to tell him what to do, and like many novices he tried too hard, forfeiting goodwill in the process. Wolfensohn's battle over the Strategic Compact—his bid for a temporary budget expansion of a quarter of a billion dollars—alienated the Bank's board for several years; the subsequent implementation of the compact caused a near revolution among staff, which bubbled up at the start of 2001, just as the Bush administration arrived in office. This friction would have been easier to justify if Wolfensohn's management reforms had been lifting the Bank to a whole new level. But, despite Wolfensohn's inspirational speeches, the expectation of a quantum leap was naïve in retrospect.

This is not to say that the management reforms achieved nothing. The two clear benefits were the decentralization of country directors and their staff and the related upgrading of the Bank's technology. It would have been harder to push decision makers out into the field if they had not been newly linked to the head office via computers and video-conferencing facilities. As of 2003, 71 percent of country directors were based outside Washington, up from nothing eight years earlier; for reasons to which I will return, this is an important development. Moreover, by 2003 Wolfensohn's early grenade throwing was long past, as was the extravagance of the Strategic Compact. The Bank's budget had fallen to a level lower than it had been at the time of Wolfensohn's arrival, in inflation-adjusted terms;[3] and two-thirds of the staff felt good about their jobs, up from a mere two-fifths in the early hand-grenade era.[4] With the belated appointment of a single deputy, Wolfensohn had found his footing in the end. His failure lay in the disruption that he caused along the way, not all of which was necessary.

WHAT OF WOLFENSOHN'S ATTEMPT to break away from structural adjustment? From his first months on the job, when he absorbed the criticisms of the Fifty Years Is Enough campaign and made his early trip to Africa, Wolfensohn understood this challenge right: the macro-economic prescriptions of structural adjustment were correct; but they were also too narrow, and they were politically toxic. The way forward lay in ramping up the rhetorical focus on poverty, in broadening the Bank's agenda beyond macroeconomic policy to challenges such as corruption, and in retreating from some especially unpopular stances,

such as the refusal to countenance debt relief. All these changes improved the Bank's image, a pressing task in the wake of the Madrid
annual meetings. But they were correct substantively, too. Wolfensohn
was right to see that the macroeconomic prescriptions of structural adjustment were not enough to deliver growth; he was right to put corruption on the Bank's agenda; and he was right to tackle debt relief. By
the mid-1990s, the refusal to countenance debt relief had locked the
Bank into defensive lending of the sort Wolfensohn confronted in Côte
d'Ivoire, and debt payments to the Bank constituted an impossible drag
on countries like Uganda.

On corruption and debt relief especially, Wolfensohn's instincts were
ahead of his peers'. Since the early 1990s, the Bank had produced
research papers on "governance," but it had never confronted corruption
in a direct, high-profile way; indeed, the Bank's chief counsel insisted
fiercely that denouncing corruption would violate the Bank's apolitical
charter. Since the early 1990s, equally, the Bank had been coming under
pressure to relieve debt. But before Wolfensohn's arrival, the Bank's
staff was wedded to the traditional argument that multilateral debt relief was wrong; moreover, the Bank's shareholders and the International
Monetary Fund opposed debt relief firmly. On both corruption and
debt relief, Wolfensohn took on fights that his predecessor had ducked.
The result was that the Bank reformed its policies faster than it would
have done without him.

Thanks to Wolfensohn's early leadership, therefore, the Bank largely
succeeded in moving beyond structural adjustment by stressing poverty,
embracing debt relief, and speaking out against corruption. The question, however, is what to make of Wolfensohn's second phase: the
period from 1999 when he and the wider development community went
beyond a tweaking of structural adjustment and offered a replacement.
The new vision of development did not repudiate the orthodox economics of the old approach. But it did replace donor conditionality with
the idea of "country ownership"; and it called upon aid recipients to

draw up comprehensive development programs ranging far beyond the macroeconomic framework, and to do so through a participatory process involving NGOs as well as government. In Wolfensohn's mind, the new vision was the one laid out in the Comprehensive Development Framework; in the mind of the Bank's staff and shareholders, it was encapsulated in the Poverty Reduction Strategy Papers that were required of poor countries from the time of the 1999 annual meetings. Both replacements were essentially the same: in this case Wolfensohn was not championing anything that the Bank would not have done without him.

Was the new approach a good idea? Perhaps its most criticized aspect is the call for comprehensiveness. Even if development is multifaceted, it's impossible to fight on all fronts at once, or so the critics charge; remember the lesson from Mao Tse Tung, as retold by Uganda's president, Museveni.[5] The attack on comprehensiveness achieved great currency in 2001, when the multiplication of mandates was listed among the causes of the Bank's management malaise, and when "mission creep" was attacked in Jessica Einhorn's *Foreign Affairs* article. But the problem with the argument for selectivity is that, at least when you're talking in grand global terms, nobody knows what to select. There is no robust body of economic research showing that particular development interventions—dam building or malaria fighting or civil-service reform—consistently relieve more poverty than other ones. It is hard enough to measure poverty, and economists vary widely on its extent.[6] It is even harder, and probably impossible, to measure the relative impact of dozens of interrelated strategies to relieve poverty across scores of countries.

The impossibility of showing which interventions trump the rest is easily forgotten, because development advocates generate a steady stream of claims to the contrary: The key to kick-starting development is said to lie in microfinance, or population control, or greater rights for women, or various other worthwhile challenges. Perhaps the most impressive recent claim of this genre comes from Hernando de Soto, a Peruvian economist, who points out that the poor often lack legal title to their land. Change that, de Soto says, and you give them collateral, and therefore a chance to borrow money and start small businesses.[7] But although de Soto's insight is important, land tenure is not a silver bullet. If the poor gain land title but women remain downtrodden, for example, half of all adults will not actually gain access to capital, and population pressure will not abate either.

There are similar problems with another kind of selectivity proposal. In a *Foreign Affairs* article published in 1997, Steven Radelet and Jeffrey Sachs of the Harvard Institute for International Development agreed that a lot of things have to go right simultaneously for development to take off; but they suggested it might be a mistake to try to achieve this on a national level. Rather than address that impossibly vast challenge, Radelet and Sachs argued, it would be better to follow Asia's strategy of creating enclaves of efficiency. Most of the East Asian Tigers created export-processing zones in which corruption and red tape were eliminated, security was reliable, and electricity and transport links were excellent. These enclaves attracted investment, and prosperity radiated gradually outward. China, for example, set up several special economic zones along its coastline, starting in 1980. Within a few years, one of the world's greatest export booms created millions of new jobs, despite the fact that China's national institutions were frequently rotten with corruption.[8] Yet the enclave argument, for all its persuasiveness, raises its own set of questions. What good are export zones if corrupt national institutions lay you open to financial meltdown? And if national institutions are corrupt, won't national politicians be tempted to extract bribes from supposedly uncorrupt enclaves? Rather like Hernando de Soto's land tenure idea, enclaves might start you down the road toward development. But in the end you can't duck the question of national governance, however daunting it might be.

Because neither the kick-start theories nor the enclave arguments are fully convincing, Wolfensohn was right that the Bank should be comprehensive. He was wrong in other ways, however. He introduced his development framework clumsily, claiming too much originality and alienating the Bank's board. He insisted that a comprehensive vision of development had to include some subjects that in truth were marginal, such as cultural heritage, and some subjects that were bitterly divisive on the board, such as religion. Most important, however, Wolfensohn's grand global development strategy tinted his perception of humbler national plans, blinding him to the fact that *at the national level* selectivity is crucial. Even if you can't get all the way to prosperity without a comprehensive approach, and even if you can't generalize globally about which type of development effort works best, countries have to make choices. Particularly in poor places where trained administrators are scarce, comprehensiveness can be disastrous.

Wolfensohn will not concede this. In one of our discussions, he assured me that successful developing countries do everything at once, and challenged me to name one intervention—education? health? electricity? roads?—that I would be happy to call unimportant.[9] But if you're thinking about a country, rather than the whole world, you *can* choose priorities. If literacy is already widespread and most people have electricity, you let the schools and the power sector coast along while you try to fix the roads; if AIDS is destroying the country, you drop other distractions and focus on containing it. The point here is that development investments, like most investments, have diminishing marginal returns: if you build a new power plant in a country that is so starved of electricity that even vital factories can't get what they need, then you'll get a huge payoff; if you build the same power plant in a country where emergency needs are already covered, the payoff will be less impressive. The right development strategy depends on what a country has already.

Because of this law of diminishing returns, it makes eminent sense for *countries* to ask themselves what their development priorities are, even if global generalizations on this subject are nonsense. Yet poor countries with scarce manpower constantly fail to absorb this point: they do not set priorities. Instead, they launch into banking reform or some other difficult venture because a donor has offered to fund it, and the result is that they dissipate the energy that should have been directed at a first-order challenge. Moreover, World Bank project teams sometimes encourage this error. After five years as the Bank's head of economic research, spanning 1997 to 2002, Paul Collier of Oxford singled out this failure to prioritize in weak countries as one the Bank's chief problems.[10]

The irony is that the Bank is perfectly suited to helping poor countries set priorities. As a friendly multidisciplinary brain trust, it understands most of the development options that confront national planners; its chief role should be to advise on which will be most fruitful. Up to a point, this is what the Bank's country directors already do, and moving them out into the field has encouraged them to see the trade-offs that face borrowers. But the country directors remain less effective than they ought to be, because they are locked in a struggle with the Bank's technical specialists—the education people, the environmental people, and so on. The managers of each specialist unit want to foist their own particular type of project on as many countries as possible; in the view of many country directors, they are little more than trade-union leaders, bent on ensuring a steady flow of work for their departments. One of the jobs of a World Bank president is to restrain the technical departments from pressing this supply-driven lending. But because he believes in comprehensiveness, Wolfensohn has played this role reluctantly. He has boosted the technical departments' budgets in some cases, increasing their ability to push projects on clients. He has subscribed to the Millennium Development Goal outlook, which imagines that all countries should aspire to meet all seven millennium targets—and never mind about their priorities.

In sum, the comprehensive development vision was right for the Bank as a whole, and right as a grand theory of human progress. After more than a decade of macroeconomic adjustment, it was time to broaden the development agenda. But the comprehensive vision was wrong at the level of individual countries, where greater selectivity is necessary.

WHAT OF THE OTHER ASPECTS of the post-structural-adjustment formula? Its best feature is the shift away from old-style conditionality and toward "country ownership." The experience with structural adjustment taught that conditions simply don't work: Remember Pakistan, which signed twenty-two loan agreements between 1970 and 1997 promising to cut its budget deficit, then failed to do any cutting at all throughout the entire period. The better approach, which the Bank rightly adopted under Wolfensohn, is to ask borrowers to select their own development targets and say when they'll reach them. If a country's targets look sensible if they reflect important development priorities, as tested against the law of diminishing returns—then the Bank should back them with a loan, reviewing the country's progress against its own benchmarks at regular intervals. By shifting from Bank-imposed conditions to country-adopted targets, the Bank has a better chance that its money will be soundly used, and that poor people will benefit.

Another part of the Bank's post-structural-adjustment formula was the shift toward participatory planning of the sort pioneered in Uganda. This innovation turned out less well than the shift away from conditions. From the time of his first trip to Africa, Wolfensohn grasped how the development dialogue needed to be broadened. Part of the reason why structural-adjustment programs were seldom implemented was that they lacked popular legitimacy. Uganda-style participatory planning is one way of building legitimacy for a national development strategy, just as consulting farmers on rural projects boosts the chances of the projects' working. But participation is no magic elixir. When it first became fashionable, consultations and discussions were seen as a chance for the Bank and governments and NGOs to bury their old arguments. But the truth is that consensus often remains as elusive as ever. In Bolivia, Jorge Quiroga's participatory efforts did not save his country from violent political unrest in the years that followed.

The elusive nature of consensus has been equally visible in Washington. By 2002, John Briscoe was telling NGOs bluntly that, although they might have participated in forging the Bank's new water strategy, their views would not necessarily prevail. NGOs, for their part, were denouncing the Bank for inviting discussion but then ignoring their opinions. A new version of this argument bubbled up again at the start of 2004. The Bank had commissioned a review of the extractive industries, and the NGO participants had dominated the proceedings. The review recommended that the Bank withdraw from all oil projects. Not surprisingly, the Bank rejected this advice—if rich countries consume oil, why shouldn't poor ones aspire to produce it?—triggering a furious outcry from NGOs. The Third Way hope was that by consulting everybody, hearing everybody, the Bank could escape the discord of the past. But this hope, like the hope of a quantum leap in managerial prowess, looks naïve in retrospect.

The truth is that participation can be constructive, but you can't expect it to work consistently. Wolfensohn was right to foster discussion with NGOs, but the Bank should have been more selective in its choice of interlocutors—discussions with the screamers from the Berkeley mafia will not get you anywhere. Equally, participatory development planning may work well in Uganda. But it may be unnecessary or unworkable elsewhere. Brazil, for example, is justifiably proud of its electoral process. Its government has a democratic mandate, so why should it convene forums of unelected NGOs to hash out its national policies? On the other hand, the idea of participation in authoritarian Zimbabwe is a nonstarter—and it's not just participation that won't work there. The idea of country ownership makes no sense either: Imagine the folly of writing condition-free blank checks to the odious President Robert Mugabe.

In some countries, in other words, the Bank's new post-structural-adjustment outlook holds out little hope. In the past, the old faith in conditions allowed you to believe that undemocratic, corrupt countries could be reformed: bribe them with a massive loan, and they will put their house in order. But if conditions don't work, you have to accept that such countries perhaps can't be helped: aid is better spent on countries that will use it wisely. The implication is that the Bank needs to give aid more selectively.

Has the Bank absorbed that lesson? Without much fanfare, it has. In the first half of the 1990s, there was no relationship between the quality of a country's institutions—measured by rule of law, democratic accountability, and so on—and the amount of IDA lending it received. But from 1995 on, countries with better governance got significantly more soft loans, whereas those without the capacity to "own" their development got significantly less money.[11] Even apparent counter-examples suggest that the Bank has learned its lesson. The Bank's loans to Chad for its oil pipeline, for example, went ahead despite Chad's poor development record. But rather than imposing conditions and praying that they would be met, the Bank helped to create a new Chadian institution to oversee the oil revenues. Equally, Scott Guggenheim's Kecamatan Development Project in Indonesia was part of this pattern. Indonesia had proved too corrupt to merit traditional lending, and there was no way that Bank conditions could change that. So Guggenheim built new institutions in the countryside that could absorb aid usefully.

. . .

THE GOOD PARTS of Wolfensohn's managerial and development reforms fit together logically. His chief managerial achievement—the decentralization of country directors—is important because it supports the chief contribution to the development agenda during his tenure— the idea of "country ownership." Thanks to decentralization, the Bank is spending less time at head office and more time listening to the real owners of development. Rather than handing down inflexible conditions from Washington, the new, decentralized Bank aims to be out there with its borrowers, figuring out how it can help. This is a humbler, less hectoring vision of the Bank: a Bank, in the end, like Linda McGinnis, the feisty country rep in Mali.

Which brings us to the third goal that Wolfensohn set himself: to shore up the Bank's relations with shareholders, NGOs, and borrowers. One could discuss each category in turn. On NGOs, as I have argued, Wolfensohn did as much as any Bank president could do; yet he found that some campaigning anti-Bank outfits do not have an off switch. On the shareholders, particularly the biggest one, Wolfensohn got off to a good start with Bosnia; he later squandered it by allowing the Stankoist Joe Stiglitz to throw rocks at the U.S. Treasury; and still later he was faced with Paul O'Neill, a sort of right-wing Stankoist. But the big point about the Bank's relations with its stakeholders is the one that animates the last part of this book, and it relates to a goal that Wolfensohn *failed* to set himself initially. Rather than trying to rebuild the Bank's relationship with all three categories of stakeholder— shareholders, NGOs, and borrowers—Wolfensohn should have been more sensitive to the trade-offs between them. And he should have put the borrowers' interests a clear first. That was what the promise of managerial decentralization and country ownership demanded.

Sixty years after Bretton Woods, the trade-offs between the Bank's competing stakeholders constitute the institution's main challenge. The rich countries that dominate the Bank's board, together with the NGOs that lobby rich Parliaments so well, want to make the Bank an agent of their own values: protect rain forests, preserve Pygmies in their "natural" habitats, send signals to China. The Bank's clients, on the other hand, have a different agenda. They want money and advice; they want the fast road to modernity. The Bank's fundamental problem is that the northerners who set its rules have no reason to exercise restraint, since they will never borrow from the Bank themselves; the borrowers, to whom the rules do unfortunately apply, have little power to change them. To respond to its clients—to fulfill the promise of "country ownership" and its new decentralized structure—the Bank needs to hold the northern rule setters at bay. Otherwise its best clients will abandon it, and the Bank's financial foundations will be in jeopardy.[12]

The northerners, to be fair, have a right to be heard. Part of the Bank's function is to further their enlightened policies. The Clinton administration was right to make the most of the Bank's help in Bosnia, and it's a pity that the Bush team did not learn from that model when it was planning Iraq's reconstruction. Equally, NGOs raise legitimate issues, and in the 1980s the pressure that the environmental movement exerted on the Bank was largely constructive. But since the 1990s, especially, the northerners have overplayed their hand. The shareholders have used the triennial IDA replenishment discussions to foist their values on the Bank's borrowers. In the IDA round concluded in 2002, for example, the donors imposed twenty-three "objectives" on the Bank and sixty-two "recommendations"—one of which was "increasing selectivity."[13] The NGOs, for their part, have presumed to tell the Bank what its policies on dams or oil investment should be, and their recommendations have been at odds with poor countries' priorities. Because of the combined pressure from northern NGOs and shareholders, the Bank's project managers labor under "safeguard" rules covering ten sensitive issues, from forestry to dam safety, from pest management to "cultural resources." No other development lender is hamstrung in this way.

The Inter-American Development Bank has safeguards in just four of these ten areas. The European Bank for Reconstruction and Development has rules in just one of them.

The northern rules, moreover, are enforced in an overbearing way, and the result is to slow the Bank's efforts to fight poverty. The Inspection Panel, which the Tibet activists used to great effect, has sometimes lost sight of the fact that the goal of the Bank is to relieve terrible suffering—and that expensive delays over technical infringements do not further that objective. The Bank's board, similarly, is too intrusive and rule bound: no private-sector institution could possibly function with such pedantic oversight. The combination of the Inspection Panel, the board, and the fear of NGO assault combine to breed a sluggish caution at the Bank, especially since no there's no profit-seeking drive pushing in the opposite direction. As a result, the institution is festooned with rules that are absurd but difficult to change, because changing would require a complex bureaucratic fight, perhaps involving board approval. If a project manager decides, for example, that a project could usefully absorb more money than originally planned, it can take nine months to gain approval from on high—so most project managers don't bother.

Looking back over some of Wolfensohn's battles, they seem like distractions from this central issue. The premise of the management reforms—that the Bank could deliver faster if only it were managed well—missed part of the point. The root cause of the Bank's slowness lies outside its doors, with the northerners who insist upon all kinds of rules, driving the Bank to tie itself up in its infernal safeguards. Equally, the early drive to encourage the Bank's managers to share their knowledge better missed the point. The lack of knowledge sharing reflected externally imposed red tape, which left little time for creativity. Other battles of the Wolfensohn era look in retrospect like disguised attempts to escape the tyranny of northern rules. The Bolivia experiment, which aimed to dilute the oversight of the Bank's board, was one such effort to escape; the Africa region's AIDS initiative, which streamlined the board's involvement by asking it to preauthorize programs, was a second one. But for much of Wolfensohn's tenure, the need to push back against northern rule setters was not clearly acknowledged. The northerners, after all, had to be charmed into replenishing IDA—and into giving Wolfensohn the second five-year term he wanted.

By late 2002, with the fight over John Briscoe's water strategy, the tension between northern stakeholders and borrowers had burst out into the open. In that episode, and in the broader push for infrastructure lending that followed in 2003, the borrowers won; and meanwhile, the Bank launched an effort to simplify its rules and stem the flight of its strong emerging-market clients. Yet the pendulum swung back only partway: the new focus on the needs of borrowers rubbed shoulders with the old efforts to please northerners. Throughout 2003 and into 2004, Jim Wolfensohn continued to talk the Millennium Development Goal talk. He burnished the Bank's image by convening one conference on the Roma people (Gypsies) and a second one on "youth" (whatever that meant). These grandiose initiatives fit with the vision of the Bank as a secretariat for the North's global ambitions. But they distract from the more important vision of the Bank, which is that it should focus its energies as much as possible on its poor clients.

To lead the Bank through its next decade, Wolfensohn and his successors must push forward with the simplification of the Bank's rules, preserving core values like environmental protection and anticorruption financial oversight, but discarding the Byzantine excess that contributes nothing to those objectives. They must consider reforming the Inspection Panel, unless it can demonstrate that the Tibet episode will never be repeated. They must push for longer-term donor commitments to IDA—the existing process of passing the hat every three years puts the Bank constantly at risk of shareholder pressure. They must ask sensitive questions about the board: Do the shareholders need permanent representatives who pester and delay the staff? What are the costs and benefits of this suffocating oversight? All these reforms would have the effect of freeing the Bank to move faster, take more risks, and deliver for the world's poorest people. The Bank's northern paymasters, who intersperse their oppressive meddling with complaints about the Bank's slowness, need to experience a Pogo moment. "We have met the enemy and he is us!" said the character in Walt Kelly's comic strip.

After sixty years of development experiments, it is time for humility among donors. The prescriptions of northerners have often failed to reverse poverty, and the most startling development successes (communist China, most notably) have come in countries that have taken donors' advice selectively. The factors that drive progress—strong institutions, stable societies, the presence of technocrats of Tumusiime's ilk—cannot be conjured up by aid donors; despite its portentous name, the World Bank is not a proxy for world government. Instead, it is a small institution relative to the problems it faces; its lending represents a fraction of total investment in its client countries; and its ten-thousand-strong staff is dwarfed by the government payrolls of major borrowers. Even though the Bank remains the world's premier development institution, and even though it is one of the rich world's best instruments for fighting economic chaos, there is a limit to what it can do, and its shareholders and NGO critics need to accept that. The Bank can play an important role in poor countries, as we have seen in Uganda. But it cannot be a magic wand for G7 summiteers, who love to gather every year and proclaim development targets.

Despite his early enthusiasm for Linda McGinnis, and despite his relationship-banker's affinity for clients, Wolfensohn could never quite embrace the idea that the Bank needed to be humble. His model and inspiration was the messianic Bank of Robert McNamara, and his response to challenges of every kind was usually to think bigger. He perceived a management problem: he threw a quarter of a billion dollars at it. He confronted the dead end of structural adjustment: he broadened the development agenda. He faced critical shareholders: he cranked up the ambitious rhetoric. He was hounded by NGOs: he promised them all kinds of partnerships. The World Bank's next president will need above all to have three qualities: managerial experience, communications flair, and fluency in the issues of development. But Wolfensohn's successor might also gain from considering his record and leaning toward the opposite approach. Think humbler. Talk smaller. Reduce the expectations of those northern stakeholders.

Is that politically possible? It will be difficult, for sure. The northern stakeholders don't want a humbler institution, just as they don't want to pay for an ambitious one. They like calling on the Bank to act on this and that; they like denouncing it for failing to deliver. But so long as they veer schizophrenically between exhortation and contempt, it will be hard for the World Bank to be what it should be—the best source of development lending and advice there is for the world's neediest people.

ACKNOWLEDGMENTS

THIS BOOK REPRESENTS debts going back two decades, to my first experiences of developing countries. After completing school in England, I took a vacation job as a truck driver's assistant in Santiago, Chile; and after two months of loading and unloading, I rode buses up the western spine of South America, through flooded northern Peru and into Ecuador, then back through the Peruvian highlands to Bolivia and Brazil. On that trip, and on later backpacking adventures in India, I grew fascinated with the topic that has come to preoccupy me as a journalist. So my first debts are to the friends who traveled with me; to the thousands of strangers who chatted with me, gave me rides, and sometimes gave me shelter; and to my parents, who showed an absence of neurosis that I shall try to match when my children are twentyish. One time I read my own name on a MISSING PERSON notice in Peru. But only one time.

Since those early travels I've had the good fortune to work at three wonderful institutions: *The Economist* of London, where I went after college; *The Washington Post*, where I have worked since 1999; and the Council on Foreign Relations, where I spent a year's leave from the *Post* in order to research and write this book. *The Economist* gave me the chance to live and work as a journalist in Africa and to spend three years in East Asia, the most spectacular development success of the postwar period. *The Washington Post* has given me a privileged window on the policy machinery of this city, where most of the grand arguments about international economics play out. The *Post* is also a great home for a journalist who wants to write about development. The newspaper, and particularly the editorial corridor that I inhabit, is driven by a hard-nosed humanitarianism; it is a fitting coincidence that Eugene Meyer, the father of the modern *Post*, was also the World Bank's first president. I'm particularly grateful to Don Graham, Eugene Meyer's grandson and the chief executive of the Washington Post Company, for accepting the unconventional suggestion that a non-American should be hired to editorialize on American politics and policy; and to Fred Hiatt, the editorial page editor, who immediately understood my enthusiasm for this book and tolerated my long absence.

The process of researching and writing *The World's Banker* was greatly assisted by the Council on Foreign Relations. Robert Orr, the Council's Washington director when I arrived, has a special interest in development, and went out of his way to make it possible for me to spend a year there. The Council's president, Les Gelb, and his successor, Richard Haass, were unfailingly encouraging, as were Mike Peters and Lee Feinstein, who ran the Studies Department when I began this project. Mike and Lee helped me to set up a study group to review parts of my manuscript, and Jessica Einhorn, dean of the School of Advanced International Studies at Johns Hopkins University, agreed to chair the proceedings. Jessica is a leading authority on the World Bank; she also runs meetings with a brisk humor, which was fortunate given that the group comprised a score of brilliant and disputatious experts. I am grateful to all of them for reading and commenting on my chapters. I am even more indebted to James Lindsay, who took over from Mike Peters as the Council's director of studies. Somehow in his packed schedule, Jim found time to read and comment on the entire manuscript.

I owe special thanks to my research associate at the Council, Amelia Branczik. Amelia immersed herself in the details of the Bank's triumphs and disasters, turning boxloads of microcassettes into interview transcripts, then arranging pieces of transcript into the chronologies on which the book's narrative is based. I hate to think of the weekends and evenings she gave up in order to meet my unreasonable deadlines, but I'm deeply grateful for the results. Her attention to detail gave birth to a special beast, the "Branczik footnote," often involving quotes from people she'd tracked down in multiple countries. Her command of Serbo-Croatian got us out of several awkward moments on our trip to Bosnia.

Neither Amelia's work nor mine would have been possible without the real heroes of any journalistic enterprise: the people who volunteer hours of their time to recall what happened and why. This book is based primarily on some two hundred long taped interviews: with World Bankers, ex–World Bankers, and people who have interacted with the institution as foes, partners, or clients. I am grateful to my main subject, James Wolfensohn, for submitting to nearly twenty hours of interviews, all of them on the record. Not many people in his sort of position offer such access without a right to review the manuscript, which he did not seek and I wouldn't have surrendered. I am also grateful to my sources in Bosnia, Uganda, and Chad as well as in London, New York, and Washington. Where possible, I have identified them in my notes, though for obvious reasons, some have preferred to remain anonymous. Particular thanks to those who provided documents, photographs, contemporaneous notes, and correspondence to supplement their memories of key arguments and events.

I have also benefited from the writings of fellow analysts. I would like to thank in particular Robert Wade of the London School of Economics, who generously shared an unpublished account of the Bank's battle with the Tibet activists, an episode that he has researched as an academic and experienced as a protagonist. Robert's many published articles helped to enrich my understanding of the Bank's dilemmas, and his appetite for narrative reconstruction sets him apart from most political scientists. Devesh Kapur of Harvard also helped to form my thinking, partly through his contribution to the Brookings Institution's two-volume history of the pre-Wolfensohn World Bank, which he coedited, and partly through numerous shorter pieces. Paul Collier of Oxford, Moisés Naím of *Foreign Policy* magazine, David Dollar of the Bank's research department, and Nick Stern of the London School of Economics (and now of the U.K. Treasury in London) have helped to shape my view of development. Thanks also to Caroline Anstey and Mark Malloch Brown, who were especially generous with their time, and to Jimmy Kolker, who had me to stay in Kampala and helped me to understand the country. Among journalists, I learned much from my *Washington Post* colleague Paul Blustein; from Stephen Fidler, Robert Chote, Martin Wolf, and Alan Beattie of the *Financial Times;* and from my ex-colleagues at *The Economist,* notably Zanny Minton Beddoes, the magazine's economics correspondent in Washington.

Zanny is more than my teacher; she is also my wife. I could never have completed this project without her. The morning after Jim Wolfensohn's seventieth birthday party, which I describe in my last chapter, Zanny gave birth to our daughter; and the morning after that she cheerfully told me to get back to my computer. Somehow she manages to be a match for all my hilarious and boisterous children—Felix, Maya, Milo, and now Molly—while at the same time dispensing editorial suggestions and doing her own job. She has the energy of six normal people, and it's to her that I dedicate this book.

Finally, I would like to thank my agent, Andrew Wylie, who helped to conceive this project and did me the great service of hooking me up with Scott Moyers of The Penguin Press. From our early discussions, Andrew made it clear that Scott would be the ideal editor for me, and I soon discovered he was right. Scott helped me to strike the difficult balance between stories and analysis, between detail and context. His intelligence is present throughout this book.

NOTES

PREFACE: THE PRISONER OF LILLIPUT

1. $2.50 is the price of a bed net plus a basic insecticide for treating it. Lawrence Barat, a malaria specialist from the Centers for Disease Control and Prevention, seconded to the World Bank, estimates that 1 million Africans die from malaria a year, and that 90 percent of those deaths involve children under five. Others, for example the Bill and Melinda Gates Foundation, put the death toll higher. Barat interview and e-mail, February 9, 2004.

2. *Faith and Credit: The World Bank's Secular Empire,* by Susan George and Fabrizio Sabelli (Boulder, Colo.: Westview Press, 1994), p. 1.

CHAPTER ONE: A TALE OF TWO AMBITIONS

1. See, for example, "Speech to Inter-American Press Association," Washington, D.C., October 13, 2001.

2. "A Partnership for Development and Peace." Keynote address delivered to the Woodrow Wilson International Center, Washington, D.C., March 6, 2002.

3. Morgenthau speech on the opening day of the Bretton Woods conference, July 1944. Quoted in George and Sabelli, *Faith and Credit,* p. 27.

4. *The World Bank: Its First Half Century,* by Devesh Kapur, John Lewis, and Richard Webb (Washington, D.C.: Brookings Institution, 1997), p. 57. Readers will see from the notes that I rely repeatedly on this magisterial work during the course of my first chapter.

5. Kapur et al., *World Bank,* p. 62.

6. The conference was advertised as being "for the purpose of formulating definite proposals for an International Monetary Fund, and possibly a Bank for Reconstruction and Development." One participant recalled how, of the fortnight or so of work at Bretton Woods, planning for the Bank probably didn't take more than a day and a half. A few years later, a plaque was placed

outside the hotel where the delegates had labored. It recorded the founding of the International Monetary Fund, but made no mention of the Bank whatever. See ibid., p. 59.

7. Ibid., p. 61.

8. Ibid., p. 63.

9. Ibid., p. 67.

10. Wolfensohn interview, April 20, 2003. See also "Man for All Reasons," by Juliet Herd, *Weekend Australian*, January 24, 1998, p. 21.

11. Wolfensohn interview, April 20, 2003. See also "The Fix-It King Everyone Wants by His Side," by Carol Leonard, *Times* (London), April 25, 1992.

12. Wolfensohn interview, April 20, 2003. See also Leonard, "Fix-It King": "I was so out of it, socially and emotionally, that I failed everything in the first year. When I left, the vice-chancellor said I was the laziest person to go through the university."

13. Wolfensohn interview, April 20, 2003. Independent verification of the way Wolfensohn came to take up fencing has not been possible; readers may wish to treat it skeptically.

14. "Jim Wolfensohn: The Beau Sabreur of High Finance," by Trevor Sykes, *Bulletin*, July 1, 1980, p. 123.

15. "Wolfensohn Left Australia for America with Just $300," by Louise Sweeney, *Christian Science Monitor*, June 18, 1980.

16. "When I was at Harvard, I got a letter from him every day. If I were a psychiatrist, I would say that he was reliving his life through me. There are very few people who have that degree of emotional support I suppose. It put a terrific weight on me." Wolfensohn interview, April 20, 2003.

17. Wolfensohn interview, March 26, 2003.

18. George and Sabelli, *Faith and Credit*, p. 33.

19. The World Bank began life with an endowment of $1.5 billion plus a "callable" promise of $6 billion.

20. Meyer was an investment banker, public servant, and father of *The Washington Post*, so he has another claim on history. However, as a *Washington Post* journalist I work for Meyer's grandson, so readers may wish to discount my view of his historical importance.

21. Richard Demuth, then assistant to the vice president. Quoted in the World Bank archives.

22. World Bank archives.

23. *The Elusive Quest for Growth: Economists' Adventures and Misadventures in the Tropics*, by William Easterly (Cambridge, Mass.: MIT Press, 2001), pp. 28–32.

24. Wolfensohn interviews, January 3, 2003, and April 20, 2003.

25. *West African Pilot,* September 5, 1961, p. 1. An account of the incident appeared on the front page of Nigeria's *Daily Express* on the same day.

26. To the equivalent of $1.9 billion, expressed in 1993 dollars. Kapur et al., *World Bank,* p. 187.

27. *Bankers with a Mission,* by Jochen Kraske et al. (New York: Oxford University Press, 1998), p. 155.

28. Wolfensohn interview, January 3, 2003.

29. Wolfensohn interview, April 20, 2003. See also "What Wolfensohn Wants," by Kevin Muehring, *Institutional Investor,* October 1, 1995.

30. Wolfensohn interview, April 20, 2003.

31. Wolfensohn interview, January 4, 2003.

32. Wolfensohn seems to remember little of these schemes, but Bernard Dewe Mathews, who worked for Schroders and has written about the history of the firm, remembers both clearly. Bernard Dewe Mathews interview, April 14, 2003.

33. Dewe Mathews interview, April 14, 2003.

34. Wolfensohn interview, January 4, 2003.

35. Carnegie Hall library; Wolfensohn interview, January 4, 2003.

36. Anthony Loehnis interview, March 6, 2003.

37. In 1963, Walt Rostow, the propounder of the financing-gap theory and by then a prominent member of Kennedy's administration, had urged the Bank to pay more attention to inequality; the Bank had refused to listen. But McNamara had been Rostow's colleague, a fellow Kennedy whiz kid, and he now proposed to implement the Rostow agenda. Kapur et al., *World Bank,* p. 207.

38. On the lack of data to support the shift away from growth in the late 1960s, see Kapur et al., *World Bank,* p. 225, especially footnote 23. For a more recent review of the data, see *Growth Is Good for the Poor,* by David Dollar and Aart Kraay (Washington, D.C.: World Bank, 2000). The authors find that "income of the poor rises one-for-one with overall growth. This general relationship between income of the bottom fifth of the population and per capita GDP holds in a sample of 80 countries covering four decades."

39. Kapur et al., *World Bank,* p. 232.

40. This was a consortium to finance agricultural research, which later became the Consultative Group on International Agricultural Research. Kapur et al., *World Bank,* p. 253.

41. "The World Bank as an 'Intellectual Actor,'" by Nicholas Stern with Francisco Ferreira, published in Volume 2 of Kapur et al., *World Bank,* p. 535.

42. Kraske et al., *Bankers with a Mission,* p. 202. See also Kapur et al., *World Bank,* pp. 22, 506.

43. "Chrysler: The Anatomy of a Loan," by Judith Miller, *The New York Times,* June 29, 1980, sec. 3, p. 1.

44. "Chrysler Issues First of Its Notes Backed by $500 Million," by Steve Lohr, *The New York Times,* June 25, 1980, p. A1.

45. Robert McNamara interview, January 16, 2003.

46. Wolfensohn interview, January 3, 2003.

CHAPTER TWO: "WORLD BANK MURDERER"

1. "A Search for Global Relevance: Patti Waldmeir on Wolfensohn's First Year at the World Bank," by Patti Waldmeir, *Financial Times,* May 30, 1996, p. 16.

2. *Bankers with a Mission,* by Jochen Kraske et al. (New York: Oxford University Press, 1998), pp. 213–15.

3. Ibid., p. 251.

4. Ibid., p. 248.

5. Ibid.

6. "The Canny Nomination of Barbara Who," *The Economist,* March 22, 1986.

7. *Hobart Rowen, Self-Inflicted Wounds, from LBJ's Guns and Butter to Reagan's Voodoo Economics* (New York: Times Books, 1994), p. 300. Cited in *The World Bank: Its First Half Century,* by Devesh Kapur, John Lewis, and Richard Webb (Washington, D.C.: Brookings Institution, 1997), p. 338.

8. In Latin America the infant mortality rate fell from 61 per 1,000 live births in 1980 to 41 in 1990. In sub-Saharan Africa the infant mortality rate fell from 115 to 101. Similarly, immunization of children under twelve months old for DPT went from 37 percent to 71 percent in Latin America, and adult illiteracy went from 20 percent to 15 percent. Figures come from the World Bank's "World Development Indicators, 2000."

9. *Faith and Credit: The World Bank's Secular Empire,* by Susan George and Fabrizio Sabelli (Boulder, Colo.: Westview Press, 1994), p. 59.

10. In another typical passage, George and Sabelli fumed that "bank projects have been known to dislocate entire communities, displace thousands of people, destroy forests, turn grasslands to desert, concentrate land and wealth in the hands of a few rich farmers or entrepreneurs—all in the name of development." Ibid., p. 2.

11. Kapur et al., *World Bank,* p. 368.

12. Kris Zedler interview, May 2, 2003.

13. *Masters of Illusion: The World Bank and the Poverty of Nations,* by Catherine Caufield (New York: Henry Holt, 1996), p. 174.

14. David Hopper, the Bank's senior vice president in charge of the environment, said: "There's no question that the monitoring by the NGOs in the US was an important factor [in the bank's decision to create the new environmental department and divisions]." Quoted in "Greening the Bank," by Robert Wade, published in Volume 2 of Kapur et al., *World Bank*, p. 654.

15. Caufield, *Masters of Illusion*, p. 180.

16. Wolfensohn interview, August 10, 2003. See also "James Wolfensohn: Financier or Cellist?," by Nigel Adam, *Euromoney*, August 1981.

17. "What Wolfensohn Wants," by Kevin Muehring, *Institutional Investor*, October 1, 1995. I also came across a letter to John Gutfreund, dated December 4, 1981, in the Wolfensohn Foundation Archives, in which Wolfensohn complained about reports that he had been ousted from Salomon's.

18. Wolfensohn interview, April 20, 2003.

19. Ibid.

20. See, for example, "Salomon Partner Cuts Back on Duties," *The New York Times*, May 12, 1981, p. D2. "After two decades in a service business, he would like to be serving himself a little more, Mr. Wolfensohn explained yesterday. 'I'm going to set up a small office, mainly to become a principal in investments, both here and in Australia,' he said." By 2003, Wolfensohn had no memory of having wanted to get away from advisory work. But several interviews published in 1981 suggest otherwise.

21. "Interview: Jim Wolfensohn," *Australian Business*, July 2, 1981, p. 75.

22. Wolfensohn interview, April 20, 2003.

23. *Gentlemen of Fortune: The World's Merchant and Investment Bankers*, by Paul Ferris (London: Weidenfeld and Nicolson, 1984), pp. 144–46.

24. Wolfensohn introduced Larry Tisch to the board of CBS in 1986, after which Tisch took control of the network. He knew CBS because he was sitting on its board, and he knew Tisch because he frequently played tennis with him on weekends in Westchester County.

25. Ray Golden interview, April 2, 2003.

26. Ferris, *Gentlemen of Fortune*, p. 147.

27. Paul Volcker interview, May 8, 2003.

28. "The Man with the Golden Rolodex," by Leah Nathans Spiro, *BusinessWeek*, April 27, 1992, p. 88.

29. Jeff Goldstein interview, April 22, 2003.

30. Golden interview, April 2, 2003.

31. "These things are not planned, they are things that sort of happen along. I get interested in them. The problem is that I have this tremendous appetite for life." Wolfensohn interview, April 20, 2003.

32. Adam, "James Wolfensohn."

33. This speculation about Wolfensohn's motives is based on several off-the-record discussions with Wolfensohn's friends from the period.

34. Gerry Rice interview, January 17, 2003. Rice was Preston's speechwriter at the World Bank.

35. Jane Armitage interview, January 24, 2003.

36. "New Leadership Style at World Bank," by Keith Bradsher, *The New York Times*, April 13, 1992.

37. "Avuncular Provider of Advice," by Michael Prowse and Peter Norman, *Financial Times*, April 27, 1992.

38. "Lewis Preston Aims to Ax World Bank's Arrogance," by Hobart Rowen, *The Washington Post*, May 24, 1992.

39. Wade, "Greening the Bank," published in Kapur et al., *World Bank*, p. 687.

40. The report's chief author was Willi Wapenhans. Prem Garg, a Bank official who served on the Wapenhans team, reckons that the quality of Bank projects in 1992 was probably no worse than it had been ten years earlier; it was just worse relative to expectations. Since Garg is not a line manager, but rather the head of the Bank's Quality Assurance Group, he has no reason to be polite about the Bank's record. Garg interview, February 2, 2004.

41. George and Sabelli, *Faith and Credit*, p. 233.

42. Caufield, *Masters of Illusion*, p. 261.

43. The internal critic was Michael Cernea. A later version of the same report, "Resettlement and Development," can be viewed at http://www.wds.world bank.org/servlet/WDSContentServer/WDSP/IB/1996/03/01/000009265_3980728143956/Rendered/PDF/multi_page.pdf.

44. For an example of the critical take, see Caufield, *Masters of Illusion*, p. 262. For an example of a balanced one, see "Moving People," *The Economist*, April 23, 1994, p. 48.

45. Meanwhile, Christian Aid declared that the Bank's structural-adjustment programs "are damaging the poorest people in debt burdened developing countries."

46. Mark Malloch Brown interview, December 5, 2002.

47. Ibid.

CHAPTER THREE: THE RENAISSANCE PRESIDENT

1. "The Salsa at the Summit: Kennedy Center Stages a Show in Miami," by Eric Brace, *The Washington Post*, December 10, 1994, p. D1.

2. Ibid.

3. Roberto Danino interview, January 22, 2003, and Wolfensohn interview, January 3, 2003.

4. Press accounts from the time also suggest that Wolfensohn had long been angling for the World Bank job. An article in the *Washingtonian Magazine* of October 1993 ("Facing the Music," by Stephen Wigler), discussing his tenure at the Kennedy Center, referred to "the often-heard rumors that he may resign, even that he is quietly campaigning to become president of the World Bank." Another article in *The Independent* of June 2, 1991 ("Crown Eludes a Kingmaker," by Peter Koenig), reports: "Several months ago, when Barber Conable stepped down as head of the World Bank, Mr. Wolfensohn's friends held their breath. Here was a position which seemed tailor-made."

5. Donna Shalala interview, January 21, 2003.

6. Mark Malloch Brown interview, December 5, 2002.

7. Gerry Rice interview, January 17, 2003.

8. This was Tuesday, January 31, 1995.

9. Jan Piercy interview, February 26, 2003.

10. Ibid.; Piercy e-mail communication, February 27, 2003.

11. *Faith and Credit: The World Bank's Secular Empire*, by Susan George and Fabrizio Sabelli (Boulder, Colo.: Westview Press, 1994), p. 1.

12. Net transfers in the year to June 1995 were $7.9 billion for the World Bank.

13. "Greening the Bank," by Robert Wade, published in Volume 2 of *The World Bank: Its First Half Century*, by Devesh Kapur, John Lewis, and Richard Webb (Washington, D.C.: Brookings Institution, 1997), p. 612.

14. World Bank data.

15. "Recent Trends in the Transfer of Resources to Developing Countries." Table prepared for World Bank Development Committee, August 29, 2001.

16. A GNP per person of $760 is the cutoff for the "middle-income" classification in the World Bank's "World Development Indicators, 2000," the source of these data.

17. "World Development Indicators, 2000," on CD-ROM.

18. Shalala interview, January 21, 2003.

19. Piercy interview, February 26, 2003.

20. Malloch Brown interview, December 5, 2002.

21. Piercy also recalls: "The day I finally had a conversation myself with Jim I was completely disconcerted. It was a snowy Saturday. I had the sense of someone with great arrogance. My first reaction was I can't imagine this sort of person being president." Piercy interview, February 26, 2003.

22. Piercy interview, February 26, 2003.

23. Jack Quinn interview, November 25, 2002.

24. Robert Picciotto interview, February 26, 2003.

25. "He knows what he would do with this institution; he has thought about it

very deeply," Rubin had told Piercy afterward. Piercy interview, February 26, 2003.

26. Robert Rubin interview, December 29, 2003.
27. For other references to George and Sabelli, see Chapter 2.
28. Wolfensohn interview, January 3, 2003.
29. Bob Nash interview, March 28, 2003.
30. "I said that the thing might be bureaucratically screwed, even if you wanted me," Wolfensohn recalls. Wolfensohn interview, January 3, 2003.
31. Malloch Brown interview, December 5, 2002.
32. George Mallinckrodt interview, March 10, 2003.
33. Wolfensohn interview, January 3, 2003.
34. Piercy interview, February 26, 2003.
35. Dow Jones News Service, March 11, 1995.
36. Piercy interview, February 26, 2003.

CHAPTER FOUR: A TWISTER IN AFRICA

1. Paul Volcker interview, May 8, 2003.
2. George Mallinckrodt interview, March 10, 2003.
3. "Wolfensohn to Retain Kennedy Center Post," by Judith Weinraub, *The Washington Post*, April 18, 1995, p. Boi.
4. My main source on Wolfensohn's early style is Jane Armitage, his executive secretary in the transition period. Armitage interview, January 24, 2003.
5. Ibid.
6. Cited in "Missionary Work," by Paul Blustein, *The Washington Post Magazine*, November 10, 1996, p. W08.
7. Kris Zedler interview, May 2, 2003.
8. Ironically, Malloch Brown was later to become boss of the United Nations Development Program.
9. Caroline Anstey e-mail, December 17, 2003.
10. Kim Jaycox interview, January 10, 2003.
11. "The Traveling Man: World Bank's Wolfensohn Seeks a Global Grasp of Its Priorities," by Clay Chandler, *The Washington Post*, June 1, 1995, p. D9.
12. This is an inflation-adjusted comparison. See *The World Bank: Its First Half Century*, by Devesh Kapur, John Lewis, and Richard Webb (Washington, D.C.: Brookings Institution, 1997), p. 696.
13. GDP per capita in sub-Saharan Africa fell 1.2 percent in 1981–90, a performance slightly worse than the 0.9 percent fall in Latin America. See the World Bank's "Global Development Finance," Table A.7, p. 186. However, measuring GDP on the basis of purchasing power parity gives a slightly

more cheerful result: the average African grew some 40 percent richer between 1980 and 1990.

14. Kenneth Kaunda of Zambia was another well meaning but misguided leader who was backed by the World Bank. According to one assessment, "The outpouring of [World Bank] loans to Zambia from 1965 to 1976, when most of the disastrous policies were being generated, took place despite the fact that they were well understood by 1974, were at least partially understood by 1971 and should have been broadly understood even earlier." "From Dutch Disease to Dutch Auction: A Retrospective Review of the Zambian Structural Adjustment Program," by Benjamin King, 1988, paragraph 106. Quoted in Kapur et al., *World Bank,* p. 698.

15. The key expression of this orthodoxy was the so-called Berg Report, named after its main author, a University of Michigan economist called Elliot Berg. After it appeared in 1981, African development ministers declared it to be "in fundamental contradiction with the political, economic and social aspirations of Africa." Kapur et al., *World Bank,* p. 718.

16. Ibid., p. 731.

17. In 1980 to 1982 the Bank chaired donor consultative groups for five African countries that met on a regular basis. By 1987, there were sixteen such groups. Ibid., p. 733.

18. Sam Carlson interview, January 17, 2003. Carlson is McGinnis's husband.

19. Internal memo from Junaid Ahmad, April 18, 1995. To prevent unfair finger-pointing, I would like to state that the internal memos cited in this chapter were not provided to me by any of the sources I name in the notes.

20. Internal memo from Linda McGinnis to Victoria Kwakwa, April 24, 1995.

21. Internal memo from Linda McGinnis to Victoria Kwakwa, April 25, 1995.

22. Internal memo from Linda McGinnis to Junaid Ahmad, June 2, 1995.

23. Linda McGinnis interview, January 29, 2003.

24. Internal memo from Hasan Tuluy to Linda McGinnis, June 15, 1995.

25. World Bank video archive. This scene, and much of this trip, was captured on video.

26. Ibid.

27. I'm grateful to Anne Alikonis, a researcher at the Council on Foreign Relations, for her inquiries into Mali.

28. Carlson interview, January 17, 2003.

29. McGinnis interview, January 29, 2003, and Carlson interview, January 17, 2003.

30. McGinnis photo collection. Along with the official video footage, McGinnis's photos provide a visual record of the visit.

31. McGinnis interview, January 29, 2003.

32. World Bank video archive. McGinnis interview, January 29, 2003. Carlson interview, January 17, 2003.

33. "The front-line people are the best people in the Bank. They are close to the client. . . . You have a totally different feel about the Bank when you are in the field with the local officers." Wolfensohn interview, January 4, 2003. Referring to Linda McGinnis and her husband, Sam Carlson, Wolfensohn said, "I loved them. It was a vision of where one could get to." Wolfensohn interview, June 12, 2003.

34. "Les Silences de Wolfensohn," *Le Republicain,* June 21, 1995.

35. Internal memo from Stephen Denning to Linda McGinnis, June 19, 1995. To prevent unfair finger-pointing, I would like to state that the internal memos cited in this chapter were not provided to me by any of the sources I name in the notes.

36. Internal memo from Stephen Denning, June 18, 1995.

37. World Bank video archive.

38. Katsu's futile remonstrations and Wolfensohn's irritation are captured on video in the World Bank's archives.

39. Olivier Lafourcade interview, January 16, 2003.

40. This taboo is recalled by many in the Bank. For example, Ritva Reinikka, the lead economist working on Uganda at the time, recalls, "I remember asking about why can't we talk about debt relief. And I was told that asking the question will create a problem for everyone because our cost of borrowing will go up." Reinikka interview, February 20, 2003.

41. Jaycox interview, January 10, 2003; Lafourcade interview, January 16, 2003.

42. Between 1980 and 1994, sub-Saharan Africa's debt nearly tripled, rising from $58 billion to $165 billion. More than a third of the growth of this debt was due to the capitalization of interest rather than fresh lending. Much of the fresh lending was triggered by the creditors' desire to avoid default. Kapur et al., *World Bank,* p. 787.

43. Ibid.

44. The multilateral share of sub-Saharan Africa's debt stock had risen from 16 percent in 1985 to 23 percent ten years later.

45. The proportion had previously been higher. By 1995, the refinancing of market-based World Bank loans with soft IDA credits was reducing the World Bank's share in debt service substantially, though the extent was unclear at the time of Wolfensohn's visit, and this did not negate the other good reasons to favor debt relief. The Bank's share of sub-Saharan Africa's debt service in the years 1991 through 1995 was 21 percent, 17 percent, 25 percent, 17 percent, and 13 percent, respectively. I am grateful to Brian Deese,

the numbers guru behind the Center for Global Development study, "Delivering on Debt Relief," for his assistance in sorting out these data from the Bank's "Global Development Finance" reports.

46. A dialogue of this sort took place in the case of Cameroon in 1994. Kapur et al., *World Bank,* pp. 785–86.

47. As late as 1994, the Bank's World Debt Tables intoned that multilateral debt relief "would entail costs to all multilateral borrowers that would far outweigh the benefits to a few."

48. Personal memo from Ravi Kanbur to Wolfensohn, My Views on Multilateral Debt, June 7, 1995.

49. Masood Ahmed, a senior Bank economist who initially treated the idea of debt relief with caution, says of Wolfensohn: "He definitely accelerated the pace at which something was done. Without him, we would have dragged this out before we managed to confront it." Since Ahmed later fell out with Wolfensohn and left the Bank, this praise carries some weight. Moreover, Ahmed's view is shared by Justin Forsyth, an Oxfam official who lobbied the Bank on debt relief during this period. Before Wolfensohn's arrival, Forsyth remembers being laughed at when he raised the debt issue with World Bank managers. But "Wolfensohn broke the logjam," says Forsyth. "I think he deserves a lot of credit for pushing it." Kevin Watkins, Oxfam's director of research, says that Wolfensohn's "political conviction, leadership, courage, and—at times—sheer bloody mindedness, were pivotal. We had been trying to get African debt on the international agenda since the early '90s—and he really opened the door." Ahmed interview, January 16, 2003. Forsyth interview, March 5, 2003. Watkins e-mail, October 30, 2003.

50. Internal memo: JDW's Meetings in London, May 19. The memo was prepared by Geoff Lamb, the World Bank's London representative.

51. Wolfensohn interview, January 3, 2003.

52. Jaycox interview, January 9, 2003.

53. Brian Falconer interview, January 15, 2003.

54. Tony Burdon interview, May 27, 2003.

55. The Bank has three principal sources of income: fees, which are charged to countries that borrow from the soft-loan IDA operations, and which are also levied on donor grants to Bank-run trust funds; profits on market-based lending; and profits on investing reserves. If the Bank ceased market-based lending, it would lose the second of these sources, forgoing $800 million or so in annual revenue. Some analysts suggest that this would not hurt too much, since the Bank would retain something like $800 million from fees plus $1 billion a year in revenue from investing reserves. But that would not be quite enough to cover the administrative budget ($1.7 billion) plus the

annual transfers that the Bank now makes to the IDA kitty ($300 million) and the HIPC debt relief fund ($240 million). Faced with this shortfall, the Bank could try to boost investment revenue by buying riskier instruments, a step that could be justified by the absence of the risk that it currently takes in its loan portfolio. But that shift to a more aggressive investment strategy would have to be approved by the Bank's shareholders, and approval might not be forthcoming. On the other hand, one can easily imagine the shareholders responding to a withdrawal from market-based lending with demands that compounded the Bank's financial crunch. Congressional critics might demand, for example, that the Bank's capital be returned to the shareholders since its original purpose—to serve as a capital base to support market lending—no longer applied. In that case, the Bank would be left with only one of its three current sources of money: fees from administering IDA and the special "trust funds." Since those fees come to just $800 million, they could cover only part of the Bank's existing operations. Moreover, there would be a knock-on effect: Because it could no longer afford to transfer $300 million a year into the IDA kitty, the Bank would also lose the fees associated with passing that money onto clients. The bottom line is that the Bank's current financial model depends on continued lending to middle-income countries. Given that the tendency to attack multilateral institutions is stronger than the tendency to bolster them, any attempt to unravel the existing arrangement would probably leave the Bank weakened.

56. The Bank's constructive role on AIDS in Brazil is noted both by Michael Merson, who headed the United Nations Global AIDS program, and by Murilo Portugal, who was then the director of the Brazilian Finance Ministry. Merson interview, November 12, 2003. Portugal interview, November 18, 2003.

57. Portugal interview, November 18, 2003.

58. Zhu Guangyao, China's representative on the World Bank's board, agrees that although the Bank's capital is incidental to China, the Bank's help in distilling best practice from international experience can be extremely valuable. Zhu interview, November 26, 2003.

59. Wolfensohn interview, January 3, 2003.

60. Mike Gillette interview, February 25, 2003.

61. Armeane Choksi interview, March 4, 2003.

62. Dow Jones International News, September 15, 1995.

63. Choksi interview, March 4, 2003.

64. Describing the Nepali NGOs in this campaign, an exhaustive article in *Cultural Survival Quarterly* mentions "the Arun Concerned Group (ACG), a coalition of human rights organizations comprised of lawyers and human

rights activists, and the Alliance for Energy, made up of engineers, economists, management experts and journalists. Both of these organizations were
described as the 'locals' in the subsequent debates over Arun. Though this
label was an important basis for mobilizing international opposition to the
project, on a national and regional level, as the founders of both organizations readily admit, this claim of 'local-ness' was easily contested." The
article goes on to note that one of the Nepali campaigners who visited
Washington to lobby against the dam had not even visited the Arun valley
where the dam was to be located. See "Defining the 'Local' in the Arun
Controversy: Villagers, NGOs, and the World Bank in the Arun Valley,
Nepal," by Ann Armbrecht Forbes, *Cultural Survival Quarterly*, October 31,
1996.

CHAPTER FIVE: MISSION SARAJEVO

1. *To End a War*, by Richard Holbrooke (New York: Random House, 1998),
   pp. 9–14.
2. *The World Bank: Its First Half Century*, by Devesh Kapur, John Lewis, and
   Richard Webb (Washington, D.C.: Brookings Institution, 1997), p. 371.
3. Kemal Dervis interview, April 29, 2003.
4. The plea in the 1950s came from Theodore Schultz, the UN economist who
   later coined the term "human capital."
5. Whether this happened would depend partly on whether shareholders
   allowed the Bank to keep its $30 billion or so in accumulated reserves. The
   shareholders might argue that if reserves were no longer needed to create a
   capital base to support market lending, the reserves should be returned to
   them. On the other hand, if they allowed the Bank to continue to enjoy the
   revenue from its reserves in addition to donations from shareholders for the
   IDA kitty, the Bank would have the benefit of an endowment, and so would
   be a cross between a big foundation and the United Nations. See also Chapter 4, note 55.
6. The Bank has twenty-four board members. The biggest shareholders get
   one representative all to themselves, but smaller countries share seats. Sub-
   Saharan Africa, for example, is represented by just two board members.
7. Kasim Omićević interview, May 23, 2003.
8. David Lipton interview, February 28, 2003.
9. Dervis interview, April 29, 2003.
10. Ibid.
11. Christine Wallich interview, March 2, 2003.
12. The leader was Ejup Ganic, the Bosniak vice president of the time. Ganic
    interview, May 23, 2003.

13. Wallich interview, March 5, 2003.

14. Zlatko Hurtić interview, May 20, 2003.

15. Wallich interview, March 5, 2003.

16. Neven Tomic, the Bosnian Croat who served as finance minister for the federation, is among those who emphasize the World Bank's role as a mediator between his side and the Bosniaks. Tomic interview, May 23, 2003.

17. Wallich interview, July 17, 2003. Dan Serwer interview, April 29, 2003.

18. Holbrooke, *To End a War,* p. 244.

19. The central government retained the rights to just two kinds of tax revenue: on overflight rights and visa fees. Most of the rest would go to the two "entities"—the Serb area, known as Republika Srpska, and the Bosniak-Croat Federation. In practice, this meant that the central government would be hopelessly weak, but Wallich and David Lipton concluded that this was the best deal they could hope for. The Operations Evaluation Department, the World Bank's internal assessor, later concluded that Dayton had "built-in obstacles to effective economic governance" (OED, p. 87). "The accords have created a perhaps uniquely weak state to serve as interlocutor and counterpart to the Bank and other external agencies" (OED, p. 25). See *Bosnia and Herzegovina Post-Conflict Reconstruction Country Case Study Series,* by Alcira Kreimer, Robert Muscat, Ann Elwan, and Margaret Arnold (Washington, D.C.: World Bank, 2000). Given the necessary weakness of the Dayton design, the success of reconstruction is all the more remarkable.

20. This is the judgment of David Lipton, the U.S. Treasury official at Dayton. Lipton interview, July 2, 2003.

21. Holbrooke, *To End a War,* p. 309.

22. Izetbegovic interview on Radio Bosna, November 22, 1995. Meanwhile, Agence-France Presse reports that, on his return to Sarajevo, Izetbegovic noted that the accord "implies the lifting of the arms embargo and *substantial economic aid* to our country" (AFP, November 21, 1995; emphasis added).

23. Haris Silajdzic, the Bosnian prime minister and key adviser to Izetbegovic at Dayton, remembers the promise of reconstruction aid as "an important factor" in the decision to accept the peace. "We were asking for some assurance because the situation we were in was very bad," Silajdzic recalls. "It was assumed that there would be some kind of assistance." Silajdzic interview, July 8, 2003. David Lipton adds that the promise of reconstruction aid from the Bank was invoked successfully several times during the Dayton negotiations in order to dissuade Silajdzic and his colleagues from walking away from the table. Lipton interview, July 2, 2003.

24. Vesna Frančić interview, May 22, 2003. Michel Noel interview, June 19, 2003. Noel was the leader of this World Bank mission.

25. Holbrooke, *To End a War*, p. 318.

26. Neven Tomic, the former federation finance minister, recalls an incident in which the European Investment Bank spent three days negotiating a loan to a road reconstruction fund that had been officially abolished. Tomic interview, May 23, 2003.

27. Sarah Forster interview, March 11, 2003.

28. Andras Horvai interview, April 23, 2003.

29. This is the conversation as recounted by Dervis, in an interview on April 29, 2003. Muratovic concurred with the account when it was read back to him. Interviews with three other participants—Wallich, Omićević, and Tomic—confirmed the substance of the exchange though inevitably not the precise language.

30. Hurtić interview, May 20, 2003.

31. Jakob Finci interview, May 20, 2003.

32. Hurtić interview, May 20, 2003. Wolfensohn had no idea he was in danger. Wolfensohn interview, June 12, 2003.

33. The Bank's error in this case is acknowledged by Xavier Devictor, the IMG official who joined the World Bank in early 1996, and by Zlatko Hurtić, the Bosnian official who also worked for the Bank later. Even Hans Apitz, the World Bank official in charge of infrastructure projects, is indirectly apologetic. In later projects, he says, care was taken to use the aid carrot to buy reconciliation. Officials who worked for rival agencies—the Office of the High Representative or the European Union—are vitriolic in their criticisms of the Bank's role in Mostar's power sector. Devictor interview, April 21, 2003. Hurtić interview, May 20 2003. Apitz interview, July 1, 2003. Massena interview, June 16, 2003. Didier Fau interview, June 18, 2003 Sir Martin Garrod interview, June 17, 2003. The Apitz, Massena, Fau, and Garrod interviews were conducted by Amelia Branczik.

34. Wallich interview, March 21, 2003.

35. The growth figures come from the World Bank's "World Development Indicators, 2003." The unemployment figures come from a report prepared for the May 1999 donors' conference hosted by the Bank and the European Commission.

36. Mirsad Kikanovic interview, May 20, 2003.

37. Omićević interview, May 23, 2003.

38. You could track down the former representatives of the Republika Srpska government; you could observe that the World Bank scarcely gave them any aid; and you could ask them to comment: "The World Bank staff was very fair," said the former Republika Srpska finance minister, Novak Kondić. In Sarajevo, you could test the waters with both Bosniaks and Croats: "In com-

parison with some of the other donors, the Bank assistance was by far the most efficient," said Zlatko Hurtić, a Bosniak; "The World Bank made fewer mistakes than the other donors," said Neven Tomic, a Croat. You could even probe an official who fought pitched battles with the Bank's staff: "The World Bank was the leading donor organization at the time," said former prime minister Muratovic. "Nobody would deny it."

39. "World Bank Gets Bosnia Aid Role," by Richard W. Stevenson. *The New York Times,* April 17, 1996, sec. A, p. 6.

40. "The World Bank's Experience with Post-Conflict Reconstruction," report by the Operations Evaluation Department of the World Bank, 1998.

41. Stevenson, "World Bank Gets Bosnia Aid Role," sec. A, p. 6.

CHAPTER SIX: NARCISSUS AND THE OCTOPUS

1. The speech was captured on video and is in the World Bank's archive.

2. See "Missionary Work," a wonderful article by my colleague Paul Blustein, *The Washington Post Magazine,* November 10, 1996.

3. *The Witch Doctors: Making Sense of the Management Gurus,* by John Micklethwait and Adrian Wooldridge (New York: Times Books, 1996), pp. 3, 281.

4. Ibid., pp. 284–86.

5. Robert Picciotto interview, February 26, 2003. Picciotto e-mails, July 20 and 21, 2003.

6. I owe this term to Michael Lewis. See *The New New Thing: A Silicon Valleyz Story* (New York: Penguin USA, 2001), p. 35ff.

7. Johannes Linn interview, June 3, 2003. Linn was the coleader of this group.

8. Jean-François Rischard interview, April 22, 2003. Caio Koch-Weser interview, May 26, 2003. Mark Baird interview, July 11, 2003.

9. Koch-Weser interview, May 26, 2003.

10. Gautam Kaji, the managing director who had selected the insurgent teams, remembers an interchange with Wolfensohn around this time. "Are you asking me to bet the ranch on this?" Wolfensohn asked. Kaji was struck by the question: How could revolutionary change demand less than that? Kaji interview, July 8, 2003.

11. Kaji interview, July 8, 2003. Koch-Weser interview, May 26, 2003. Wilfried Thalwitz, who retired just after the Hay-Adams retreat, had no memory of these interchanges when interviewed, but did not deny them. He died some weeks later. Thalwitz interview, July 17, 2003.

12. Kaji interview, July 8, 2003. Rachel Lomax, now number two at the Bank of England, is the only serious protagonist who declined to be interviewed for this chapter. Her friends say this is because her year at close proximity to Wolfensohn was so unpleasant that she prefers not to talk about it.

13. Kaji interview, July 8, 2003.

14. On April 8, 1996. Wolfensohn addressed the Middle East and North Africa region staff. "I came back exhausted, physically and emotionally," he told them. World Bank video archive.

15. Wolfensohn "just did not have the moral courage to stand up to all of us and tell us we were wrong and we could go jump in the lake if we did not agree." Armeane Choksi e-mail, July 17, 2003.

16. "If I look back I should have been infinitely more decisive," Wolfensohn admitted in one interview, "but I had to balance support for the old guard, not blowing the place up, and bringing about change at the same time." Wolfensohn made this point several times in interviews, and at some length. The passage quoted above comes from a conversation on March 26, 2003, during which Wolfensohn added: "I thought I couldn't throw out the old guard. . . . I was frankly scared to see everyone go, for fear of losing control of the organization. It's a fair comment to say that the management structure was opaque and I was not decisive enough."

17. Ngozi Okonjo-Iweala interview, June 27, 2003.

18. Steve Denning interview, May 2, 2003. Denning has written a book about his ideas: *The Springboard: How Storytelling Ignites Action in Knowledge-Era Organizations* (Boston: Butterworth-Heinemann, 2001). See in particular p. 6.

19. "Steve will say we didn't back him. He's right!" Gautam Kaji says frankly, adding that Denning's crusade appeared more linked to his need for a new job within the Bank than to the virtues of knowledge management. Kaji interviews, July 8, 2003, and January 14, 2004.

20. For example, six vice presidents signed a joint letter to Preston appealing a decision by the management committee not to back an anticorruption initiative. Preston rebuked the letter writers in harsh terms for attempting to go around established processes. On the other hand it is true that Bank managers could pursue their own agendas by persuading shareholders to give them special trust funds, as Kemal Dervis did on Bosnia.

21. "People and Development." Address by James D. Wolfensohn, October 1, 1996.

22. Martine Haas, an assistant professor at Cornell University who has studied the Bank, comments: "It was pretty avant-garde for the Bank to get into knowledge management so early. They were behind the consulting firms, but equivalent to the rest of the corporate sector. And much earlier than the rest of the public sector." Haas interview, June 4, 2003.

23. Mark Baird, an astute Bank official who later played a central role in the reforms, said after his retirement, "The chaos broke the mold of the institution. A lot of ideas percolated." Baird interview, July 11, 2003.

24. Awarded in 1993 for "Distinguished and Pioneering Philanthropy" in the fight against AIDS.

25. Moisés Naím interview, March 5, 2003.

26. Micklethwait and Wooldridge, *The Witch Doctors*, pp. 277–79. The authors also note that in 1995 a management theorist suggested that the *Harvard Business Review* should come with a skull and crossbones on the cover and the warning "not to be taken by the public sector." See p. 289.

27. This judgment is shared by no less a person than Mark Baird, the author of the compact. According to Baird, "Jim was more negotiating a deal than writing a strategy." Asked what was the trigger for the Strategic Compact, Gautam Kaji answered: "It was, how do you dress up this damn thing because we're going to need this extra money." Baird interview, July 11, 2003. Kaji interview, July 8, 2003.

28. "He was fully in control, almost relishing the battle," Mark Baird recalls; "This was the one time he enjoyed dealing with the board," which he usually regarded as a committee of second-rate obstructionists. Baird interview, July 11, 2003.

29. Wolfensohn was also reversing the expectation created by his candidacy. In 1995, *The Economist* had commented: "An early front-runner was James Wolfensohn, who, were this a political campaign, would be considered the candidate of the 'Austerity' party. An investment banker who has been publicly campaigning for office, he hopes to cash in on frustration with the Bank's bloated staff, and has pledged to enact further cuts in personnel on top of the 10–15% reduction over the next three years that Mr. Preston had already announced." "The World Bank—Party Games," *The Economist*, March 11, 1995.

30. Mohamed Muhsin, the chief information officer who managed this process, had a strategy for coping with the Wolfensohn tornado. "We kept reminding him of what we agreed," Muhsin recalls. "The tactic with him has always been to keep him focused on the plan. . . . If not you give him the luxury of being all over the map and raising the ante." Muhsin interview, June 26, 2003.

31. Mark Malloch Brown interview, February 11, 2003.

32. *Who Says Elephants Can't Dance? Inside IBM's Historic Turnaround*, by Louis V. Gerstner Jr. (New York: HarperCollins, 2002), p. 189.

33. Ibid., p. 188.

34. Ibid., p. 213.

35. In 1999, OED damaged its reputation by changing its view on which of its indicators meant most—a change designed to save the Bank's management from embarrassment.

36. Fearing a damning inspection, the members of one infrastructure department started to "pre-QAG" each other.

37. Wolfensohn himself sometimes ignored his own policy, appointing vice presidents for political reasons.

38. In 2002, an ex–World Bank economist named Surjit Bhalla launched a furious attack on the Bank's poverty numbers, claiming they exaggerated human misery. It turned out that Bhalla had calculated poverty using countries' national statistics, whereas the Bank relied on data from household surveys. According to a careful review of this debate, the Bank's methods were better, but the larger point is clear. If it is hard to measure poverty, it's even harder to measure different ways of fighting it. See "Bhalla Versus the World Bank: An Outsider's Perspective," by Jeromin Zettelmeyer, *Finance & Development*, June 2003, pp. 50ff.

39. An example of this uncertainty can be found in the debate over education projects. When Jim Wolfensohn arrived in office, the latest World Bank annual report stated confidently that "the rate of return to primary education investment in developing countries is 18 percent," and that this was "a much higher return than from most investments in the industry and infrastructure sectors." (See "The World Bank Annual Report 1995," p. 18.) But six years later a departing World Bank economist named William Easterly published a book called *The Elusive Quest for Growth*. A whole chapter was devoted to demolishing the idea that education projects boost development.

40. Xavier Devictor remembers the paralysis of that period: "When you are on the verge of a reorganization . . . you basically don't go on mission because you don't know what's going to happen when you're not there. You start wondering about whether there are options in other regions. . . . You spend less time trying to help your clients." Devictor interview, April 21, 2003.

41. Referring to the early chaos of the matrix system, Wolfensohn said: "If I were doing it again, I would have the columns and bars of the matrix report in to the same person, which is what I have now." Wolfensohn interview, April 20, 2003.

CHAPTER SEVEN: THE CANCER OF CORRUPTION

1. Wolfensohn interview, August 8, 2003. Several of Wolfensohn's close colleagues at the Bank made the observation that he wanted to compete intellectually with the institution's research establishment.

2. Peter Eigen, the World Bank's former representative in Kenya, grew so frustrated with the Bank's refusal to confront corruption that he left to set up Transparency International, a corruption watchdog, in 1993. Several of his former colleagues wanted the Bank to back his experiment with a donation,

but this was opposed as a violation of the Bank's apolitical charter by the chief counsel.

3. "It was a very personal kind of association between the Bank and the technocrats of Indonesia. All of us involved with the program, for better *and* worse, felt that kind of emotional commitment." Ben Fisher interview, July 23, 2003. Fisher was an official in the Bank's Jakarta office during much of the 1990s.

4. Fisher interview, July 23, 2003. Fisher managed the logistics of Wolfensohn's trip.

5. Wolfensohn interview, August 8, 2003.

6. Wolfensohn interview, January 4, 2003.

7. Jan Piercy, the U.S. director on the Bank's board, confirms Wolfensohn's impatience with Indonesia's corruption at the time. Piercy interview, September 21, 2003.

8. Stephen Dice, an official in the Bank's Jakarta office, recalls that the Bank had begun challenging corrupt bidding and other abuses in projects before 1996. Dice interview, July 8, 2003. With gathering insistence from 1995, a new arrival in the Jakarta office, Scott Guggenheim, was drawing attention to corruption in rural projects. Guggenheim interview, August 29, 2003.

9. Dennis de Tray, the head of the Bank's Jakarta office, said in his leaving speech in 1999: "I have watched our technical people become extraordinarily frustrated with the government because they can't impose their highly Western, aggressive, conflictual program that requires people to admit their errors and be very open and transparent. These are antithetical to the cultural foundation of much of this country. That's a fact—it's not good or bad, just a fact. I had many times to tell my colleagues, '*be patient—this is their country, their culture. We have to figure out how to operate in it, not the other way around.*'"

10. The country director was Marianne Haug, who tried in the summer of 1996 to win promotion to vice president and was rebuffed. Her setback was widely known, enabling the "trusting" faction within the Bank's Indonesia team to defy her view that the loan to the state banks should be frozen. The battle ended with authority over the loan being removed from one of Haug's Washington-based department heads and transferred to the Bank's resident representative in Jakarta, who in this case followed orders from Haug's superiors. Haug interview, September 8, 2003. Off-the-record interviews supported Haug's version. Looking back, Wolfensohn admits this error. "I was not successful and probably not forceful enough . . . in allowing the Bank to carry on business as usual in Indonesia. I think that before the crisis the Bank should have done more what I did in the case of [Kenya's president]

Moi, which is when we discovered he was not going to do a goddamn thing we stop lending. And in retrospect that's what I should have done in Indonesia, but I didn't. And I should've." Wolfensohn interview, August 8, 2003.

11. "The Chastening," by Paul Blustein, *PublicAffairs,* 2001, p. 96.

12. For example, Scott Guggenheim, an anthropologist in the Bank's Jakarta office, was under the impression that Winters worked for the Asian Development Bank when he talked to him. "At the time Winters was staying at the house of my future wife. He asked me how much the corruption was. Try to take a guess. So I pulled a number out of a hat. It was an off-the-cuff guess. I said it was 30 percent. He then published it, and once the number was out there people start confirming. Then it starts to look like a Chinese crossword puzzle; no matter which way you look at it the number comes to 30 percent. Count it up, down, sideways, diagonally; 30 percent. I still don't believe that number. You get a huge range that goes from 10 percent to 90 percent." Guggenheim interview, August 29, 2003.

13. "Much of the Indonesia office staff was very upset. . . . It makes us all look naïve and foolish, when we know what's happening. . . . I think Dennis was frankly a bit taken aback by the staff reaction." Dice interview, July 8, 2003.

14. The principal author of the memo was Stephen Dice, and when it achieved notoriety later it became known as the "Dice memo."

15. Vikram Nehru interview, July 24, 2003. Nehru was the Bank's lead economist in Jakarta, and I am grateful for his help in understanding the dynamics of the crisis. The economist who bet his own money on the rupiah was a member of Nehru's staff.

16. *In an Uncertain World: Tough Choices from Wall Street to Washington,* by Robert Rubin and Jacob Weisberg (New York: Random House, 2003), p. 222.

17. Blustein, "Chastening," pp. 103–4.

18. De Tray expounded on these issues in an unpublished retrospective article on the crisis.

19. In his leaving speech in 1999, de Tray said: "What we missed was that Indonesia's success did not manifest itself in bad economic policies but in an inability to influence institutional policies. That is what I view as the major shortfall in our vision in Indonesia. It is not that we did not know that institutions were weak—we most certainly did. It was that we—or at least I—really didn't understand how critical those weaknesses would be in the transition from Suharto to post-Suharto."

20. This simile was apparently first cooked up by Paul Volcker, the former Fed chairman who visited Jakarta at the time.

21. This line was cited by four different off-the-record sources.

22. At a meeting on December 23, 1997, held to discuss South Korea's meltdown, Wolfensohn fretted about becoming "little brother to the IMF." Contemporaneous note by a Bank official.

23. Ibid.

24. Ibid. This meeting was the Strategic Forum of January 7, 1998.

25. Wolfensohn adds, "Stiglitz had been recommended to me by the U.S. administration, including Larry Summers. . . . When he started going off about them, they came back to me and said who is this son of a bitch you have working for you? I said, well, he happens to be the person you recommended to me." Wolfensohn interview, August 8, 2003.

26. Technically, IMF money flows to the central bank, not to the government's budget. But by increasing central banks' foreign-currency reserves, IMF loans soften austerity. Governments can finance extra public spending by issuing bonds that are bought by the central bank. Normally the central bank might have to print money to do this, and this would be inflationary. But IMF credits allow the central bank to buy the bonds without printing money. With the exception of the early stage of the Thai crisis, when the IMF mistakenly imposed budget austerity, IMF lending during the crisis was intended to cushion public spending, making the World Bank's efforts to differentiate its role in large part rhetorical.

27. The internal briefing prepared for Wolfensohn's visit lists a number of objectives, including "Clearly differentiate Bank's role from IMF."

28. Wolfensohn interview, January 3, 2003.

29. Fisher interview, July 23, 2003. Mark Malloch Brown interview, August 5, 2003.

30. Ibid.

31. Fisher interview, July 23, 2003. Nehru interview, July 24, 2003.

32. "Speak No Evil: Why the World Bank Failed to Anticipate Indonesia's Deep Crisis," by Marcus W. Brauchli, *Wall Street Journal,* July 14, 1998, sec. A, p. 1.

33. "World Bank Memo Depicts Diverted Funds, Corruption in Jakarta," by Glenn R. Simpson, *Wall Street Journal,* August 19, 1998, sec. A, p. 14.

34. Kim Versak interview, July 8, 2003.

35. Internal memo from de Tray to Jean-Michel Severino, September 4, 1998.

36. "I'm driving along in some rural clove-growing area. I'm on vacation in the eastern islands, with some driver from the hotel, and the driver says how wonderful the IMF is for getting the cloves out from the first family. The Bank was seen as complicit with Suharto; the fund came in with hands clean

in a crisis. The IMF got all credit, but by stealing Bank ideas." Lant Pritchett interview, August 6, 2003.

37. Guggenheim interview, August 29, 2003.

38. The Bank official in the car was Lant Pritchett. Pritchett interview, August 6, 2003.

39. The successor was Mark Baird, a tough Bank official who had been the point man on the Strategic Compact.

40. Guggenheim interview, August 29, 2003.

41. Fisher interview, July 30, 2003. Fisher was the organizer of the visit.

CHAPTER EIGHT: UGANDA'S MYTH AND MIRACLE

1. Wolfensohn's comments on July 13, 1998, are recorded in contemporaneous notes by a World Bank official.

2. Wolfensohn told his Bank colleagues of the exchange with Camdessus on September 28, 1998. Contemporaneous notes by a World Bank official.

3. This interchange took place on September 10, 1998. Contemporaneous notes by a World Bank official.

4. "JDW v. anxious that say as little as possible to the press. If cornered must present united view. *Not one critical quote.*" Contemporaneous notes of a vice presidents' meeting on September 28, 1998, taken by a World Bank official.

5. This was Marianne Haug, the former Indonesia country director who had wanted to confront Suharto's corruption.

6. Marianne Haug interview, October 22, 2003.

7. These coffee figures come from a retrospective review of the Bank's relationship with Uganda conducted by the Bank's internal watchdog, the Operations Evaluation Department.

8. The measurement of poverty is bedeviled by disputes over its definition, but these numbers are taken from perhaps the leading authority on the subject, the World Bank's Martin Ravallion. See in particular "How Did the World's Poorest Fare in the 1990s," by Shaohua Chen and Martin Ravallion, World Bank Policy Research Working Paper, August 2000.

9. Kim Jaycox interview, January 13, 2003.

10. Veena Siddharth interview, May 5, 2003.

11. Jim Adams interview, March 19, 2003.

12. According to Warren Nyamugasira, an NGO leader who attended a Consultative Group in the early 1990s, "We could not speak unless spoken to. The whole structure was designed to underline the dependence of the Africans upon the donors." Nyamugasira interview, May 15, 2003.

13. Ezra Suruma interview, May 16, 2003.

14. The first household survey, which showed that 56 percent of Ugandans lived in poverty, had been conducted in 1992. But there was no follow-up survey until 1997, so in 1995 the trends in poverty were uncertain.

15. Jim Adams interview, September 30, 2003.

16. Suruma interview, May 16, 2003.

17. "I came to the job thinking that the Bank had to be more responsive. The department had a style that was a bit standoffish. We're the Bank. We're the experts. We tell you what to do. I came with the strong view about the importance of government ownership and giving the government space to exert that ownership." Adams interview, March 19, 2003.

18. Adams interview, September 30, 2003. See also *Participation, Deliberation, and Policy Reform: Theory and Evidence from Bolivia,* by Kevin Morrison and Matthew Singer, presented at the Latin American Studies Association Conference in Dallas, Texas, March 27–29, 2003.

19. The economist was Walter Elkan of Durham University, who was rare among development specialists in the early 1970s in recognizing the virtues of markets over planning. Tumusiime appeared to reject Elkan's teaching at the time, but an appreciation of markets surfaced later on in his thinking. Elkan interview, May 27, 2003.

20. Emmanuel Tumusiime-Mutebile interview, May 13, 2003.

21. Allister Moon interview, February 5, 2003. Damoni Kitabire interview, February 14, 2003.

22. According to Jim Adams, "Tumusiime is the best counterpart I've ever worked with. He could be rough. He always made it clear he was your equal." Adams interview, March 19, 2003.

23. "I told him, look, we know you are going to fail, allow us to continue preparing for when your program fails." Tumusiime-Mutebile interview, May 13, 2003. Tumusiime's willingness to stand up to Museveni is almost unique in the Ugandan government. According to Damoni Kitabire, who worked under Tumusiime for seventeen years, "If he thinks the president is wrong he will call him and tell him to his face. Which is really really rare." Kitabire interview, February 14, 2003.

24. Perhaps the most influential visitor was Paul Collier of Oxford, who later became head of research at the Bank. Tumusiime recalls one meeting between Collier and Museveni: "He basically explained the quantity theory of money. And Museveni has learnt it, really seen it in policy terms, as too much money chasing too few goods. And that has been very helpful to me. I don't have to teach Museveni the dangers of unsound finance." Tumusiime-Mutebile interview, May 13, 2003.

25. Allister Moon, one of the British advisers who worked for Tumusiime,

remembers: "He would happily have me in meetings with the cabinet. Precisely because he was so confident he could use foreigners so well. His attitude was, first, I'm perfectly prepared to listen to you and second I'm perfectly prepared to disagree with you." Damoni Kitabire, a Ugandan member of Team Tumusiime, sums up his attitude: "If you can do the job, and you can do it on time, and do it well, I don't care where you come from and I don't care if you are black or white." Moon interview, February 5, 2003. Kitabire interview, February 14, 2003.

26. Mark Henstridge interview, March 7, 2003. Henstridge worked for Team Tumusiime, and kindly reviewed a draft of this chapter.

27. "There's no doubt that Jim Adams transformed the relationship between the Bank and Uganda. I think he took the cue from Jim Wolfensohn." Tumusiime-Mutebile interview, May 13, 2003. According to Louis Kasekende, then a senior Bank of Uganda official, "The Bank was learning from its mistakes. It learnt that too many conditions did not work. . . . Jim Adams listened to us. He related to us. . . . At a more general level even Wolfensohn himself was ready to give the Africans a chance to be in charge and learn from past mistakes." Kasekende interview, January 30, 2003. It is worth noting that the Ugandans were not polite about all donors. According to Tumusiime, "Some are bad. Others are outright useless."

28. This interchange is captured in a documentary film made about the Bank in Uganda: *Our Friends at the Bank,* directed by Peter Chappell.

29. Ibid.

30. This was Mark Baird, later point man on the Strategic Compact and country director in Indonesia.

31. Zie Gariyo, the leader of the Uganda Debt Network, a prominent NGO, remembers that it was the Bank that saw to it that NGO leaders were invited to the conference. The Bank's resident representative, Brian Falconer, asked Gariyo for a list of 80 NGO representatives who should be invited. Both Gariyo and Warran Nyamugasira, a fellow NGO leader, recall how the spectacle of World Bank experts presenting sophisticated papers on poverty went some way to softening their suspicion that the Bank cared only about growth. Nyamugasira interview, May 15, 2003. Gariyo interview, May 17, 2003.

32. Tony Burdon interview, May 27, 2003.

33. The consultant was Zerubabel Ojoo. The spreadsheet wizard was Mimi Klutstein-Meyer. Three World Bank economists helped to design the survey and analyze the data: Emmanuel Ablo, Mathew Verghis, and Ritva Reinikka.

34. Ritva Reinikka interview, February 20, 2003. Zerubabel Ojoo interview, May 13, 2003. Keith Muhakanizi interview, May 16, 2003. See also "How Research Can Assist Policy: The Case of Economic Reforms in Uganda," by

John McKinnon and Ritva Reinikka, *World Bank Research Observer* no. 2, pp. 267ff.

35. *Assessing Aid: What Works, What Doesn't, and Why,* by David Dollar and Lant Pritchett (Washington, D.C.: World Bank/Oxford University Press, 1998).

36. See "Uganda's Universal Primary Education: The Role of Electoral Politics, Fiscal Stability and Information Campaign Against Capture." Background paper for "World Development Report, 2003."

37. A bit later, in June 1999, Adams moved from Washington to run the Uganda and Tanzania programs from the Bank's office in Tanzania.

38. Muhakanizi interview, May 16, 2003. Muhakanizi is a prominent Tumusiime lieutenant who oversaw the participatory poverty survey.

39. For an example of the lessons drawn from the "Ugandan model," see *Aid and Reform in Uganda,* by Torgny Holmgren et al. (Kampala, Uganda: Economic Policy Research Center, 1999), p. 46. Analysts from outside the Bank—especially those in the NGO movement who had long criticized the strict conditionality associated with structural adjustment—were even more prone to cite the Ugandan model in this way.

40. "There are certain things we have done to tie our hands behind our backs, because these are agents of restraint. That conditionality is good. Fiscal consolidation, the reduction of the budget deficit, was a necessary condition for restoring macro stability. And until the government's hand was tied it was not going to allow fiscal consolidation. . . . So if there are no domestic agents of restraint, the IMF and World Bank must provide the restraint, there are no two ways about it. Conditionality has a role." Tumusiime-Mutebile interview, May 13, 2003.

41. See "Changes in Poverty and Inequality," by Simon Appleton, in *Uganda's Recovery: The Role of Farms, Firms and Government,* edited by Ritva Reinikka and Paul Collier (Washington, D.C.: World Bank, 2001), p. 84.

42. Between 1988 and 1998, the World Bank approved a whole string of loans to Uganda. There was an Economic Recovery Credit worth $125 million, an Agricultural Sector Adjustment loan worth $115 million, and three Structural Adjustment Credits worth a total of $330 million. There was only one loan with poverty in the title, and it was worth a modest $28 million. Yet over this period more than one in ten Ugandans was lifted out of poverty.

43. Coffee's impact on national poverty rates is cited in "Building Poverty Reduction Strategies in Developing Countries," a paper prepared for the Bank's Development Committee in September 1999.

44. This observation comes from Allister Moon, a Tumusiime lieutenant who later joined the World Bank and promoted participation in chaotic Georgia. Moon interview, February 5, 2003.

CHAPTER NINE: A FRAMEWORK FOR DEVELOPMENT

1. Javed Burki, the former vice president for Latin America and the Caribbean, remembers: "If it had not been presented in the spirit of eureka, Wolfensohn's contribution would have been excellent." Burki interview, October 17, 2003. Numerous other sources recalled that Wolfensohn's excessive claims to originality alienated his audience.

2. Javed Burki is among those who remember the reluctance of senior staff to tell Wolfensohn his ideas weren't new. Burki interview, October 17, 2003.

3. The senior official was Jack Boorman, the head of the IMF's Policy Development and Review Department.

4. Burki interview, October 17, 2003.

5. "In the Salomon Brothers partners' meeting in the morning, at eight o'clock in the morning, you would have all the managing partners frequently screaming and yelling at each other and the smoke was flying from cigars and the language was terrible, and what the fuck are you doing here, and what is this over there, and I used to find this coming from Schroders unbelievable, but wonderful because everything was on the table. I mean nothing was on the table at Schroders, it was all polished. But the beautiful thing about Salomon was that you had these fights, but the thing you knew was that the guy that had just called you an ignorant son of a bitch, when the client came in or there was a challenge to the firm you could be absolutely certain he would defend you to the death. Absolutely certain. That is the one thing about Salomon that I cherished." Wolfensohn interview, August 10, 2003.

6. Wolfensohn cited Tanzania's example in his next annual meetings speech, delivered on September 28, 1999.

7. See the World Bank's "World Development Report, 2000/2001," pp. 280–82.

8. The other founder of AES was the levelheaded Roger Sant. If Koch-Weser had cultivated Sant as much as Bakke, he might have avoided trouble.

9. The term was borrowed from GE and IBM, which had pioneered this form of brainstorming.

10. Isabel Guerrero interview, April 7, 2003.

11. Quiroga's speech is captured on video. I am also grateful for several off-the-record conversations with Bank officials who recalled the meeting.

12. "Quiroga was not sufficiently deferential. He was excited about his own ideas." Burki interview, October 17, 2003.

13. The paper was coauthored by Nick Stern, Stiglitz's successor as World Bank chief economist. Their article appeared in a volume entitled *Development Strategy and Management of the Market Economy*, edited by Edmond Malinvaud et al. (Oxford: Clarendon Press, 1997). The French director who circulated the article was Jean-Claude Milleron.

14. The Italian director was Franco Passacantando. Jan Piercy, the U.S. director, recalls: "Jim got very curt. He took it so personally. Franco had to say it two or three times." Piercy interview, October 23, 2003.

15. Pablo Guerrero, a Bank official who presented the Comprehensive Development Framework status report at the meeting, recalls that the mention of the Berlin meeting was the last straw. Guerrero interview, October 27, 2003. (Pablo Guerrero is Isabel Guerrero's cousin.)

16. See "Wolf at the Door," by Robert Chote, *Financial Times,* April 14, 1999, p. 18.

17. These are the verdicts of Alberto Leyton, a Bolivian official who served as an adviser to Quiroga and who was involved in the implementation of the program. Leyton interview, October 22, 2003.

18. Elected in 1997, the Blair government turned the Overseas Development Administration, which had been a junior partner to the Foreign Office, into a full-fledged government ministry called the Department for International Development; and Britain's aid budget jumped nearly one-fifth over the next three years. Coming to power in 1998, Gerhard Schröder's government reversed Germany's traditional hostility to debt relief, and now the Germans vied with Britain for the status of chief cheerleader.

19. To preserve the idea that the World Bank and the IMF never have to go without repayment (and therefore to protect the Bank's credit status), the debt-relief scheme created a trust fund that repaid the Bretton Woods institutions in lieu of repayment from developing countries. The trust fund was partially financed by the taxpayers of the rich countries and partly by a transfer from the Bank's operating income.

20. This was the view of a senior aide to House of Representatives Speaker Dennis Hastert. See "Giving In on Foreign Aid Bill, G.O.P. Finds an Election Issue," by Tim Weiner, *The New York Times,* November 5, 1999, sec. A, p. 28.

21. This interchange is lodged in the memory of Kevin Watkins, Oxfam's director of research. Watkins e-mail, October 30, 2003.

22. "Jim said to me after we left that he felt very much like the little Jewish boy that they all felt they needed to educate (convert?) to a more moral/ethical stance." Caroline Anstey e-mail, December 17, 2003.

23. Justin Forsyth of Oxfam recalls that Wolfensohn reacted defensively to calls for deeper debt relief rather than embracing the campaigners as allies in furthering his cause. "He reacted with hostility to people who said it ought to go further, even though he himself had originally wanted it to go further." Forsyth interview, March 5, 2003.

24. See "Delayed Debt Relief Will Cost Uganda Dearly" (letter from Mr. J. S. Mayanja-Nkangi), *Financial Times,* March 10, 1997, p. 22.

25. Tony Burdon interview, May 27, 2003.

26. The outcome was shaped by the fact that key players in the debt discussion knew Uganda intimately: Britain was the country's biggest bilateral donor, and was keen to apply its lessons broadly; Oxfam and other NGOs had long embraced Uganda as their poster child; and Ugandan NGO representatives visited Europe at the invitation of British NGOs to lobby on the debt issue. Masood Ahmed, the Bank's senior negotiator on debt relief, recalls Uganda's influence: "We kept on referring to it as the Uganda Model." Uganda's influence was also helped by the fact that Paul Collier, the Bank's director of research, knew Uganda's leadership intimately. Meanwhile, Tony Burdon, who had worked for Oxfam in Uganda at the time of Wolfensohn's 1995 visit and later joined the board of Jubilee 2000, recalls: "The example of Uganda was there all the time. The Poverty Action Fund was well known. The PEAP was well known globally as a model. The consultative process, the participatory poverty survey—all were well known globally as an approach. All the donors were using Uganda as an example." Ahmed interview, March 26, 2003. Burdon interview, May 27, 2003. Zie Gariyo interview, May 17, 2003.

27. *Assessing Aid: What Works, What Doesn't, and Why,* by David Dollar and Lant Pritchett (Washington, D.C.: World Bank/Oxford University Press, 1998), p. 1.

28. "Organizing for Empowerment: An Interview with AES's Roger Sant and Dennis Bakke," by Suzy Wetlaufer, *Havard Business Review,* January–February 1999, p. 111.

29. An interest in management literature permeated Clinton's "New Democrats" and Blair's "New Labour." Clinton's reinventing government initiative was an attempt to apply management theory to the workings of the federal government. In October 1995, Blair sent his entire shadow cabinet to Templeton College, Oxford, to spend a weekend learning about management theory.

CHAPTER TEN: FROM SEATTLE TO TIBET

1. "The Non-Governmental Order," *The Economist,* December 11, 1999.

2. Ibid.

3. Wolfensohn interview, January 4, 2003.

4. Justin Forsyth interview, March 5, 2003. Forsyth represented Oxfam in Washington.

5. Bruce Rich interview, January 22, 2003. Rich attended the dinner with colleagues from the Environmental Defense Fund. The vice president was Ismael Serageldin.

6. Mark Malloch Brown interview, August 5, 2003. Malloch Brown had been reading Chapter 3 of Niall Ferguson's *Empire: The Rise and Demise of the British World Order and the Lessons for Global Power* (New York: Basic Books, 2003). See in particular pp. 138ff.

7. The Bank did finance second phases for two large dams—in Lesotho and in China—during this period, but it did not initiate new ones. Alessandro Palmieri interview, December 8, 2003.

8. "Skewered in Seattle," by John Micklethwait and Adrian Wooldridge, *Los Angeles Times*, December 5, 1999, p. M1.

9. Summers did want to use Wolfensohn's reappointment to secure Stiglitz's departure. But he stopped short of making this condition explicit to Wolfensohn, since Wolfensohn might have called his bluff, circumventing the Treasury via his ties to the White House and the Bank's European shareholders.

10. "The Insider: What I Learned at the World Economic Crisis," by Joseph Stiglitz, *New Republic*, April 17, 2000.

11. Stiglitz appeared on *The NewsHour with Jim Lehrer*.

12. See "U.S. Hegemony and the World Bank," by Robert H. Wade, *Review of International Political Economy* 9, no. 2, May 2002, pp. 201–29.

13. Notably T. N. Srinivasan of Yale and Angus Deaton of Princeton.

14. *Growth* Is *Good for the Poor*, by David Dollar and Aart Kraay (Washington, D.C.: World Bank, 2000).

15. Stiglitz was among those who believed Wolfensohn was moving to the right under U.S. pressure. "Jim did want to differentiate the Bank from the IMF, but since the April protests he has backtracked," he told *Institutional Investor*. See "Wolfensohn Agonistes," by Deepak Gopinath, *Institutional Investor*, September 2000, p. 147.

16. The following section on China draws substantially from Robert Wade of the London School of Economics, who generously shared his unpublished description of the Bank's Qinghai adventure. Having interviewed many confidential sources whom Wade presumably also interviewed, I reached conclusions similar to his.

17. See "How Did the World's Poorest Fare in the 1990s," by Shaohua Chen and Martin Ravallion, World Bank Policy Research Working Paper, August 2000, Table 2. It's worth noting that Surjit Bhalla, an Indian economist, suggests that the poverty-fighting record has been better than the Bank's numbers suggest. According to Bhalla, the incidence of extreme poverty worldwide fell from 44 percent to 13 percent between 1980 and 2000—the

number for 2000 being considerably lower than the Bank's estimate of 23 percent. Whatever the truth of this debate, there is no doubt that the world's progress against poverty has depended to a large degree on progress in China.

18. The task manager was Petros Aklilu.

19. The Tibet campaigner was Kate Saunders. Saunders e-mail, December 12, 2003.

20. Tibet Information Network, "News Updates," April 27, 1999, available at http://www.tibetinfo.net/newsupdates/nu270499.htm. The story also asserted that the Bank would be investing "hundreds of millions of dollars" in the Qinghai project, even though the real number was $40 million.

21. See "World Bank's China Western Poverty Reduction Project Summary Paper," May 28, 1999.

22. The Bank's critics sometimes argued that the settlement area was culturally Tibetan because it was in a part of the Qinghai that was classified as a "Mongolian-Tibetan Autonomous Prefecture." But this did not mean that Mongolians or Tibetans predominated: three-quarters of the people living in the prefecture were Han Chinese. It was not only the activists who made much of the "autonomous prefecture" label. The U.S. executive director emphasized it at the board meeting on June 24, 1999, when she voted against the Qinghai loan. It is also worth noting that even if you considered the sub-prefecture level, the claim that the settlers would be arriving in a "culturally Tibetan" area did not stand up. Dulan County, which would play host to the settlers, was 53 percent Han and only 23 percent Tibetan. See Table 2 in ibid.

23. The letter was dated May 28, 1999. The lead organization was the Center for International Environmental Law.

24. The press release was put out jointly by the International Campaign for Tibet, Friends of the Earth, and the Center for International Environmental Law.

25. See letter from Wolfensohn to Rep. James McGovern, June 24, 1999.

26. Harrison Ford's wife had written a movie script about Tibet. She was part of Wolfensohn's social circle in Jackson Hole. "I'm very good friends with Harrison Ford and Melissa. And they were leading charges against the Bank. They'd call me up because they would be embarrassed about it. Richard Gere was involved. He sent me a book of his pictures. . . . Nancy [Pelosi] is another very good friend of mine. And her kids are friends with my kids. So there were a lot of friendships here. . . . Before I came to the Bank I had been a supporter of the Dalai Lama and I knew the Dalai Lama. . . . He still regards me as a friend." Wolfensohn interview, August 9, 2003.

27. One Oxfam official remembers attending an NGO retreat in October 1995, soon after Oxfam had shared a platform with Wolfensohn. Her roommate

during the retreat, a woman from a German NGO, refused to talk to her during the three-day period. Veena Siddharth interview, May 5, 2003.

28. John Ackerly of the International Campaign for Tibet, the group that filed the Inspection Panel case, remembers that the banner was erected by Students for a Free Tibet. "Personally I didn't really agree with the tactic. I was even worried that people hanging the banner could cause a backlash. It would be seen as grandstanding. The message was unnuanced, it had the word *genocide*, which I didn't agree with either." Kate Saunders, of the Tibet Information Network in London, was also uncomfortable with the use of the contentious term *genocide*. Meanwhile, Phuntsog Wangyal of the Tibet Foundation in London actively favored World Bank involvement in Tibetan development. "Westerners have this romantic ideal of the Tibetans living in their tent, burning dung for fuel. Tibetans in Tibet like any other human beings prefer a better standard of living, health care, and education," he observed, plausibly. Since Wangyal spent his youth engaged in armed resistance to Chinese occupation and subsequently represented the Dalai Lama in London, he speaks with some authority. But his voice was drowned out by the extreme wing of the Tibet movement. Ackerly interview with Amelia Branczik, October 30, 2003. Saunders interview with Branczik, November 14, 2003. Wangyal interview and e-mail with Branczik, November 18 and December 29, 2003.

29. The bill containing this falsity was introduced in September 1999 by Rep. Christopher Cox, Republican of California. Wade, unpublished.

30. The American was Daja Meston. At the time it seemed possible that he had been pushed from the window, but it turned out that the pressure of intensive interrogation had driven Meston to attempt escape. Ackerly interview with Branczik, October 30, 2003.

31. A manager present at the Jackson Hole retreat comments, "Most people are intimidated by Wolfensohn, no matter what they say. He has you by the hair and the balls at the same time." A second manager who was present comments, "That wasn't unusual. When something went wrong he always took it out on someone."

32. Wade, unpublished.

33. Ibid.

34. Ibid.

35. Ibid.

36. Wolfensohn interview, January 4, 2003. One senior Bank official adds: "We were secretly hoping that the Chinese would withdraw so that the problem would go away."

37. Jan Piercy, the U.S. board director, recalls, "We knew going into the board meeting that the effect of conditional acceptance would be for China to

withdraw, which it did. That was scripted." She adds that the United States did not want the project to go ahead, because congressional opinion was so hostile that proceeding despite an American no vote would have been disastrous for IDA. Piercy interview, September 22, 2003. Piercy's version is supported by one senior Bank official, who points out that the United States was lobbying European directors to vote against the project. On the other hand, Wade suggests that the United States hoped that the project would go ahead, even though it felt it had to satisfy Congress by voting against it.

38. "Cost of Doing Business: Fiduciary and Safeguard Policies and Compliance," by Dan Ritchie (unpublished World Bank Study), July 16, 2001.

39. This appears to have surprised some Tibet activists. Wolfensohn recalls: "Within days [after the Bank's withdrawal from the Qinghai project] I had the same NGOs coming to me and saying, 'Well now what are they doing?' And I'd say, 'How the fuck do I know what they're doing? You just got us out of there!' 'And are they going to follow the environmental requirements?' they would ask. I'd tell them, 'You're out of your minds. Here we were with an agreement with them to do all these things. We'd pushed them very far, the Chinese. They were ready to accept all these things.' I said, 'You had all this, and then you pushed it over the edge and you expect us to come in and take responsibility. Are you crazy?'" Wolfensohn interview, August 9, 2003.

40. The project manager was Julia Bucknall. Bucknall interview, January 27, 2003.

41. "There are so many rules and safeguards now that it is becoming very expensive for some borrowers to use us," Wolfensohn told the *Financial Times*. "World Bank Chief Under Fire After Chinese Project," by Stephen Fidler and Sathnam Sanghera, July 14, 2000, p. 10.

CHAPTER ELEVEN: WAKING UP TO TERROR

1. Paul O'Neill interview, March 15, 2002.

2. The impact on the Bank's finances resulting from withdrawal from middle-income countries would depend on whether shareholders allowed the Bank to keep its $30 billion or so in accumulated reserves. The shareholders might argue that if reserves were no longer needed to create a capital base to support market lending, the reserves should be returned to them. On the other hand, if they allowed the Bank to continue to enjoy the revenue from its reserves in addition to donations from shareholders for the IDA kitty, the Bank would have the benefit of an endowment, and so would be a cross between a big foundation and the United Nations. See also Chapter 4, note 55.

3. Moreover, time was to prove the late 1990s exceptional: in 2002 and 2003, Brazil was frozen out of the capital markets for almost a year, and was forced to rely upon official lenders like the Bank in the interim.

4. Meltzer argues that there *is* a cost to the Bank's shareholders, in that the Bank's market-based lending is underwritten by rich countries' promise to recapitalize the Bank in the event that borrowers default. Extending this promise carries a theoretical cost. However, it is only theoretical. There is no evidence that bond markets place any real value on these quasi-loan guarantees: neither the United States nor any of the Bank's other backers are being made to pay higher interest rates on their own borrowing because of the guarantees they have extended to the Bank. Meltzer also argues that, since there is a limit to the Bank's capacity to lend, loans to middle-income countries crowd out loans to poorer ones. But this is a theoretical objection, too. Except during the emerging-market crisis, the Bank has not recently been in danger of hitting its prudential lending limits. Its problem has been the opposite: declining demand for its lending. Allan Meltzer interview, November 25, 2003.

5. As noted in Chapter 4, the Bank helped Brazil to put in place a successful AIDS program in the early 1990s, and around the same time it improved the design of Brazil's land reform. The Bank's constructive role on AIDS in Brazil is noted both by Michael Merson, who headed the United Nations Global AIDS program, and by Murilo Portugal, who was then the director of the Brazilian Finance Ministry. Merson interview, November 12, 2003. Portugal interview, November 18, 2003.

6. Meltzer had known Taylor since Taylor had been a young economics professor; indeed, Taylor's most famous academic paper had appeared in a journal that Meltzer edited. The article was "Discretion Versus Policy Rules in Practice," by John B. Taylor, published in the *Carnegie-Rochester Conference Series on Public Policy* 39, pp. 195–214. Meltzer interview, November 25, 2003.

7. John Taylor, the international point man at the Treasury, was not told of the change, and he went to Wolfensohn's home and found it dark and empty. Taylor interview, November 20, 2003.

8. O'Neill refused to be interviewed for this book, though I had some access to him in 2001 and 2002 when I was working at *The Washington Post*. However, three people with insights into his thinking in early 2001 told me separately that he was out to replace Wolfensohn.

9. In early 1999, the head of the staff association took one of the managing directors on two walks through the Bank's offices. They made one tour at seven A.M. and another at nine P.M. A remarkable number of the people who'd been there early in the morning were still there in the evening. Jamil Sopher interview with Amelia Branczik, October 28, 2003.

10. IBRD Monthly Staffing Report, January 6, 2003, p. 5.

11. "I forced an appointment with him: I said, I'm nominated by the United States, I am president of the Bank, we do live in Washington, and you're

going to the Development Committee [which was to meet during the Bank's spring meetings a bit later]." Wolfensohn interview, August 9, 2003.

12. Note that the choice of time period is important here. As mentioned in the previous chapter, between 1987 and 1998 the total number of people in poverty failed to decline at all—though to be fair it did not increase either, despite rapid growth in the world's population.

13. Nick Stern interview, December 5, 2003.

14. Wolfensohn interview, August 9, 2003.

15. Ibid.

16. Morallina George, the head of the Bank's staff association, recalls: "Staff realized that they needed to show some solidarity and band together to strengthen the Bank against this." George interview with Branczik, November 5, 2003.

17. Jamil Sopher, the one-time head of the staff association, remembers a colleague saying: "We bitch, we bitch, we bitch, nothing has improved, this is a terrible place, I'm putting in my time, I'll leave when I can, but I'm tired of bitching." Sopher interview with Branczik, October 28, 2003.

18. As I describe in Chapter 12, the impetus to expand the Bank into health came from outside the institution also. In the early 1990s, public health officials at the World Health Organization fought to get the Bank involved in fighting AIDS, knowing that they were failing by themselves.

19. Wolfensohn recalls: "It was a huge kick in the stomach. It was a low point for me. I think maybe the only time I thought of getting out was when that article was written. I don't recall any period that I was more unhappy than then." Wolfensohn interview, August 9, 2003.

20. "At a Difficult Time, Spiritual Adviser Aided First Lady's Search," by Bob Woodward, *The Washington Post*, June 23, 1996, p. A01.

21. "I think all my friends would tell you that throughout my life I have been extremely sensitive to criticism." Wolfensohn interview, August 9, 2003.

22. Ibid.

23. Ibid.

24. Ibid.

25. These names come from three well-placed sources. McPherson was considered before Reed, though the timing is hazy. When asked about both names, John Taylor, the top international man at the Treasury, said he could not comment, but then commented that "you sound like you're talking to people about these things who really know." Taylor interview, November 20, 2003.

26. The CNN cameraman was John Bodnar. His recollections helped to reconstruct this sequence. I am also grateful to three others who were there: Nick Stern, Jane Holden, and Caroline Anstey.

27. This has been documented in the case of Pakistan by Jessica Stern of Harvard. See her book *Terror in the Name of God: Why Religious Militants Kill* (New York: Echo, 2003).

28. This report was based partly on work done by the Bank, led by Enrique Rueda-Sabater.

29. The speech was delivered on March 6, 2002, at the Woodrow Wilson Center for Scholars in Washington, D.C.

30. "My concern as an American as well as president of the World Bank was that I did not want the U.S. and in particular George Bush to go down to Monterrey and run into torrents of criticism when the mood was for everybody to commit some additional funding. It was a very rare intervention, but I did go over to the White House and I did say this is not me begging for money. But you cannot let the president go down there with empty words. You just cannot. I think I was somewhat effective." Wolfensohn interview, August 10, 2003.

31. Caroline Anstey e-mail, December 15, 2003. Anstey was the Bank's head of press and chief message strategist at the time.

32. Wolfensohn interview, August 10, 2003.

33. This count comes from Steve Radelet, the U.S. Treasury official who worked on the U.S. government's performance criteria. See *Challenging Foreign Aid: A Policymaker's Guide to the Millennium Challenge Account,* by Steven Radelet (Washington, D.C.: Center for Global Development, 2003), pp. 20–21. Radelet interview, December 5, 2003.

34. See "Reducing Child Mortality: Can Public Health Deliver?" by Jennifer Bryce, Shams el Arifeen, George Pariyo, Claudio F. Lanata, Davidson Gwatkin, Jean-Pierre Habicht, and the Multi-Country Evaluation of IMCI Study Group, *The Lancet* 362, July 12, 2003. Michael Clemens of the Center for Global Development in Washington adds that the median poor country closed the gap between its maternal mortality rate and zero at a rate of just over 1 percent per year during the 1990s, but attaining the Millennium Development Goal of reducing maternal mortality by three-quarters would require cutting maternal mortality at a rate of over 5 percent a year—an impossible acceleration. See "The Trouble with the MDGs: Confronting Expectations of Aid and Development Success," by Michael Clemens, Charles Kenny, and Todd Moss, Center for Global Development Working Paper 40, posted on May 10, 2004, at www.cgdev.org.

35. See Table 2.15 in the World Bank's "World Development Indicators, 2004," p. 94.

36. For a detailed argument as to why the millennium goal of universal primary enrollment will not be attained, see "The Long Walk to School: Inter-

national Education Goals in Historical Perspective," by Michael Clemens, Center for Global Development Working Paper 37, posted on March 16, 2004, at www.cgdev.org. The evidence presented by Clemens suggests that the typical developing country closes the gap between its primary-school enrollment rate and full enrollment by 4 percent a year. The Millennium Development Goals assume that Africa can close the gap at four times that rate, an achievement that's never been seen in the history of development.

CHAPTER TWELVE: A PLAGUE UPON DEVELOPMENT

1. "Death Watch: The Global Response to AIDS in Africa; World Shunned Signs of the Coming Plague," by Barton Gellman, *The Washington Post*, July 5, 2000, p. A01. Gellman's article is a journalistic masterpiece.

2. Kim Jaycox, the Bank's vice president for Africa in the late 1980s and early 1990s, recalls no interest from the Bank's board on AIDS. Richard Skolnik, director of health programs in South Asia during the 1990s, has the same recollection, adding that the Bank's staff arranged briefings for board members on AIDS that were sparsely attended. Jaycox interview, December 10, 2003. Skolnik interviews, December 9, 2003, and March 2, 2004.

3. The WHO director general who recognized the threat of AIDS was Halfdan Mahler. His successor, who refused to recognize the threat of AIDS, was Hiroshi Nakajima. Gellman, "Death Watch."

4. The intelligence official was Katherine J. Hall. Ibid.

5. Ibid. In a retrospective admission that the AIDS effort had been preposterously small, President Bush pledged in 2003 to spend $15 billion over five years on international AIDS programs, a twenty-four-fold increase from the figure a decade earlier, measured in nominal dollars.

6. One exception may have been Uganda. Kim Jaycox recalls urging Uganda's president, Yoweri Museveni, to distribute condoms to his armed forces; soldiers are required to wear helmets when they go into battle, and they should be required to wear them, too, when they go into the bedroom, Jaycox suggested. Shortly thereafter, Museveni took a newly vigorous stance on HIV prevention. Jaycox interview, December 10, 2003.

7. The meeting took place on October 9, 1990. The organizer of the presentation was Hazel Denton, senior project economist in the Population, Nutrition, and Health Division of the West Africa Department. The Nigerian minister was Dr. Olikoye Ransom-Kuti. Contemporaneous notes from Hazel Denton and Denton interview, December 3, 2003. Later the Bank did prepare an AIDS project in Nigeria, but the preparations were disrupted when political turmoil drove the Bank to freeze its relationship with the country.

8. Katherine Marshall e-mails, December 9 and December 10, 2003. Marshall was the director of the Sahel department between 1990 and 1994.

9. "Project Performance Assessment Report: India National AIDS Control Project," July 2, 2003. Operations Evaluation Department. See p. 5 for slow disbursement and p. 2 for the suggestion on sex with foreigners.

10. In several countries the Bank built smallish AIDS components into broader health projects. Denton e-mail, January 23, 2004.

11. I was the *Economist*'s Africa correspondent at the time, and Stamps fed me terrifying numbers on HIV prevalence rates. The resulting article was the most unpopular piece I wrote during my posting in Zimbabwe.

12. A Nexis search of the world's major newspapers for stories mentioning "HIV," "World Bank," and the word "Preston" within twenty words of "AIDS" turned up just one story. This turned out to be a reference to a speech on AIDS given in 2003 in the Bank's Preston Auditorium.

13. In 1995, the Bank's Annual Report noted defensively that it had lent more than $800 million to fifty-one HIV projects over the past ten years, but this is less than it appeared; it was another way of saying that AIDS had accounted for less than half a percent of the Bank's portfolio. "World Bank Annual Report, 1995," p. 18.

14. The World Development Report did point out that AIDS should be prioritized because it kills people in their prime. But the leadership of the health sector within the Bank remained reluctant to elevate AIDS above other diseases.

15. Jaycox interview, December 10, 2003.

16. One reason for disbelief was that the AIDS data came from towns, and it was wrongly assumed that rural prevalence would never rise below very low levels.

17. "Poor Man's Plague," *The Economist*, September 21, 1991, p. 21.

18. "AIDS Forecast Focuses on Third World; WHO Predicts Epidemic Will Ebb in West as African Death Toll Soars," by Malcolm Gladwell, *The Washington Post*, June 17, 1991, p. 1.

19. "AIDS in Latin America—A Special Report; In Deception and Denial, an Epidemic Looms," by James Brooke, *The New York Times*, January 25, 1993, p. 1.

20. These quotes are from a memo signed by the Bank's legal adviser Louis Forget and human development director Richard Feachem. The memo is cited in Gellman, "Death Watch."

21. Richard Feachem claims that the failure to boost lending was partly because of the reorganization that gripped the Africa region in 1996, and partly because the philosophy of country "ownership" made it harder than ever to push unwanted issues. Feachem interview, March 5, 2003. By contrast,

Keith Hansen notes that all donors including the Bank made the mistake of losing focus after the arrival of antiretroviral therapy in rich countries in 1996 reduced the sense of alarm there, and also as it appeared that the early round of AIDS projects had achieved little. Hansen interview, November 21, 2003.

22. A Nexis search of the world's major newspapers for stories mentioning "HIV," "World Bank," and the word "Wolfensohn" within twenty words of "AIDS" turned up just four stories during Wolfensohn's first four years at the Bank. Only one of these quoted Wolfensohn speaking out about AIDS; the other three contained no signs of his concern for the subject. By contrast, the same search for the four years starting June 1, 1999, turned up 146 stories.

23. See *Intensifying Action Against HIV/AIDS in Africa: Responding to a Development Crisis* (Washington, D.C.: World Bank, 2000), p. 35. I am indebted to Noah Eaker of Dartmouth College, who kindly analyzed a series of World Bank reports on AIDS for me.

24. Looking back, Wolfensohn acknowledges this error. "I think I was too slow before then [1999] to be honest. . . . I don't think I gave it the urgency I should have." Wolfensohn interview, December 15, 2003.

25. "I had found that there was virtually nothing going on in the fight against AIDS. The Bank programs were desperately bad. I heard the numbers, which hit me as hard as anyone else. They were a massive call to action." Hans Binswanger interview, November 13, 2003.

26. Binswanger was the first openly HIV positive Bank employee; as of 2003, he remained the only one. Binswanger interview, November 13, 2003.

27. Debrework Zewdie interview, December 9, 2003. Hans Binswanger and Keith Hansen, Madavo's special assistant at the time, also remember the demographic conference as a defining moment. Binswanger interview, November 13, 2003. Hansen interview, November 21, 2003.

28. "When I went to the Geneva conference I was totally shocked, and I was also shocked by the low quality of our programs, the very few that we had." Binswanger interview, November 13, 2003.

29. Binswanger interview, November 13, 2003. Zewdie interview, December 9, 2003.

30. After leaving WHO, Mann founded the *Health and Human Rights* journal. He also organized the first world conference on health and human rights, at Harvard in 1996.

31. The study was *Confronting AIDS: Public Priorities in a Global Epidemic,* by Martha Ainsworth and Mead Over (New York: Oxford University Press, 1999).

32. After his death in a plane crash in 1998, *The New York Times* obituary quoted Mann: "Against AIDS we will prevail together, for we will refuse to be split, or to cast into the shadows those persons, groups and nations that are affected." September 4, 1998.

33. Zewdie interview, December 9, 2003.

34. Ibid.

35. The need to avoid coming up with an AIDS stance that sounded like structural adjustment apparently weighed on Zewdie. Invited to make a closing statement in an interview published in May 2003, she chose to sign off with the following point: "There is periodically a lot of misunderstanding between what the Bank does now, specifically in fighting the HIV/AIDS epidemic, and what the Bank used to do years ago in structural adjustment programs." Zewdie interview with International AIDS Economic Network, www.iaen.org, conducted on April 29, 2003.

36. This report was "Intensifying Action Against HIV/AIDS in Africa: Responding to a Development Crisis."

37. Zewdie interview, December 9, 2003.

38. Wolfensohn interview, December 15, 2003.

39. Alex Shakow interview, December 19, 2003, and e-mail, December 23, 2003. Shakow was the secretary to the Development Committee, responsible for putting together its agenda.

40. Zewdie interview, December 9, 2003. Binswanger interview, November 13, 2003.

41. An internal summary of the Bank's December 2002 Corporate Day meeting cites a figure of $50 million, but this seems to be a global figure rather than an African one.

42. In November 2002, the head of Ethiopia's National AIDS Secretariat admitted: "We did not adequately establish the institutional arrangements that enabled effective absorption of funds of that size when the loan of $59.7 million dollars was secured [from the World Bank] two years back. Institutionally, we did not have that capacity to deal with the funds that came to the country." See "Interview with Negatu Mereke," UN Integrated Regional Information Network, Nairobi, November 27, 2002.

43. The verdict that National AIDS Councils were generally not an improvement on what came before is shared by Helene Gayle, the AIDS program director at the Bill and Melinda Gates Foundation, and by J. Stephen Morrison of the Center for Strategic and International Studies, who runs a program on AIDS in Africa. Andrew Cassels of the World Health Organization agrees: "The trouble with the idea of creating new bureaucratic bodies is that they don't work. They don't have clout unless they have a budget."

Gayle interview, February 28, 2004. Morrison interview, December 11, 2003. Cassels interview, March 12, 2003.

44. Skolnik interview, March 2, 2004.

45. "We have not delivered," Wolfensohn said, "and we simply must raise our game." Internal summary of the Bank's December 2002 Corporate Day meeting.

46. Armin Fidler interview, November 24, 2003. Fidler was the health sector manager responsible for Europe and Central Asia.

47. By early 2004, disbursements in the Africa programs stood at around $200 million. In Ethiopia, where the Bank's money had been stuck in the capital at first, some six thousand NGOs and community outfits had received grants from the Bank by early 2004.

48. Mike Merson, the former head of the Global AIDS program at WHO and a fierce critic of the world's failed response to AIDS, regards the Bank's effort in Russia as a triumph, given the local resistance to action that the Bank encountered. Merson interview, November 12, 2003. It's also worth noting that other donors also found fast progress elusive. In Botswana, for example, a high-profile coalition involving the Gates Foundation and the Harvard AIDS Foundation set out to see what could be accomplished in a small and efficient country with plenty of political commitment to fighting AIDS; in 2003, three years after the effort's announcement, less than 8 percent of the population knew whether or not it had the virus and just nine thousand patients had entered the government's antiretroviral programs—more than were being treated in any other African nation, but still a fraction of Botswana's estimated 350,000 cases. See "Reluctance to Face Tests Slows Botswana AIDS Fight," by John Donnelly, *Boston Globe*, November 8, 2003, p. A1.

49. Peter Heywood interview, November 19, 2003. Heywood was the Bank's AIDS expert stationed in Delhi.

50. "Performance Project Assessment Report," OED, pp. 14, 17. To be sure, the improvements reflected a variety of influences, not just the Bank, and untangling causation is unfortunately impossible. However, the Bank's money provided the majority of the financing for the Indian national AIDS program in this period.

51. On harassment of AIDS workers, see "Epidemic of Abuse," a report by Human Rights Watch, July 2000. See also "Rights-India: Criticism Aimed at AIDS Program as Workers Jailed," by Ranjit Devraj, Inter Press Service, May 29, 2000. According to this report, in one incident in 2000, a World Bank–backed NGO produced an AIDS-education pamphlet that used sexually explicit language. The pamphlet's authors were jailed, and the news-

papers were full of angry quotes about the imposition of "alien" World Bank values in India's Himalayan north, a region so tradition-bound that menstruating women are forced to live in cattle sheds.

52. "Performance Project Assessment Report," OED, p. ix.

CHAPTER THIRTEEN: BACK TO THE FUTURE

1. I am grateful to John Briscoe for a long and wonderful conversation, and for a copy of his report to Jim Wolfensohn on his Bangladesh experience. The report was subsequently published as "Two Decades of Change in a Bangladeshi Village," by John Briscoe, *Economic and Political Weekly* 36, no. 40, October 6, 2001.

2. It was not just that NGOs figured low down the villagers' list of reasons for their progress. One large NGO called Proshika had been actively hostile to the source of their good fortune. It had produced a glossy video with images of sick women and children, whose misery was the fault of the embankment—or so viewers were told. Briscoe, "Two Decades of Change."

3. These figures measure financial commitments, not numbers of projects, though the trend would be the same either way.

4. Social-sector lending had come to $4.2 billion in FY95, or 18 percent of total lending. In FY99, it came to $7.3 billion, or 25 percent of the total.

5. Formally speaking, the Indian government withdrew the project. But that was after the Bank's top management requested that it do so.

6. As Briscoe points out, there was a cruel irony in this. The borrowers *least* able to afford the Bank's stringent conditions were the ones with no alternative sources of capital—and therefore the ones that had no choice but to accept them.

7. In Chad, Exxon operated through a subsidiary called Esso Exploration and Production Chad, Inc. Moreover, in 1999, Exxon merged with Mobil. The resulting push-me-pull-you is called the Exxon Mobil Corporation, although, just to keep you guessing, a lot of the company's literature refers to Exxon-Mobil, all one word. For simplicity's sake, I refer throughout this chapter to "Exxon."

8. Katherine Marshall interview, December 23, 2003. Marshall was the director of the Bank's Sahel department at the time.

9. This seems a fair assertion, given that Wolfensohn pulled the Arun dam in Nepal when he was forced to take a decision on it early in his term. However, it is worth noting that Exxon lobbied the Bank at a high level. After his arrival, Wolfensohn spoke to Exxon's president, and this may have dissuaded him from stopping the project in his early years. In the hypothetical case of Exxon initiating contact with the Bank in 1996, it is hard to know whether

high-level lobbying would have tipped Wolfensohn in favor of beginning work on the project.

10. Marshall interview, December 23, 2003. The Bank also worried that, in an environment of exploding private capital flows, the rationale for a public-sector lender was to catalyze private investment in countries that would not otherwise get it. Chad presented an opportunity to do that.

11. I toured Exxon's Chad operations in October 2003, and spoke at length to Ellen Brown and Miles Shaw and other company executives. The story of the molasses comes from Ron Royal, Exxon's chief in the country.

12. The Bank threatened to walk out in 1998, for example, after a mission from the International Finance Corporation, the Bank's private-sector arm, drove along part of the pipeline route and found that it did not follow the route of existing infrastructure as closely as Exxon had claimed, and that it bisected a sensitive forest. Shabhaz Mavaddat interview, January 23, 2004.

13. One Bank official recalls: "They were a better implementing agency than we usually deal with. One reason we moved away from infrastructure was that these are complex projects and at some point the implementer misses something and then you are not in compliance and you pull out."

14. The rebel group was named Armed Forces for a Federal Republic, or FARF. Its leader was Laokein Barde.

15. The southern leader was Ngarlegy Yorongar.

16. Allegedly, one particularly rare tulip bulb was traded for a working brewery at the height of the bubble.

17. The Bank's research department held a well-attended seminar on its aid effectiveness findings in December 1996, and briefed Wolfensohn on them in the spring of 1997. David Dollar e-mail, December 31, 2003.

18. This IDA credit was worth $17.5 million. A second capacity-building credit, worth $27.3 million, was approved along with the rest of the pipeline project the following June.

19. Perhaps the clumsiest of all the critics was Friends of the Earth, whose website later stated that "the World Bank loaned $3.6 billion for this controversial project in June 2000." This overstated the Bank's involvement by at least tenfold. In a report called "Broken Promises," issued in June 2001, Friends of the Earth also opposed the project on the grounds that it involved oil and would contribute to global warming.

20. Elf's takeover earlier in 1999 by TotalFina may also have played a role.

21. The war-room meeting was led by Praful Patel, who features later in the chapter. Rashad Kaldany interview, January 22, 2004. Mavaddat interview, January 23, 2004.

22. In the end the consortium consisted of ExxonMobil (40 percent of private equity), Petronas (35 percent), and Chevron (25 percent).

23. The World Bank lent $90 million to Chad's government to finance its small stake in the project, and also lent $100 million to the consortium through its private-sector arm, the International Finance Corporation. Robert Calderisi e-mail, May 25, 2004.

24. The human rights leader was Delphine Djiraibe of the Chadian Association for the Promotion and Defense of Human Rights.

25. Pelosi was concerned that the environmental management plan for the pipeline be publicly disclosed 120 days ahead of the vote by the Bank's board, since she herself had authored the congressional measure that made this a condition for U.S. approval of Bank projects. But the Bank and Exxon were careful to comply with her rule. Mavaddat interview, January 23, 2004.

26. Section 2 of the Bank's Articles of Agreement on "Dealings Between Members and the Bank" is quite clear: "Each member shall deal with the Bank only through its Treasury, central bank, stabilization fund or other similar fiscal agency, and the Bank shall deal with members only by or through the same agencies." Section 10 also prohibits "political activity": "The Bank and its officers shall not interfere in the political affairs of any member; nor shall they be influenced in their decisions by the political character of the member or members concerned. Only economic considerations shall be relevant to their decisions, and these considerations shall be weighed impartially in order to achieve the purposes stated in Article I." In practice, Bank officials appear before the U.S. Congress only at the request of the Treasury. Robert Calderisi e-mail, May 25, 2004.

27. Note, however, that the Bank loans to Chad for the pipeline (as distinct from the loans for capacity building) did not come from IDA.

28. See, for example, "Damming Evidence: The Pros and Cons of Big Earthworks," *The Economist*, July 17, 2003.

29. "The Use of a Trilateral Network: An Activist's Perspective on the Formation of the World Commission on Dams," by Patrick McCully, *American University International Law Review* 16, no. 6, pp. 1453ff. See in particular p. 1465.

30. See "External Views on the World Bank Group's Draft Water Resources Sector Strategy: How They Were Elicited, What They Are, and How They Will Be Addressed," August 2002.

31. The presentation was entitled "Investment Lending and the MDGs," and it was shown to the top managers at Corporate Day on November 1, 2002.

32. Briscoe interview, August 6, 2003. The Nordic director was Finn Jonck.

33. Guangyao Zhu interview, November 26, 2003. Chander Vasudev interview, December 22, 2003. See also "Infrastructure Business: Key Trends and Issues," a statement by Chander Mohan Vasudev and Guangyao Zhu, executive directors for India and China, February 13, 2002.

34. On January 31, Bush said he would not; on February 24, he reversed himself. On March 6, he said he would demand a vote on a second resolution because "it's time for people to show their cards." On March 17, he decided he would not demand a vote after all.

35. "The Snags of Multilateralism," *The Economist*, March 22, 2003.

36. In a legal sense, the first UN resolution was probably enough to authorize war. But in a political sense, the failure to secure a second resolution deprived the invasion of the UN's blessing.

37. Wolfensohn interview, June 12, 2003.

38. "U.S. Plans for Iraqi Economy Hit Friction," by Paul Blustein, *The Washington Post*, April 11, 2003, p. A34.

39. For a while Bank officials argued that an earlier UN resolution (661) imposing sanctions on Iraq prevented it from sending missions to conduct a needs assessment, claiming that it would be illegal for the Bank to pay hotel bills in the country. This legalism reflected the Bank's desire to await a political consensus before acting.

40. "Mr. Wolfensohn's Criteria," *Wall Street Journal*, August 5, 2003, p. A8.

41. In an interview soon after the phone call, Wolfensohn said: "John Taylor still is hostile. He calls up saying I need $4 to $5 billion for Iraq so I've sent the lawyers over to tell him that we can't write a check for $4 to $5 billion. We need to lend to someone who recognizes the debt and we need a legal framework. I said let's not argue about $4 to $5 billion until we have those two preconditions right. He got very angry. . . . I come back [from Iraq] and I get an attack in the *Wall Street Journal* and I get a call from Taylor. . . . I do not believe it was coincidence." Wolfensohn interview, August 9, 2003.

42. The World Banker was Dr. Alya Sousa, an Iraqi national and UN employee who was seconded to the Bank's Baghdad office.

43. The press tour was organized by the World Bank, but most of my interviews in Chad (including the one in Kome Atan) were done independently.

44. Rashad Kaldany interview, January 22, 2004.

CHAPTER FOURTEEN: A LION AT CARNEGIE

1. This point was first argued by Moisés Naím, the editor of *Foreign Policy* magazine. See "The World Bank: Its Role, Governance and Organizational Culture," available on the website of the Carnegie Endowment for Inter-

national Peace, at http://www.ceip.org/files/Publications/worldbankpaper.asp?from=pubauthor.

2. The survey also put this proposition to Bank staff: "In the World Bank Group, staff are rewarded according to their job performance." Only 44 percent of the survey's respondents agreed with that statement.

3. This comes from a World Bank internal document: SecM2003–067, October 23, 2003. Including pension contributions, FY03 administrative expenditures were 88 percent of FY95 in real terms. Excluding pension contributions, they were 96 percent of the earlier level.

4. In 1997, when the Bank's official staff survey asked whether morale was high, only 40 percent said yes. In 2003, 71 percent responded positively.

5. See Chapter 8, page 223.

6. As described in Chapter 6, in a note, in 2002 an ex–World Bank economist named Surjit Bhalla attacked the Bank's poverty numbers, claiming they exaggerated human misery. The Bank's methods were better, but the larger point is clear. If it is hard to measure poverty, it's even harder to measure different ways of fighting it. See "Bhalla Versus the World Bank: An Outsider's Perspective," by Jeromin Zettelmeyer, *Finance & Development*, June 2003, pp. 50ff.

7. *The Mystery of Capital: Why Capitalism Triumphs in the West and Fails Everywhere Else*, by Hernando de Soto (New York: Basic Books, 2000).

8. "Asia's Reemergence," by Steven Radelet and Jeffrey Sachs, *Foreign Affairs* 76, no. 6, November/December 1997.

9. Wolfensohn interview, April 20, 2003.

10. Paul Collier interview, January 19, 2003.

11. David Dollar of the World Bank's research department has asked how different donors respond to a one standard deviation improvement in rule of law and one standard deviation improvement in democracy (both indexes are created independently of the World Bank). In the first half of the 1990s IDA lending did not respond at all. In the second half of the decade it more than doubled. Compared to other multilateral donors, IDA was the second most responsive. Extending his research into 2000 to 2002 but using a slightly different measure of good governance, Dollar finds that a one standard deviation increase in policy quality leads to an increase of IDA support of 80 percent—slightly lower than in 1995 to 1999, but still higher than for any other donor in Dollar's sample except Denmark's government. See "The Increasing Selectivity of Foreign Aid, 1984–2002," by David Dollar and Victoria Levin, World Bank Working Paper, February 2004.

12. Versions of this argument have been made by Devesh Kapur of Harvard and Robert Wade of LSE. See, for example, Kapur's "Do As I Say Not As I Do:

A Critique of G-7 Proposals on Reforming the MDBs," available at http://ksghome.harvard.edu/%7E.drodrik.academic.ksg/G24Kapur.pdf; or Wade's "The World Bank and Its Critics: The Dynamics of Hypocrisy," an unpublished paper on file with the author. I am also indebted to David Dollar for pointing me in this direction.

13. Kapur, "Do As I Say." One of these objectives was to fight money-laundering by boosting the legal framework for prosecuting financial crime. This is not a priority for developing countries trying to fight poverty.

INDEX

Abidjan, Côte d'Ivoire, 101
Adams, Jim, 216–18, 222–23, 226–28, 230, 359–60
AES, 240–41
Afghanistan, 311
  nation building in, 2, 118, 126, 363
  terrorists in, 304
Africa, 5, 6, 73, 89–92, 101, 106, 107
  agriculture in, 90, 345
  AIDS in, 90, 215, 314–34, 352, 391
  Bank's mission in, 2
  Bank's program for, 44
  debt problem of, 106
  IMF loans and, 106
  McNamara's policies toward, 89–90
  1990s stagnation in, 90
  oil in, 23, 91, 106, 347, 350
  poverty reduction in, 214
  state-backed industries in, 45
  Wolfensohn's policies toward, 90–92, 157–58, 218, 222, 228
  Wolfensohn's trips to, 89, 92–105, 108, 111–12, 146, 215–16, 233, 303–4, 312, 333
  see also specific countries
African Development Bank, 70
agriculture, 6
  in Africa, 90, 345
  in Chad, 345
  McNamara and, 34–37, 118
Ahmed, Masood, 253, 257
AIDS, 1, 3, 5, 13, 14, 72, 118, 295, 313–34, 383
  in Africa, 90, 215, 314–34, 352, 391
  Bank denial about, 318–19

  in Brazil, 112, 350, 360
  in Congo, 314–15
  first cases of, 314
  IDAs and, 329
  increase in cases of, 315, 317–18, 322–23
  in India, 316–17, 331–33, 360
  NGOs and, 323–24, 332–33
  Preston and, 317–18
  in Russia, 331–33
  in South Africa, 320, 360
  in Uganda, 109
  U.S. government spending on, 315
  WHO and, 314
  Zewdie's report on, 327–28
  Zewdie's strategy on, 323–25, 328–30, 332–33
  Zewdie's workshop on, 321–22
  see also World AIDS Conference
Air Force One (film), 116
Alcoa, 289, 291, 305
Alternative Forum, 61
American Enterprise Institute, 291
Amin, Idi, 213, 217, 219
Amnesty International, 348
Angelou, Maya, 66
Angola, oil in, 347
Annan, Kofi, 376
Anstey, Caroline, 137
Appraisal Mission, 149
Argentina:
  Bank loans to, 148
  IMF and, 363
  inflation in, 45

Articles of Agreement, of World Bank, 16
A SEED (Action for Solidarity, Equality, Environment and Development), 61–62
Ashkenazi, Vladimir, 31, 33
Asia, 45, 90
  Bank's mission in, 2
  economic strategy of, 382
  financial crisis in, 177–207, 360
  IMF and, 186–91, 193, 209
  poverty reduction in, 214, 218
  see also specific countries
Asian Development Bank, 70
Assessing Aid, 175, 270, 310, 351
Atelier Couture Non-Violence, 370
Australia, 17, 19, 28, 376
Autheman, Marc-Antoine, 170–73, 190
Autonomous University, 61

Baghdad, 4
Baker, James:
  Conable and, 43
  Gulf War and, 363
  as possible Bank president, 300–301
Bakke, Dennis, 241–43, 247, 255
Balkans, 9, 121, 124, 362–63
Ballet Gran Folklorico de Mexico, 66
Bamako, Mali, 93, 94, 97–98
Bangladesh, 336–39, 357
Bangladesh Rural Advancement Committee (BRAC), 338–39
BankAmerica, 42
Bank for Reconstruction of the United and Associated Nations, *see* World Bank
Bank Swirled, 88, 296
Bankwide Operations Committee, 149
Barenboim, Daniel, 31–33
BBC, 369
Beastie Boys, 274
Beatrix, Queen of Holland, 374, 376
Bedié, Henri Konan, 102–3
Beijing, China, UN Conference on Women in, 113
Benin, 96
Berger, Sandy, 374
Bernstein, Leonard, 32
Bicakcic, Edhem, 141

Binswanger, Hans, 324, 327, 329
  African AIDS pandemic and, 320–21
  Community Driven Development of, 323, 330, 337
  at Geneva AIDS conference, 322–23
Blair, Tony, 249, 255–56, 302
Bloomberg, Michael, 376
Bolivia, 238–48, 254, 258–59, 328–29, 386, 390–91
  AES as model for, 240–41, 243
  Bank loans to, 247
  Bank visit to, 245
  corruption in, 243
  debt relief in, 249
  IDA credits of, 244–45
  inequality in, 239
  NGOs and, 338–39
  riots in, 46, 258
Bono, 307–9
Bosnia, 6, 73, 117–44, 169, 234, 363, 366–67, 388–89
  Bank trips to, 123–24, 129
  Dayton conference and, 126–30, 132, 140, 362, 366
  debts of, 134
  donors' conference and, 129–31
  loans to, 135–36, 138–39
  as member of Bank, 135–36, 138
  NGOs and, 119, 143, 168
  reconstruction in, 126, 132, 135, 163, 168, 191, 207
  Serb debt payment in, 140–41
  U.S. negotiating team in, 117
  Wolfensohn and, 117–18, 120, 126, 135, 136–39, 207, 388
Bosniak-Croat Peace Deal (1994), 140
Bosniaks, 140
  attacks on, 124–26
  Bank reconstruction of towns of, 125–26
  Dayton talks and, 129, 131
  meeting with Wallich of, 125–26
Botswana, AIDS in, 317, 330–31
Branczik, Amelia, 370
Bratton, William, 151, 161
Brazil, 358, 360, 386–87
  AIDS in, 112, 316, 350, 360

Bank loans and, 111, 120, 290
currency crisis in, 210, 212
dam project in, 356
financial crisis in, 207
IMF and, 210, 363
inflation in, 45
NGOs and, 386–87
Polonoroeste in, 48
private capital in, 73, 120
Bremer, Paul, 365
Bretton Woods conference at, 15, 17, 20, 60, 61, 388
Briscoe, John, 336–37, 340, 356–61, 391
NGOs and, 356–59, 361, 386
Brody, Ken, 75
Broinowski, John, 29–30
Brookins, Carole, 301, 303
Brown, Ellen, 344–47, 353
Chad poverty study of, 345–46
NGOs and, 344
Brown, Gordon, 306–7
Bujagali, Uganda, dam project in, 7–8
Burdon, Tony, 109, 251
Burki, Javed, 236
Burundi, 96
Bush, George H. W., 257
appointment of Preston by, 56–57
Clinton defeat of, 63–64
Bush, George W., 12, 379
alliance with Bank of, 305
Bono and, 309
contempt for Bank of, 4, 123, 287, 312, 363, 389
Monterrey summit and, 307–8
September 11 terrorist attacks and, 11, 14, 303–4
unilateralism of, 362
BusinessWeek, 53

Camdessus, Michel:
debt relief and, 115
on long-term development, 209
Suharto meeting of, 189–90
Cape Verde, 148
Care, 265, 286
Carlson, Sam, 96–97, 100
Carnegie Hall, 3, 32–33, 52–55, 175, 374

Carter, Jimmy, 40, 42, 49
Castro, Fidel, 26
Centers for Disease Control, 158
Central Intelligence Agency, 318
Chad, 341–56, 359, 368–73
agriculture in, 345
author's trip to, 368–73
Bank's oil revenue plan for, 352
Chicken Price Index in, 345
Congressional Black Caucus and, 355
Dutch disease and, 350–51
Ellen Brown in, 344–47, 353
Environmental Defense Fund in, 347–48, 353–56
Exxon in, 342–50, 368–73
human rights record of, 353
IDA money and, 343, 352
mangoes in, 349
military clash in, 347–48
NGOs and, 343–44, 346, 348–49, 352–54, 356, 369–71, 373
oil in, 342–56, 369–73, 387
pipeline completion in, 369, 372–73
political dissent in, 348
politics in, 342, 351–52
population of, 341
poverty in, 342, 345
Pygmies in, 342–43, 346, 353
road construction in, 344
Chase Bank, 29
Chenery, Hollis, 71
on "optimum growth," 35
Cheney, Dick:
unilateralism of, 362
Wolfensohn and, 287
Chevron, 354
China, 179, 270–85, 290, 359–61
arrest of journalists in, 278
Bank loans and, 27, 73, 111, 120, 148, 270, 334
dam project in, 271–85, 340–41, 348–49, 354, 356
economic boom in, 382, 392
Ministry of Finance of, 359
NGOs and, 273–77, 279–83, 388
poverty reduction in, 214, 270, 311
private capital in, 120

Chirac, Jacques:
    AIDS and, 326
    Exxon and, 349
Christopher, Warren, 129
Chrysler, 3, 37–39, 49, 52, 108, 310
    Wolfensohn's work for, 38–39
Clausen, Alden "Tom," 69
    background of, 42
    McNamara's antipoverty rhetoric
        downgraded by, 46–47
    Preston and, 57
Clinton, Bill, 64, 65–66, 72, 82, 116–17, 143,
        255–57, 286–88, 297, 374, 389
    debt relief and, 249
    Oklahoma City bombing and, 302
    Qinghai dam and, 274
    and search for Bank president, 69, 71,
        73–75, 77–81
    State of the Union 1996 speech of, 262
Clinton, Hillary, 300
CNN, 302
coffee, in Uganda, 213–14, 220, 229–30
cold war, 26, 130
Collier, Paul:
    criticism of Bank by, 384
    Museveni and, 254
communism, 2, 16, 26
Community Driven Development, 323, 330
Comprehensive Development Framework,
        235–38, 248, 254–55, 257, 259, 287, 299,
        311–12, 328, 381
Conable, Barber, 55, 69
    appointment to Bank of, 43
    emphasis on poverty by, 47
    failed management reform under, 157
    ignorance of Bank of, 43, 49
    managerial reform by, 150
Concert of the Americas, 65–66
Congo:
    AIDS in, 314–15
    bank loans to, 148
    Ugandan invasion of, 258
    see also Zaire
Congo-Brazzaville, 96
    oil in, 347
Congress, U.S.:
    AIDS in, 326
    debt relief and, 249
        Iraq reconstruction and, 366
        World Bank Inspection Panel and, 276
        see also House of Representatives, U.S.
Congressional Black Caucus, 355
Conthe, Manuel, 292
Côte d'Ivoire, 112
    development agencies' conference in,
        235–36
    Wolfensohn's first trip to, 92, 101–5, 108,
        380
Council on Foreign Relations, 366
Croats:
    attack on Bosniaks by, 124
    Bank reconstruction of towns of, 126
    Dayton talks and, 128, 140
Cruz, Celia, 66
Cuba, 26

Daimler-Benz, 77
Dalai Lama, 275
Dam, Ken, 294
Danino, Bobby, 66–67
Darling & Co., 28
Dayton, Bosnia peace conference in, 126–30,
        132, 140, 362, 366
debt relief, 105–8, 112, 114–15, 252
    Uganda and, 113, 215, 249, 251–52
    Vatican and, 250
    Wolfensohn and, 112–15, 146, 212, 248–50,
        263, 380
Deby, Idriss, 372
de Larosière, Jacques, 115
Denmark, 22
Denning, Steve, 158–60
Depression, Great, 17
Dervis, Kemal, 117, 121–26, 129, 132–38, 363
    at Bosnia dinner, 125
    Bosnian loans and, 134–36
    Wolfensohn and, 137, 156
de Soto, Hernando, 382
de Tray, Dennis, 183–88, 190–91, 195–96, 203
    Bank's board and, 184, 186
    corruption memo of, 185–86, 201
    on Indonesia, 184, 188
    at Indonesian NGO conference, 199
    and Jakarta demonstrations, 199–200
Development Committee, of World Bank,
        254, 269, 293, 305, 328

Diana, Princess of Wales, 151
disease, 2, 35
    see also AIDS
Dominican Republic, 46
Douglas, Michael, 66
Drucker, Peter, 151
du Pre, Jacqueline, 32–33, 54
Dutch disease, 350–51

East Timor, nation building in, 2, 118, 126,
    143
Economist:
    on AIDS, 318
    Conable and, 43
    on Wolfensohn, 262
education, 383
    in Bangladesh, 338–39
    in Uganda, 224–27, 311
    universal, 288, 298, 307
Einhorn, Jessica, 297–98, 381
electricity, 58
Elf, 347, 354
Emergency Recovery Project, 134
Emergency Social Fund, of World Bank,
    141
Enron, 66
Environmental Defense Fund, 286, 353–56
    on Chad, 347–48, 352–56
    Wolfensohn's dinner with, 347
environmentalism, 2, 5, 14, 58, 72, 297, 389,
    391
    in Chad, 347–49, 369
    dams and, 7, 340
    Gore and, 80
    Inspection Panel and, 276
    MacNeill and, 279
    Mobilization for Global Justice and,
        265–66
    National Environmental Action Plans
        and, 70
    NGOs and, 48
    Piercy and, 74
    Seattle protest and, 261–63
    Wolfensohn and, 74, 234, 265
Equatorial Guinea, oil in, 347
Ethiopia:
    AIDS in, 321, 328, 330–31
    National AIDS Councils in, 330–31

Europe:
    Bank loans to, 21–22
    and choice of Bank president, 43, 69
    see also specific countries
European Bank for Reconstruction and
    Development, 390
European Union, 142
    Bosnia and, 362
Export-Import Bank, 75
Exxon, 343–50, 368–73
    Bank and, 343, 346, 349
    Chad celebration of, 372–73
    Chirac and, 349
    construction in Chad by, 344, 369
    Ellen Brown and, 344–47, 353
    Moundou attack and, 347–48

fascism, 2
Fatepur, Bangladesh, 336–39
    average lifespan in, 336
    economic improvement of, 337–38
Federal Reserve, 42, 51, 74, 374
Fidler, Stephen, 299–300
Fifty Years is Enough campaign, 61, 65, 82,
    87, 119, 162, 194, 211, 261, 264, 272, 343,
    379
Final Executive Project Summary, 149
Financial Times, 58, 66–68, 82–83, 251, 293,
    296
Fischer, Stan, 71, 189, 192, 195, 210, 268
Fisher, Ben, 198–99
Ford, Harrison, 116, 275
Ford Motor Co., 52
Foreign Affairs, 297, 381, 382
Foreign Policy, 298–300, 306
Forster, Sarah, 132
Forum of Indian Leftists, 264
France, 131
    development beliefs of, 357
    Iraq War and, 362–63, 365
Friends of the Earth, 59, 286

Gabon, oil in, 347
Gandhi, Indira, 34–35
Garcia Marquez, Gabriel, 84
Gates, Bill, 307
Gay and Lesbian Organization of Bank
    Employees, 320

Gay Men's Health Crisis Award for
    Distinguished and Pioneering
    Philanthropy, 54
George, Krome, 291
George, Susan, 47, 78
Germany:
    debt relief and, 249
    Iraq War and, 363, 365
    postwar recovery of, 27
    in World War II, 2
Gerstner, Lou, 166
Ghana, 45, 91
Gilman, Benjamin, 277
Gingrich, Newt, 72, 88–89, 151
Giuliani, Rudy, 161
Golden, Ray, 51, 53–54
Goldman Sachs, 75
gold standard, 14
Goldstein, Jeff, 54
Gore, Al, 72, 374
    AIDS protesters and, 320, 328
    reinvention of government by, 151,
        163
    Wolfensohn and, 77–78, 80, 374
Grameen Bank, 338–39
Grant, Jim, 69
Great Britain:
    creation of Bank and, 15
    debt relief and, 115, 249
    donations to Uganda by, 253
    Iraq War and, 364
    Uganda's independence from, 213
Great Depression, 17
Greenspan, Alan, 192, 296, 374
Guerrero, Isabel, 240–44
Guggenheim, Scott, 202–5, 233
    empowerment of Indonesian villagers by,
        225, 233, 337
    Kecamatan Development Project of, 205,
        387
Gulf War, 363
Gutfreund, John, 49
Gyari, Lodi, 275–76
Gypsies, 391

Habibie, B. J., 200–202
Haiti, 146
Harvard Business Review, 255

Harvard Institute for International
    Development, 382
Harvard University, 70, 73
    Business School of, 3, 19–20, 23, 38
    John F. Kennedy School of Government
        of, 54
Hasan, Bob, 189
Helms, Jesse, 275
Helton, Arthur, 366
Herfkens, Eveline:
    in Bosnia, 137
    O'Neill and, 305
HIV, 314, 316, 332
    see also AIDS
Hoagland, Jim, 209
Holbrooke, Richard:
    at Dayton conference, 126–30, 362
    Mount Igman accident and, 117
    UN AIDS session planned by, 320
Holland, *see* Netherlands
House of Representatives, U.S., 47, 277
Howard Hughes Medical Institute, 54
Hubbard, Glenn, 290
Hussein, Saddam, 118
Hussein, Shahid, 113

Iacocca, Lee, 37
IBM, 166
IDA, *see* International Development
    Association (IDA)
illiteracy, 1, 35
    Bank's battle against, 14, 118, 295
    in Indonesia, 178
Independent Journalist's Association, 204
India, 290, 358, 360–61
    AIDS in, 316–17, 331–33, 360
    Bank loans and, 16, 120
    campaign against poverty in, 34–35, 311
    Narmada Valley development in, 58–59,
        340
    NGOs and, 340
    private capital in, 120
    Wolfensohn's trip to, 23, 331
Indian Council on Medical Research, 316
Indonesia, 6, 60, 177–206, 210, 215–16, 233,
    337
    average income in, 177
    Bank loan to, 181, 208

canal project in, 198–99
corruption in, 178–84, 187–89, 194, 200,
    202–5, 319
currency regime of, 184
currency slide of, 186, 188, 191, 197
economic collapse of, 184
Guggenheim's empowerment of villagers
    in, 225, 233, 337
illiteracy in, 178
IMF and, 186–96, 201
Kecamatan Development Project in, 205,
    387
monopolies in, 189–90
NGO conference in, 196–98
NGOs in, 178–79, 184, 196–98, 201, 205
open capital flow of, 194
regional and ethnic conflicts in, 177
student protests in, 199–200
Suharto's resignation in, 200, 204
telecommunications project in, 180
unemployment in, 184
Wolfensohn's visits to, 178–80, 190,
    195–99, 207
inflation:
    Bank loans and, 26, 182
    in Latin America, 45
    in pre–World War II Europe, 2
    in Uganda, 213–14, 221–22, 226
Initial Executive Project, 148–49
Integrated Rural Development Projects, 253
Inter-American Development Bank, 70,
    309, 389
International Campaign for Tibet, 275–76
International Development Association
    (IDA), 111, 119–20, 162, 254–55, 263–66,
    276–77, 285, 288, 306, 341, 387, 389, 391
    AIDS and, 329
    Bolivia and, 244
    Bosnia and, 135–36
    Chad and, 343, 352
    Côte d'Ivoire and, 102, 104–5
    creation of, 26–27
    U.S. Congress and, 275–77
International Finance Corporation, 148
International Labor Organization, 35
International Monetary Fund, 4, 71, 123, 199,
    207, 249–50, 262
    Africa and, 91, 106, 112, 114–15, 217, 220

aid to South Korea by, 192, 194
Argentina and, 363
Asia and, 186–91, 193, 209
Asian financial crisis and, 186–94, 209
Bank and bailouts of, 192, 211
Bosnia and, 363
Brazil and, 210, 363
Comprehensive New Development
    Framework and, 232, 235, 236
debt relief and, 380
Indonesia and, 186–96, 201
lending policy of, 44–45
loans to Pakistan of, 182
Mobilization for Global Justice protests
    of, 264–68
origin of, 2, 15
Oxfam's criticism of, 60
purpose of, 2, 118
riots triggered by, 46
Russia and, 209
Stiglitz's attack on, 193–95, 210,
    266–67
Thailand and, 192–94
Uganda and, 217, 220
Washington Post on, 209
International Rivers Network, 7, 82
Iran:
    oil in, 351
    revolution in, 36–37
Iraq, 123
    reconstruction of, 2, 4, 118, 123, 130,
        364–67, 389
    U.S. invasion of, 362–64
Islam, 11
Izetbegovic, Alija, 128–29, 137

Jackson Hole, Wyo., Wolfensohn's house in,
    116
Jakarta:
    Bank office in, 177, 179, 183, 191, 202
    Wolfensohn's visit to slum of, 198–99
Jakarta Post, 185
James D. Wolfensohn Inc., 50–54, 74, 78
    Fuji-Wolfensohn branch of, 54
    J. Rothschild, Wolfensohn & Co. branch
        of, 54
    sponsorship of Kennedy Center Fellows
        program by, 66

Japan:
    debt relief and, 249
    development beliefs of, 357
    influence of, 3
    postwar recovery of, 27
    in World War II, 2
Jaycox, Kim, 89, 102, 109, 112–13, 157–58
    argument with Wolfensohn of, 104–5, 108
Jennings, Peter, 76, 374
John F. Kennedy Center for the Performing
    Arts, 3, 54, 55, 65
    Fellows program of, 66
Jones, Quincy, 65
Jordan, Vernon, 66, 74, 374, 376
JP Morgan, 56–57
Jubilee 2000, 251–52

Kaji, Gautam, 152, 154, 155–57, 190, 236
Kampala, Uganda, 215, 217, 222, 251, 258
Kanbur, Ravi, 107–8, 268–69, 280
Karadzic, Radovan, 140
Katsu, Shigeo, 102
Katwe, Uganda, 109, 112, 215, 258
Kecamatan Development Project, 205, 387
Kennedy, Edward, 376
Kennedy, John F., 27, 94, 255
Kenya, AIDS in, 319, 328, 330
Keynes, John Maynard, 15–16
Kikanovic, Mirsad, 142
Kirgiz Republic, 374
Knight, Andrew, 55
Koch-Weser, Caio, 152–54, 155, 157, 240–41,
    243, 245
Kome Atan, Chad, 370
Konaré, Alpha Oumar, 95–98, 102
Koro-Koro, Mali, 98
Kosovo, nation building in, 2, 118, 143
Krueger, Anne, 71
Kwakwa, Victoria, 92–93

Lafourcade, Olivier, 101, 103, 105
Lamb, Geoff, 61
Laos, 340, 359
Latin America:
    Bank loans and, 16
    Bank's mission in, 2
    Bank's program for, 44
    debt problems of, 56, 106

economic growth of, 46
1990s revival in, 90
state-backed industries in, 45
Wolfensohn's trip to, 113
see also specific countries
Latvia, 176
Leahy, Patrick, 307
Le Figaro, 130
Lindsay, Larry, 290
Lipton, David, 122–23, 127, 130, 193
Loehnis, Anthony, 53
Lomax, Rachel, 155, 236
Luxembourg, 22

Ma, Yo-Yo, 376
McCarrick, Cardinal, 309
McCarthy, Joseph, 14
McCloy, John, 21
McGinnis, Linda, 92–94, 96–97, 99–100,
    392
    as model for Bank, 108, 132, 143, 153, 215,
    388
    Wolfensohn and, 99
Mack, Connie, 277
McKinsey, 153, 155, 168
McNamara, Robert, 28, 42, 46–48, 61, 71, 74,
    81, 87, 119, 150, 234, 254, 392
    Africa policy of, 89–90
    agriculture and, 34–37, 118
    Bank ambitions of, 34–37, 41, 85, 118, 307
    NGOs and, 393
    oil shock and, 44, 209
    Piercy's visit to, 76–77
    Wolfensohn's relationship with, 39–40,
    67, 82
MacNeill, Jim, 279
McPherson, Peter, 301
Madavo, Callisto, 322
Madrid, Bank protests at, 60–65, 72, 101, 110,
    208, 257, 261, 263, 286, 343
Major, John, 130, 151
Majot, Juliette, 82
Malawi, 110, 227
Malaysia, 197
Mali, 92–93, 132, 215, 388
    NGOs in, 96
    poverty in, 93
    Wolfensohn's trip to, 94–101, 143, 303–4

Mallinckrodt, George, 81–82, 85
Malloch Brown, Mark, 61, 76, 78–79, 81–83,
    88–89, 165, 209–10, 264
  anger at Wolfensohn of, 236–37
  denunciation of NGOs by, 62–63
  at Jakarta press conference, 198
Manila, 36
Mann, Jonathan, 314, 324, 326
Mao Tse Tung, 223, 381
Marek, Michael, 69
Marshall Plan, 22
Martin, Jurek, 82
Medjugorje, reconstruction conference in,
    126
Meltzer, Allan, 289–91, 294, 298
Menuhin, Yehudi, 247
Metzler Bank, 81
Mexico, 45, 158, 337
  Bank loans and, 111
  peso crisis of, 71, 73, 81
Meyer, Eugene, 21
Middle East, 10
Millennium Development Goals, 5, 307, 311,
    334, 384, 391
Miller, William, 38
Minnelli, Liza, 66
Mobilization for Global Justice, 264–68,
    286
Mobutu Sese Seko, 96
Monterrey, Mexico, summit in, 307–8,
    310–11
Morgenthau, Henry, 14–15
Morocco, 46
Morse, Bradford, 58
Morse, David, 35
Moundou, Chad, military clash in,
    347–48
Mount Morgan, 29
Mozambique, 339, 368
Mugabe, Robert, 387
Multi-Country HIV/AIDS Program,
    329
Multilateral Investment Guarantee Agency,
    148
Muratovic, Hasan, 135–36, 138–39
Museveni, Yoweri, 213–17, 220, 222–26, 312
  attack on Congo by, 258
  and coffee liberalization, 213–14

Collier as adviser to, 254
  on Mao Tse Tung, 223, 381
Mustapha, Mahamat, 371

Naím, Moisés, 299
Nairobi, Kenya, 35–36, 307
Namibia, 321
Nash, Bob, 79
National Association of Professional
    Environmentalists, 8
National Cathedral, 11
National Symphony Orchestra, 65
NATO, 123
Nepal, 62
  dam project in, 113–14, 263, 334
  NGOs and, 114
Netherlands, 22
  Dutch disease and, 350–51
Neville-Jones, Pauline, 130
New Development Framework, 212, 218,
    224, 231–34, 242
  see also Comprehensive Development
    Framework
Newman, Frank, 69
New Republic, 266–68
New York Philharmonic Orchestra, 32
New York Times, 61
  on AIDS, 318
  environmental ad in, 353
  on Preston, 57–58
  Wolfensohn and, 39, 83
Nicholl, Peter, 164
Niger, 96, 351
Nigeria, 31
  AIDS in, 315, 328
  author in, 368
  Wolfensohn's trips to, 23–26, 32, 176, 213,
    328, 331
Nile river, 7
nongovernmental organizations (NGOs),
    6–7, 70, 88, 99, 133, 162, 193, 248, 259,
    263, 268, 284–85, 334, 340–41, 381, 386,
    388–89, 392
  AIDS and, 323–24, 332–33
  in Bangladesh, 338–39
  Bank's abolition called for by, 59
  Bolivia and, 240
  Bosnia and, 119, 143, 168

nongovernmental organizations (NGOs)
(*cont.*)
   Brazil and, 386–87
   Briscoe and, 356–59, 361, 386
   Chad and, 343–44, 346, 348–49, 352–54,
      356, 369–71, 373
   Ellen Brown and, 344
   increase of, 262
   in India, 340
   Indonesian, 178–79, 184, 196, 201, 205
   Inspection Panel and, 276–77
   in Laos, 340
   McNamara and, 393
   Madrid protests of, 60–65, 72, 101, 110
   Mali and, 96
   Malloch Brown's denunciation of, 62–63
   in Nepal, 114
   poverty statement of, 47
   protests of, 47
   Qinghai dam and, 273–77, 279–83, 312
   in Uganda, 7–9, 109–10, 113, 215, 217–18,
      224, 228–29, 312
   Wolfensohn's relations with, 87, 102–3,
      114, 145–46, 155, 176, 201, 206, 207, 215,
      233, 262–65, 269, 286, 296–97, 319, 356,
      377, 386, 388
   see also specific NGOs
Noor, Queen of Jordan, 374
Norway, AIDS grant of, 322
Nyerere, Julius, 90

Obote, Milton, 213, 217
Office of the High Representative, 132, 142
O'Hara, Pat, 57, 68
oil, 351, 386, 389
   Africa and, 23, 91, 106, 347, 350
   Arab embargo of, 36, 44
   in Chad, 342–56, 369–73, 387
   in Holland, 350–51
   Iranian revolution and, 36–37, 209
Olympic Games, 1956, 19
Omicevic, Kasim, 122, 142–43
O'Neill, Paul, 289–91, 293–97, 305, 308–9,
      363, 365, 367, 388
   visit to Bank of, 305–6, 308
   Wolfensohn and, 289, 291, 293–97, 305–6,
      308–10
Ord Minnett Thomson, 28

Osborne, Frederick, 19
Oxfam, 60, 62, 109–10, 114–15, 178, 215, 248,
      251, 253, 265, 277, 286, 288

Packer, Kerry, 53
Pakistan, 182
Pale, Bosnia, 140–41
Paris, Uganda donors' conference in, 216–17,
      220
Patel, Praful, 359–60
Peace Orchestra, 376
Pearl Harbor, Japanese attack on, 14
Pelosi, Nancy, 273, 275, 355
Pentagon, terrorist attack on, 302
Peru, 34, 45, 66
Petronas, 354, 372
Piercy, Jan, 68–69, 73, 74, 76–80, 82
Piot, Peter, 315, 326
Policy Framework Paper (PFP), 236, 238
Polonoroeste, 48
Population, Health and Nutrition
      Department, of World Bank, 35
Population Council, 39, 74
Porter, Michael, 73
Pottinger, Lori, 7
Poverty Eradication Action Plan, 224, 230,
      252
Poverty Reduction Strategy Papers, 254–55,
      257, 259
Powell, Colin, 296, 363
Power Corporation, 29
Pre-Appraisal Mission, 149
Preston, Lewis, 66, 79, 82, 86–87, 136, 149,
      159, 163, 257
   AIDS and, 317–18
   background of, 56
   Balkans and, 117–21
   Clausen and, 57
   death of, 68
   environmentalism and, 265
   at Madrid conference, 60–63
   managerial reform by, 150
   resignation of, 69
   search for successor to, 68–69, 71, 73
   weak communication skills of, 70
Progressive Librarians Guild, 264
Pronk, Jan, 131
Puente, Tito, 66

Putin, Vladimir, 363
Pygmies, 342–43, 346, 353, 388

Qinghai, China, dam project in, 271–85,
    340–41, 348–49, 354, 356
    Wolfensohn and, 273–79, 281
Quality Assurance Group, of World Bank,
    167
Queen Elizabeth (ship), 19
Quinn, Jack, 77, 80
Quiroga, Jorge, 239–47, 258, 386
Quixote Center, 264

Radelet, Steven, 382
Rainforest Action Network, 61, 353, 356
Raymond, Lee, 347, 354
Reagan, Ronald, 42, 44, 60, 254
Reed, John, 301
Regional Operations Committee, 149
Rheem International, 23, 25, 28
Rice, Condoleezza, 296, 304, 308–9
Rice, Gerry, 68
Rich, Bruce, 263
Richardson, Gordon, 30
Richardson, Peggy, 30
Rischard, Jean-François, 152–53, 159–60
Rockefeller, David, 29
Rockefeller Foundation, 39
Rohatyn, Felix, 75
Roosevelt, Eleanor, 300
Roosevelt, Franklin Delano, 2, 11, 14, 17
Rose, Leonard, 33
Rostow, Walt, 22, 27
Rostropovich, Mstislav, 53
Rothschild, James, 17
Rothschild family, 18
Rowen, Hobart, 58
Rubin, Robert, 69, 75–76, 82, 164, 307
Ruckus Society, 286
Rural Development Department, of World
    Bank, 35
Russia:
    AIDS in, 331–33
    Bank loans to, 71–73, 148, 163
    financial crisis in, 207, 211
    IMF and, 209
    Iraq War and, 363
    Wolfensohn's trip to, 331

Sabelli, Fabrizio, 47, 77
Sachs, Jeffrey, 382
Salomon Brothers, 37–38, 49–50, 237
Salzman, David, 65–66
Samuelson, Paul, 16
Sandstrom, Sven, 157, 159, 278, 280, 291, 360
Sarajevo, 117, 124, 126–27, 130–33, 139–40, 145
Saudi Arabia, 304
Schrempp, Juergen, 77
Schröder, Gerhard, 249, 256
Schroders, 30–34, 85, 310
Schultz, Theodore, 26
Seattle, Wash., protests in, 260–61
Sen, Amartya, 175, 248
Senate, U.S., 47, 59
September 11, 2001, terrorist attacks of,
    11–14, 301–4, 307, 310, 334
Serbs:
    attack on Bosniaks by, 124
    Bank reconstruction of towns of, 126
    Dayton talks and, 128, 140–41
Serwer, Dan, 126
Severino, Jean-Michel, 190
Shalala, Donna, 67–68, 74
Shaw, Miles, 346–48
Shell, 353–54
Sierra Club, 348
Singh, I. J., 146–47
Snow, John, 364
South Africa, 110–11, 120–21, 123, 283–84,
    290, 360
    AIDS in, 320, 360
South Korea, 289
    Bank and, 192–93
    Bank loan to, 208
    economic crisis in, 191
    IMF aid to, 192
Soviet Union, 2, 16, 130
    industrialization of, 22
    see also Russia
Sprinkel, Beryl, 44
Srebrenica, massacre in, 124–25, 132
Stages of Economic Growth, The (Rostow),
    22–23, 27
Stamps, Tim, 316
State Department, U.S., 304
Stern, Ernie, 105, 117, 136, 155
Stern, Isaac, 33

Stiglitz, Joseph, 71, 175, 209, 246, 269, 374, 388
    attack on IMF of, 193–95, 210, 266–68
Stockholm:
    UN environment conference at, 74
    Woods's speech at, 27
Stone, Julius, 18
Strategic Compact, 162–67, 169–70, 213, 245,
    291, 378–79
Strong, Maurice, 29, 39, 74, 82
Sudan, 46
    author in, 368
    terrorists in, 304
Suharto, Madame Tien, 178
Suharto, Mohamed, 177–81, 185, 187–89, 195,
    199, 254
    Bank loans to, 196
    resignation of, 200, 204
    sickness of, 188–89
Suharto, Tommy, 178, 189
Summers, Lawrence, 71, 75, 123, 192, 285, 324,
    333
    as Bank president candidate, 78, 82
    criticism of Wolfensohn by, 269, 297–98
    on development banks, 143, 367
    Stiglitz and, 195, 268
    Strategic Compact and, 164
Summit of the Americas, 65
Swedish Society for Nature Conservation, 8
Sydney Boys High School, 18

Tajikistan, 148
Talbott, Strobe, 374
Tanzania, 90, 95, 213, 219, 238, 253
Taylor, John, 290, 366
Teddy's Laundry Service, 20
Tehran, 31
terrorism:
    causes of, 304
    see also September 11, 2001, terrorist
        attacks of
Thailand, 183–84, 186
    AIDS in, 325
    Bank loan to, 208
    currency turmoil in, 184, 191
    IMF and, 192–94
    private capital in, 73
    unemployment in, 184
    Wolfensohn's visit to, 197

Thalwitz, Wilfried, 154
Thatcher, Margaret, 44, 60, 254
Third Way, 249–50, 255–57, 259, 269, 286,
    292, 386
Tibet, Tibetans, 6, 271–82, 354–55,
    390–91
Tibet Information Network, 271–72
Timbuktu, Mali, 93
Toffler, Alvin, 151
Transparency International, 179
Treasury, British, 306
Treasury, U.S., 70, 194, 268–69, 295, 298, 310,
    388
    Bosnia and, 122–23, 125, 143
    hostility towards Bank by, 4, 164, 207, 210,
        288–91, 293–95, 305
    Iraq and, 4, 123, 366
    South Korean bailout and, 192
Treaty of Paris, 362
Truell, Peter, 82
Tsering, Bhuchung, 275
Tuluy, Hasan, 94
Tumusiime-Mutebile, Emmanuel, 219–22,
    226–31, 251, 253, 259, 312, 352, 392
    background of, 219
    at Consultative Group meetings, 220
    at Ugandan poverty conference, 224
Twin City Bank, 39

Uganda, 213–31, 233, 251–53, 258–59, 268, 359,
    381, 385–86, 392
    AIDS in, 109, 215, 319, 323, 325
    Bank loans to, 115
    budget process in, 221–22
    Bujagali dam in, 7–8
    changes of government in, 213
    coffee market in, 213–14, 220, 229–30
    Congo invasion by, 258
    debt relief in, 113, 215, 249, 251–52, 380
    education in, 224–27
    foreign economists in, 220–21
    income in, 214
    inflation in, 213–14, 221–22, 226
    Ministry of Education in, 225
    Ministry of Finance in, 220
    NGOs and, 7–9, 109–10, 113, 215, 217–18,
        224, 228–29, 312
    Planning Ministry of, 220

Poverty Eradication Action Plan in, 224, 230, 252

poverty reduction in, 217

road construction in, 222–23

Wolfensohn's policies towards, 218, 222–23, 228, 251

Wolfensohn's trip to, 92, 108–10, 113, 211, 215–16, 251

UNAIDS, 319, 322, 326

unemployment, 2

UNESCO, 298

UNICEF, 69, 91, 315

United Nations, 4, 70, 118, 120, 125, 307

Conference on Women of, 113

Development Program of, 58, 91, 215

Food and Agricultural Organization of, 35

International Labor Organization of, 35

Iraq resolutions of, 362–63

Uganda and, 215

United States:

African poverty and, 1–2

and choice of Bank presidency, 43, 69

debt relief and, 115

influence of, 3

Iraq invasion by, 362–64

unipolarism of, 4–5

Urban Development Department, of World Bank, 35

USAID, 70

Vatican, 230

Venezuela, 31

oil in, 351

Verey, Michael, 33–34

Vieira de Mello, Sergio, 366

Vietnam War, 27, 35–36

Vogue, 174

Voices of the Poor, 253

Volcker, Paul, 42, 51–52, 74, 85, 137, 374

Wade, Robert, 279–80

Wallich, Christine, 122–27, 130–31, 138, 144, 169, 363

at Bad Ragaz conference, 135–36

at Dayton peace conference, 128

Serbian debt payment to, 140–41

Wall Street Journal, attacks on Bank by, 4, 200–201, 204, 365–66

Walters, Barbara, 374

Warburg, Siegmund, 30, 31

Ward, Barbara, 39

war on terror, 304

Warsaw, Bosnia meeting in, 121–22, 123

Washington Opera, 65

Washington Post, 58, 86

AIDS and, 315, 318

on Concert of the Americas, 66

on Hillary Clinton, 300

on IMF, 209

West African Pilot, 25

White, Harry Dexter, 14–16

WHO, see World Health Organization

Who Says Elephants Can't Dance? (Gerstner), 166

Wilde, Oscar, 172–73

Winans, BeBe, 66

Winans, Cece, 66

Winters, Jeffrey, 184–85, 203

Wintour, Anna, 174

Wolfensohn, Adam, 376

Wolfensohn, Dora, 17

Wolfensohn, Elaine Botwinick, 67, 81, 93, 97, 102–3, 196, 199, 205, 294, 299, 301

African clinic named after, 99–100

desire to leave Australia of, 29

at Indonesian NGO conference, 197–98

marriage of, 20

move to Australia of, 28

Wolfensohn, Hyman "Bill," 17–18, 20, 54

Wolfensohn, Jim, 1, 9–10, 23, 73, 84–85, 257, 269, 334–35, 337

affability of, 174

Africa policies of, 90–92, 157–58, 218, 222, 228

Africa trips of, 89, 92–105, 108, 111–12, 146, 215–16, 233, 303–4, 312, 333

AIDS and, 313–14, 319, 323, 328–29, 331, 334

ambition for Bank's long-term strategy of, 208–9

antipoverty speech of, 210–12

appearance of, 49

appointment as Bank president of, 81–83

argument with Bank board of, 245–47

Wolfensohn, Jim (*cont.*)
argument with Jaycox of, 104–5, 108
athletic talents of, 1, 19, 41
Autheman's speech and, 170–73
background of, 3, 17–20
Bank bureaucracy and, 148–50
as Bank president candidate, 74–81
Bank reform and, 151–55, 157–70, 339–40,
  377–93
Bank schedule of, 87
Bank speech of, 145–47
Bank staff complaints about, 88, 292–93,
  296
behavior at board meetings of, 170–71
Bolivia and, 239, 244–45
Bosnia and, 117–18, 120, 126, 135, 136–39,
  207, 388
Bush aid package and, 309–10
business practices of, 53–54
on Carnegie Hall board, 32–33
charity work of, 50–51, 54, 376
Chrysler work of, 38–39
Clinton friendship of, 116–17
corporation of, 50–54, 66, 74, 78
on corruption, 176, 181, 183, 353–54
Côte d'Ivoire trip of, 92, 101–5, 108, 112
at Darling & Co., 28–29
drive of, 54–55, 86–87
duality of, 376–77
economists and, 176–77
Einhorn's criticism of, 297–98
Environmental Defense Fund dinner
  with, 347
environmentalism and, 74, 234, 265
Exxon and, 343, 354–55
fight against corruption by, 176–77, 185
first press conference of, 88–89
fishing trips of, 53
Foreign Policy criticism of, 298–300, 306
IMF bailouts and, 192
Indian trip of, 23, 331
at Indonesian NGO conference, 197–98
insecurity of, 114
internal bleeding of, 38
Iraq visit of, 4, 365–66
Iraq War and, 365
Jakarta visits of, 178–80, 190, 195–99,
  205–7

job worries of, 299–301
lack of strategy of, 174–75
Latin America trip of, 113
at Madrid conference, 210–12
Mali trip of, 94–101, 112
managerial goal of, 377–79
marriage of, 20
at meeting with Malloch Brown, 209–10
meeting with managers of, 112–13
meeting with Quiroga of, 244
Monterrey summit and, 307–8
moves to New York of, 31, 38
musical interests of, 1, 17, 20, 30–33, 41,
  50–51, 66, 375
New Development Framework essay of,
  212, 224, 231–34
NGOs' relations with, 87, 102–3, 114,
  145–46, 155, 201, 206, 207, 215, 233,
  262–65, 269, 296–97, 319, 356, 377, 386,
  388
Nigerian spying accusation against,
  24–25
Nigerian trips of, 23–26, 32, 176, 213, 328,
  331
O'Neill and, 289, 291, 293–97, 305–6,
  308–10
passion for development of, 41
Qinghai dam and, 273–79, 281
relationship with McNamara of, 39–40
return to London of, 33
Roma conference of, 391
Russian trip of, 331
salary of, 86
Salomon Brothers and, 37–38, 49–50, 237
Salomon payout of, 50
at Schroders, 30–34, 37–38
September 11 speech of, 12–14, 17
seventieth birthday party of, 374–76
South Africa trip of, 110–11, 120, 283
Stiglitz and, 195, 268
Strategic Compact and, 162–67, 169–70,
  213, 245, 291, 378–79
structural adjustment at Bank by, 380–85
Summers's criticism of, 297–98
at Summit of the Americas, 65–67
temper of, 80, 85–86, 137–38, 156–57,
  164–65, 169, 174, 299
theory of presidency of, 99

Third Way strategy of, 256, 260
Uganda donors' conference hosted by,
    216–17
Uganda policies of, 218, 222–23, 228, 251
Uganda visit of, 92, 108–10, 113, 211, 215–16,
    251
war on terror view of, 304
youth conference of, 391
see also Comprehensive Development
    Framework
Wolfensohn, Sara, 301, 376–77
Wolfensohn Family Foundation, 31–32
Woods, George, 27, 310
World AIDS Conference, 321–22
World Bank, 1–2, 5, 84–85, 334–35
    AAA credit secured by, 22
    Africa and, 23, 89–92, 101, 106, 107
    Africa department of, 23, 92
    AIDS and, 313–34
    AIDS report of, 326–27
    Articles of Agreement of, 16
    board meeting schedule of, 161–62, 378
    Briscoe's water strategy and, 360–61
    budget of, 163
    bureaucracy of, 146, 148–50, 170, 390
    Central Asia and, 311
    Clinton's search for president of, 69, 71,
        73, 80–81
    decentralization at, 388
    Development Committee of, 254, 269,
        293, 305, 328
    early projects of, 22–23
    economic research of, 70–71
    effort to simplify rules of, 391
    Emergency Social Fund of, 141
    Exxon and, 343, 346, 349
    fight against corruption by, 176–77, 178,
        180, 184–85, 202–4
    fragility of, 4
    George H. W. Bush's presidential
        appointment to, 55–57
    human capital projects of, 26
    illiteracy battled by, 14, 118, 295
    image of, 47
    IMF bailouts and, 192, 211
    imperialism of, 35
    Inspection Panel of, 276–77, 279–81,
        284–85, 350, 390–91
    Integrated Rural Development Projects
        of, 253
    interest in politics of, 95
    Iraq War and, 363
    as "knowledge bank," 160
    lending policies of, 44–45, 70, 385
    loans to Europe of, 21–22
    McNamara as head of, 28, 34
    McNamara replacement chosen at, 39–40
    macroeconomic policies of, 37, 177, 196,
        208, 211, 379–81, 385
    Madrid protest of, 60–65, 72, 101, 110, 208,
        257, 261, 263, 286, 343
    matrix reform at, 168, 292
    meeting at Hay-Adams of, 154, 157
    Meltzer's criticism of, 289–90, 294, 298
    methods of, 20–21
    Millennium Development Goals and, 5,
        307, 311, 334, 384, 391
    mission in Asia of, 2
    Mobilization for Global Justice protest
        of, 264–68, 286
    Narcissus analogy of, 171–73
    National Environmental Action Plans of,
        70
    new headquarters of, 59–60
    1995 loans of, 72
    oil shock and, 44–45
    O'Neill's criticism of, 289–91, 293–97,
        305–6, 310
    origin of, 2, 14–16
    overextension of, 36
    Oxfam's criticism of, 60
    participatory development and, 346
    political attacks on, 44
    Polonoroeste and, 48
    Population, Health and Nutrition
        Department of, 35
    Poverty Reduction Strategy Credit of,
        259, 263
    presidential selections of, 41–44
    under Preston, 56–60
    primary school drive of, 288
    private sector ideas at, 167–68
    project-based investment lending of,
        359–60
    public image of, 145–46
    purpose of, 2–3

World Bank (*cont.*)
  Quality Assurance Group of, 167
  and reform in poor nations, 44–46
  reform of, 151–55, 157–70, 339–40, 377–93
  riots triggered by, 46
  Rural Development Department of, 35
  Sahel department of, 315–16
  search for Preston's successor at, 66–69
  September 11 terrorist attacks and, 302
  South Africa and, 110–11
  spending at, 165
  staff complaints about, 292–93
  Strategic Compact of, 162–67, 169, 170,
    213, 245, 291
  stress on poverty of, 34–35
  structure of, 21
  Third Way and, 249–50, 255–57
  UNAIDS and, 319, 322, 326
  and universal education, 288, 298, 307
  unsatisfactory projects of, 59, 149–50
  Urban Development Department of, 35
  U.S. Treasury hostility towards, 4, 122, 164,
    207, 210, 288–91, 293–95, 305
  Wolfensohn's appointment as president
    of, 81–83
  Wolfensohn's candidacy for president of,
    74–81
  Wolfensohn's clash with board of, 85–87
  Wolfensohn's first press conference at,
    88–89
  Wolfensohn's reforms at, 151–55, 157–70,
    339–40, 377–93
  World Development Report of, 71, 268,
    317, 322
  Zhang's criticism of, 359–60
  see also Comprehensive Development
    Framework; International
    Development Association (IDA);
    Wolfensohn, Jim; *specific countries*

World Bank Group, 148
World Commission on Dams, 357–58
World Development Report on Poverty,
  268, 280–81
World Health Organization (WHO), 314,
  318–19, 324
World Trade Center, attack on, 11, 301–3
World Trade Organization, 260–62, 265
World Vision, 215, 286
World War I, 17
World War II, 15, 17, 56
World Wildlife Fund, 262
Wright-Patterson Air Force Base, 127,
  128

Yeltsin, Boris, 71, 162
Yom Kippur War, 36

Zaire, 46, 96
  see also Congo
Zambia, 46, 96, 111, 253
  malaria in, 158
Zedillo, Ernesto, 306
Zedler, Kris, 47–48, 88
Zewdie, Debrework, 321
  AIDS report of, 327–28
  AIDS strategy of, 323–25, 328–30,
    332–33
  AIDS workshop of, 321–22
  Bank's AIDS report and, 326–27
  at Geneva AIDS conference, 322–23
  Multi-Country HIV/AIDS Program of,
    329
Zhang, Shengman, 285, 359, 360, 371
Zhu Rongji, 179
Zimbabwe, 387
  AIDS in, 316–17, 319, 324
  author in, 368
Zukerman, Pinchas, 376

ABOUT THE AUTHOR

SEBASTIAN MALLABY has been a *Washington Post* columnist since 1999. From 1986 to 1999 he was on the staff of *The Economist*, serving in Zimbabwe, London, and Japan, and serving as the magazine's Washington bureau chief. He spent 2003 as a fellow at the Council on Foreign Relations and has written for *Foreign Affairs*, *Foreign Policy*, *The New York Times*, and the *New Republic*, among others. Born in England and educated at Oxford, he lives in Washington, D.C., with his wife and children.